D1558568

The Ultimate Guide:
WOODWORKING
Furniture Projects, Carpentry, Tools

The Ultimate Guide:
WOODWORKING
Furniture Projects, Carpentry, Tools

Original title: Guía práctica de la madera

© 2001 Gorg Blanc, S.L.
All rights reserved throughout the world
Muntaner, 515, ático
08022 BARCELONA

PROJECT MANAGER:
Jordi Vigué

SCIENTIFIC COORDINATOR:
Vicenç Gibert i Armengol

EDITORIAL: MATERIALS:
Jordi Graell i Vilà
Joaquín Montón Lecumberri

EDITORIAL: TOOLS, WOODWORKING, CABINETMAKING:
Vicenç Gibert i Armengol
Jordi Graell i Vilà
Francesc Jordana i Riba
Rodrigo Lazcano Hormaechea
Judith Ramírez i Casas

PROJECT MAKERS:
Eduard Vall.llosera i Camí
Pedro Carrero Román

PHOTOGRAPHY:
Estudi Enric Berenguer

Photographic sources:
Gorg Blanc photographic archive
Universitat Politècnica de Catalunya photographic archive
Jordi Vigué
Francisco Po Egea
Chassan
Stock Photos

JACKET:
Estudi gràfic Gorg Blanc

DESIGN AND PAGE MAKEUP:
Estudi gràfic Gorg Blanc
Paloma Nestares
Noemí Blanco

ILLUSTRATIONS:
Jordi Segú

Illustrations advisers:
Miquel Ferrón
Myriam Ferrón i Viñas
Vicenç B. Ballestar

TECHNICAL DRAWINGS:
Salvador Obiols i Comas
David Garrés i Cervantes

ACKNOWLEDGEMENTS:
Pere Roig
Balius, Centres comercials de ferretería i bricolatge
Carpintería de Josep Soria Ramírez
Aismalibar, S.A.
Castorama
Akí

English edition:

TRANSLATION:
Rosetta International, London
Parts: Dr. Albrecht Tribukait, Köln

TYPESETTING:
Rosetta International, London
Parts: Katrin Story Jurgenson, Lauffen/Neckar

COORDINATION:
Hans-Joachim Maschek-Schneider, Köln

PRINTING:
Brepols, Belgium

© 2001 Dumont Buchverlag, Cologne
Dumont monte UK, London

ISBN 3-7701-7047-4

All rights reserved

Printed in Belgium

All the instructions given in this book have been carefully checked for accuracy. However, in the context of product liability or other legislation, the possibility of the existence of mistakes cannot entirely be excluded. Accordingly the instructions are provided without any guarantee by the authors or publisher. In particular, the authors and publishers accept no liability for any loss, damage or injury which may occur directly or indirectly as a result of following the instructions given or from individual behaviour or from failure to observe appropriate precautionary measures and safety guidelines. Any corrections will be gratefully received.

Dumont monte UK, 565 Fulham Road, London SW6 IES, GB

contents

materials 11

• • Wood   12
• • • Origins of wood 12
• • • • State of the world's forests 12
• • • • Changes in the wooded areas of the earth 14
• • • Wood formation and wood growth 15
• • • • Anatomy of wood 15
• • • • Growth structure 17
• • • • Particular features of growth 18
• • • • Growth of the branches 18
• • • Wood production 19
• • • • Felling, preparing and classifying timber 19
• • • • • The right season for felling trees 20
• • • • • Age of felling for various trees 20
• • • • Tree felling and forestry management 20
• • • • • Partial felling 20
• • • • • Reproduction felling 20
• • • • • Selective felling of chosen trees 20
• • • • Raw and sawn timber 22
• • • • • Rough timber 22
• • • • • Sawn timber 22
• • • • Systems for converting a log into planks 23
• • • • Drying 23
• • • • • Drying methods 24
• • • • • Drying plants 25
• • • • • Drying with warm air and steam 25
• • • Characteristics of wood 26
• • • • Composition and structure of wood 26
• • • • Physical properties 27
• • • • • Anisotropy 27
• • • • • Water content 27
• • • • • Water content of wood 27
• • • • Swelling and shrinking 29
• • • • Density 30
• • • • Homogeneity and durability 31
• • • • Flammability and combustibility 31
• • • • Mechanical properties 32
• • • • • Elastic deformation 32
• • • • • Flexibility 32
• • • • • Hardness 32
• • • • • Strength 33
• • • • • Resistance to splitting 33
• • • • • Resistance to wear 33
• • • • • Resistence to shock 33
• • • • • Resistence to tension 33
• • • • • Resistence to compression 34
• • • • • Resistence to bending 34
• • • Wood species 35
• • • • Timber species 35
• • • • • Conifers or gymnosperms 35
• • • • • Deciduous trees 35
• • • • • Softwoods 36
• • • • • Hardwoods 36
• • • • Catalogue of woods 38
• • • • • Amaranth 38
• • • • • Boxwood 38
• • • • • Buninga 38
• • • • • Ebony 38
• • • • • Holm oak 38
• • • • • Laurel 38
• • • • • Lignum vitae 39
• • • • • Sucupira 39
• • • • • Wenge 39
• • • • • Cinnamon 39
• • • • • Satinwood 39
• • • • • Courbaril 39

• • • • • Jacaranda 40
• • • • • Hickory 40
• • • • • Jagua 40
• • • • • Liquidamber 40
• • • • • African walnut 40
• • • • • Olive 40
• • • • • Elm 41
• • • • • Guatambu 41
• • • • • Red pine 41
• • • • • Rewa rewa 41
• • • • • Oak 41
• • • • • Teak 41
• • • • • Wacapou 42
• • • • • Sipo 42
• • • • • Birch 42
• • • • • Maple 42
• • • • • Mahogany 42
• • • • • Red cedar 42
• • • • • Cherry 43
• • • • • Eucalyptus 43
• • • • • Ash 43
• • • • • Beech 43
• • • • • Imbuia 43
• • • • • Iroko 43
• • • • • Makore 44
• • • • • Mansonia 44
• • • • • Larch 44
• • • • • Walnut 44
• • • • • Rio Rosewood 44
• • • • • Pear 44
• • • • • Scots pine 45
• • • • • European plane 45
• • • • • Ramin 45
• • • • • Sapele 45
• • • • • Utile 45
• • • • • Abarco 45
• • • • • Spruce 46
• • • • • Poplar 46
• • • • • Amboyna 46
• • • • • Avodire African 46
• • • • • Chestnut 46
• • • • • Cedar 46
• • • • • Dibetou 47
• • • • • Limba 47
• • • • • Maranti 47
• • • • • Okoume 47
• • • • • Indian rosewood 47
• • • • • Parana pine 47
• • • • • Douglas fir 48
• • • • • Sen 48
• • • • • Redwood 48
• • • • • Tamo, Japanese ash 48
• • • • • Tepa 48
• • • • • Balsa 48
• • • Wood in commerce 49
• • • • Traditional commercial terms 49
• • • • New products 49
• • • • • Prepared timber 49
• • • • • Wood mouldings 50
• • • • • Imitation beams 50
• • • Wood protection and preservation 51
• • • • Protective products 51
• • • • • History 51
• • • • • The properties of wood preserving products 52
• • • • • Categories of risk 52
• • • • Classification of wood preservatives 54
• • • • • Water-soluble preservatives 54

• • • • • Emulsions 54
• • • • • Organic solvents 55
• • • • • Natural organic treatments 55
• • • • Application of preservatives 56
• • • • Preventative treatments 56
• • • • • Moist wood processes 56
• • • • • • Replacement of wood's own sap 56
• • • • • • Diffusion 57
• • • • • • Complementary methods 57
• • • • • Dry wood processes 57
• • • • • • Without autoclave 57
• • • • • • Autoclave systems 58
• • • • • • With autoclave without pressure 59
• • • • • Curative treatments 59
• • • Wood diseases and parasites 60
• • • • Abnormal growth 60
• • • • • Eccentric heartwood growth rings 60
• • • • • Twin sapwood 60
• • • • • Ring check 60
• • • • • Faults in the pattern of growth rings 60
• • • • • Hollow heartwood 60
• • • • • Shakes 60
• • • • • Cock's claw 61
• • • • • Cup check 61
• • • • The effects of xylophagous insects 61
• • • • • Old house borer (Hylotrupes bajulus) 61
• • • • • Powderpost beetle (Lyctus brunneus) 61
• • • • • Woodworm (Anobium punctatum) 62
• • • • • Termites (Reticulitermes lucifugus) 62
• • • • • The carpenter bee 62
• • • • Fungal attack 62
• • • • • Xylophagous fungi 62
• • • • • Chromogenic fungi 62

• • Manufactured products 63
• • • Blockboard 63
• • • Plywood boards 63
• • • • Normal plywood boards 63
• • • • Extra-thick plywood boards 64
• • • • Plywood with phenolic resin coating 64
• • • • Plywood with non-slip coating 64
• • • • Vibration-absorbing plywood 64
• • • • Resin-impregnated high-density
plywood boards 65
• • • • Resin-impregnated high-density
plywood boards for floor covering 65
• • • • Resin-impregnated high-density
plywood boardsfor facade cladding 65
• • • • Fire-resistant resin-impregnated high-density
plywood boards 65
• • • • Bullet-proof resin-impregnated high-density
plywood boards 65
• • • Particle boards 66
• • • • Medium density fibreboard (MDF) 66
• • • • Hardboard (HDF) 66
• • • • Chipboard 66
• • • • Tubular chipboard 67
• • • • Tubular chipboard with
sound-insulation properties 67
• • • • Cement-bonded chipboard 67
• • • • Pressed boards made from wood shavings 67
• • • Other types of wood panels 68
• • • • Parallel Strand. Lumber (PSL) or Parallam™ 68
• • • • Malleable boards 68
• • • • Multi-layered boards 68
• • • • Building panels for indoor use 69
• • • • Facade cladding 69

• • • Floor coverings 69
• • • • Mosaic parquet floor 69
• • • • Solid wood 70
• • • • Plywood 71
• • • • Parquet for floating floors 72

tools 73

• • Hand tools 74
• • • Measuring tools 74
• • • • Rules 74
• • • • Squares 74
• • • • Steel rules 74
• • • • Bench rules 74
• • • • Sliding bevel 75
• • • • Mitre gauge 75
• • • • Vernier callipers 75
• • • Marking tools 75
• • • • Wood pencils 75
• • • • How to improvise a rule 75
• • • • Awls 76
• • • • Marking gauges 76
• • • • Compasses and dividers 77
• • • Cutting tools 77
• • • • Handsaws and backsaws 77
• • • • Frame saw 78
• • • • Mitre saw 79
• • • • Ripsaws 79
• • • • Crosscut saw 79
• • • • Backsaws 79
• • • • Coping saws 80
• • • • Compass and keyhole saws 80
• • • • Saws with interchangeable blades 80
• • • Tools with a cutting edge 81
• • • • Guided cutting tools: planes 81
• • • • • Planes 81
• • • • • Jointer or try plane 81
• • • • • Jack plane 81
• • • • • Smoothing plane 82
• • • • • Planes with curved soles 83
• • • • • Metal planes 83
• • • • • Toothing plane 83
• • • • Moulding planes 84
• • • • • Shoulder plane 84
• • • • • Rebate plane 84
• • • • • Fluting plane 84
• • • • • Moulding plane 85
• • • • • Ploughing plane 85
• • • • • Tongue-and-groove plane 85
• • • • Freehand cutting tools 86
• • • • • Firmer chisels and bevel edge chisels 86
• • • • • Mortise chisels 87
• • • • • Gouges 87
• • • Tools for drilling and screwing 88
• • • • Awl 88
• • • • Gimlet 88
• • • • Brace 88
• • • • Drill bits 88
• • • • Hand drill 89
• • • • Screwdrivers 89
• • • Hammers and nail extractors 89
• • • • Hammer 89
• • • • Mallet 90
• • • • Pincers 90
• • • • Pliers 90
• • • • Nail set 90

• • • • Claw 90
• • • • Cramping tools 91
• • • • G-cramps and corner cramps 91
• • • • Strap, web or band cramp 91
• • • • Bar cramp 92
• • • • Edge cramp 92
• • • • Sash cramp 92
• • • • I-beam bar cramp 92
• • • Smoothing, shaping and finishing tools 93
• • • • Rasps 93
• • • • Files 93
• • • • Scraper 93
• • • • Round or rat-tail rasp and file 93
• • • • Spokeshave 94
• • • • Half-round spokeshave 94
• • • • Sandpaper 94
• • • • Steel wool 94

• • Portable power tools 95
• • • Compound mitre table saw 95
• • • Portable power drill 96
• • • Vertical drill stand 96
• • • Portable jigsaw 96
• • • Portable circular saw 97
• • • Orbital sander 97
• • • Power edge router 97
• • • Portable planer 98
• • • Power router 98
• • • Portable biscuit jointer 99
• • • Screwdriver with rechargeable battery 99
• • • Portable power drill with rechargeable battery 99

• • Maintaining and sharpening hand tools 100
• • • Keeping tools clean 100
• • • Sharpening 100
• • • Honing 101
• • • Setting saw teeth 101
• • • Saw sharpening 101
• • • Sharpenng the blades of
guided cutting tools (e.g. plane blades) 101
• • • Sharpening the blades of
freehand cutting tools (e.g. chisels) 102
• • • Sharpening a scraper 102

woodworking 103

• • The woodworker's skills 104
• • • The workshop 104
• • • The workbench 104
• • • Storage arrangements 106
• • • The project 108
• • • Preliminary sketches 108
• • • Making a template from a drawing
of a curved component 108
• • • Making templates from a measured drawing 109
• • • Various templates 110

• • Basic woodworking techniques 111
• • • Smoothing the wood 111
• • • Marking out 112
• • • Marking a horizontal line 112
• • • Truing up a piece of wood 112
• • • Marking an angle 113
• • • Marking a cutting line 113
• • • Using a marking gauge 114
• • • Drawing circles 114

• • • Sawing 115
• • • • Square cuts 115
• • • • Making an angle cut 116
• • • • Cutting a rectangular opening 116
• • • • Cutting a curved opening 116
• • • • Cutting a curve 117
• • • • Cutting a curve without marking the surface 117
• • • • Cutting a concave curve 118
• • • • Cutting a rebate with a chisel 118
• • • Drilling 119
• • • • Drilling a vertical hole in a piece of wood 119
• • • Joints 119
• • • Edge joints and connectors 120
• • • • Splined edge-to-edge joint 120
• • • • Double splined edge-to-edge joint 121
• • • • Double splined edge-to-edge joint 121
• • • • Splined edge-to-edge joint reinforced with tenons . 121
• • • • Edge-to-edge biscuit joint 121
• • • Tongue-and-groove joint 122
• • • • Twin tongue-and-groove joint 123
• • • • Alternating tongue-and-groove joint 123
• • • • Moulded tongue-and-groove joint 123
• • • • Tongue-and-groove joint with mortise and tenon . . 123
• • • Corner and cross joints 124
• • • • T-halving and corner-halving joint 124
• • • • Cruciform halving joint 125
• • • • Stopped halving joint 125
• • • • Stacked cross joints 125
• • • • Clamp halving joint 125
• • • • Wedged twin through mortise and tenon joint 126
• • • • Central bridle joint 127
• • • • Forked bridle joint 127
• • • • Bridle joint with bevelled edges 127
• • • • Loose-wedged mortise and tenon 127
• • • Corner bridle joint 128
• • • • Stopped twin corner bridle joint 129
• • • • Mitre joint with stub, invisible or hidden tenon . . . 129
• • • • Corner mortise and tenon joint 129
• • • • Stopped corner bridle joint 129
• • • Through dovetail joint with single pin 130
• • • • Dovetail halving joint 131
• • • • Slotted dovetail joint 131
• • • • Skewed twin dovetail and tenon joint 131
• • • • Dovetail pins 131
• • • Dowel joints 132
• • • • Types of dowels 133
• • • • Glued butt joint with
wooden pegs 133
• • • • Corner butt joint with dowels 133
• • • • T-shaped butt joint with dowels 133
• • • Splice joints 134
• • • • Splice joint with right-angled tenon 134
• • • • Bridle splice joint 135
• • • • Bridle splice joint with pointed head 135
• • • • Splice joint with alternate tenons 135
• • • • Angle bridle splice joint with tongue 135
• • • • Splice halving joint with simple false tenon 136
• • • • Splice halving joint with dovetail false tenon . . . 137
• • • • Splice halving joint with dalse tenon,
tongue and rebate 137
• • • • Angled splice halving joint
with false tenon 137
• • • • Splice joint with twin false tenon 137
• • • • Splice joint with square tenon 138
• • • • Quartered splice bridle joint 139
• • • • Cruciform splice joint 139
• • • • Double splice bridle joint 139

• • • • • Splice joint with four tenons 139
• • • Preliminary and final assembly 140
• • • Correct use of softening 140
• • • Joining two boards edge-to-edge using bar cramps . 140
• • • Assembling a frame using bar cramps 141
• • • Assembling a frame using mitre
        or corner cramps 142
• • • Holding a right-angled butt joint in
        position while it is fixed 142
• • • Cramping using C-shaped springs 143
• • • Assembly using a circular band cramp 143
• • • Cramping a joint using a
        home-made tourniquet 143
• • Glued joints and metal fixings 144
• • • Diagonal nailing 144
• • • Fixing moulding with concealed panel pins 144
• • • Screwing components together 145
• • • Fixing with coach bolts 146
• • • Butt jointing man-made boards with screw connectors 147
• • • Gluing two pieces together 148
• • • Gluing two pieces together side by side 148
• • • Gluing a laminate or veneer to a man-made panel . . 149
• • • Gluing the edges of man-made panels 151
• • Sanding 152
• • • Hand sanding 152
• • • Power sanding 154
• • Fitting hinges 155
• • • Fixing a hinge without a recess 155
• • • Fixing a recessed hinge 157
• • Finishes 158
• • • Applying filler 158
• • • Cleaning the surface 160
• • • Applying a grain-filling sealer 160
• • • Applying knotting 161
• • • Applying wax 161
• • • Applying wood stains 162
• • • Applying varnish 164
• • • Applying paint 165
• • • Lacquer 166
• • • Distressing or ageing 167
• • Fixing metal closures (locks, bolts, knobs and handles) 168
• • • Fitting a sliding bolt 168
• • • Fitting a cupboard lock in the front face
        of a panel door 169
• • • Fitting a lock in the edge of a door 171
• • • Fitting a bolt to glazed doors or French windows . . . 174
• • • Fitting escutcheons and pull handles 176
• • • Escutcheons for door handles and locks 176
• • • Knobs and handles 176
• • • • Fitting a surface-mounted pull handle 176
• • • • Fitting a recessed handle 178
• • • • Fitting a door knob with integral
        surface-mounted backplate 179
• • • • Lipping 180
• • • • Metal lipping 180
• • • • Fitting solid wood lipping to a chipboard panel . 182
• • • • Solid wood lipping with mitred corners 182

• • Making projects 184
• • • Woodworking 185
• • • Garden fence 185
• • • Garden gate 190
• • • Trellis 198
• • • Trestle 206
• • • Wine rack 214
• • • Laying wood flooring 222
• • • • Composition of wood floor

• • • • with a solid wood top layer 222
• • • • Composition of laminated floating
        wooden flooring with a sub-layer of wood 223
• • • • Size and packaging if ready-made wood
        or laminated plank flooring 224
• • • • Skirting boards and other uses of wood 224
• • • • Laying a wooden floor 225
• • • • A special jointing system 226
• • • • Some installed floors 227
• • • Assembling kitchen units and bathroom furniture 229
• • • Pre-fabricated components and hinges for
        assembling a kitchen or bathroom cabinet 230
• • • Typical assembly procedure for a kitchen cabinet . . . 231
• • • Installing the finished cabinets 237

cabinetmaking 239

• • Cabinetmaking skills 240
• • Cabinemaking joints 240
• • • Corner joints for panels 240
• • • • Splined wood corner joint for man-made panels 241
• • • • Corner joint for panels with
        interior wood reinforcement 241
• • • • Lap joint for panels 241
• • • • Curved splined wood corner joint 241
        Curved tongue-and-groove wood corner joint 241
• • • Longitudinal joints 242
• • • • Longitudinal joint with a single central dowel 242
• • • • Three-dowel joint 243
• • • • Rounhd peg joint 243
• • • • Screw joint 243
• • • Dovetail joints 244
• • • • Lapped dovetail joint 244
• • • • Double-lapped dovetail joint 245
• • • • Secret dovetail joint 245
• • • • Secret mitred dovetail joint 245

• • Cabinetmaking skills 246
• • • Marquetry 247
• • • Turning 251
• • • Carving 255

• • Furniture making 259
• • • Hall 260
• • • Chest 260
• • • Clock 274
• • • Coat stand 290
• • • Bedroom 300
• • • Bed 300
• • • Bedside table 310
• • • Living room 320
• • • Coffee table 320
• • • Decorative frame 332
• • • Table lamp 342
• • • Decorative items 358
• • • Pipe stand 358
• • • Book stand 368
• • • Decorative figure: clown 390
• • • Useful items and toys 394
• • • Shelving 394
• • • Toy box 399
• • • Chessboard 404
• • • CD rack 414
• • • Toy aircraft 422

• • Restoring furniture 432

*A*nyone who has had the opportunity of understanding and working with the noble material that is wood will already know that its lifeblood is the sap which runs through its interior, and that the central part of the trunk is always described as the heart. Allow me to use a play upon words to express a tender regard for this material which is so widely appreciated and beloved by woodworkers, since it is only possible to work with it if one has a large amount of creativeness and a great heart.

Almost since the origins of mankind, humans have been accompanied by objects and tools made from wood. This is why people feel such a special attraction to this material which is so satisfying, a fact demonstrated by its continuing and abundant presence in the everyday environment, a position it will undoubtedly continue to hold in the future.

The philosophy which has inspired the structure of the sections of this book follow the example of the growth of a young tree, in which the wood which exists under the bark grows with the passing of time, as the soft growth rings of the spring wood give way to the harder, darker features of the late summer wood. Using this simile of the tree, this book may be seen as an innovative design which describes the techniques of the craft, interlaced with the experience of skilled workmen, as a means of conveying a comprehensive survey of the various techniques of woodworking. It respects the need to appeal to the many readers who will approach the techniques shown with different degrees of knowledge about wood and the ways of handling it.

The knowledge within this book starts from wood itself, an extremely diverse, varied material even as between species which have identical growth patterns. For this reason it is helpful to be able to identify the different species in relation to the type of wood, its

hardness, texture, colour and other significant characteristics. The basic practical skills of the woodworker are illustrated, as are the various tools used in handling and preparing wood.

On the basis of this knowledge of materials and tools, the main woodworking tasks and operations are described, revealing a whole series of details which, without being particularly noticeable in themselves, are fundamental to the proper execution of any project, lending an indefinable air of quality to the completed work.

Finally, in the section of the book devoted to cabinet-making, it is shown how a cabinetmaker is something more than a woodworker, often making use of other techniques related to his own, such as turning, carving, marquetry and furniture restoration.

We hope and believe that readers wanting to practise and improve their skills will find solutions to all the difficulties and problems which can arise in woodworking among the basic exercises and detailed project instructions described in this book.

I would like to thank each and every one of the professionals who have made up the creative team for the valuable contributions they have made by sharing their knowledge and experience, their enthusiasm and their spirit of cooperation, which has enabled us to accomplish this extensive work with pleasure and delight. Without their invaluable participation it would not have been possible to complete it.

There are few moments so agreeable as those spent in contemplating a completed work in whose creation one has taken such special satisfaction, as I have in the case of this book. It is my hope and desire that this pleasure will be shared many times by everyone who, with the help of this book, succeeds in transforming formless pieces of wood with their own hands into object swhich contain and express part of themselves.

Vicenç Gibert i Armengol

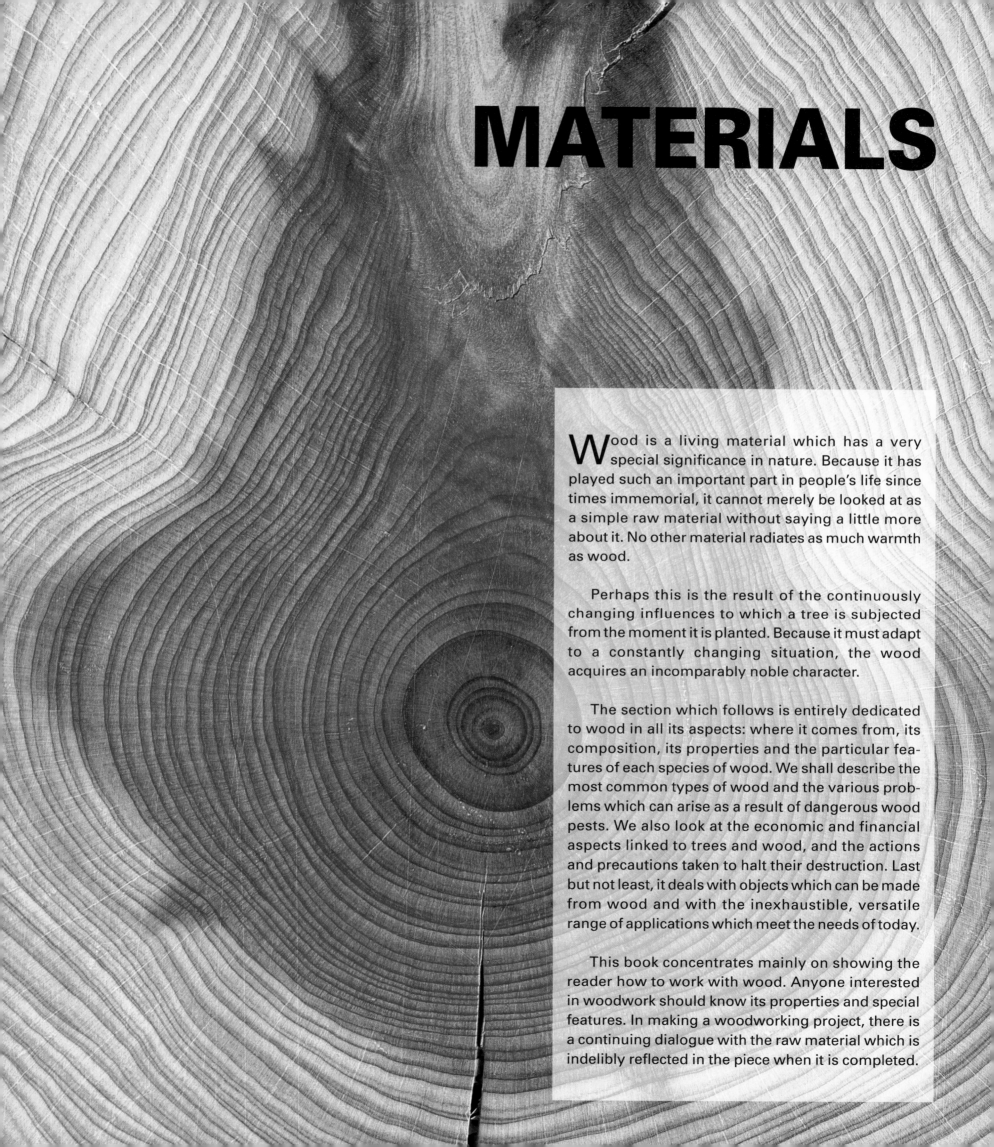

MATERIALS

Wood is a living material which has a very special significance in nature. Because it has played such an important part in people's life since times immemorial, it cannot merely be looked at as a simple raw material without saying a little more about it. No other material radiates as much warmth as wood.

Perhaps this is the result of the continuously changing influences to which a tree is subjected from the moment it is planted. Because it must adapt to a constantly changing situation, the wood acquires an incomparably noble character.

The section which follows is entirely dedicated to wood in all its aspects: where it comes from, its composition, its properties and the particular features of each species of wood. We shall describe the most common types of wood and the various problems which can arise as a result of dangerous wood pests. We also look at the economic and financial aspects linked to trees and wood, and the actions and precautions taken to halt their destruction. Last but not least, it deals with objects which can be made from wood and with the inexhaustible, versatile range of applications which meet the needs of today.

This book concentrates mainly on showing the reader how to work with wood. Anyone interested in woodwork should know its properties and special features. In making a woodworking project, there is a continuing dialogue with the raw material which is indelibly reflected in the piece when it is completed.

Wood

Each species of wood has its own particular properties of durability, colour and resistance which in the course of history have determined in a decisive manner the enormous range of application of this precious, unique material. Experience has shown that not all types of wood are the same. Their behaviour changes depending on how it is used, in other words what is used for. Therefore, in order to get the best out of wood, it must be chosen with care so that its properties are exploited to the full in order to meet the requirements of the task it is intended to perform.

Since time immemorial wood has been used in the building of houses both for the walls and the roof. For centuries it has also been used to make pieces of furniture (whether for storage, residential or other general purpose), as raw material to embellish objects (such as furniture or for purely decorative purposes such as carvings), to make pieces of equipment for every day life (containers, tools and other appliances) and to make many other objects (such as musical instruments, ships and toys).

Depending on the purpose for which the wood is used, different techniques are used. Between the simple board or beam and a perfect piece of furniture lies a whole range of woodworking techniques.

Wood is not just a material. Studying the wood itself, where it comes from and all that happens to it from the time the tree is felled to the end result, it becomes apparent that it conceals a whole world of its own. The first pages of the book are a window onto the world of trees: how it is treated, processed and prepared for use in woodwork.

12

Origins of wood

Wood is produced by trees and is the primary component of the trunk and branches. Because trees grow mainly in forests, these must be considered the original, natural habitat as far as the origin and formation of the wood is concerned.

The present conditions of forests throughout the world are therefore examined with particular attention to their level of survival and replacement, and the degree to which proper management techniques could preserve them.

State of the world's forests

Every two years the Food and Agriculture Organisation (FAO) of the United Nations publishes a global report entitled the State of the World's forests. According to this report, in 1995 almost one quarter of the earth was covered with trees, with a total of 3,454 million ha (8,535 million acres) of forest. The man-made forests which are included in these above-mentioned figures only make up 3% of the all the forests, the remaining 97% being natural or semi-natural woods. Of these 55% are in the developing countries and 45% in the industrialised world.

From a climatic point of view, there are two main groups which occupy roughly the same surface area: the tropical and sub-tropical forests in the warm zones and the temperate forests of the colder regions of the north.

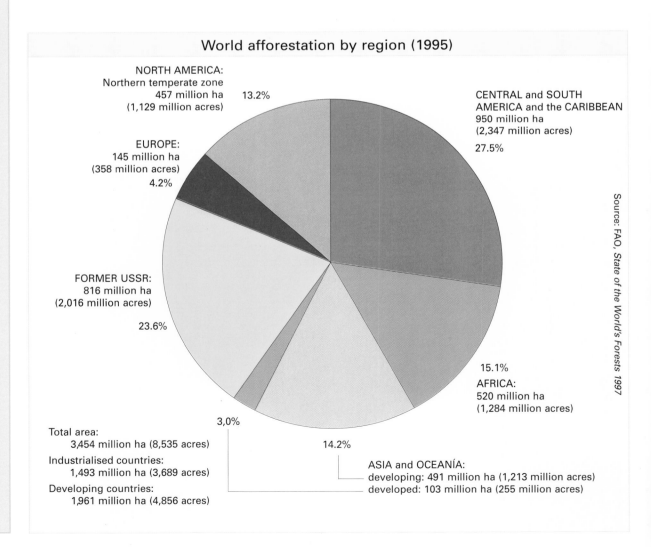

World afforestation by region (1995)

NORTH AMERICA: Northern temperate zone 457 million ha (1,129 million acres) 13.2%

CENTRAL and SOUTH AMERICA and the CARIBBEAN 950 million ha (2,347 million acres) 27.5%

EUROPE: 145 million ha (358 million acres) 4.2%

FORMER USSR: 816 million ha (2,016 million acres) 23.6%

15.1% AFRICA: 520 million ha (1,284 million acres)

3,0%

14.2%

ASIA and OCEANÍA: developing: 491 million ha (1,213 million acres) developed: 103 million ha (255 million acres)

Total area: 3,454 million ha (8,535 acres)
Industrialised countries: 1,493 million ha (3,689 acres)
Developing countries: 1,961 million ha (4,856 acres)

Source: FAO, State of the World's Forests 1997

Not all trees are equally good for all purposes. The durability, colour and other characteristics of its wood determine its suitability for specific kinds of use.

As well as being an entity in its own right and an important part of the natural environment, a tree is also a supplier of timber, the raw material for a large number of different purposes.

Whether it is a copse or a plantation or a forest, a group of trees occupies a relatively small surface area, yet it represents a storehouse from which wood can be extracted, indispensable for the construction of buildings and other things of great value to the human race.

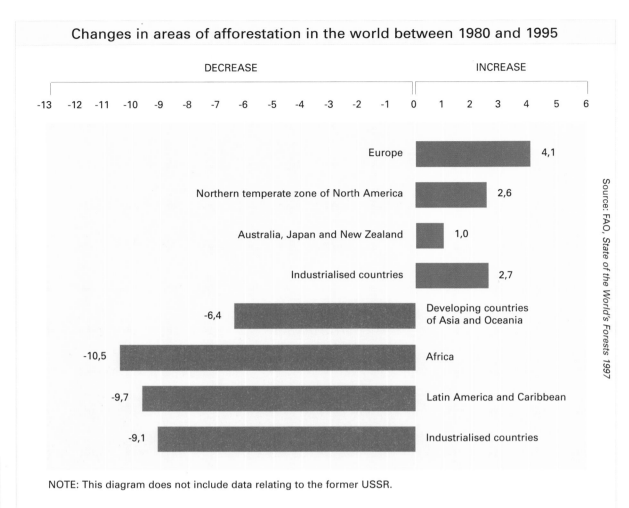

Changes in areas of afforestation in the world between 1980 and 1995

DECREASE   INCREASE

-13 -12 -11 -10 -9 -8 -7 -6 -5 -4 -3 -2 -1 0 1 2 3 4 5 6

Region	Value
Europe	4,1
Northern temperate zone of North America	2,6
Australia, Japan and New Zealand	1,0
Industrialised countries	2,7
Developing countries of Asia and Oceania	-6,4
Africa	-10,5
Latin America and Caribbean	-9,7
Industrialised countries	-9,1

Source: FAO, *State of the World's Forests 1997*

NOTE: This diagram does not include data relating to the former USSR.

14

Changes in the wooded areas on earth

Because of the loss of forests resulting from deforestation on one hand and the gains resulting from reforestation or restocking of forests on the other, the distribution of wooded areas throughout the world does not remain constant but changes continuously. However, from a world-wide point of view the total area covered with forests is decreasing steadily. Based on the SOFO-report of the FAO published in 1997 , the following tendencies have been observed: a large loss of forests in the developing countries of 200 million ha (500 million acres), as opposed to a small increase of wooded areas in industrialised countries of 20 million ha (50 million acres) between 1980 and 1995.

Over this period there was a slight reduction in the rate of loss of forests in developing countries and a larger increase in reforestation in industrialised countries. The period 1980 to 1990 saw an annual overall loss of 15.5 million ha (39 million acres) while in the period of 1990 to 1995 a total of 13.7 million ha (34 million acres) of forest were lost throughout the earth every year. Whether this encouraging trend will continue to improve will only become clear when the next figures are issued.

The main reason for the reduction of wooded areas, especially in the tropics, is the expansion of subsistence agriculture in Asia and Africa as well as the extensive economic programmes in Latin America and Asia which involves the deforestation of large areas for housing, agricultural development and improvements in infrastructure.

In contrast, the continuous increase in wooded areas in industrial countries is due mainly to reforestation and restocking of existing forests.

In addition, a natural regeneration in areas where agriculture is becoming less important has been recorded. Although the felling of trees in industrial countries is more than compensated for – at least in quantity – by the reforestation and restocking of existing forests, the worldwide trend of decreasing wooded areas shows no sign of being reversed.

In recent years, the planet has experienced an alarming reduction of the area of forest as a result of the expansion of agriculture, programmes of large scale economic development, speculation and the absence of ecological conscience. The result has been to bring about a substantial reduction in the amount of timber available, and several species are now threatened with extinction.

Wood formation and wood growth

In order to have a better understanding of wood, it is first necessary to have a close look at how trees grow. Like herbaceous plants and shrubs, even the tallest trees start life as tiny seedlings. In favourable surroundings and conditions, trees can grow taller than any other living things.

This is mainly the result of biological peculiarities which are only found in trees: a tall size, the formation of strong, resistant, protective bark and a longer life expectancy than most other living things.

Trees grow almost everywhere on earth, having developed and adapted to the area and climate in which they grow. The differences in climate, soil and other growing conditions have led to the development of a large number of families and species. There are trees which not grow no taller than 2 m (6 ft 6 in) while others easily reach a height of 100 m (330 ft).

Trees can live for a very long time. The trees with the longest life expectancy are those which grow in mountainous regions where the cold, ice and snow slow down the growing process. Some trees are more than a thousand years old.

Anatomy of wood

Wood has a complicated structure. As in all living things or creatures, the basic element is the cell. Cells of the same type or with the same function develop tissues which together form the woody mass which consists of various cell types, the so-called wood elements. Wood fibres are formed by the superimposition of elongated cells, connected to each other, which in turn form the starting point for the development of bundles and tissue. The process of lignification is the result of a series of transformations. Lignin is stored in the cellulose structure of the cell walls. This gives them a particular strength. The heartwood is formed in the older parts of the tree whose vessels are no longer used to conduct water, the task carried out by the sapwood.
As a result of the stored tanning agents, miner-

The trees which are found in high mountain regions are those which live longest. This is the result of the cold, snow and ice which reduce the rate of growth to a much slower level, only detectible after many years.

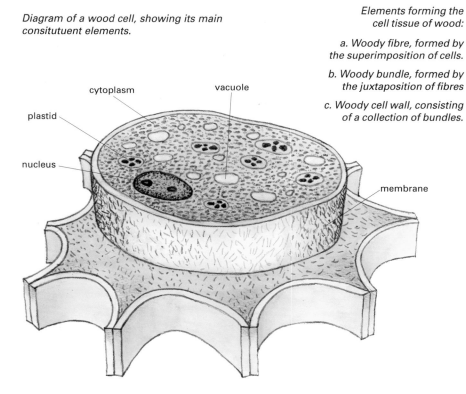

Diagram of a wood cell, showing its main consitutuent elements.

cytoplasm

vacuole

plastid

nucleus

membrane

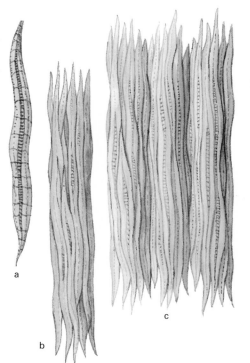

Elements forming the cell tissue of wood:

a. Woody fibre, formed by the superimposition of cells.

b. Woody bundle, formed by the juxtaposition of fibres

c. Woody cell wall, consisting of a collection of bundles.

a

b

c

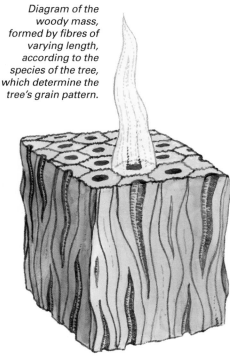

Diagram of the woody mass, formed by fibres of varying length, according to the species of the tree, which determine the tree's grain pattern.

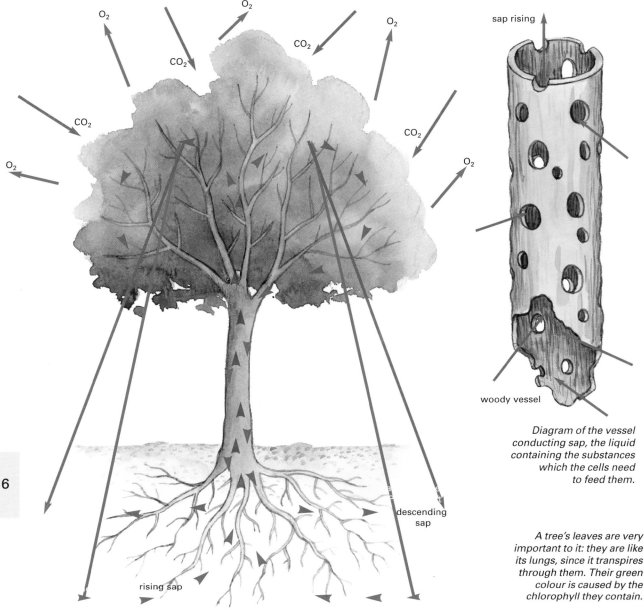

als, pigments and other substances the ripe wood, also known as heartwood, becomes considerably harder and frequently also denser and darker which also protects it from decomposition. However not all trees develop a heartwood core. Depending on the species, the fibres which determine the veining or wood grain vary in length. The main tissue of a tree is divided as follows:

- the epidermis or protective tissue.
- the supporting tissue
- the cambium or sapwood

The latter is extremely important because its task is to carry the water enriched with minerals and other elements from the soil in the form of rising sap through the woody sapwood to the leaves where it is further enriched by other nutrients through photosynthesis. This cycle is completed when the processed sap is carried down through the inner living bark and distributed throughout the tree to be stored or to form new tissue. The sap keeps the tree alive because it promotes the development and formation of branches, leaves and fruit.

Diagram of the vessel conducting sap, the liquid containing the substances which the cells need to feed them.

Diagram showing the natural process of interaction between the , through photosynthesis. The tree absorbs carbon dioxide (CO_2), which it needs for its sustenance. With the action of chlorophyll, this is turned into oxygen (O_2), which is given off at the end of the process; this is of particular benefit to the animal kingdom including man.

A tree's leaves are very important to it: they are like its lungs, since it transpires through them. Their green colour is caused by the chlorophyll they contain.

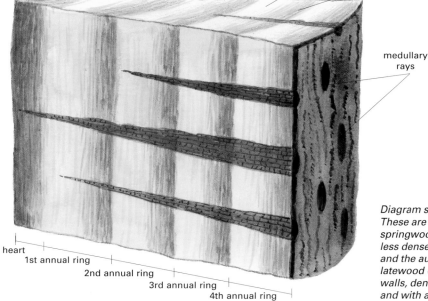

Diagram showing growth rings. These are formed by the springwood or earlywood (pale, less dense and with large vessels) and the autumn wood or latewood (stiffer, with supporting walls, denser than the earlywood and with a darker colour).

Diagram of a tree trunk with its
component elements.

bark phloem Cambium Sapwood Heartwood

The location of a tree, whether it is near water or in a completely dry terrain, has a decisive influence on its wood's texture,
hardness and resistance to particular attacking agents.

The leaves are an important organ of the tree. Their function is to absorb vital carbon dioxide. In human terms, leaves are to the tree what lungs are to people, the roots are the entrance to the digestive system and the sap is the blood.

Growth structure

Wood structure will be referred to again later in the book but it is important at this point to clarify a few points here in order to understand the process of growth better.

When the cross-section of a trunk is closely examined, the concentric structure of the trunk is immediately apparent. It is arranged as follows:
• The bark, an impervious tissue which encloses the trunk and also serves as a protective layer for the tree.
• Under the bark lies the inner bark, a thin layer of tissue through which the sap rises.
• Between the inner bark and the wood is the cambium, the only layer of cells which divide during the growth period whereby new wood cells are produced towards the inside and phloem cells (a component of the bark) towards the outside. In this way, the new wood envelopes the already existing core.
• The young wood is situated within the cambium, a layer of cells. Its function is to carry the sap up the tree and store nutrients. These elements of the tree will be described in greater detail in the next section on the characteristics of wood.

In spring, trees grow and produce wood which is
less dense and with broad vessels.

In autumn, the wood produced by trees is
denser, its vessels are narrower and its colour
is darker.

17

Structure of a trunk depending on its type of growth

Slow

This structure is typical of mountain trees which have to undergo extreme cold, snow and ice. As a result their rate of growth slows down and they are very long-lived. The growth rings are close together.

Fast

This structure is typical of trees from temperate climates. The wood is less dense, and as a result it is not so strong and prone to many kinds of pests and diseases. Such trees live much less long.

Eccentric

This structure is typical of trees which have suffered some accidental circumstance which affects them on one side in particular: sun, cold, wind etc. The situation can occur equally with mountain trees and those of temperate zones.

• The earlywood or spring wood which is the first layer formed. It is made up chiefly of broad vessels which carry the sap up to the leaves. It is light coloured, soft and not very dense.
• The latewood or autumn wood consists mainly of wood fibres and narrow vessels. It is darker coloured and denser.

Earlywood and latewood together form an annual ring.

The environment in which a tree grows is an important factor in its development and the conditions prevalent during each growth phase are clearly reflected in the annual rings. By analysing these annual rings, their thickness, colour and other features it is possible to discover what the growing conditions were.

Trees growing on fertile soil develop wider annual rings than they would on poor soil. In addition, the width of the annual rings reflect the speed of growth. Fast-growing trees usually have wide annual rings while slow-growing trees have narrow rings.

When a tree is felled, it becomes immediately obvious whether the annual rings are identical throughout. Trees which have been subjected to high winds from a particular direction will develop eccentric, oval rings which are wider on one side than the other.

Seasonal variations also influence the growth of the tree and determine how strongly marked an annual ring will be. In extreme conditions such as prolonged drought, growth may stop and lead to the formation of false annual rings. Infestation by insects, fire or frost damage are recorded in the shape of injuries.

In temperate zones the main growth takes place in spring when the largest leading vessels are produced. At the beginning of autumn, narrower cells are produced. A few weeks later growth stops completely and will only resume the following spring.

Particular features of growth

Chlorophyll, the green pigment of plants, also plays an important part in this system, giving leaves their green colour and ensuring photosynthesis whereby water from the soil, taken up by the roots, is combined with carbon dioxide from the air, using light energy absorbed by the chlorophyll. This also makes it possible for nutrients important to the growth of the tree to be taken up and stored.

The wood of a tree will reflect all the influences and conditions to which the tree has been subjected during its lifetime. This is particularly apparent in the annual growth rings.

In order to understand the various growth phases better, it is worth looking closely at the transverse section of a trunk, preferably as close to the base as possible. The following elements will be apparent:

The season of spring is one of great activity for a tree, both internally and externally. This is when it begins a new growth cycle into which it throws all its energy and available resources.

Seasonal changes have a decisive influence on the growth of trees. In winter, the tree, though still living, is in a dormant state and its vital activities are at a minimum in order to save energy.

Growth of the branches

Environmental conditions are not only reflected in the rings but also in the development of the branches. These conditions are clearly reflected in the branch markings in the wood. When a branch is alive and develops leaves its tissue is connected to the trunk. When a branch dies the new tissue is no longer connected to it in spite of the fact that the it is still attached to the main trunk. The subsequent annual rings merely close up slowly around it. Branch markings show where there used to be branches. Living branches, are described as connate or fixed branches because their fibres are growing together with the surrounding wood. It is true that dead branches are also surrounded by tree fibres but they are no longer connected. Dead branches are easily detached from the trunk by the slightest knock, forming knot holes. Markings of branches and twigs or knots are undesirable but unavoidable in wood. However, by correct pruning it is possible to restrict the number and size of branches or twigs to a minimum.

Wood production

The structure and composition as well as the season when the tree is felled all play an important part in the production of quality wood. By felling is meant the separation of the tree from its base, in other words just above ground level. The wood is sorted at a collecting point in the forest where the branches are cut off the trunks. The bark is then removed. The trunks are then cut to a certain length, sorted out and stacked up ready for transport.

Trees should only be felled when they have reached a certain development and maturity. A tree which is very young has too much softwood. It is vulnerable to insect infestation, warps and cracks very easily. On the other hand, in trees that are too old the oldest part, the heartwood, is often rotten or destroyed.

Felling, preparing and classifying timber

Tree felling is carried out by professional lumberjacks. Several methods are used depending on the environmental conditions. Trees can be felled by traditional hand methods with an axe and a hand saw, or by special power saws powered by petrol or a diesel generator, or by special vehicles which fell the tree mechanically.

After being felled, the branches and twigs are removed with an axe or chain saw. Conifers are also immediately debarked. Ideally, the trunks are taken out of the forest as soon as possible. The trunks can be transported by draught animals, by diesel; tractors or by water, whereby the logs are collected together as enormous rafts. The processes of felling, harvesting, sawing and sorting timber are carried out by large companies which are responsible for removing the branches, debarking the logs, cutting them to size and classifying them before they are stacked and transported.

During this first phase all softwood must be debarked before being sawn up so that the water present in the wood can evaporate more

When a tree is cut down, the timber is sorted and piled up according to its classification while it waits to be transported to the place where it will be processed.

19

Piles of logs which have been through various operations of sorting and and classification, waiting to be transported to the next stage.

After sorting it is important that trees should not wait long before they are moved, because at this stage they are exposed to a number of possible threats which could seriously damage them.

The age trees when felled varies according to the species and the climate region in which they are found. The table at the bottom of this page lists some different trees and the ages at which they are normally felled. The range of years indicated are only guidelines.

When sorting is completed, the great forestry companies use the rivers to transport the timber at very low cost. Large quantities of logs are delivered in this way to the processing plants, where the timber is dried, sawn into planks and converted to convenient sizes.

quickly. On the other hand hardwood, which is often used for veneer, is not usually debarked immediately in order to avoid the formation of cracks through excessive drying out.

The right season for felling trees

The best season for tree felling is at the end of the winter before the start of the new growing period which starts in spring. Felling trees during the dormant winter season has the advantage that very little sap is carried through the tree at that time and that there is no danger of wood damage from insects or fungi.

If at all possible, trees should never be felled in summer because when the sapwood is full of sap it also attracts damaging organisms, attracted by the nutrients and minerals present in the sap. After being classified, the logs should be transported to the timberyard as soon as possible. There they remain during the winter months so they can be processed further during the spring and summer.

Age of felling for various trees

SPECIES	YEARS
Acacia	20–60
Black poplar	30
Birch, white poplar, alder	40
Maple, cedar, cherry, sycamore	50
Larch, ebony, elm, pine	70–80
Fir, ash, walnut, lime	100
Beech	100
Chestnut, cypress, holm oak, oak	80-250

Tree felling and forestry management

For many centuries woods and primeval forests were exploited without supervision of any kind because it was thought that natural resources were unlimited and that nature's own regenerative power would compensate for its exploitation and destruction by man. Although there are still places today where forests are cleared and trees are felled, the situation has greatly improved. It is now known that natural resources can become exhausted if no precautions are taken. This is why it was essential that forestry management policies should be developed.

The demand for wood by saw mills, paper mills and other sectors of industry is constantly increasing. Although it is necessary to be able to meet this growing demand in the future, this demand must be contained within the limits of the natural cycle of wood production. That means that every year only as many trees should be felled as can be replaced. Experience has shown that many more trees must be planted than will be needed later because a number of them will fall prey to rodents, insects and other pests and diseases, thus failing to survive to maturity. In addition, the weakest specimens are normally thinned out in order to make more room for the stronger trees which will then be able to develop better. The young trees which have been thinned may be used for fencing and pit props in coal mines, while the smaller pieces are often sold as firewood.

Forestry management which deals with the cultivation of forests applies scientific techniques to achieve maximum growth at minimum cost.

The methods used in organised tree-felling include partial felling, reproduction cutting and selective felling.

Partial felling

In the case of partial felling the forest is divided into sections which are felled alternately following a rotation system. In this way a constant yield is sustained and it becomes possible to introduce other types of trees. A section is chosen where the trees will be felled while the surrounding sections remain untouched to protect the soil and the environment. The area where the trees have been felled will be artificially restocked or allowed to grow back naturally again. After the trees in this section have grown to a certain height and developed sufficiently, the trees in the next section can be felled.

Reproduction felling

This method is used mainly in forests with species of trees which reproduce easily and which do not require any particular care. The entire forest can be completely felled, leaving only a few trees here and there as parent trees to ensure reproduction and subsequent reforestation. The main problem with this kind of approach is the excessive, undesirable density of the young self-seeded trees which is a known drawback of natural reforestation. That is why the young forest must be thinned once or twice in order to ensure that the remaining trees have sufficient space to develop properly.

Selective felling of chosen trees

This method allows the plantation of mixed forests which preserves the variety of species of the eco-system because selective felling of selected trees protects the animal and plant world as well as the soil. Selective felling is practised mainly in areas of ecological and

Stages of partial felling

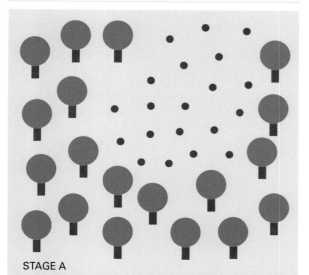

STAGE A

An area to be felled is chosen, leaving adjacent areas untouched. so that the forest is preserved and the overall habitat does not suffer.

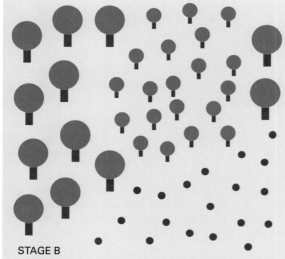

STAGE B

The area felled in Stage A has been naturally or artificially replanted and continues to grow. Meanwhile, an area adjacent to the original one is felled.

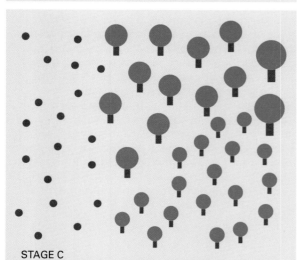

STAGE C

The trees planted in the area felled in Stage A are growing and the area felled in Stage B has also been replanted. Meanwhile the trees are felled in the area adjacent to those already felled earlier.

Stages of reproduction felling

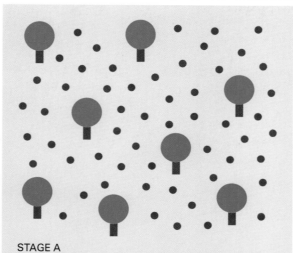

STAGE A

An area is selected in which a large number of trees are felled. Only a few fully-grown examples are left to act as parent trees which will seed themselves in the area felled so that it becomes replanted.

STAGE B

Once the trees seeded by the parent trees have established themselves, the parent trees themselves are felled in order to leave more room for the growth of the new trees.

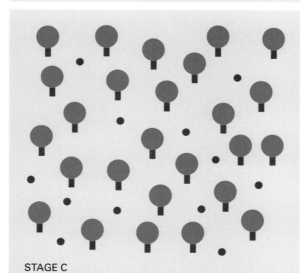

STAGE C

The forest is cleared once or twice, removing the less healthy and robust trees to encourage the growth of the better trees which will ultimately be felled.

Stages of selective felling

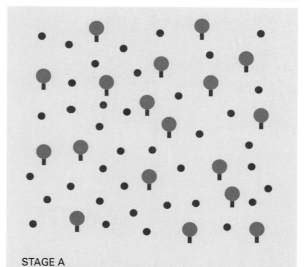

STAGE A

In a nominated area of the forest the fastest-growing trees are felled, leaving the strongest to continue to grow and become stronger.

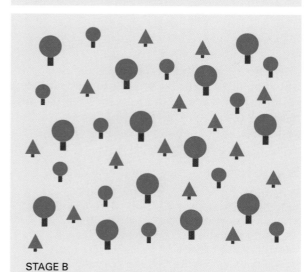

STAGE B

While the trees not felled during Stage A continue to grow, the forest is replanted with one or more new species which will grow with them.

STAGE C

While the trees planted in Stage B to fill the gaps in the forest are now well-established and growing well, those remaining from Stage A are felled, since by now they will have reached a level of vigorous maturity.

21

tourist interest because this type of felling does not create large, bare areas which could interfere with beauty of the landscape. Individual fully developed trees are felled while the younger trees are left to grow and develop. The existing gaps are filled by replanting. When the newly planted trees have reached a certain height, the other trees which have by now reached maturity are felled. After felling, the trees are taken to the saw mill where they are cut to the required shape and size.

The longitudinal sawing of a trunk is always arranged to provide the maximum amount of wood, with the smallest number of cuts and avoiding waste as much as possible.

Raw and sawn timber

The term raw timber is used to designate debranched, debarked timber, sometimes sawn lengthways or merely split, but in any case timber which has not been further processed. This is used as a basic material for further commercialisation. Sawn timber is wood sawn parallel to the axis of the trunk, into square or rectangular pieces such as beams, thick planks and boards. They may be sawn with a sharp edge (square edged) or left with a waney edge. In some parts of the world this is still done with reciprocating gang saws with one or more blades working either vertically or horizontally. Elsewhere, band saws are gaining ground.

Rough timber

When buying rough wood, the most important point is the intended purpose. Raw timber is divided according to the quality of the wood and the part of the trunk it comes from, which controls its knottiness.
• Quality classification: Grades range from A to C and are based mainly on the degree of knottiness . A tree trunk is sawn from bottom to top into several sections (the lower trunk, middle trunk and top trunk), the number of branches gradually increasing towards the top of the trunk. The mostly knot-free wood from the lower trunk and middle trunk is ideally suited to cabinetmaking while the more branched wood from the top part of the trunk is used mainly for building purposes.
• Size classification: because the trunk is not equally thick everywhere, an average diameter has been fixed. The classification according to size ranges from L0 (under 10 cm/4 in) to L6 (60 cm/24 in and over). The wood volume is calculated on the basis of the length of the rough timber and the diameter of the trunk. The price of rough timber cubic metre is based on the quality and size classification.

Sawn timber

Sawing takes place in saw mills using hand controlled or computer controlled sawing machines, the latter sometimes equipped with measuring programmes to reduce wastage to a minimum. On arrival at the saw mill, the trunks are first debarked on an edger, a machine which removes the bark and possible defects, if this has not been already been done in the forest. Nothing is wasted in a saw-mill; the bark is chopped up and used as fuel in the saw mill itself or used in horticulture to fertilise or improve the soil. The trunk is measured and cut according to its intended use. Beams and planks intended for outdoor use need to be longer than those for indoor uses, such as wainscoting. With vertical gang saws which can be fitted with as

Logs after leaving the debarking machine.

many as 30 blades, it is possible to saw an entire trunk in one pass. Band saws and circular saws are also used. The length of the finished pieces is in fact pre-determined by the original size and shape of the tree. For instance, if a tree is very tall but the trunk is markedly cone-shaped towards the top (the diameter of the trunk decreasing towards the top), there will also be a larger number of shorter pieces.

At the end of this process and if destined for building purposes, the saw timber is sorted according to size and shape, placed on a conveyor belt in bundles and run past a radial saw which trims the ends to ensure that all the pieces are the same length.

The rectangular cut pieces may be *undressed* which means that the surfaces have not been planed after sawing, known in the trade as rough timber. The timber may also be *dressed* which means that the surfaces have been smoothed down by machine planing. With high quality hardwood timber, often used to make veneer, the butt is usually cut as logs and sold as such.

Veneer

The very thick trunks of exotic trees and others suitable for veneer are debarked with a special debarking machine so that the trunk can later be sliced off in thin layers. Another way of cutting veneer is to cut the timber to the right size with a band saw and peel thin layers of veneer from the trunk with a veneer lathe, which works like a very large parallel pencil sharpener. There is another very time-consuming method which involves sawing thin sheets from the trunk. However, this method is hardly used today because of the high percentage of waste.

Systems for converting a log into planks

All types of cutting are designed to use as much of the trunk as possible with as many usable pieces while reducing wastage to a minimum. In doing this, it is important to cut the wood in such a way that the wood does not warp during drying.

Drying

After the trunks have been felled, sawn, cut to the required length and sorted according to size, the timber is dried. Freshly sawn wood contains a lot of moisture while the sap which is still present in the vessels and fibres may attract pests and fungi which could damage the wood. The wood will contract and change shape during the drying process.

When wood is dried its moisture content decreases until it is in balance with that of the environment in which it will be used. This will achieve the following:
• Stabilisation to keep shrinkage and warping of the wood to a minimum

The various ways of sawing a trunk

Cut for a large whole piece
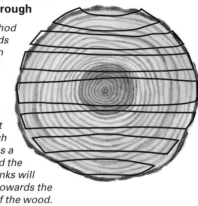
This provides a fairly uniform central beam of large size. The trunk is cut with a saw which cuts four faces at right angles to each other. The four edges cut off may provide planks if the size is large enough.

Parallel or through and through
With this method planks and boards are obtained from the whole width of the log. The disadvantages are that the central piece will contain the heart of the trunk which will be uneven as a result, and the remaining planks will tend to warp towards the outer sides of the wood.

Radial cuts
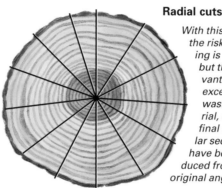
With this method the risk of warping is reduced, but the disadvantage of an excessive waste of material, once the final rectangular sections have been produced from the original angled cuts.

Cross cut
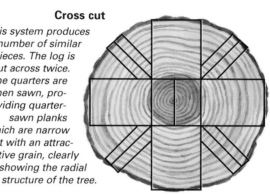
This system produces a number of similar pieces. The log is cut across twice. The quarters are then sawn, providing quartersawn planks which are narrow but with an attractive grain, clearly showing the radial structure of the tree.

Cantibay cut
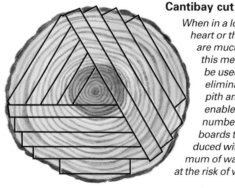
When in a log the heart or the pith are much altered, this method can be used which eliminates the pith and enables a good number of wide boards to be produced with a minimum of waste, but at the risk of warping.

Quartersawing
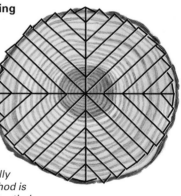
This is one of the best ways of converting a log into planks without warping because the cuts are at right angles to the growth rings. This yields a larger number of narrower boards but they are of high quality and beautifully figured. This method is used with choice timbers.

Alternating cuts
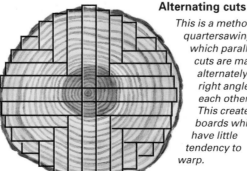
This is a method of quartersawing in which parallel cuts are made alternately at right angles to each other. This creates boards which have little tendency to warp.

Square cutting
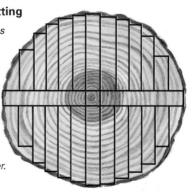
This method provides planks with cuts at right angles to the growth rings, reducing the tendency to warp. A transverse cut removes the central area containing the pith, resulting in boards which are narrower.

23

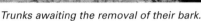

Trunks awaiting the removal of their bark.

Collection of thick trunks, that is, trunks which are over 30 cm (12 in) in diameter and cut to a length of 10 to 15 m (33 to 50 ft).

• Prevents an invasion of putrefying fungi who need over 20% moisture in the wood to survive
• A reduction in weight which is very important for transport
• Increased strength of the wood

A newly felled trunk may contain twice its weight in water. The moisture contained in the wood is measured as a percentage and indicates the amount of moisture compared to the dry wood. If a piece of wood weighing 150 g (6 oz) in total would contains 100 g (4 oz) of wood when completely dry, then its moisture content is 50%. In the table below on the right are a few moisture percentages suitable for specific purposes.

Drying methods

• Air-drying: This method involves stacking up the wood neatly so that it can dry in the air. The pieces of wood to be dried are separated from each other by strips of wood so that the air can circulate around freely everywhere. Because air-

Logs on the saw table after measurement, ready to be sawn into pieces as decided.

drying takes a very long time, it is important to have large stacking areas.

Air-drying is easy and cost-effective and produces excellent result, although sometimes there are problems with pest infestation and fungi. However, only a certain level of drying can be achieved in this way, so air-dried wood is not immediately suitable for indoor use. The colour of wood does not change with this method of drying. The time it takes to dry depends on the climatic conditions, the type of wood and the thickness of the planks. Softwood takes about two years to dry while hardwood can take up to six years.

The faster-drying softwood is stacked in early summer while hardwood which take a longer time to dry is stacked in winter to slow down the drying process and thus prevent the formation of cracks and warping.

After a few months it is advisable to continue the drying process in closed woodsheds with good ventilation in order to protect it from direct sunlight and strong wind. When drying in sheds it

is important that the ventilation openings should be placed in the direction of the prevailing wind so that the wind can blow through the whole breadth of the stacked wood . After drying the planks are stacked on top of each other without strips of wood separating them.

The timber is considered sufficiently dry when the residual moisture content of the wood is between 13 and 20%.
• Kiln drying: One of the most important factors when drying wood artificially is that the drying process should be started immediately after felling so that the water-loss can take place under controlled conditions. With artificial drying, drying time is reduced to a few weeks in contrast to the months and years it takes with air-drying. The result is wood with normal moisture content, that is a residual moisture content of 10 to 15%. The methods using artificial drying make it possible to produce dry wood with a moisture content of 10 to 15% in a very short time which is not possible with air-drying alone.

Relative humidity levels of wood

USE OF WOOD	MAX. %
Hydraulic works	30
Very humid conditions	25–30
Exposed to weather, not covered	18–25
Open covered works	16–20
Closed covered works	13–17
Closed rooms with heating	12–14
Open rooms with heating	10–12

Advantages of artificial drying

- Destroys all insects and larvae
- Avoids fungi and rot
- Not subject to climatic conditions
- The wood is quickly dried at low energy cost, if the waste wood is used as fuel for the drying ovens
- Greater control of the air speed, humidity and temperature
- The drying process is continuous
- Takes up much less space than natural drying
- If the process is properly controlled, warping of the timber is avoided

Disadvantages of artificial drying

- Requires costly plant and equipment
- Can harden the outer layers of the wood
- If there is any technical or human error, there is the risk of ruining the whole of the consignment being dried.

View of a continuous saw mill working on a trunk, dividing it into separate parts according to the uses and properties expected from the resulting planks.

After spending two months in the open air, the drying of the wood is continued in open or closed sheds so that the pieces of timber are protected from the sun but exposed to ventilation with dry wind.

Drying plants

There are two main types of drying installations: room kilns and ventilation kilns.

The most commonly used drying systems are those using warm air and steam (convection drying), followed by those using direct or indirect heat transmission. High-frequency drying is rarely used because of its high cost; it is reserved for expensive, rare woods.

Drying plants consist of one or more air-tight sealable rooms or chambers through which air circulates, its temperature and humidity are carefully controlled.

Drying with warm air and steam

It is generally assumed that artificial drying with warm air is a variation of natural drying. The timber is stacked in a room or ventilation kiln and warm air is pumped in which quickly absorbs the moisture. In theory this method is simple but in fact it is a very complicated procedure because serious damage can occur if the wood is dried too quickly. The difference between the humidity in the air and the moisture in the wood must be controlled at all times. There are two ways of achieving this:
• By blowing in warm air at a constant temperature. The process starts with a high level of humidity in the air which is achieved by pumping steam into the room. It continues until the moisture content in the wood has dropped to a certain level. This prevents the moisture levels in the wood dropping too quickly.
• By changing the temperature and humidity level. This method involves humid, very lightly warmed air being pumped into the kiln to start with. The air temperature is then gradually raised and the humidity slowly reduced in order to reduce the risk of warping and cracking. The process must be watched very carefully to avoid serious damage to the wood. There are many variations on this method which is generally held to be an improvement on one or other aspect of the previous method: faster drying, greater efficiency, better control, and so on.

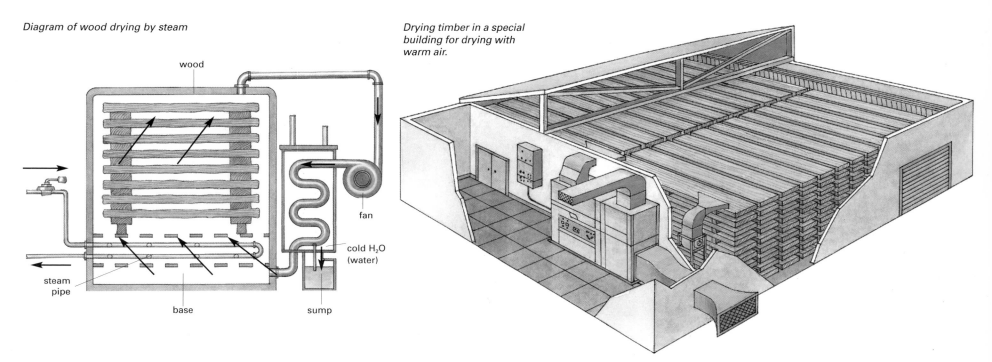

Diagram of wood drying by steam

wood

fan

cold H_2O (water)

steam pipe

base

sump

Drying timber in a special building for drying with warm air.

Characteristics of wood

Wood is a complex material whose properties are determined not only by its composition but also by its structure, that is, the way in which the various wood elements are arranged. It is indeed the arrangement of these elements which influences the sometimes apparently illogical behaviour of wood. But it is important to remember that wood is not a material produced by mankind for its own purposes but a natural product, gathered from the trunk and branches of trees whose primary purpose is not to produce wood for people. Also the variations resulting from this contribute to the great usefulnes of wood and to its character as a material.

Wood is not a homogeneous material. It is made up of different types of specialised cells which form its tissue. This tissue carries out the basic functions of the tree such as carrying the sap, converting and storing nutrients as well as forming a robust support structure which gives the tree its solidity. In this section the composition, microstructure and macrostructure of wood is described in more detail.

Composition and structure of wood

Wood is a heterogeneous, fibrous material which is produced by a living thing, a tree.

The wide range of uses and qualities of different kinds of wood is the result of the particular properties given it by the structure and composition of the cells which make up the tree. It is the vegetable origin of wood which distinguishes it from mineral matter, and makes it such a variable material.

The organic constituents of wood

Cellulose:	40–50%
Lignin:	25–30%
Semi-cellulose:	20–25% (carbohydrates)
Resin, tannin, fats:	remaining %

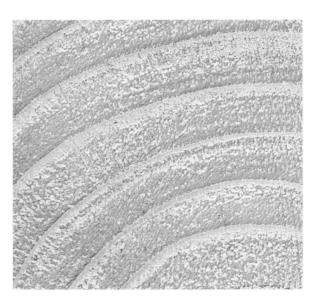

The trunk of a conifer, with the growth rings, clearly showing the difference between spring wood (earlywood) and autumn wood (latewood).

Cross section of a trunk showing a strong contrast between the lighter area of the sapwood and the darker tone of the heartwood.

Trunk of wood from the plane tree with very densely distributed medullary rays.

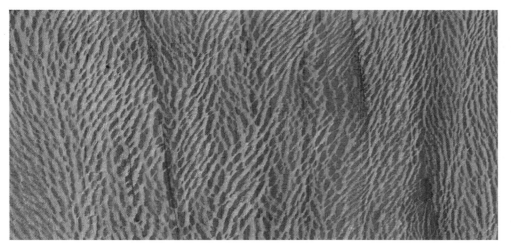

Trunk of a holm oak tree with its medullary rays.

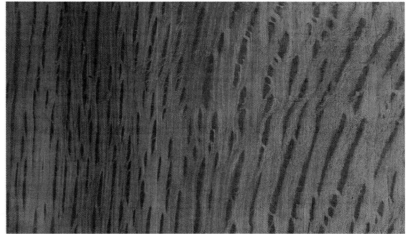

CROSS SECTION OF A TREE TRUNK SHOWING ITS VARIOUS PARTS

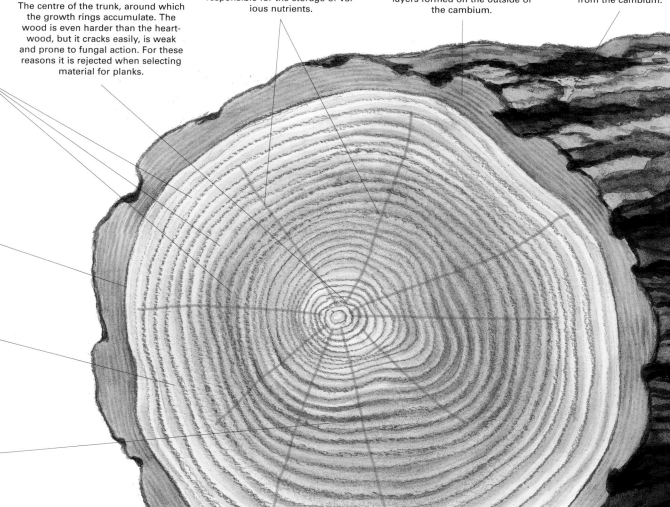

Growth rings

These are approximately concentric rings of alternate like and dark tones which are visible in transverse sections of the truck. These correspond to the layers which are formed by the cambium in the spring (light in colour, broad vessels) and in late summer (dark colour, narrow vessels), during the growth period which generally occurs annually. The width varies according to the type of tree and the kind of climate the tree has undergone. It provides very interesting information relating to the chronology of the tree and also the events which may have affected it. The rings are formed by the large cells of the early-wood and the smaller ones of the latewood.

Pith

The centre of the trunk, around which the growth rings accumulate. The wood is even harder than the heart-wood, but it cracks easily, is weak and prone to fungal action. For these reasons it is rejected when selecting material for planks.

Medullary rays

These are formed by cells arranged radially, at right angles to the growth rings, and they are responsible for the storage of various nutrients.

Phloem

The inner layer of the bark, responsible for conveying the descending sap. It is built up of layers formed on the outside of the cambium.

Cortex

The outer bark which protects the tree. It is formed by dead cells originating from the cambium.

Cambium

The fine layer of cellular material which occurs between the bark and the sapwood. It is this which is responsible for the growth of the tree. It creates the dark bark on one side and the light sapwood on the other.

Sapwood

New material whose cells transport or store the nutrients which support the tree. It is very moist. Since it contain food, it is very prone to insect attack and decomposition caused by micro-organisms. This wood is not recommended for work demanding stability and durability.

Heartwood

Old wood, that is, the oldest part of the trunk which forms the main support of the tree. It is usually very dry, harder and darker than the sapwood. It consists of old growth rings and occupies the greater part of the trunk. With the passage of years, the pores which once conveyed the sap are filled with various materials. It is the most appreciated wood, since it is dense and durable.

27

Physical properties

Anisotropy

Wood is an anisotropic material because it is made up of fibres which are arranged in one particular direction. This means that it does not have the same physical and mechanical properties in all directions. These properties change depending on the direction in which a force is exerted.

There are three main directions with their own properties:

- **Axial direction:** The longitudinal direction, that is, parallel with the axis of the tree. It is in this direction that the tree has its best properties, looked at from a commercial point of view.

- **Radial direction:** Perpendicular to fibres and parallel to the rays.

- **Tangential direction:** Also perpendicular to the fibres but parallel to the growth rings.

Water content

Water is the carrier used by the plant for the transport of nutrients. Moisture is the most important property of wood since it influences all its other properties, both physical and mechanical, and also its ability to deal with, moderate and resist biological attack by pests, fungal growth and disease. This is why it is important to know the relative humidity together with the hygroscopic properties of wood before using it, because the moisture level may be responsible for possible physical and mechanical changes. This could affect decision of which would to use.

Water content of wood

The humidity or moisture content of a piece of wood is calculated as follows: the difference between the moist weight and the dry weight is divided by the dry weight and multiplied by 100. This gives the moisture content of a piece of wood expressed as a percentage.

It is important to be aware that moisture levels are not the same in all parts of a tree. Wood is hygroscopic which means that. depending on the level of humidity in the atmosphere, it absorbs or exudes water. With time a stable moisture content is achieved automatically, determined by the ambient temperature and humidity. If these conditions change, the moisture

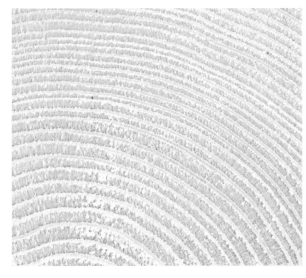

Transverse section of coniferous wood.

Radial section of coniferous wood.

Tangential section of coniferous wood.

Transverse section of deciduous wood.

Radial section of deciduous wood.

Tangential section of deciduous wood.

Presence of water in wood

Water of constitution or combined water	This forms part of the chemical constituents of wood. It is an integral part of the woody material and it can only be removed by destroying the material itself (for example, by burning).
Water of impregnation or saturation	This impregnates the cell walls, filling their sub-microscopic and microscopic spaces. It comes inside the cell walls, being the cause of wood shrinking when it is lost and swelling when it is recovered. It can be removed by heating to 100–110° C (212–230° F).
Free water	This fills the cells or tubes (vessels, tracheids etc.). It is absorbed by capillary action..

• Once free water has been eliminated from the wood, it cannot be replaced by being in a humid atmosphere. To replace it, it must be soaked in water. Free water has no effect on the physical content of the vessels and it has no influence the swelling or shrinkage of the wood, or its mechanical properties.

• The two last types, water of saturation and free water, constitute the moisture content of the wood. Humidity is the amount of water in the wood expressed as a percentage.

State of wood at various levels of % humidity

Soaked wood	Up to about 150% (immersed in water).
Green wood	Up to 70% (standing timber or just felled).
Saturated wood	30% (without free water, coinciding with FSP).
Semi-dried wood	From 30% to 23% (sawn timber).
Commercially dried wood	From 23% to 18% (in the open).
Air-dried wood	From 18% to 13% (sheltered from the rain).
Desiccated wood (very dry)	Less than 13% (dried naturally or in a dry climate).
Dehydrated wood	0% (in an oven at 103° C/217° F. Unstable state).

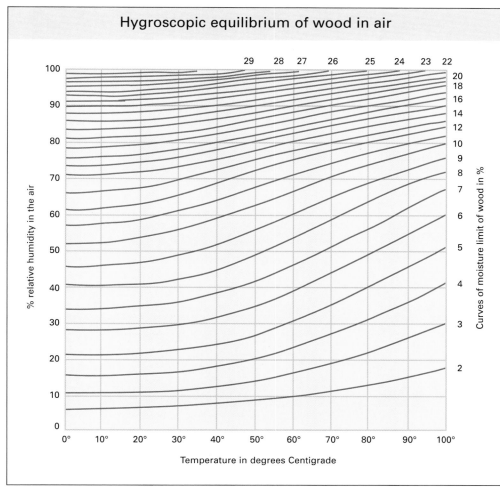

Hygroscopic equilibrium of wood in air

% relative humidity in the air

Curves of moisture limit of wood in %

Temperature in degrees Centigrade

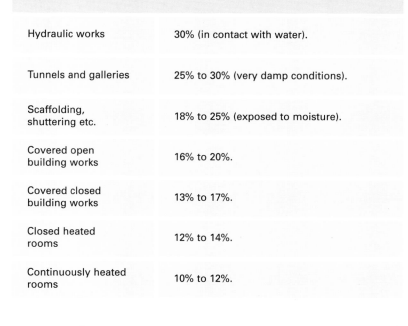

Optimum humidity of wood for various uses

Hydraulic works	30% (in contact with water).
Tunnels and galleries	25% to 30% (very damp conditions).
Scaffolding, shuttering etc.	18% to 25% (exposed to moisture).
Covered open building works	16% to 20%.
Covered closed building works	13% to 17%.
Closed heated rooms	12% to 14%.
Continuously heated rooms	10% to 12%.

Swelling and shrinkage

This describes the capacity of wood to alter its volume when humidity levels change. This only happens below the fibre saturation point. If the wood increases in volume as a result of absorbing moisture it is described as swelling, while if it

content in the wood also changes in order re-establish the balance with the ambient air.

Wood first releases its free water during the drying process. This loss of water takes place without any changes in the physical and mechanical properties of the wood. Even when the free water has evaporated there still remains water in the cell walls (bound water). It is only when the bound water begins to decrease through evaporation or drying that the physical and mechanical properties of the wood begin to change; its hardness and most aspects of its mechanical resistance increase while the wood decreases in volume as a result of the reduced volume of the cell walls.

Now the moisture content depends on the ambient hygrothermic conditions. Each elevation in the temperature and relative humidity of the air corresponds to a moisture content in the wood of between 0% and 30% (the approximate fibre saturation point or FSP) which is known as *hygroscopic equilibrium moisture content*. The fibre saturation point, that is the saturation point of the cell wall, indicates the maximum moisture content of

wood after evaporation of the free water. If it is below this point wood will only be able to absorb free water when immersed in water.

The fibre saturation point is very important. It is the point at which there are no more changes in volume, resistance and so on. The fibre saturation point is reached at approximately 30% moisture content, although there may be small differences between one species and another.

Wood with a low saturation point has stable mechanical properties when used in humid surroundings. In surroundings with a low humidity it warps when there are changes in humidity levels. Wood with a high saturation point is mostly used in surroundings whose humidity level is much lower than its fibre saturation point, unless it is under water. This kind of wood hardly warps or shrinks when humidity levels change. When the equilibrium moisture content is 12%, it is described as normal moisture content. This figure has been chosen because it is the moisture content of wood grown in the temperate zone at an average temperature of 20° C (68° F) and an ambient relative humidity of 65%.

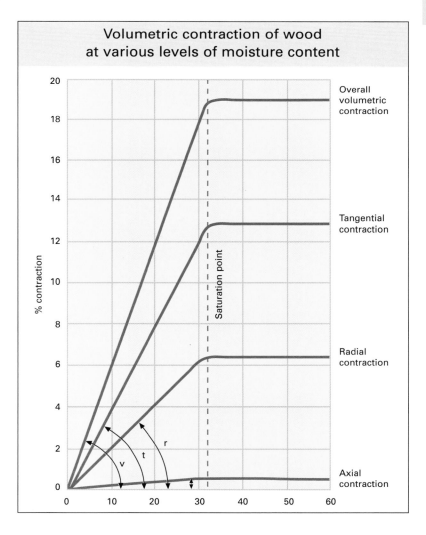

Volumetric contraction of wood at various levels of moisture content

% contraction

Saturation point

Overall volumetric contraction

Tangential contraction

Radial contraction

Axial contraction

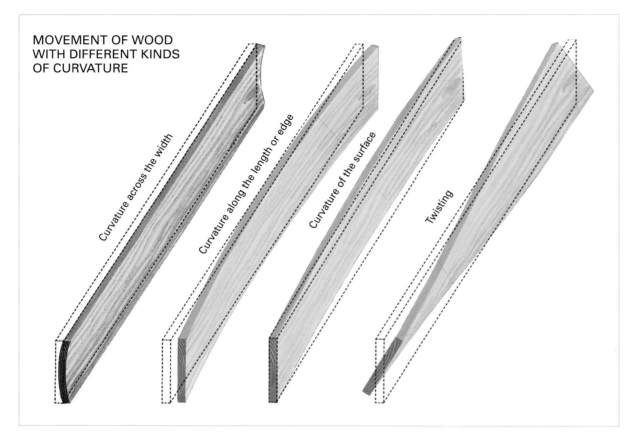

MOVEMENT OF WOOD WITH DIFFERENT KINDS OF CURVATURE

Curvature across the width

Curvature along the length or edge

Curvature of the surface

Twisting

change (0.1%) need not be taken be taken into account, unlike the variations in the radial direction which range between 2% and 4%. In the tangential direction (growth rings) shrinkage is usually 1.5 to 2 times larger than it is in the radial direction. The difference in shrinkage between radial and tangential directions is the cause of the warping and cracking which occur during drying. There are a few types of wood in which the swelling and shrinking are almost equal in both radial and tangential directions. These types of woods do not crack or warp even when shrinking a lot if they have been dried correctly.

The shrinkage and warping in a symmetrical board can be as follows depending on the cut: longitudinal warping on the short side, transverse warping, longitudinal warping of the side and twisting (difference between the tangential and radial shrinkage).

The warping and shrinking of the wood is more pronounced towards the outside of the trunk than in the middle, boards tending therefore to warp in the direction of the sapwood (because this is where the largest amount of water is absorbed).

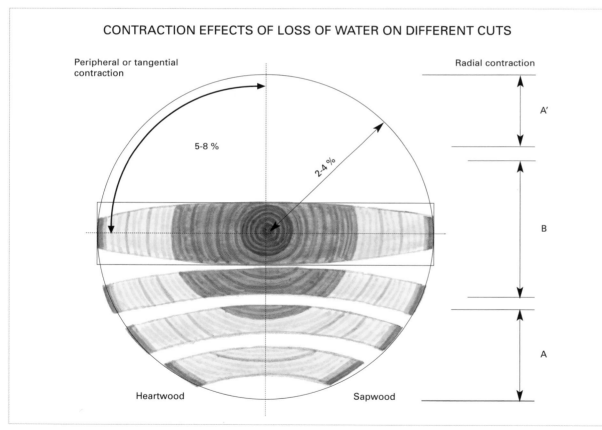

CONTRACTION EFFECTS OF LOSS OF WATER ON DIFFERENT CUTS

Peripheral or tangential contraction

Radial contraction

5-8 %

2-4 %

A'

B

A

Heartwood

Sapwood

Density

Density is defined as follows:

Density = weight divided by volume

Wood is a porous material, in other words it contains cavities (vessels) which play a part in the definition of density. In view of the porous nature and the changes in weight and volume determined by the moisture content, it is important that the conditions under which density is measured should be defined more precisely.

If account is taken of all the cavities when determining the volume a rough value for density is obtained.

If only the pure wood mass is considered (ignoring the volume of the pores), the pure density is obtained. Pure density (without taking the pores into account) is the same in all types of wood, equalling 1.55 g/cm². This is the theoretical maximum limit which wood can reach when the cell cavities have been reduced to nil. The different rough density of the various types of wood is therefore based on the proportionate volume of cavities.

It is very important to know the rough density (taking the pores into account) because it gives an approximate representation of the physical and mechanical behaviour of the wood. If the wood has a high rough density, it means there are few pores and a lot of resistant matter. Rough density is calculated from the weight of the wood and the volume of all its cavities. There is a relation – although not a linear one – between rough density and the resistance of wood.

decreases in volume because of loss of moisture it is described as shrinking.

The volume of the wood increases proportionately to the level of humidity to approximately 25% moisture content in the wood. Beyond that, the volume continues to increase but increasingly slowly until the fibre saturation point is reached. After that the volume remains constant (maximum swelling). The changes in volume are the result of linear changes in the three directions: axial, tangential and radial, whereby the swelling and shrinking resulting from the anisotropic nature of wood is clearly marked in the respective direction. Wood changes only very little in the longitudinal fibre direction. As a result, this

Classification of wood according to specific gravity

TYPE	CONIFEROUS	DECIDUOUS
Very light	0.4	0.5
Light	0.4 to 0.5	0.5 to 0.65
Medium	0.5 to 0.6	0.65 to 0.8
Heavy	0.6 to 0.7	0.8 to 1.0
Very heavy	>0.7	>1.0

Homogeneity and durability

Wood is homogeneous when the structure and composition of the fibres in all its woody parts are uniform (for instance: pear wood, apple wood, lime wood, box wood or maple). Non-homogeneous wood types include:
• Wood with very strongly developed pith (for instance, chestnut oak, ash and plane).
• Wood whose growth rings show considerable differences between early and late wood (for instance: fir).
Homogeneity is a very variable property because it depends on many factors: surroundings, type of wood, type of felling, general conditions, drying method, fluctuations of humidity, soil conditions (wood keeps a long time in loamy soil and moist sand but only a short time in sand and chalky soil), water (wood lasts for a long time in fresh water), treatment before use, protection after processing (paint, varnish), and so on.
The higher the density of wood, the more durable it is. Durable woods include for instance: chestnut oak, oak, mahogany, beech.

Flammability and combustibility

Wood burns, a feature which is considered a virtue when it is seen as a fuel. However, from a building and interior design point of view it is serious drawback. However, because it

Transverse section of a very homogeneous wood, box.

Cross-section of a very heterogeneous wood, holm oak.

Flammability of wood

Highly inflammable	Pine, fir, willow, black poplar, alder, etc., and almost all resinous trees
Fairly inflammable	Beech, mahogany, chestnut, cedar etc
Not very inflammable	Holm oak, ebony, box, larch etc.

Ignition of wood

Dry wood		wet wood
Wood with bark and branches	burn(s) better than	debarked wood without branches
Small pieces		large pieces
Vertical pieces		horizontal pieces

burns from the outside to the inside, it can sometimes have a longer survival time in a fire than steel girders would. According to the standard classification of degree of flammability of building materials, wood is in the B2 category (normally flammable). However, the application of chemicals and waterproofing agents on outer surfaces can also increase the fire resistance of wood.

When wood burns the cellulose which produces the plant fibres reacts with oxygen. What is left behind is a small residue of ashes, produced by the lignin and mineral salts. Wood will burn almost completely if there is enough oxygen and the temperature is very high. If there is not enough oxygen and the temperature is not very high, wood will only burn partially. In this case the cellulose becomes dehydrated (the water is removed from the wood) and the wood is transformed into soft charcoal which has little resistance. Dry wood ignites spontaneously at a temperature of 300° C (572° F).

Hard wood burns superficially and slowly with a small flame. Soft wood burns brightly with large flames. The differences are less marked when the pieces of wood are not very thick.

Mechanical properties

Elastic deformation

Under stress wood becomes deformed as formulated by Hooke's Law, which says that each increment of stress produces a proportional increment of strain. If the proportional limit is exceeded, wood only recovers part of the strain, remaining permanently deformed to a certain degree. If the stress continues to increase the wood will break. The resistance of a material, including wood, is determined by ratio of stress to strain which is known as the modulus of elasticity. It indicates the resistance against elastic deformation. The higher the modulus of elasticity, the smaller the deformation under stress, which means also means that the material is less elastic.

The modulus of elasticity of wood depends on the type of wood, the moisture content, and the type, nature, direction and duration of the stress. It usually increases with greater rough density is and decreases with higher moisture content in the wood.

exceed its proportional limit without breaking immediately. This is why it is ideally suited for objects with curves such as furniture, wheels, centring, musical instruments and so on.

Green, young or heated wood is more flexible than dry or wood and has a higher proportional limit.

Bending is made easier by warming the inside of the wood (the fibres shrivel) and wetting the outside with water (the outer fibres become elongated). This process must be carried out very slowly.

Nowadays, flexibility is increased by treating the wood with steam.

Hardness

The hardness of wood is its ability to resist penetration by foreign objects into its surface (nails, screws, chisel, saw etc.).

The hardness of wood is determined by the composition of its fibres and its structure, the type of tree, the part of the trunk in question and the age of the wood. These result in invariable properties.

Flexibility

Some types of wood can bend or become deformed in a longitudinal direction without breaking. If they are elastic they recover their original shape when the stress is removed. Wood has an amazing ability to

Examples of flexibility	
Flexible woods	Ash, elm, fir, pine.
Non-flexible woods	Holm oak, maple, hardwoods in general.

Illustration of the flexibility wood can achieve.

Main determinants of hardness in wood
• The hardest woods are also the heaviest.
• The heartwood is harder than the sapwood.
• Green wood is softer than dried wood.
• Fibrous material is harder than that which is not.
• The woods with most vessels are softest.
• The hardest woods polish best.

Examples of hardness in wood	
Very hard	Ebony, box, holm oak.
Hard	Cherry, maple, oak, yew.
Medium	Beech, walnut, chestnut, pear, plane, acacia, mahogany, cedar, ash, teak.
Soft	Fir, birch, alder, pine.
Very soft	Black poplar, lime, willow, balsa/

Strength

This is the wood's resistance against a force applied perpendicularly against the fibres which tends to break the wood.

To break the wood perpendicular to the direction of the fibres, a relatively high force is required. To split or cut wood parallel to the fibres, only a minimum of force is required.

Resistance to splitting

This refers to the wood's resistance against a force applied in direction parallel to the fibres when cutting or chopping wood.

Wood has a tendency to crack or split in the direction of the fibres. The blade of an axe easily penetrates the wood because its force overcomes the cohesive power of the fibres (the axe splits but does not cut). This characteristic is quite evident when chopping firewood: it is easy to split the logs in the direction of the fibres. Green wood splits more easily than dry wood.

If wooden components must be assembled with screws or nails it is important that the wood used should not split easily.

Examples of splitting capability of wood	
Easy to split	Chestnut, larch, fir.
Hard to split	Elm, maple, birch.
Splintery	Ash.

Resistance to wear

There are types of wood which undergo a loss of material when subjected to erosion or abrasion.

Resistance to abrasion is strong in a direction perpendicular to the fibres, smaller in tangential ones and very small in radial ones.

Resistance to shock

This is the resistance of wood to a particular shock. Resistance is highest when the blow occurs parallel to the direction of the fibres and smaller when in a transverse or radial direction.

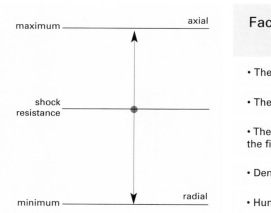

Factors influencing shock resistance
• The type of wood.
• The size of the piece.
• The direction of impact in relation to the fibres.
• Density.
• Humidity.

Charpy pendulum to measure resistance of wood to shock.

Resistance to tension

The resistance to a force which is exerted in the direction of the fibres of the wood. Wood is ideally suited for being used under tension loads (in the longitudinal direction of the fibres). This property is only limited by the difficulty of transfer the tensile forces to the individual components. This means that problems may occur at the joints.

If tension is exerted in the longitudinal direction of the fibres, the degree of deformation is lower than in the case of a compressive load, especially so far as plastic deformation is concerned. This means that the brake of a piece of wood resulting from tension load can be considered

Factors affecting resistance to tension	
Humidity	Resistance to tension along the grain increases in a more or less proportionately as the saturation point of the fibres approaches 10%, with an increase of 3% for each 1% drop in humidity. Between 8 and 10% humidity it is at its maximum, after which it reduces slightly.
Temperature	The effect of temperature is less on tension along the grain than with other types of force.
Knots	Knots affect the strength tremendously, since the diversion of the fibres round the knot has a great effect on resistance. So, small knots which reduce compression resistance by 10% will reduce the tensile strength by 50%. Knots also cause the tension to be irregularly distributed.
Fibre (grain) direction	It can be said that the angle of the fibres has a much greater effect on tension than compression. An angle of 15° reduces the tensile strength by 50% and at 30° it is one-fifth of what it would be if the fibres were parallel.

as a fragile break. The resistance of wood to a tensile load in the longitudinal direction of the fibres is high. This is due to the cellulose molecules which make up the cell walls.

In practice there are a number of limitations if wood is to be subjected to tensile load. There are compression loads such as drill holes and so on in those places where two components have been joined which can lead to a break because of shearing tension, so that the wood's high tensile strength cannot be fully be utilised. In addition, this resistance is also greatly affected by knot holes as well as by the run of the grain which may strongly reduce it as the compression load decreases.

Resistance to compression

Compression strength is the resistance to a force which is exerted parallel or perpendicular to the wood fibres.

Because wood is used for constructional as well as decorative purposes but also plays an important part in the construction of buildings, its compression strength is very important. The compression strength of wood is not always the same. It is lower than the tensile strength in the longitudinal direction of the fibres, the ratio being of the order of 0.5. But it may vary between 0.25 to 0.75 depending on the type of wood.

Factors influencing compression resistance

Angle of the fibres	The effect of reduction of resistance in itself is somewhat less than in tension.
Density	There is a linear relationship, so that the greater the density the greater the resistance.
Humidity	The influence is almost nil at the saturation point, and increases from this point as humidity is reduced. Between a humidity of 8 to 18%, the variation is virtually linear.
Knots	Its influence is less than it has on tensile strength

Classifications of woods according to UNE

VALUE	CONIFEROUS	DECIDUOUS
Small	Less than 35.	Less than 45.
Medium	From 35 to 45.	From 45 to 75.
Large	More than 45.	More than 75.

This classification is made according to the unit resistance C to the axial compression N/mm²

Classification of wood according to values obtained in a tensile test at 12% humidity

Small resistance	Less than 25 N/mm².
Medium resistance	Between 25 and 45 N/mm².
Strong resistance	Greater than 45 N/mm².

Resistance to bending

This is the resistance of the wood against a force exerted at right angles to the direction of the fibres. To test this, the wood is supported at both ends and a load is applied in the middle, perpendicular to the axis. This causes the wood to bend, the top side becoming shorter and the bottom side longer. The resulting axial bending stresses are greatest at the ends of the wood, decreasing towards the middle. The applied force and bending of the neutral axis are measured with special instruments. Because the compression strength of wood is lower than its tensile strength, the top surface of the beam where the pressure is applied will brake first while the bottom, which is subjected to tension, will break later. If it is bent further it will produce a typical longitudinal splintery break.

Influences affecting reaction to bending

Angle of the fibres	This is very similar to resistance to tension. The reduction of bending resistance is appreciable from an inclination of 1/25, while in compression it reduces from 1/10, while in cross-section it has hardly any resistance.
Specific gravity	There is a linear relationship between resistance to bending and density. In cases where this relationship is not followed it is the result of woods which contain a high level of resin.
Humidity content	Resistance to bending is at a maximum with a humidity of 5%, diminishing resistance from that moisture level until FSP. The difference between 8 and 15% can be considered linear.
Temperature	Resistance to bending decreases as the temperature increases. This increase is greater than the increase caused by humidity.
Knots	The influence of knots varies according to their position. It is greater with increasing bending moments and it has more effect in an area under tension than in one under compression. In summary, the influence increases according to the tension its area undergoes, and since knots suffer more as the tensile pressure increases, tension has more effect than compression.

34

Wood species

The trees of the forests and jungles of the world are divided among an immense variety of species with a correspondingly different characteristics. Many factors have an influence on the specific qualities of trees, but three of them are of particular importance:

• **Temperature**: No tree or plant can grow at temperatures below 0° C (-32° F) or above 55° C (131° F).
• **Humidity**: Trees need water to grow; the quantity and quality of ground water as well as the rain pattern are essential conditions.
• **Wind**: When the intensity of the wind is combined with the humidity of the air and the tree's height, wind becomes a crucial factor which can determine the length of a tree's life.

For a tree to develop normally, it needs to get enough rain and be in a climate that does not inhibit its growth, either through low temperatures or through dehydration, which may occur at high temperatures. The extent to which each of these factors affect the tree will determine its specific qualities.

Timber species

Conifers or gymnosperms

These have the following characteristics:

• Their appearance is fairly uniform: branches forming a leafy crown on top of a clear bole.
• The structure of the wood of conifers is homogeneous. This characteristic is why it has become so widely used for making furniture.
• The wood of conifers is light, normally soft and easy to work. For this reason, the wood of conifers is described as 'softwood', although the term include woods which are physically hard, such as yew.
• A transverse cut across the trunk reveals the growth rings, each consisting of light, thin-walled earlywood tissue alternating with darker, denser latewood tissue.
• A knot-free radial cut reveals resinous wood with parallel rings of almost equal width when is examined. A tangential cut displays wavy patterns concentrically arranged upon a flat grain.
• The growth of conifers decreases during the year, and as the temperature drops it does not stop. For this reason, the trees do not shed their leaves in the autumn and they are therefore evergreen.
• About 650 species have been classified in over 50 classes, each grouped in 8 families.
• Conifers often grow as monocultural groups covering large areas.
• As softwood is homogeneous and easy to work, it is the type most often used for a large variety of purposes.

Deciduous trees

These have the following characteristics:

• A transverse cut through the trunk of a deciduous tree, rings typically formed of pores or vessels are seen, intersected by perpendicular radial lines originating in the pith.
• By contrast, in a radial cut the growth rings appear to be continuous and nacreous; these figures are called silver rays or silver grain, and have a very attractive appearance.
• The appearance of tangentially cut wood is the poorest and least attractive.
• The knotted, shiny, veined surface of hardwood makes it ideal for decorative purposes.
• The complex structure influences the mechanical properties of the wood, which are closely related to its density.
• Deciduous trees stop growing during the winter, causing the leafs to fall, and they start growing again in the spring when the new leaves sprout, leading to flowering.
• More than 1,400 deciduous species of trees have been catalogued, counting the commercially important monocotyledons and dicotyledons.

The atlas cedar is an evergreen that can reach 40 meters height and has a bluish green colour.

Among the angiospermeae, the black poplar is the most widely commercially used.

Evergreen timber

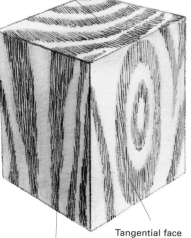

Transverse face

Tangential face

Radial face

Deciduous timber

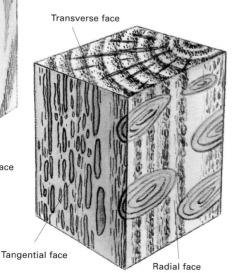

Transverse face

Tangential face

Radial face

SOFTWOODS

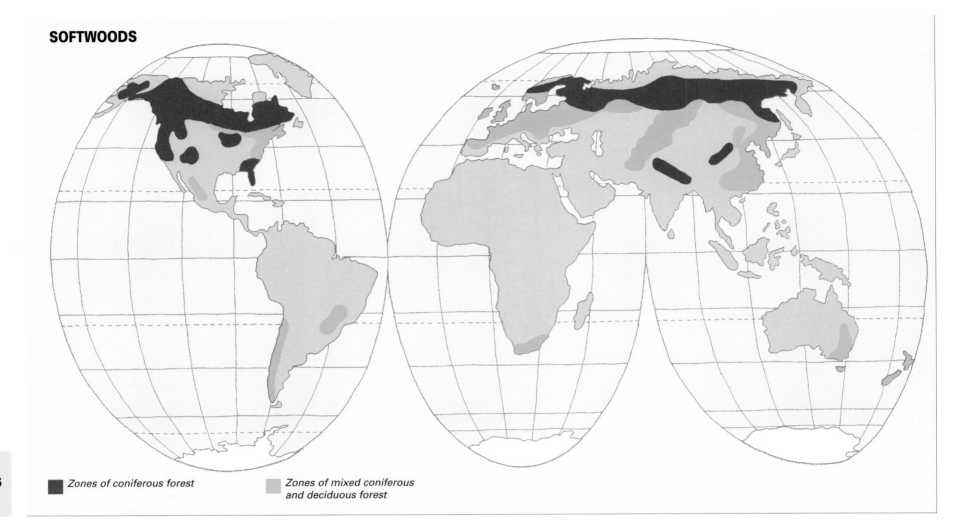

■ Zones of coniferous forest

▨ Zones of mixed coniferous and deciduous forest

Softwoods

Softwoods come from coniferous trees and usually have a low specific gravity. Coniferous trees belong to the class of gymnosperms, plants that produce naked seeds not enclosed in an ovary, but not all of these trees match a unique prototype. In general they all are tall, slender, and pointed. Softwood is usually pale coloured, ranging from yellow to brownish red. The texture is well defined as a result of the contrast in intensity between the winter and summer growth rings. Softwoods are mostly found in zones of cold and moderate temperatures, in the arctic, sub-arctic and temperate regions of northern Europe and America, reaching as far as the south-eastern United States. Coniferous trees grow fast and have tall and straight trunks which makes them ideal for plantations.

Being faster growing, they are less expensive than hardwood. They are widely used for construction, cabinetmaking, as well as to provide wood pulp for papermaking and cardboard.

Hardwoods

Hardwoods come from deciduous trees and usually have a high specific gravity (balsa wood is a notable exception). They belong to the class of angiosperms, having their seeds enclosed in ovaries that become fruit after being fertilised.

Most of these trees grow in temperate and tropical zones. They are deciduous, shedding their leaves in the fall.

Hardwood is normally more durable than softwood, and shows larger variations in colour, texture, and grain. It is also much more expensive; some of the hardwoods; the unusual and exotic ones in particular reach very high prices, and are often used in the form of veneers of high value to cover inferior wood.

Hardwoods are used in construction and for manufactured products. The most important factor in their growth is the climate, which explains their location on the world map.

Hardwood is generally of slow growth and in spite of reforestation programs, younger specimens do not equal older ones in quality.

Softwood from conifers represents an important source of wealth for countries with large areas of land covered by forests.

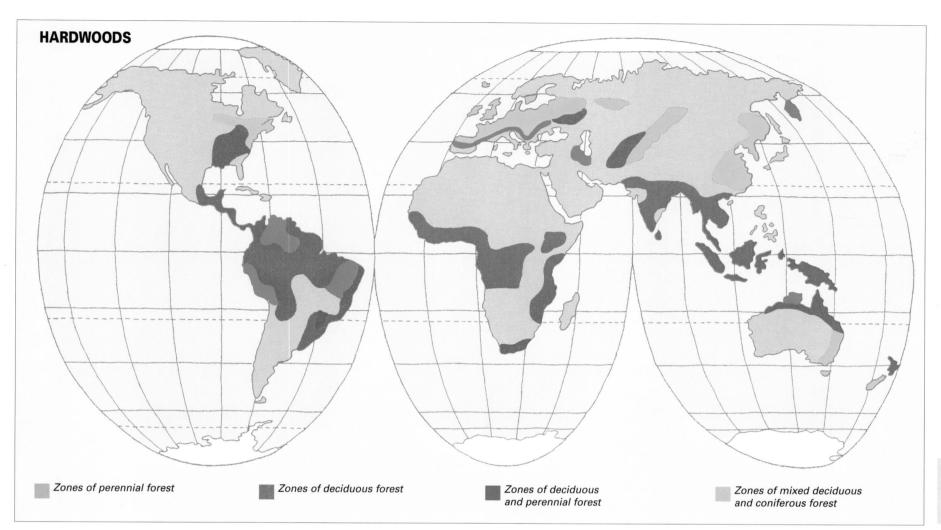

HARDWOODS

Zones of perennial forest

Zones of deciduous forest

Zones of deciduous and perennial forest

Zones of mixed deciduous and coniferous forest

Properties of different timber types

Wood	Density kg/m³		Height in m	Diameter. in cm	Wood	Density kg/m³		Height in m	Diameter. in cm
	dry	green				dry	green		
EUROPE					**NORTH AMERICA**				
Fir	450	635	45	140	Birch	700	840	20	60
Poplar	500	900	40	110	Maple	750	875	30	80
Chestnut	580	720	40	80	Common Larch	850	1030	30	40
Cherry	689	800	20	70	Douglas Fir	480	670	80	100
Holm oak	873	1060	40	85	Redwood	430	-	110	800
Maple	570	630	-	60	Tepa	440	-	8	-
Ash	630	950	40	60	Ara tree	500	650	18	50
Beech	700	900	30	70					
Walnut	670	810	20	200	**CENTRAL and**				
Olive	780	1100	10	60	**SOUTH AMERICA**				
Elm	690	950	40	80					
Pear	730	830	10	40	Amaranth	920	1020	30	100
Pine	540	750	25	60	Cinnamon	900	1000	-	-
Red Pine	500	900	40	75	Mahogany	720	900	30	70
Plane	580	1085	25	80	American Cedar	380	720	-	-
Oak	630	1085	40	110	Courbaril	850	-	-	-
					Jacaranda	850	900	19	100
					Rio Rosewood	850	1000	-	-
ASIA and OCEANIA					Lignum Vitae	1100	1250	10	70
Box	912	1016	8	10	Brazilian Pine	560	850	40	-
Ebony	936	1100	8	30					
Eucalyptus	-	-	80	90	**AFRICA**				
Indian Laurel	900	950	30	100	Scented Mahogany	750	850	40	140
Indian Rosewood	850	1000	-	-	Bubinga	950	1100	30	-
Rewa Rewa	770	800	30	50	Sipo (Utile)	750	900	40	120
Sen	600	650	25	100	African Walnut	900	1150	20	250
Tamo (Japanese Ash)	-	570	-	-	Okoume	486	500	40	-
Teak	1000	1100	10	40	Sapele	750	900	30	100
					Utile	650	700	60	200
					Makore	850	950	80	200

conversion table: 1 inch=2.54 cm – 1 cm=0.3937 inches – 1 m³=35.315 cubic feet – 1 cubic yard=0,765 m³ – 1 kg=2.2 pounds – 1 pound=0.454 kg

Oak is among the most widely used hardwoods.

AMARANTH

very hard

Origin
South America, especially Brazil and Guyana; Central America and Mexico

➤ **Characteristics:** In contact with the air, this yellowish brown heartwood turns violet which gives it its alternative name, purple heart. A very heavy, resistant, elastic, tough wood. Because the sapwood is vulnerable to xylophagous (wood-eating) pests it is necessary to remove it. It dries well and once dry it is stable and maintains its shape. Because of its high density it is difficult to cut and work and it is not suitable for turning or nailing.

➤ **Applications:** Heavy constructions (piers, bridges, pilasters) and work requiring significant durability and compressive strength. Selected fine woodworking, decorative veneers, luxury turned ware and coachbuilding. Its bark has been long used for tanning.

➤ **Finishing:** Easy to polish and varnish.

BOXWOOD

very hard

Origin
Southern Europe, Asia Minor and western Asia

➤ **Characteristics:** The largest specimen are found in Turkey, Russia and Asia. Of a yellowish ivory colour, it is a slow growing, short bush. The wood is heavy and compact, with a uniform and fine texture, having a close grain, straight and sometimes irregular, with almost invisible stripes. The growth rings are hardly visible and it must be dried carefully, as it reacts strongly to temperature changes and distortion. Among European woods it is the heaviest and hardest, and very hard to work.

➤ **Applications:** Engraving, inlaid work, turned ware, flutes, cutlery, tool handles, rulers, inlays and small sculptures. Excellent for carvings requiring very fine detail.

➤ **Finishing:** Finishes well, with a fine wax-like surface

BUBINGA

very hard

Origin
Equatorial zone of West Africa, especially Cameroon, Gabon and Zaire (Democratic Republic of Congo); almost extinct

➤ **Characteristics:** Heartwood of red or dark brown colour, with intensely coloured stripes, mostly purple or black. With time and light it darkens. Heavy and resistant to parasites. The texture is fine, smooth, slightly coarse and has a marked grain, sometimes irregular and interlaced. Not easy to work. When cut or carved it gives off a fetid odour that irritates the mucous membrane. Due to its beauty it is very much appreciated in Japan.

➤ **Applications:** Appreciated in fine carpentry, it makes beautiful veneers. Excellent for quality turning, furniture and implements.

➤ **Finishing:** Good varnished and finished.

EBONY

very hard

Origin
Celebes, Madagascar, Cameroon, Mozambique, Nigeria, Gabon, India, Mauritius and Ceylon

➤ **Characteristics:** The sapwood is of a pinkish white colour while the heartwood is black, interlaced with blackish brown, while the grain is even blacker. Together with African Wenge it is one of the blackest woods available. Much appreciated because of its scarcity. Fine pore wood, compact, scented, dense and heavy. It has a fine and smooth texture with straight, irregular or undulated grain. Working it requires great skill due to its brittleness. Once dry it is hard to saw. Easily polished.

➤ **Applications:** luxury indoor decorations, quality furniture, black keys for musical instruments and decorative items. Cutlery handles, turned ware, inlaid floors. Door handles, billiard cues and inlaid work.

➤ **Finishing:** Varnishing may be difficult but the final appearance is good.

HOLM OAK

very hard

Origin
Europe and North America

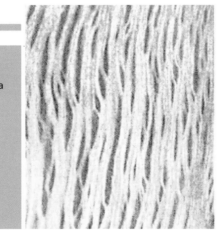

➤ **Characteristics:** Heavier and harder than red oak. Its colour is a light brown ochre with a beautiful silvery grain and eccentric piths forming yellow plates. It has yellow pores, a fine and uniform texture and with a figure corresponding to the growth rings. Hard to dry and bend. It tends to crack.

➤ **Applications:** Ordinary construction work (posts, fences), farming tools, carpentry, carriage work, wine barrels, wooden floors and cabinetmaking.

➤ **Finishing:** Easy to smooth but due to the open pores it is hard to varnish to a smooth surface.

LAUREL

very hard

Origin
India, Burma and Ceylon

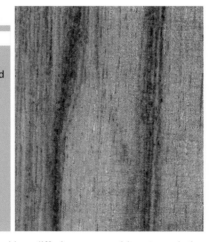

➤ **Characteristics:** Very differing sap- and heartwood, the former being pinkish and the latter a brownish orange. It is similar to European walnut. Very decorative, sparsely striped, thick texture and straight, sometimes irregular fibres. Heavy and dense, thick logs are difficult to dry. It twists, breaks and cracks easily. Strong but difficult to saw and work. Not very resistant to humidity and termites.

➤ **Applications:** Because it is greasy, varnishing can be difficult and it does not glue well. Used as a veneer or solid wood in stairways, doors and coatings.

➤ **Finishing:** Though difficult, varnishing gives it a beautiful look.

LIGNUM VITAE

very hard

Origin
Exclusively found in the Brazilian coast woods

➤ **Characteristics:** probably the heaviest wood known. Its sapwood ranges from pale yellow to light brown and contrasts with the colour of its heartwood, which goes from dark to reddish brown with purple reflections of great beauty. Compact and heavy, it requires special tools to be cut. Its grain is straight and its texture firm, smooth and uniform.

➤ **Applications:** Exterior construction, naval construction, bridges and musical instruments. Violin bows, canes and umbrella handles. Luxury cabinetmaking and veneers.

➤ **Finishing:** It presents a good, soft finish. Excellent for varnishing.

SUCUPIRA

very hard

Origin
The whole Amazon region of Venezuela and Brazil

➤ **Characteristics:** It has a pinkish brown heartwood. One of the densest and heaviest woods known. Very resistant to parasite action, it offers good mechanical resistance.

➤ **Applications:** It is used for furnishing and, because of its hardness and resistance, for exteriors and parquet floors.

➤ **Finishing:** Because of its high colour and resin content, finishing is often difficult.

WENGE

very hard

Origin
Diverse tropical regions of Africa, mainly Cameroon and the Belgian Congo

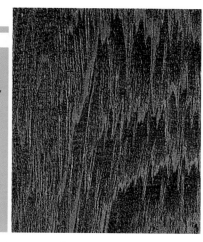

➤ **Characteristics:** Its sapwood can be almost white while the heartwood is a dark yellowish brown with almost black grain. When exposed to air, it oxidises quickly and acquires a blackish, greyish tone. Very strong and fine wood with open pores. Decorative but heavy, with great resistance to mechanical pressure as well as friction. It resists blows and high temperature. Difficult to polish and varnish, even gluing is difficult This wood is resistant to practically all animal and vegetal parasites, as well as humidity. Nice and easy to work.

➤ **Applications:** It is used in cabinetmaking, parquet floors, cutlery handles and various tools. Because of its highly decorative properties it is used in quality furnishings.

➤ **Finishing:** It varnishes well.

39

CINNAMON

hard

Origin
South America, Amazon basin, Central America up to the Yucatan peninsula.

➤ **Characteristics:** Because the sapwood is vulnerable to xylophagous pests, it is useless. The heartwood is of a brownish yellow colour with a brownish black grain. A heavy, dense wood, its workability is good.

➤ **Applications:** Exterior construction. Shipbuilding industry and furniture that requires durability and resistance.

➤ **Finishing:** Varnishing can be difficult.

SATINWOOD

hard

Origin
East India and Ceylon

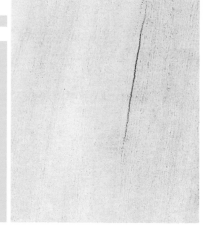

➤ **Characteristics:** Heartwood and sapwood are very similar, their colour being yellowish brown with a golden grain that makes its veneer very beautiful. It is very hard to work, and the dust irritates the mucous membrane, which makes protection necessary.

➤ **Applications:** Furniture industry. Indoor decorations and coatings.

➤ **Finishing:** Gives a good finish.

COURBARIL

hard

Origin
Parts of Mexico, Central America and the western Amazon basin

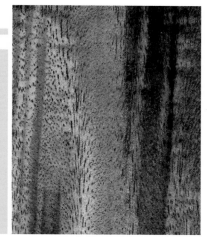

➤ **Characteristics:** Sapwood and heartwood are quite different, with colours ranging from yellowish white to a combination of attractive colours (from orange brown to black violet), here especially the grain. Heavy, dense, flexible and elastic wood. It must be dried slowly if deformation is to be avoided. It is hard to cut and needs special tools.

➤ **Applications:** Indoor and outdoor construction. Furniture, although veneer is hard to make. Shipbuilding and parquetry.

➤ **Finishing:** Varnishing gives a good finish.

JACARANDA

hard

Origin
Brazil and Cuba;
some species
also in India

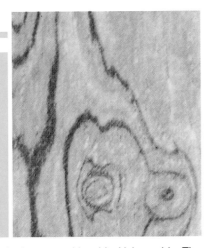

➤ **Characteristics:** Its heartwood is a blackish marble. The growth rings are quite unattractive because the blackish grain is eccentric to the rings. Scented wood that burns well, due to the glossy resin in its vessels.

➤ **Applications:** Luxurious fine carpentry and turned ware.

➤ **Finishing:** It takes varnish, wax and lacquer well.

HICKORY

hard

Origin
North America,
especially
eastern Canada;
United States
and Mexico

➤ **Characteristics:** Sapwood and heartwood differ. The sapwood is white or pale brown while the heartwood is reddish brown. Has a slight silver ray and a smooth greyish grain. Very resistant with a coarse texture. The grain is generally straight, but can be irregular or undulated. Hard but not difficult to work.

➤ **Applications:** Because of its remarkable toughness, it is used in cars, coachwork and implements. Also for tool handles and sporting goods, such as golf clubs and skis. Chairs, curved furniture and decorative veneers.

➤ **Finishing:** It varnishes and polishes with difficulty, but finishes well.

JAGUA

hard

Origin
Tropical areas of
Central and
South America

➤ **Characteristics:** Sapwood and heartwood differ. The heartwood is of a palish grey with a pink overall tone. Almost no figure, fine and of very high density.

➤ **Applications:** Bends easily, can be used as a substitute for beech and ash. Sporting goods and turning.

➤ **Finishing:** Varnishing and polishing present no difficulties.

40

LIQUIDAMBER

hard

Origin
South-eastern
United States,
Mexico and
Central America

➤ **Characteristics:** Its sapwood is whitish in colour while the heartwood is reddish brown grey with marked grain. It must be dried slowly to avoid the risk of warping.

➤ **Applications:** Furniture manufacturing, as a veneer and sometimes in plywood.

➤ **Finishing:** Good varnished and sandpapered.

AFRICAN WALNUT

hard

Origin
Western Africa,
from Ivory Coast
to Gabon

➤ **Characteristics:** similar to walnut in colour, grain and fibre, but despite its name it is from the African Mahogany family, with which it shares its texture and weight. It dries fast and well. Once dry it is very stable, easy to cut and work. Its interlaced fibre makes it necessary to work with care to avoid tearing. Somewhat resistant to humidity and fungus, but not to termites. Its fibre is straight and normally does not show knots.

➤ **Applications:** As solid wood for furniture manufacturing. As a veneer for large areas. Turned ware.

➤ **Finishing:** Good to finish, especially with varnish or wax.

OLIVE

hard

Origin
Typical tree of
southern Europe,
especially the
countries in the
Mediterranean
that present a
warmer climate

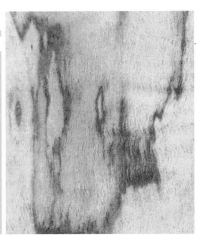

➤ **Characteristics:** Dense and resistant, with the sapwood very similar to the heartwood. It has a greenish yellow colour with irregular dark brown grain combined with stains. Presents a fine texture with sometimes interlaced and irregular fibres. The drying is slow, and it tends to crack and split. Has a high density and a moderate resistance to fungus. Olive roots have an attractive figure and big silver rays. It is silky to the touch.

➤ **Applications:** Due to its ease of sawing and pleasant working qualities it is used for indoor and furniture veneers, mouldings, door panels, inlaid floors and chests. It does not split when nailed. Used also for turned ware, wood engraving, cabinetmaking and sculpture.

➤ **Finishing:** Can be difficult to varnish.

ELM

hard

Origin
Central and southern Europe, including the whole Northern Hemisphere

➤ **Characteristics:** Semi-heavy. Depending on the type, the wood ranges from semi hard to hard. It is brown with an occasional reddish tint. It has very fine vessels with a subtle radius, which makes them almost invisible. Some species, like the red american elm, are exceptionally soft and workable. The texture can be rough but is usually acceptable. Long lasting and nor liable to fungus.

➤ **Applications:** Solid and veneered cabinetwork, vehicle bodies and fenders. Items that are continually exposed to water, such as fishing boats or ship structures. Also used in hydraulic work.

➤ **Finishing:** The grain is tight and irregular. Hard to plane, polish or varnish, although easily glued.

GUATAMBU

hard

Origin
South America, especially Brazil, Paraguay and Venezuela

➤ **Characteristics:** Its heartwood colour ranges from yellow to lemon yellow and it has a whitish sapwood. Its fine grey grain is almost imperceptible. Heavy wood of fine and regular texture. Easy to work with all kinds of machinery.

➤ **Applications:** Good quality veneers, interior decoration, furniture and different turning.

➤ **Finishing:** Best results by spraying, but also easily glued and stained.

RED PINE

middle hard

Origin
Atlantic Coast of the United States into the Gulf of Mexico and 200 km (125 miles) inland

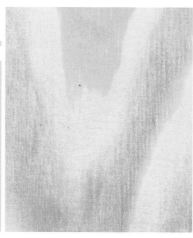

➤ **Characteristics:** Considered one of the most important resinous woods worldwide. It is pinkish yellow coloured with a yellowish orange resin grain. It is heavy but flexible, and due to its great resin content, resistant to external agents. Very easy to work.

➤ **Applications:** Cabinetmaking, furniture, house interiors and general construction. While living it is used to produce turpentine.

➤ **Finishing:** Very good.

41

REWA REWA

hard

Origin
New Zealand and southern Australia

➤ **Characteristics:** The colour of the heartwood ranges from golden yellow to a very pale pink. A radial cut presents a very decorative pattern, similar to birch, but much more marked and with larger speckles. It has great resistance and durability. Easy to work.

➤ **Applications:** It is used as decorative wood for various purposes. Furniture fabrication and interior coating.

➤ **Finishing:** It offers good finishing possibilities.

OAK

hard

Origin
Europe, also Asia, North Africa and North America

➤ **Characteristics:** It is one of the trees with a very long life span, reaching up to 500 years. Its heavy wood has great resistance, stiffness and durability. The European species present brown or brownish yellow tones and fundamentally straight fibre, which sometimes is unpredictably interlaced. The American species present pale brown or pinkish tones and straight fibre; it differs, according to how it is sawn, which is usually straight or in quarters. In the last case it has medullary rays, particularly in the European species, which go through the whole grain pattern. It reacts with ferrous metals such as nails and becomes stained.

➤ **Applications:** Fine quality carpentry, both in the solid and as veneer, parquet floors, carvings, panels, in naval industry, construction and making wine and beer barrels.

➤ **Finishing:** Good response to wax finishing or varnish, either matt or glossy.

TEAK

hard

Origin
It is indigenous to Burma, Thailand and India, but also grows in Malaysia, Indonesia and Zambia

➤ **Characteristics:** One of the most outstanding woods in the world for quality work. The natural range of colours varies from a golden yellow to a dark brown, with a whitish sapwood and a dark grained brownish ochre heartwood. Once sawed it darkens due to air exposure. With its very oily nature, its resistance to water is excellent. It has a good parasite resistance. Once dried it is stable and long-lasting.

➤ **Applications:** For ships and other purposes that involve exposure to the wet, such as outdoor furniture, there is nothing better. Fine carpentry making and surfaces that require resistance to acidic products. Decorative veneers.

➤ **Finishing:** The traditional finish is several layers of flax seed oil, today Danish oil or teak oil. Its oily nature can provoke problems such as bubbles or formation of ripples with some finishing products.

WACAPOU

hard

Origin
Tropical regions of South America

➤ **Characteristics:** Its sapwood is whitish and its heartwood goes from olive to a dark chocolate brown. Very oily and heavy wood, water resistant and difficult to work.

➤ **Applications:** Excellent for naval constructions. Also used in parquet floors as well as interior and exterior carpentry in general.

➤ **Finishing:** Varnishing works very well.

SIPO (UTILE)

medium hard

Origin
Equatorial Africa, mostly Guinea

➤ **Characteristics:** Similar in strength to mahogany but with a dark reddish colour. It has fine pores with an iridecence of changing colours and shine towards the middle, similar to sapele. Easy to saw and handle.

➤ **Applications:** Luxury furniture and high quality decorations because of its beautiful wood figure.

➤ **Finishing:** Varnishing shows excellent results.

BIRCH

medium hard

Origin
Northern Hemisphere in Europe, Canada and the northern United States, Central Europe and northern Asia

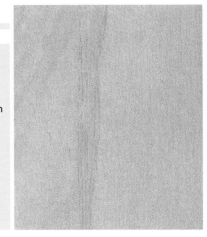

➤ **Characteristics:** fFne textured wood, almost white in colour, with a pale yellow heartwood. The closed straight or sometimes intricate grain occasionally presents an attractive pattern, but it generally lacks particular effect. It can be as heavy as oak and as hard as ash, but is more resistant. It does not crack nor corrode but can become worm-holed in humid climate.

➤ **Applications:** Because of its excellent mechanical properties and its whitish colour, it is more commonly used as plywood rather than as a solid construction material. But it is also used in furniture and panel manufacturing and, because of its smooth surface for handles and carvings.

➤ **Finishing:** Any natural finishing. Its close texture requires only a few layers.

42

MAPLE

medium hard

Origin
Canada and north-eastern Untited States (Oregon), less in Europe and Japan

➤ **Characteristics:** Of high density, similar to beech, it bends well. Its tensile and impact strength are like beech. It does not crack and it polishes and dyes well. The fibre is straight, sometimes striped with tones ranging from creamy white to light brown. The sapwood is whiter and the heartwood brownish pink, with growth rings lightly marked. Of high durability indoors. Needs to be treated if outdoors.

➤ **Applications:** Dance, parquet and inlaid floors, shoe heels, parts for pianos and other musical instruments. Turned ware, panels, fine carpentry, tool handles, coachwork and veneers.

➤ **Finishing:** Because of its closed grain, it accepts most finishes and grain filling is not necessary. Protective treatment against fungus and insects is recommended. Inlaid floors should be worked with a spray gun.

MAHOGANY

medium hard

Origin
Central America, between Honduras, Mexico and the Caribbean Islands, Southeast Asia, West Africa and Brazil

➤ **Characteristics:** These are specific to its origins. The heaviest and hardest comes from Cuba, the softest from Nigeria and West Africa. Narrow whitish red sapwood and brownish cinnamon or brownish pink heartwood. African mahogany is darker than the eastern American one, paler, but usually the tone is between brownish gold and pale pink. Uniform ribbon striped, sometimes with surface speckles. Small and firm grain. Highly resistant, does not warp and is not attacked by insects.

➤ **Applications:** The great cabinetmaking in the Europe of the 17th and 18th century was mainly executed in solid mahogany. Today it is used in quality cabinetmaking and for musical instruments.

➤ **Finishing:** With the least possible colouing, to highlight its beautiful natural tone. Wax, oil, french polish.

RED CEDAR

medium hard

Origin
Western United States and eastern Asia

➤ **Characteristics:** It emits a camphor-smelling aromatic scent. The sapwood is yellowish and the heartwood greyish brown. It changes colour outdoors. The American type has a dense grain, although it is spongy and has a cedarlike colour. The burl resembles leopard skin. Apart from the roots it is easily workable.

➤ **Applications:** Veneer used in luxury furniture, roof shingles, outdoor coatings, greenhouses and sheds. The root is used for carving in fine woodwork.

➤ **Finishing:** Varnishing is difficult, but it finishes well.

CHERRY

medium hard

Origin
Originally from Europe, today also found in the United States, Asia Minor and the Caucasus

➤ **Characteristics:** The brownish pink heartwood darkens with time and the fine, tight and straight grain is dark brown. It is stiff, bends and glues well and can be polished. Extremely hard wood, and often difficult to work. Its high hydrotropism diminishes with steam dying. It must be dried with care because it warps. Once dry it is stable and outdoor resistant.

➤ **Applications:** Fine cabinetmaking because of its fine finish. When tempered in acid or lime water for 24 hours it turns a deep red. String instruments and ships interior, chairs, and small implements (cigar holders, carvings), gear teeth, turning and inlaid work.

➤ **Finishing:** Natural wax, oil and french varnish.

EUCALYPTUS

medium hard

Origin
Australia, Tasmania, New South Wales and various parts of Oceania

➤ **Characteristics:** Similar to tangentially sawed oak wood, but it lacks the silver grain of the former. It has a thick bark of 2–3 cm (¾–1¼ in). A medium weight, fast drying wood, its superficial cells tend to shrink. It is quite solid and can be sawn and worked easily. Vulnerable to humidity it must be treated for outdoor use. Good flexibility.

➤ **Applications:** General carpentry and furniture manufacture. Veneers and plywood, compressed wood plates, sporting goods, packaging and turned ware. Fast-growing, it is also used to provide wood pulp for the paper industry.

➤ **Finishing:** Good finish, but not suitable for high quality work.

ASH

medium hard

Origin
Medium altitude forests, sharing them with oak in Europe. Similar species in the United States and Japan

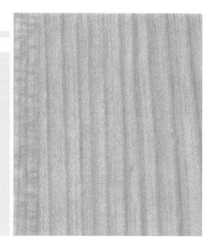

➤ **Characteristics:** Strong and tough wood, fast drying and very stable, resistant to impact and vibrations and known for its stiffness. The texture is creamy with a lightly pink whitish, grey or brownish tone, beautiful grain and marked growth rings. It works and saws well but can tear during planing. It can be bent. It is not long-lasting and is without treatment not suitable for outdoor usage.

➤ **Applications:** Due to its elasticity and toughness it is used for curved furniture and other items. Its hardness and impact strength makes it good for sporting goods such as hockey sticks, baseball bats, tennis racquets and gymnastic apparatus. Also used for tool handles (hammers, axes and pikes), curved ship parts, axis, and wagon and car frames.

➤ **Finishing:** Easy to polish and varnish.

43

BEECH

medium hard

Origin
Temperate northern Europe, shares forests with oak. North America and Japan

➤ **Characteristics:** wWitish or brownish pale pink colour, darkens when treated with steam. Fine and uniform texture, straight grain and small wood rays. Dries fast but tends to warp. Once dry, moves considerably with changes in humidity. Heat resistant, bends well. Darkens in contact with water and putrefies fast, which makes it unsuitable for outdoors. It planes well and does not split easily, ideal for carvings or to dress. Must be drilled before nailing.

➤ **Applications:** Furniture, especially when curved or with turnings and technical items. Veneers and hard block paving, home implements ranging from tool handles to chair frames to ladles, also toys and chests.

➤ **Finishing:** The best finishes do not change the beautiful colour and grain, such as wax, colourless varnish. Solvent based dyes can burn it.

IMBUIA

medium hard

Origin
South America, especially Brazil

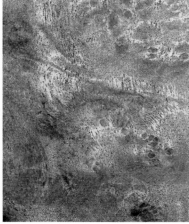

➤ **Characteristics:** Sapwood and heartwood differ markedly in colour, ranging from the brownish yellow of the former to the yellowish brown to olive of the latter. Easy to work and resistant to insects.

➤ **Applications:** Frequently used in furniture manufacturing, especially in Brazil. Plywood and veneers.

➤ **Finishing:** Finishing is not difficult.

IROKO

medium hard

Origin
West Africa, especially Equatorial Guinea

➤ **Characteristics:** itl colour is pale greenish yellow to honey brown and darkens with age and in contact with air, tending to even the colour. The look is rough, tough and against the grain it is sometimes moiré. Resistant to water and insects. The wood is greasy, with open pores and interlaced grain. It is one of the few woods encountered in large dimensions on the lumber market. Easy to saw and work.

➤ **Applications:** Indoor and outdoor carpentry, solid shipbuilding and furniture pieces, where it is often used as a substitute for Asian teak, although it is lighter and less scented. Beams, veneers, doors and floors.

➤ **Finishing:** Good finish.

MAKORE

medium hard

Origin
Tropical Africa, especially Guinea, Ghana, Nigeria and Ivory Coast

➤ **Characteristics:** The sapwood presents a white to pink colour, while the heartwood is brownish pink, depending on age and tree size. A dense, stable and fine porous wood. It irritates the mucous membrane so it must be worked with care. Easy to saw, polish and varnish.

➤ **Applications:** Veneer manufacturing, used as substitute for mahogany in furniture manufacturing. Outdoor carpentry, stairways and indoor decorations. Exterior marine plywood, luxury cabinetmaking and coachwork.

➤ **Finishing:** Good to polish, varnish and dye.

MANSONIA

medium hard

Origin
Tropical Africa, especially Ivory Coast, Nigeria, Cameroon and Ghana

➤ **Characteristics:** Its sapwood is a whitish yellow, the heartwood brown with a few soft stripes. Fine and regular wood, lacks pores. Sometimes replaces walnut. In contact with air and light it changes colour, turning lighter and pale brown. Dries fast and although it tends to crack, it is very durable. Hard to work, but allows good polishing. The dust may affect workers with skin, eye, throat or nose irritations.

➤ **Applications:** Fine luxury cabinetmaking, veneers, plywood and parquetry. Rifle butts and moulds, also floors.

➤ **Finishing:** Easy to finish.

LARCH

medium hard

Origin
All of North America and Europe

➤ **Characteristics:** It has a brownish red bark with very few branches. The trunk is smooth and without knots. Its intense orange yellow colour darkens with light and time. The growth rings are wide and marked. Among the coniferous trees, it has a low resin content, although some species have plenty, which makes drying difficult. Once dry it is resistant to humidity and invulnerable to insects. Due to its high calcification it dulls tools rapidly.

➤ **Applications:** ils resistance to humidity makes it ideal for water-based constructions, shipbuilding, bridges and outdoor constructions. Also beams, stairways etc.

➤ **Finishing:** Good to finish and varnish.

44

WALNUT

medium hard

Origin
Originally from the Middle East, now characteristic of temperate and warm zones of the Northern Hemisphere, mainly Europe and North America

➤ **Characteristics:** Semi-heavy wood, dries slowly and with good mechanical properties, bends easily. The colour is a greyish brown with almost black grain. Irregular but straight fibre, with small undulations and a medium to thick texture. The heartwood is light coloured when young and turns a dark brown, almost black when old. The sapwood colour ranges from brownish grey to pale grey. Good resistance to fungus. It does not crack nor cleave easily.

➤ **Applications:** Together with oak, it is one of the most appreciated European woods. Solid walnut is used in luxury cabinetmaking, furniture, turnery, carving, panels and inlaid work, High quality veneer and coatings. The veneer can be from the trunk or the root. Veneer coming from the trunk can be cut transversially to the grain to obtain an unusual figuring.

➤ **Finishing:** Traditionally wax, varnish and oil for a matt or slightly glossy finish.

RIO ROSEWOOD

medium hard

Origin
Fundamentally found in Brazil and Argentina.

➤ **Characteristics:** It has a white yellow sapwood and beautifully coloured heartwood; tobacco brown to chocolate, violet or blue veins and grain, which are sometimes black and big bright patterned. It is a fine fibred, very heavy wood, not difficult to dry or to be chemically treated, although the heavier species must be carefully handled. It is characteristic for its strong scent.

➤ **Applications:** With its beautiful grain pattern, its various tones and its scent it is extremely highly appreciated for expensive furniture making. Also used for luxury interiors, boxes, musical instruments and decorative items.

➤ **Finishing:** Wax is the most traditional and best finish.

PEAR

medium hard

Origin
All central and southern Europe. Some species are also found in Asia.

➤ **Characteristics:** The sapwood is white, the heartwood pale pink to salmon coloured with darker grain. Uniform medular radius appear on the subtle grooved surface, which makes them barely visible. The wood is susceptible to worm, and tends to warp.

➤ **Applications:** Gighly appreciated for turning, excellent for carving, for musical instruments and fine cabinetmaking.

➤ **Finishing:** It takes polish and varnish well.

SCOTS PINE

medium hard

Origin
Northern Europe and northern Asian important mountain ranges

➤ **Characteristics:** ii is considered the best resinous wood. Its sapwood is a pinkish yellow colour and the heartwood reddish brown, which in time turns yellow. The very characteristic grain is in young wood light and in adult wood reddish. Easy to work, glue and finish, though varnishing may turn difficult due to the high resin content.

➤ **Applications:** Quality furniture. Cabinetmaking in general. Construction work, doors, windows etc.

➤ **Finishing:** It gives a good appearance when finished.

EUROPEAN PLANE

medium hard

Origin
Northern Europe

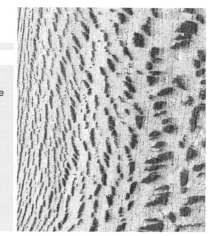

➤ **Characteristics:** tTe heartwood is light reddish brown, with larger darker, extremely visible rays. When tangentially sawn in quaterts a characteristic lacy grainis revealed.

➤ **Applications:** Used for mouldings. In general it has the same applications as birch: toy making, boxes and inlaid floors. Fine carpentry. It makes very attractive veneers.

➤ **Finishing:** Good and diverse, acceptable sanded, uniform, easy to dye and varnish.

RAMIN

medium hard

Origin
Southeast Asia, north western Borneo, Java and the Philippines

➤ **Characteristics:** the sapwood is whitish yellow and the heartwood pale ivory.The wood tends to darken with time. It has a mildly fine and smooth texture. The grain is straight. As it is greatly attacked by vegetable and animal parasites it needs to be protected through impregnation. It is easily workable but splits very easily.

➤ **Applications:** Solid sections, mouldings. Furniture and interior cabinetmaking, turnery toys, carvings, inlaid floors and veneers.

➤ **Finishing:** It presents a good finish.

45

SAPELE

medium hard

Origin
Tropical African regions like Ivory Coast, Ghana, Cameroon, and eastern regions of Zaire and Uganda

➤ **Characteristics:** The sapwood and heartwood are clearly differentiated by the pink yellow colour of the sapwood and the red, cinnamon brown colour with golden highlights of the heartwood which forms a linear grain. In time it darkens, turning a tobacco colour. It is resistant and durable. A soft and scented wood that, once dried, is not very stable because the interlaced fibre influences the drying and changes its properties. Easy to work and very much used in Europe. For its appearance, density, fineness and dark colour it is used as African mahogany.

➤ **Applications:** Because of its easy workability, it is used for both exterior and interior quality carpentry and furniture. Naval construction, and decorative veneer making.

➤ **Finishing:** Generally it has perfect finishing performance.

UTILE

medium hard

Origin
Tropical Africa, especially Zaire, Ivory Coast, Gabon, Cameroon and Guinea

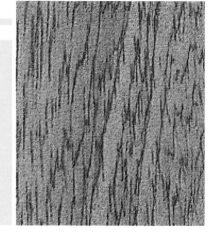

➤ **Characteristics:** A pinkish brown that turns into a reddish brown and darkens when exposed to air. Its grain is generally interlaced which makes a characteristic blackish stripe when radially cut. Compact, mild textured wood. With similar characteristics to mahogany, and in stability and stiffness superior to sapele, it is one of the most appreciated African woods. It is a threatened species. Easy to work.

➤ **Applications:** It is used as a mahogany replacement. Much used in the furniture industry, and for counter tops, interior and exterior carpentry and cabinetmaking. Ship construction, inlaid floors and veneers. Used for sculptures because it is easily carved.

➤ **Finishing:** Good to finish, polish, varnish and stain.

ABARCO

soft

Origin
Central America, especially Colombia, Venezuela and Brazil

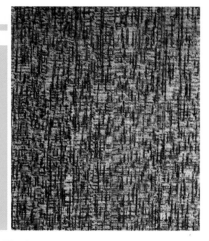

➤ **Characteristics:** The heartwood is brownish red to dark red colour, with a slightly marked grain. Its high silica content makes it hard to cut. The texture is average, the grain straight and sometimes interlaced. It is easily worked.

➤ **Applications:** Naval construction, furniture and counter plaques. Fine indoor carpentry, coatings and panelling. Carvings, pianos and veneers. Because it is mostly exported from Colombia, it is known as Colombian mahogany.

➤ **Finishing:** Offers a good finish.

SPRUCE

soft

Origin
Central and southern Europe, between the Pyrenees and Russia, especially in mountainous regions. Some parts of North America, East and Central Asia

➤ **Characteristics:** Wood colour ranging from creamy white to ochre, with a charecteristic and almost indistinct sapwood texture; porous small and sinuous close grain of a reddish brown colour with a light pink to brown tone. Easy to work, light, porous and elastic wood. It has a weak odour like all resinous woods. It is very strong and durable outdoors because it is hydrophobic. It does not resist abrupt changes of climate; it can produce surface mould and become vulnerable to fungus. Its dry and porous fibre makes it a fast drying wood.

➤ **Applications:** Often used for construction and wood carving. Furniture, framework, cases, various parts of musical instruments. Not long ago it was still being used for shipbuilding, in particular to construct masts and small sailing boats.

➤ **Finishing:** easy and suitable for varnish.

POPLAR

soft

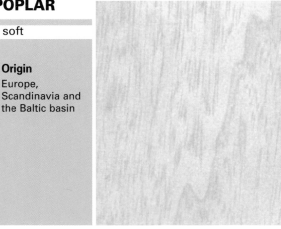

Origin
Europe, Scandinavia and the Baltic basin

➤ **Characteristics:** The wood colour ranges from white to grey. It has a tendency to warp and crack. Not very resistant to water. It grows fast and is easy to work.

➤ **Applications:** Venetian window blinds and furniture insides such as drawer bottoms, cabinet doors and plywood.

➤ **Finishing:** It reacts well to simple finishing.

AMBOYNA

soft

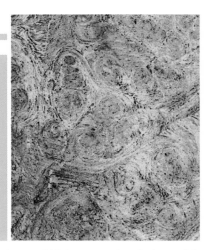

Origin
Equatorial tropics from India to the Philippines and Indonesia, in particular from the Moluccas

➤ **Charcteristics:** It has a whitish sapwood and a brownish pink yellow to red heartwood. The same species as mahogany, its scent is similar to that of vanilla. Although of small size, the roots produce excellent veneers due to its beautiful small and skin-coloured figure. It is easy to work.

➤ **Applications:** With its appreciated burls, it is used for fine cabinetmaking, for decorative items and musical instruments. A very fine veneer is obtained from its roots.

➤ **Finishing:** Every type of finish, all very attractive.

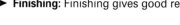

46

AVODIRE AFR.

soft

Origin
West Africa, especially Ivory Coast

➤ **Characteristics:** tTe sapwood and heartwood are very similar in colour, a pale light yellow. Has a soft look with few nerves and closed grain. It is vulnerable to parasites. Easy to work.

➤ **Applications:** Fine carpentry, light carpentry, mouldings, musical instruments and veneer manufacturing.

➤ **Finishing:** Finishing gives good results.

CHESTNUT

soft

Herkunft
Mediterranean zone, central and northern Europe (Switzerland, Germany and Austria) and southern England

➤ **Characteristics:** A brownish red colour with a coarse texture, wide fibres and structure. Similar in characteristics to oak but with no visible silver rays. Sapwood has a much lighter colour than heartwood. It reacts with ferrous metals due to its high acid content. It can be split easily and is water resistant. Insects do not do it much harm. It is more easily worked than oak, although planing is difficult. It can be bent, and once dry is very stable.

➤ **Applications:** Turned ware and tool handles, stairway construction. Used as an oak substitute in carpentry and turning. All types of furniture (tables, chairs, cabinets etc.), especially for outdoor use and also for kitchen furniture doors. Frequently used for coffins, wine barrels, posts and stakes.

➤ **Finishing:** Very easy.

CEDAR

soft

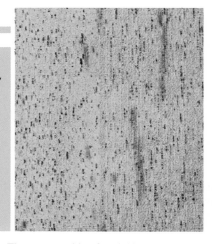

Origin
Central America, from Mexico to Brazil

➤ **Characteristics:** The sapwood is of a pinkish colour, the heartwood brownish pink with a violet and purple glare. One of the most important Brazilian timbers, it is exported to all of Europe. American cedar is also called cedrala; it is not a cedar but belongs to the class of dicotyledonous angiosperms, and is not to be confused with the Himalayan cedar which belongs to the pine family. The texture of American cedar is thick, light and sometimes resinous. It dries fast and once dry, is very stable, strong and light. It is easily worked.

➤ **Applications:** Light construction and fine carpentry, furniture and home implements. Racing boats and plywood.

➤ **Finishing:** Finishes well.

DIBETOU

soft

Origin
Tropical parts of West Africa, especially Sierra Leone and Nigeria. Also found on the Philippines

➤ **Characteristics:** Heartwood and sapwood are similar in colour, ranging from pale grey to golden hazelnut. It has a regular grain and sometimes stripes. Darkens with light and is outdoor resistant. In some countries it is used as a walnut substitute. Very vulnerable to termites, which attack it assiduously. Sometimes stained holes appear, a product of worms. Easily cut.

➤ **Applications:** The veneer obtained from these trees is attractive and appreciated. Due to its good carving properties, it is often used in fine carpentry. Sand-papering may be difficult because its cross fibres may break. For carving and moulding.

➤ **Finishing:** Varnishing is normal.

LIMBA

soft

Origin
Tropical West Africa, especially Sierra Leone and Guinea

➤ **Characteristics:** Sapwood and heartwood have the same colour, an ivory pale yellow with a very soft, somewhat darker grain. Close grain and straight fibres. Darkens with light and works easily.

➤ **Applications:** Due to its atmospheric vulnerability it is no suitable for outdoor use. Normally used as plywood, for moulds and in carpentry.

➤ **Finishing:** Good and decorative finishing.

MERANTI

soft

Origin
Eastern Asia

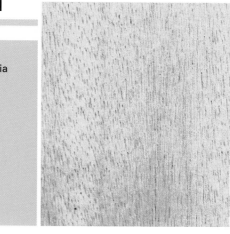

✦ **Characteristics:** four known types exist, each with a different colour, ranging from white (semi-hard wood) to yellow to pale pink to dark pink (soft wood). Its lack of hardness makes it easy to work.

➤ **Applications:** Foremost for windows, but also decorative veneer, plywood and floors.

➤ **Finishing:** It does not require a special finishing.

47

OKOUME

soft

Origin
Abundant in tropical and western Africa; Gabon, Equatorial Guinea, Cameroon and Congo

➤ **Characteristics:** The heartwood is of a salmon pink colour. The grain or figure is less marked. A wood with cross fibres and not good for sawing, sandpapering and varnishing. The fine texture has a straight fibre. Okoume has a high silica content. It is rarely sawn, due to its abrasive action on saws and other cutting equipment. It is relatively soft and water resistant.

➤ **Applications:** Mainly used for indoor plywood panels, indoors and low quality chests. Veneering of doors, furniture and screens.

➤ **Finishing:** Veneers give an excellent finish.

INDIAN ROSE-WOOD

soft

Origin
Eastern India, Thailand, Indonesia, Sri Lanka and Java

➤ **Characteristics:** The sapwood has a white yellow colour with a tone of pink. Its heartwood, when fresh, gives out a pleasant rose-like scent and has a very intense colour that ranges from dark violet blue to orange, forming a very marked grain. It presents dark purple to black grooves. The wood is very heavy, a little rough and fine textured. It has interlaced grain which forms grooved stripes. It is easy to work, but the finish becomes difficult with certain products.

➤ **Applications:** Quality furniture and luxury decoration. Musical instruments. Naval construction. Cutlery handles. Veneers, turned pieces and inlaid floors. Luxury cabinet-making.

➤ **Finishing:** It allows good finishing which gives an elegant and attractive appearance.

PARANA PINE

soft

Origin
Northern coast of Argentina and Brazil. Also found in some regions of Paraguay

➤ **Characteristics:** Ochre straw coloured wood that sometimes has a bright red grain. Uniform and fine textured, almost lacking growth rings, with straight knotted fibre. It is difficult to dry and requires precautions to avoid crooks and ruptures. Its strength, although less, is similar to white pine. It dries quickly and is easy to work manually as well as mechanically.

➤ **Applications:** It provides very long knot-free planks, suitable for interior works such as stairways. Also used for quality furniture.

➤ **Finishing:** Very easy.

DOUGLAS FIR

soft

Origin

North America. Mostly found along the North American Northern and Pacific coasts. Also found in the United Kingdom

➤ **Characteristics:** Also known as Oregon pine, this has a whitish sapwood and a pinkish yellow heartwood, with a different silver ray in spring and autumn. Turns darker with time. It is one of the most outstanding coniferous trees. Its wood dries quickly and has a good mechanical resistance towards humidity. It has a rough and very pronounced grain. It is resinous, light and with very marked growth rings. Out of it are obtained very large dimensioned, regular and knot-free planks. Easy to work.

➤ **Applications:** Of great utility in fine carpentry, both interior and exterior. Also used in naval construction and wooden house building. Its very important plywood is used for structures.

➤ **Finishing:** It has a reasonable appearance.

SEN

soft

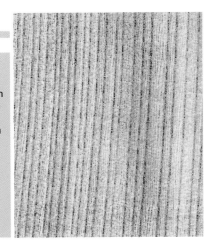

Origin

Mainly Japan, but also found in Sri Lanka, Korea and certain regions of China

➤ **Characteristics:** This wood has a whitish sapwood and a light yellowish brown heartwood. It does not have many patterns, just a subtle darker longitudinal stripe. It presents a porous ringed structure which makes it like ash, but without its hardness. If its growth is slow it may become brittle making it unsuitabe for nailing, and it cannot be used for exteriors. It contracts while drying but does not leave ridges. Soft and workable.

➤ **Applications:** Interior decoration. Vessel industry and turnery items. Furniture making, decorative surfaces, handles abd hilts, diverse tools. Veneers and counter veneers.

➤ **Finishing:** Good to finish and stain.

REDWOOD

soft

Origin

North America, mostly the western United States

➤ **Characteristics:** The light yellow-white sapwood and the heartwood are equal. The heartwood is reddish brown colour, straight grained with a very distinct contrast between winter ansd summer wood. Its growth is slow as can be seen on the very pronounced rings. It has the appearance of light brownish fir, darekening when exposed. Its texture varies from fine to relatively coarse. It is a good drying light wood that becomes stable after it is dried. The wood is not resinous and is a protected species. It is easy to work.

➤ **Applications:** interior and exterior carpentry (shingles and coatings), naval construction, furniture frame work. Fine interior carpentry, coffins, posts and veneers. Ideal for glass houses, garden furniture and country houses. Not adequate for structural works.

➤ **Finishing:** It gives an acceptable finish.

48

TAMO, JAPANESE ASH

soft

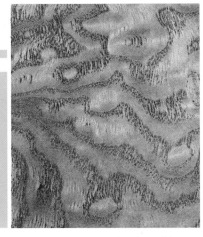

Origin

Southeast Asia, Japan, Korea and the China's Manchuria region

➤ **Characteristics:** ils white sapwood and pale red heartwood does not present great textural differences. It has a darker colour than the European ash, but the grain is more marked and the colour deeper. Easy to use, it has good mechanical properties.

➤ **Applications:** Due to its beautiful figuring it is used for fine carpentry, high quality furniture and decorative veneers.

➤ **Finishing:** It gives a beautiful finish.

TEPA

soft

Origin

Southern mountain ranges of Chile and Argentina

➤ **Characteristics:** Sapwood and heartwood do not show great differences. The colour is yellowish ivory which turns darker when exposed to light. Its uniform and barely visible pattern or silver ray present some grey shading. Workable with any tool or machine.

➤ **Applications:** Packages, boxes. Door and window frames.

➤ **Finishing:** It gives a good finish and varnishes well.

BALSA

very soft

Origin

South America

➤ **Characteristics:** The colour ranges from ivory to beige to pale pink. It is a fast growing tree, the lightest softest and most springy of the commercial woods. Its grain is straight, it does not cut well, it saws worse, and it is not recommended for wood carving.

➤ **Applications:** Most suitable for thermal and acoustical insulation, liquefied gas transport, stage decorations, flotation aids, models, packaging and model planes.

➤ **Finishing:** Very easy.

Wood in commerce

Usually solid wood has already been processed when it comes on the market, which means that it has already been cut to standard measurements. The tree trunks have been sawn and converted into sawn timber, sold as boards with parallel surfaces, and in the case of dressed timber with side edges trimmed.

Timber is available in the following form: beams, scantling, squared timber, planks, boards, laths, strips, borders, edging, veneer, roof rafters, solid wooden boards, stakes and posts.

Timber is divided into categories, based on the size of the cross-sectional area across the grain or its strength (related to the thickness). Nowadays, besides the standard sizes of sawn timber, almost all timber merchants will be able to cut the wood to the required measurement and deliver it.

The standard measurements of timber vary from country to country and sometimes even from region to region. The specifications usually depend on the particular type of wood. The measurements are generally given in centimetres. But in Anglo-Saxon countries Imperial measures are often included in spite of the fact that the metric system has already been officially introduced.

Cross-sections of
planed pine and fir
(commercial dimensions in Sweden and Finland)

thickness	width (mm)									
(mm)	22	34	45	70	95	120	145	170	195	220
9				X	X					
13				X	X	X	X			
16	X	X	X	X	X	X	X			
19				X	X	X	X	X		
22			X	X	X	X	X	X	X	X
28			X	X	X	X	X	X		
34		X	X	X	X	X	X	X	X	
45			X	X	X	X	X	X	X	X
70				X	X	X	X	X	X	X

Traditional commercial terms

Beams: long, thick, rectangular pieces of wood with sharp edges whose larger sectional cross-cut side is at least 200 mm (8 in) wide.
Scantling: a piece of sawn timber with a cross-sectional area larger than 32 cm² (5 sq in). The original round log must be cut cross-wise to the heart.
Squared timber: sawn timber with square or rectangular cross-section with sides wider than 60 mm (24 in), and with the larger cross-cut side at least three times as large as the small one.

Cross-sections of
sawn pine and fir
(commercial dimensions in Sweden and Finland)

thickness	width (mm)									
(mm)	25	38	50	75	100	125	150	175	200	225
12				X	X					
18				X	X	X	X			
19	X	X	X	X	X	X	X			
22	X	X	X	X	X	X	X	X	X	X
25	X	X	X	X	X	X	XX	X	XX	X
32				X	X	X	X	X	X	X
38		X	X	X	X	X	X	X	XX	X
44					X	X	X			
47				X	X	X	X	X	X	X
50			X	X	X	X	XX	X	XX	XX
63					X	X	X	X	XX	XX
75				X	X	X	X	X	XX	XX
100					X		X		X	

Planks: saw timber at least 40 mm (16 in) wide with a cross-cut side twice as side as the smaller cross-cut side.
Boards: sawn timber with a thickness of at least 8 mm (⅓ in) and not more than 40 mm (1¾ in) and a width of more than 80 mm (3⅛ in).
Slats: sawn timber with cross-sectional area of 32 cm² (5 sq in) and a maximum width of 80 mm (3⅛ in).
Moulding, edging: these are ready-made, shaped strips of wood with a range of profiles used for decoration, covering, framing, edging and so on which are available on the market.
Veneer: thin sheets of wood with thickness of 0.55 mm to 3.5 mm (1/64 to ⅛ in), available in various lengths and widths.
Rafters: long wooden beams, used to make roof-trusses. They are cut from knot-free timber and are much used in the building trade.
Solid wood boards: these are produced as a semi-finished product with a thickness ranging from 16 mm upwards (⅝ in) which are used in many sectors of the industry. For instance, three-ply sheets of wood known as blockboard is available in many types of wood and used to make furniture, cupboards and the like. Thee transverse middle layer resists against warping and distortion. These boards are often made from beech but also from other types of wood. They are made up of strips of wood roughly 2 to 5 cm (¾ to 2 in) wide and 10 to 20 cm (4 to 8 in) long with a thickness of 2 to 5 cm (¾ to 2 in) glued together. The thin to medium thick boards are generally used for general work surfaces, kitchen work tops, table tops etc. The thicker sheets are for stairs and other similar purposes.
Posts: although strictly speaking they are not sawn timber, posts are a very important product of the timber trade. They are made from dry, de-barked round wood. Their moisture content is at the most 15%. They are used mainly for telephone and electricity poles. The wood must be well-treated and well proportioned. The diameter varies between 10 and 18 cm (4 and 7 in) depending on the length. Smaller posts are available for use in gardens.
Railway sleepers: these were specially developed for the railways but today in that use they have been replaced by steel or concrete sleepers. Recycled, they have been very popular in gardens and parks, but they are now less favoured because of being treated with creosote which in some circumstances can be a health hazard.

New products

This section describes the many products which are available at builders' merchants and do-it-yourself stores in addition to those traditionally available.

These products are often ready-to-use parts which are pre-treated and pre-prepared, such as mouldings, edgings, skirting boards, plinths, frames and other profiled wood.

Prepared timber

Any woodworker can buy rough-sawn timber and plane it smooth, square and to size. However, there is a whole range of ready-cut, shaped wood of various sizes, ready for immediate use. One of the most important distinguishing features is the treatment of the surface. To avoid much of the effort of planing,

Sawn planks of timber, not planed.

timber planed all round ('POR') is readily available. It will still need finishing, but the amount of work involved is very much less.

Various sections of planed wood.

Sizes of planed timber*			
SECTION (in mm)	LENGTH (in cm)		
	ref. 180	ref. 240	ref. 270
20 x 20	155	305	360
20 x 115	650	1 300	1 555
20 x 145	810	1 625	1 895
25 x 25	220	435	510

*These tables contain examples of the sizes available

Sizes of rough-sawn timber*			
SECTION (in mm)	LENGTH (in cm)		
	ref. 180	ref. 240	ref. 270
19 x 32	205	275	355
25 x 30	220	300	330
25 x 48	280	360	400
50 x 50	490	650	730

Moulded edging

A wide range of moulded edging is available on the market which can be used for decorating ceilings, walls, pillars and so on.

As an alternative, polyurethane moulding is available which imitates the appearance of real wood very convincingly

Drawing of a room with various wood mouldings.

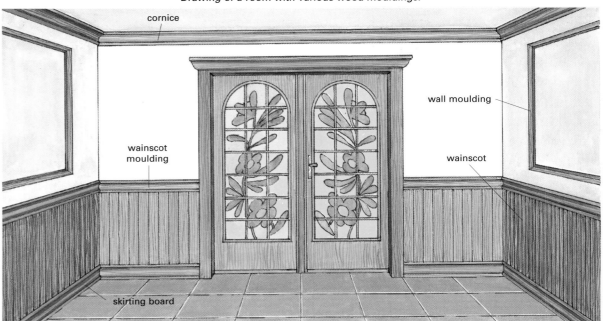

cornice

wall moulding

wainscot moulding

wainscot

skirting board

Various wood mouldings

Imitation beams

These are almost perfect imitations of old beams made from polyurethane. If well-made and properly fitted, they are hardly distinguishable from real wood beams to the layman's eye, and they are much easier to buy and fit. Most imitation beams are made to look like ancient beams with all the natural imperfections of age such as cracks, broken edges, knots and woodworm holes, and carefully varnished or stained as to look like real beams. Most are hollow and U-shaped so they are also very light.

Imitation beams

Wood protection and preservation

Protective products

History

Wood is a very fragile material which is constantly exposed to various sources of danger: damp, fungi or wood eating insects. In the course of time, a number treatments have been developed which are either preventative or curative in order to guarantee the durability of wood.

Today it is a matter of course for any woodworking when planning and constructing a piece to consider what kind of damaging influences it may later be subjected to. The appearance and care or maintenance of the object will also play a part in the choice of the finish.

Because there is no product that is suitable for all types of wood, it is important to consider each project separately. No wood, however hard, is resistant to every possible external influence, so it is very important to select the right treatment. However there is another important aspect to consider, namely the health of people and animals as well as the protection of the environment. Indeed, not all products which protect wood are good for people's health and the environment.

It is important to have some knowledge of the subject in order to be able to choose the right product. Even when buying industrially pre-treated wood, it is important to know what this treatment consisted of. In this way you will be able to decide whether the wood needs to be treated at all or whether the wood needs further protective treatment in order or ensure the durability of a piece.

The protection of wood is a subject which has interested man for a very long time. The spears and arrowheads found near animal remains thousands of years ago have shown that even in prehistoric times wood was hardened through carbonisation which also protected it.

In the Bible, in the first book of Moses, there are some early references to the protection of wood when Noah was told by the Lord to go and build the ark: 'And the Lord said unto Noah: go forth and build an ark from spruce and build store-rooms inside it and coat it with pitch inside and out'. This use of pitch and tar was to seal the overlapping planks of the vessel so that not water could penetrate. The Mesopotamians already knew about pitch 4,000 years ago.

In the 1st century AD Pliny the Elder wrote his *Historia Naturalis* which remained a source of important information until the 18th century. In it he described how to make oleaginous, pitch-like substances, explaining how effective they were against insects and fungi.

It was only in the Renaissance that chemical compounds were produced, based on the chlorides and other salts of mercury, arsenic and so on. Leonardo da Vinci recommended the use of these substances to protect sculptures and carvings as well as wooden buildings from wood-eating insects.

As early as the 17th century, scientists had discovered ways of obtaining oils and tar from the distillation of wood. This means that wood preserving products as they are understood today already existed at that time. In the 19th century, the subject of wood preservation was

Already in the 1st century AD Pliny the Elder described the techniques for protecting wood against insects and fungal attack, using oily, pitch-like materials. The picture shows a miniature from a medieval copy of the Historia Naturalis *('Natural History') of Pliny the Elder, in the Biblioteca Medicea-Laurenciana, Florence.*

During the Renaissance period, the polymath Leonardo da Vinci (born Vinci, Tuscany, 1452, died Le Clos-Lucé, Amboise, 1519) wrote that to protect wood, particularly large carved works of sculpture, against attack by wood-eating insects, it should undergo chemical treatment based on mercuric chloride or other salts of mercury, arsenic, etc. The illustration shows a self-portrait of Leonardo, preserved in the Biblioteca Real, Turin.

explored scientifically and in 1913, the English scientist Kyan carried out the first serious experiments. In 1832, he patented a method whereby the wood was immersed in a solution of corrosive sublimate (mercuric chloride). This method became known as kyanisation. In the same year, the French scientist Bréant carried out experiments in an autoclave (a hermetically closed vessel used for chemical reactions at high pressure) in which wood and other substances could be made water-resistant.

Because ship building was making amazing progress at the time and wood was subjected to extreme conditions in a marine environment, the development of techniques and methods for preserving wood was very important. In 1838, tar oil in the form of creosote, produced in an autoclave, was patented by Bethell. This marked the beginning of large-scale industrial wood preservation. The largest buyers of this new product were the railway companies, the coal mining industry and, last but not least, shipyards and the shipping industry.

It is true that these wood preserving products left stains on the wood and often emanated extremely unpleasant, long-lasting smells. This is why they were not used in housing construction and ornamental woodwork. Here varnish would be used on top of a coating of vegetable oil such as linseed oil which obviously meant that the wood did not last very long in the open air.

In about 1920, the Danish scientist Sigurd Dyrup began looking for a new wood preserving product. The features he sought were that it should not smell strongly or unpleasantly, nor stain the wood surface as dark as creosote did; at the same time it should not leave a film behind as traditional varnishes did because this soon wore off, leaving a residue. He began to explore the potential of pigments, resins, fungicides and insecticides. While mixing these with an organic solution so that they could penetrate the wood, he created what was to be a breakthrough in the preservation of wood. His treatment left no film behind while protecting the wood against aggressions of all kinds.

The properties of wood-preserving products

Looking at the development of wood preserving products over the last few centuries, it is evident that an ideal product would provide the wood with protection against many different kinds of attack. These prerequisites are listed in the box on the right.

This list highlights the fact that one product alone cannot meet all the requirements, so that the woodworker must weigh up which

The materials used in the construction of houses, particularly those in the rustic style, include large quantities of wood. Being exposed to the air (as in the case of this type of roof), much of it may be exposed to weather conditions and harmful insects which threaten it continually. Concealed timber is also at risk from insect and fungal attack. This is why adequate protective treatment is essential.

Desirable properties of wood preservation products

- It should be toxic to fungi and insects (fungicidal and insecticidal) but not toxic to humans or warm-blooded animals.
- It should belong-lasting and resistant to washing, evaporation and sublimation.
- It should be chemically stable over a long period of time.
- It should be readily available on the market and easy to find.
- It should be safe to use.
- It should be easy to apply.
- It should not corrode metals.
- It should penetrate wood well.
- It should not make the wood more inflammable.
- After application, it should be possible to paint or varnish the wood or apply a similar finish.
- It should not give off unpleasant odours.
- It should be colourless, if the finish planned for the wood is intended to preserve its natural colour.
- It should respect the environment, not contaminate it and it should be possible to recycle the materials treated with it.

Categories of risk

The risks to which wood may be subject in certain conditions depends partly on how it has been processed and also on the wood's own resistance and on the wood-preserving treatments it has undergone.

As a rule of thumb, it may be said that wood with a moisture content lower than 20% is not very likely to be attacked by fungi. On the other hand, for wood-eating insects which thrive in the same climatic conditions as fungi, the level of moisture alone is not a decisive factor. They attack both dry and moist wood.

Although it is true that not all wood is used in the building trade, the classification of wood and the attacks to which it may be prone is very useful because they are applicable to these types of wood used in other fields and for other purposes.

product is best suited to the particular requirements of the situation in which the wood will be used, and is most appropriate for the species of wood under consideration.

Types of risk to avoid for wood used in buildings

Humidity

Wood should keep the same relative humidity as it had when it was installed, always less than 20%. With few exceptions, there is no risk of rot and fungal attack. However wood-eating insects can appear at any time during the larva cycle.

Examples: wood block flooring, staircases, floor boards, interior doors, joists, studs, interior wood lining, wood walls, etc.

Accidental humidity

There is always the possibility of accidental humidity through condensation or water leaks which present a potential risk of attack by fungi and insects if the ventilation is inadequate. Apart from this, wood-eating insects can appear at any time during the larva cycle.
Examples: areas near waste pipes, plumbing leaks, leaking roofs, etc.

Intermittent humidity

In this situation wood is exposed to a varying relative humidity approaching 20% and there is therefore a tendency towards rot and attack by wood-eating insects.

Examples: external woodwork, cladding, shutters, doors, windows, etc.

Permanent humidity

The wood is continually subject to conditions unfavourable to its preservation, so that it has a relative humidity of about 20% all the time. This puts it is at permanent risk from rot and insect attack.

Examples: piles, fences, palisades, basements, cellars, garden constructions, swimming pools, saunas etc.

External woodwork, such as doors, windows, shutters and so on, is particularly vulnerable to the action of wet and the deterioration brought about by changing weather conditions during the seasons. Given the serious conditions it has to survive, it is vital that the wood used should have been treated to give sufficient protection.

Apart from the kitchen, the bathroom is the place in a house or apartment where wood undergoes the harshest conditions. The steam and humidity are an enemy which is constantly destructive. It is therefore essential to use wood treated to survive the conditions it will encounter for all the wooden fittings in the bathroom.

Classification of wood preservatives

Water-soluble preservatives

These products consist of mineral salts dissolved in water at a pre-determined strength. The concentration of the solution depends on how strong the protection needs to be, whether further application is foreseen, and what type of wood is involved. They are made up of three main components:
• The active ingredients are the salts of elements such as fluorine, boron, arsenic, copper, zinc etc. which act as insecticides or fungicide.
- Additive products: These are salts with binding properties designed to fix the active ingredients in the wood. They must not be washed out or evaporate under any conditions.
- Water as the solvent.
There are several water-soluble wood preservatives which can be classed as follows, depending on their formula:
Classification based on biocidal properties
• Fungicide or insecticide, or both combined.
Classification based on fixing method:
• Products which penetrate fast and do not wash out easily. To ensure that they penetrate well into the wood they are applied using a

special process. Copper-chromium-arsenic are typical compounds.
• Products which penetrate slowly. They do not penetrate so quickly into the wood as the previous compounds and are better suited for water-proofing dry wood in an autoclave, or in the case of moist wood, in a diffuser. Chromium-fluorine and chromium-boron-fluorine compounds are those most commonly used.
• Leachable products without fixing salts.
These are generally used on moist wood to ensure a good depth of penetration using a special diffusion process, but also through short immersion or spraying only superficial protection is needed. Water-soluble wood preservatives are good for all types of wood which are continuously exposed to the moisture in the soil or set in brickwork or masonry (fences in fields, orchards and gardens, beams and rafters, etc.).
Advantages: These are very effective chemical compounds using water which is a very cheap solvent. The wood treated with these products hardly changes in colour and remain clean-looking for a long time. Plastic components which may later be attached to the wood will not be affected and paint may also be applied on top. Products which do not wash out are

used mainly in agriculture. Objects which come into contact with wood treated with these products do not become stained and there is no increase in flammability.
Disadvantages: Because these wood preservatives are applied on moist wood or the wood has become moist through the treatment, it is important that the wood should be allowed to dry out afterwards. This may lead to some warping of the wood. Also, treatment in an autoclave is very expensive.

Emulsions

These are substances not soluble in water which require the addition of an emulsifying agent to ensure good dispersion in water. In the trade they are known as emulsions. They form a link between the water-soluble wood preservatives and those using an organic solvent. What they have in common with the former is the way in which they penetrate into the wood, but like the latter they include active metallic salts. They are divided into fungicide and insecticide emulsions, but there are some products which combine both functions. They come as a liquid concentrate in which the wood may be immersed or which, if required,

Types of protective treatments by level of penetration

Surface protection	The average dept of penetration by the preservative is 3 mm (1/8 in), and not less than 1 mm (½₂ in) at any point of the area treated.
Average protection	The average depth of penetration by the preservative is over 3 mm (⅛ in) but under 75% of the thickness of the wood treated.
Deep protection	The average depth of penetration by the preservative is equal to or more than 75% of the thickness of the wood treated.

Systems of timber protection

TYPE OF PROTECTION	TREATMENT	APPLICATION	RISK
Water-soluble	Preventative	Spray Autoclave (vacuum pressure)	1,2,3,4
Emulsion	Preventative	Spray Brush	1,2
Dissolved in organic solvent	Preventative	Spray Brush Immersion Autoclave	1,2
	Curative	Spray Brush Injection	1,2,3
Natural organic	Preventative	Autoclave	1,2,3,4

Risk factors: 1) Not prone to damp but vulnerable to insects 2) Prone to damp 3) Weather-resistant but not in contact with the soil 4) In constant contact with the soil or with moisture

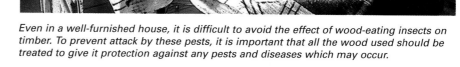

Even in a well-furnished house, it is difficult to avoid the effect of wood-eating insects on timber. To prevent attack by these pests, it is important that all the wood used should be treated to give it protection against any pests and diseases which may occur.

55

can also be sprayed onto dry or moist wood.
Advantages: Emulsions do not alter the colour of the wood and allow subsequent painting if desired. Glue may also be used if necessary and metal and plastic are not affected by them. Flammability is not increased and does not stain the objects they come in contact with.
Disadvantages: because these products are applied to moist wood and because they wet it further the their watery consistency, the wood may warp, crack or shrink during the drying process.

Organic solvents

These are ready-to-use solutions of very complex compounds which are made up of three main elements:
• Active agents: compounds which belong mainly to the organic chloride group (phenol chloride, naphthalene chloride etc.), organo-metallic compounds (copper and zinc salts) and organo-phosphoric compounds. Some of these compounds are extremely poisonous both to people and animals and since the 1980s have been the subject of much legal argument because wood preservatives containing pentachlorophenol (PCP) and lindane

(Gamma HCH) are now known to emanate gases into the atmosphere which are then breathed in by people and animals. Many health problems are said to be caused by the neurological toxicity of these substances which has led to the use of pentachlorophenol and lindane being banned in many countries. Both have been replaced by less toxic but slightly less effective substances such as dichlofluanide and TBTN (tributyl naphthalene) compound.
• Additives: These are compounds ensuring the stability of the product and the penetration of the active ingredients into the wood.
• Organic solvents: They are usually the results of distillation of crude oil. They are either insecticides or fungicides or both and they can be applied by brush or spray. Alternatively the wood can be immersed briefly. If deeper penetration is required the pressure-vacuum method is used for dry wood. Because the wood remains dry using this method, treatment can be carried out after the object has been built.
Wood preservatives dissolved in organic solvents are divided into two categories:
Preventative treatments: Impregnation, water-repellent biocidal wood preservative.
Curative treatments: These are used in the event of infestation by insects such as woodworm.

Natural organic treatments

These organic wood preservatives are produced by the distillation of coal tar or wood, or by the pyrolysis of petroleum. The best-known of these products is creosote, a waste product produced by gasworks and blast furnaces.
They are complex chemical oil compounds which can only be used on dry wood.
Because of the particular properties of these products the wood is impregnated by hot or cold immersion or under pressure in an autoclave, or by brush.
Advantages: they are particularly effective against wood-eating insects and because of their excellent adhesive power they remain effective for a very long time. They do not affect metal.
Disadvantages: they are highly poisonous and give off a strong, unpleasant smell for a very long time. They leave grease marks and other stains and only dry very slowly. Treated surfaces cannot be painted immediately, and creosote shows through paint and has a bad effect on plants. Finally, using an autoclave is difficult and expensive.

Like the bathroom, the kitchen is the other room in the house where the woodwork is particularly vulnerable to the effects of humidity. Wood to be used for furniture in the kitchen must be treated properly to protect it from the consequences of the inevitable humidity generated by the steam of cooking.

Types of wood treatment

Protective treatments			
	Moist wood processes	Sap-replacing processes	
		Diffusion processes	
		Complementary processes	
			Painting and spraying
			Sprinkling tunnel
Preventative treatments		Processes without autoclave	Free sprinkling
			Prolonged immersion
	Dry wood processes		Hot-cold immersion
			Empty cell system
		Autoclave processes with pressure	Rüpping system
			Lowry system
			Full cell system
			Bethell system
		Autoclave processes without pressure	Full cell system
			Vacuum-vacuum system
Curative treatments			

Application of preservatives

There are several different methods used to apply wood preservative. The purpose is to remove the possible sources of danger which may threaten the wood, including that used in buildings or other items already constructed. The choice of method will depend on the nature of the wood preservative and/or the desired level of protection. It is also important to decide at what stage during construction the treatment should take place, because this also has a bearing on the choice of method. Wood preservatives can be applied before or after the item is built. They are divided into two groups:

• Preventative treatments: These are applied to healthy wood before or after it is used in constructing a building or other item so that it is protected from possible dangers.
• Curative treatments: These are intended to rid the wood of existing infestation or damage and protect it against future attacks.

Preventative treatments

The way in which a wood preservative is applied depends on whether the object has already been constructed, whether the wood has already been treated either industrially or in the workshop, and what its future use is likely to be.

Preventative wood preservatives can be divided into two groups:
• A product which is applied to moist wood
• A product which is applied to dry wood.
This distinction is extremely important because before it can be used for construction or other purposes the wood first undergoes some natural seasoning. This slow drying process results in a wood whose cells and cell walls have been altered in such a way that many of the nutrients on which wood-eating insects feed will have been removed.

Moist wood processes

Replacement of the wood's own sap

This process involves the replacement the wood's sap by a wood preservative. The most commonest method is known as the Boucherie process. Originally the trunks were attached to supports, the thin ends always being placed at

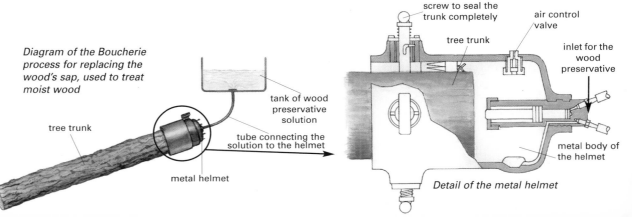

Diagram of the Boucherie process for replacing the wood's sap, used to treat moist wood

tree trunk

tank of wood preservative solution

tube connecting the solution to the helmet

metal helmet

screw to seal the trunk completely

air control valve

tree trunk

inlet for the wood preservative

metal body of the helmet

Detail of the metal helmet

the bottom. A metal 'helmet' was placed over the thicker end, from which a thin tube led to a container filled with wood preservative, placed about 10 m (33 ft) above the trunk. The so-called helmets closed off the ends of the tree, the protective fluid penetrating the wood because of the height difference and thus displacing the tree's own sap. Eventually the tree's sap flows out at the bottom end of the trunk. As time went by, the original process was gradually improved and refined, and above all the duration of the process was considerably shortened. This was achieved by using compressors and suction apparatus, increasing the pressure.

Diffusion

This method consists of pouring a highly concentrated wood preservatives onto the surface which penetrate a little way into the wood. It then combines with the wood cells so that eventually the whole piece of wood becomes gradually impregnated. The basic idea of this method is that two similar solutions of different concentrations are mixed together and after a time form a homogenous solution. The moisture contained in the wood carries the wood preservative from the surface of the wood to the inside.
There are several stages in this process:
- Partial drying of the wood (when the interior of the wood is still very moist)
- Superficial impregnation and the actual diffusion, followed by the drying process.
The following aspects affect the diffusion process:
• Properties of the wood (texture, moisture content etc.)
• Concentration of the wood preservative
• Treatment temperature
The method consists of applying the product to the wood and as soon as it is absorbed, carrying out the actual diffusion. This is only possible with relatively moist wood. The wood preservatives used are water-soluble and consist either of a concentrate or a paste with fluorides or borates. The compound bisodium-octo-borate was first used for this purpose in 1949, when the method became known as timberisation.
Advantages:
- Complete penetration by the wood preservative
- The method is relatively cheap.
- It takes less time to achieve a certain level of protection than other methods such as the lengthy immersion method.
Disadvantages:
No other products can be used that might trigger further chemical reactions creating new compounds which could influence the solubility and thus prevent the diffusion of the chemical compounds in the wood.
- When using water-soluble substances which

must preserve this property, this method can only be used on indoor wood types which are not subjected to moisture.
- This method takes longer than it would using an autoclave.
There are many variations on this method: normal diffusion, osmosis system (one-sided diffusion), belt system, hole system, double diffusion system, sling system etc.

Complementary methods

These are exclusively applicable to wood which has been treated in an autoclave and also has a high moisture content. In preparation for the chemical treatment, the wood must first be partly dried which implies that the drying process must be carried out in an autoclave. The treatment itself then takes place immediately without the wood being removed from of the autoclave. The treatment can combine several methods:
Steam + vacuum + impregnation
The wood is placed in the autoclave and subjected for several hours to a steam pressure of 1–2 kg/cm^3 and a temperature of 120° C (248° F). The pressure is then reduced to atmospheric level which creates a high vacuum. Because the temperature of the moisture inside the wood is still very high as a result of the previous heating process, it is extracted out of the wood. Because the boiling-point of water in a vacuum is several degrees lower than normal, the wood dries out in the end.
After the wood has dried, several autoclave-impregnation procedures are carried out. Because these procedures can be combined, it is possible to save a few stages because two vacuum procedures can take place one after the other.

Dry wood processes

Without autoclave

• Systems involving spraying or brushing
The simplest system consists of applying the wood preservative with a brush. This purely superficial system means that very little preservative is required and because of the capillarity of the wood only a small amount of the substance penetrates the wood, leaving only a thin surface layer which is toxic. The product penetrates deepest into the wood when it is brushed on in the direction of the fibres: on average 1 to 5 mm (½₂ to ³⁄₁₆ in), depending on the resistance and level of absorbency. In order to ensure that the wood absorbs enough of the preservative, it must be applied three times with the previous layer being allowed to dry before the next one is applied. Three such stages correspond to one spraying session. The great advantages of this method are that it is relatively cheap and

Any external wooden construction is in permanent danger of deterioration, whether by natural element of erosion, the activity of insects, or the rapid ageing brought about by the weather. It is therefore essential to use properly treated wood for this kind of use, and to give it preventative maintenance on a regular basis.

that it is fairly easy to carry out. However, the disadvantage is that the degree of protection is not very high.

• Sprinkling tunnel
Compared to the other systems described above, this system provides much more effective protection. This method consists in passing the pieces of wood lengthways through a tunnel. From small openings placed all along the tunnel, the wood preservative is sprinkled onto the wood. The arrangement of these holes is such that all sides of the wood, including the ends parts, are sprinkled, thus achieving a homogenous protection of the wood.

This method can cause atmospheric pollution the atmosphere, and to minimise this the remaining wood preservative not absorbed by the wood can be collected and filtered. The in-depth protection is also better than that provided by the brush-on method because the penetration and retention levels are higher.

• Short wood preservative bath
With this method the wood is completely immersed for a certain length of time at room temperature in bath filled with wood preservative. Depending on the type of wood and size, the immersion time can range from a few seconds to ten minutes. The protection achieved by this method is relatively superficial. Any wood preservative can be used with this method which is mainly used for dry wood. Comparing this immersion method

with the systems described above, it must be said that it achieves a higher although still superficial degree of wood protection. The disadvantages are obvious; it is more expensive with larger amounts of wood preservative being needed and it is clearly not suitable for smaller pieces of wood.

• Prolonged wood preservative bath
This method is similar to the previous one but the duration of immersion in the wood preservative is longer. The wood is immersed for at least 10 minutes but it may be for as long as several weeks or months. This basically very simple method ensures an extremely high degree of protection but the very long time spent in the wood preservative bath is an important disadvantage compared with the modern, efficient, reasonably short industrial methods.

• Hot-cold wood preservative bath
Compared to the previous system, this particular method is a clear improvement because not only is the immersion time much shortened but the penetration and retention of the wood preservative is increased. The pieces of wood are immersed in different baths, filled with wood preservative (hot-cold). The hot bath causes the air stored in the wood to be expelled in the form of bubbles, although some air remains trapped in the wood. The hot bath is followed by the cold bath where the remaining air escapes and the already existing vacuum is increased. Because the wood preservative takes the place of the air which has just escaped, the penetration and absorption of the product are greatly improved.
Advantages: complete penetration of the wood is achieved within 24 hours.
Disadvantages:
• In many cases only organic wood preservatives can be used.
• High cost because it requires a permanent installation.

Short immersion system, using dry wood without an autoclave.

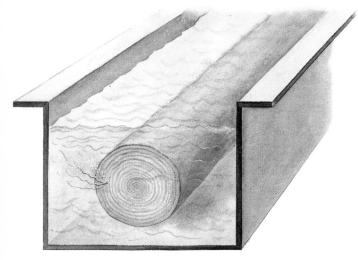

Autoclave systems

The autoclave methods are divided into two groups:
• The group in which the wood preservative is made to penetrate the wood by applying pressure
• The group where no pressure is involved.
The first group is further sub-divided into two sub-groups:
• System with empty cells.
• Systems with full cells.

• Empty cell system
Wood preservative is pushed through the capillary network of the wood surface by applying pressure which traps the air in the wood in the form of micro-bubbles. Later when the pressure is reduced , the compressed air pushes out the wood preservative. What is left are almost empty cells whose cell walls are impregnated with wood preservative.
Advantage: this system does not increase the weight of the wood noticeably and the precise amount of the product needed is used without any waste.

• Rüpping system
This method was patented in the United States in 1902 and involves the following stages:
- Placing dry wood in a cylinder which is then sealed.
- Steaming, vacuum-treating and drying the wood if moist.
- Raising the pressure in the cylinder. The pressure depends on the porosity of the timber and the level of protection required. On average, the pressure is 4 to 5 kg/cm²
- Introduction of the wood preservative into the cylinder.
- Raising the pressure to so-called 'normal pressure' level. This depends on the type of wood and how much wood preservative must be retained. On average the pressure is 10 to 15 kg/cm². It is important to ensure that the pressure ratio is right for the type of wood. For instance, pine-wood or the wood of light broad-leaved trees may simply collapse without warning if the pressure and temperature of the wood preservative introduced into the tunnel are too high. In the case of these kinds of wood, the pressure should not exceed about 9 kg/cm².
- Maintaining the 'normal pressure' at the same level for a certain time (depending on the criteria mentioned above).
- Lowering the pressure to atmospheric level.
- Removal of the wood preservative which has come out of the wood.
- Removing the treated wood from the impregnated cylinder.
The most interesting feature of this method, compared with all the others, is that pressure produced by a compressor is applied from the very beginning when the wood is first intro-

duced in the cylinder, before the wood preservative is added.
Advantages: Excellent penetration and low retention of wood preservative in the wood.
Disadvantages: The wood preservative in the impregnation device placed in the cylinder is dispensed under relatively high pressure. If in addition the temperature of the wood preservative is raised when pumped into the cylinder, there is a risk of explosion or ignition under certain circumstances.

• Lowry-system
The difference between this system and the Rüpping system lies in the fact that in this system the internal pressure is not raised before the introduction of the wood preservative into the impregnation tank. In this system the wood preservative is introduced into the tank at the same time as the pressure is increased. This causes the air to be compressed out of the wood which then resumes its volume when the pressure is reduced back to atmospheric level. This simplifies the collection of the unused wood preservative. More wood preservative is collected at the stage of the final emptying. As a rule, oily products (creosote and organic products) are used at a particular temperature. The pressure (as far as time and amount is concerned) depends on several factors: the type of wood, the size and also the moisture content of the wood to be treated. The pressure ranges between 9 and 15 kg/cm².
Advantages:
- Unlike the Rüpping system, a superimposed cylinder is not required.
- Because the wood preservative is not pumped in at a high temperature, there is no danger of explosion or fire.
- Both the level of penetration and the retention are considerably higher than with the Rüpping system. With similar levels of retention, penetration is even higher.
Disadvantages:
- More preservative is needed to achieve a similar level of protection as that achieved with the Rüpping system.

• Full cell system
The aim of this system consists in achieving a high level of retention of wood preservative in the wood cells, so noticeably smaller amounts of the product can be recovered than with the empty cell system. If the objective is for the wood to absorb the largest amount of wood preservative, the wood is first treated in a vacuum before filling the impregnation tank with wood preservative. In this way the wood cells will be filled with the maximum possible amount of wood preservative.

• Bethell system
With this system any kind of wood preservative can be used. It consists of the following stages:

- Placing the dry wood in the impregnation chamber which is then hermetically sealed.
- Creating an initial vacuum which can vary in duration and intensity depending on the type of wood and level of protection required.
- Adding the wood preservative to the impregnation chamber.
- Raising the internal pressure to a working pressure of 8 to 15 kg/cm^2.
- Maintaining this pressure for a certain time, up to 6 hours if necessary, depending on the type of wood.
- Returning the pressure to atmospheric level. With this method very little air remains in the wood because of the initial vacuum. If the pressure is raised again, there will be hardly any air left in the wood. But this barely reduces the level of retention of the wood preservative.
- Removing the product which has not been absorbed.
- Applying a final vacuum of varying duration and intensity but with a higher pressure and longer duration than the initial vacuum. This is to collect some of the excess wood preservative and to clean the wood surface.
- Restoring the atmospheric pressure.
- Removing the excess wood preservative, recovered after the final vacuum stage, from the impregnation chamber.

The initial vacuum extracts the air enclosed in the capillary network of the wood which increases the depth of penetration of the wood preservative when the chamber is filled. The pressure which is then raised to working level encourages this process. In many cases the product is completely absorbed by the wood which is therefore completely saturated. The final vacuum process balances out the difference in pressure between the atmospheric pressure and internal pressure which prevents any possible exudation of the preservative in the future.

With autoclave without pressure

This includes all the methods which involve an autoclave and wood preservative but without exerting any pressure on the wood.

• Full cell system
The autoclave systems without pressure mainly include full cell methods, in particular those using the double vacuum system.

• Vacuum-vacuum system
This popular modern system is one most widely used throughout the world, especially in the treatment of building timber and wood intended for outdoor and indoor woodwork (parquet floors, rafters, beams etc.).
It consists of the following stages:
- Placing the dry wood in the impregnation chamber.

Impregnation tank used in the Lowry empty-cell process, one of the pressure autclave systems

- Activating the initial vacuum whose intensity and duration vary depending on the type of wood and required level of protection.
- Filling the impregnation chamber with wood preservative so as to cover the wood completely. The level of vacuum is then reduced and the atmospheric pressure restored.
- Leaving the wood for a period in the wood preservative. The length of time depends on the type of wood and desired level of protection.
- Removing the wood preservative which has not been absorbed by the wood.
- Activating the final vacuum whose intensity is greater and duration longer. In fact, it should last until the desired level of retention

of wood preservative has been achieved.
- Restoring the atmospheric pressure.
- Removing the remaining wood preservative, exuded during the final vacuum.
- Removing the wood from the impregnation tank.

The vacuum-vacuum system uses an organic wood preservative which combines insecticides and fungicides as well as water-repellent wax and resin. The wood must be dried to the correct level and left for a few days in the open after treatment so that the fumes of the solvent contained in the wood preservative can evaporate and the active substances can become fixed in the wood. This waiting time is one of the disadvantages of this system.

59

Curative treatments

These are methods used to deal with wood already used in construction or to make furniture which has been affected by fungi or wood-eating insects. The aim is not only to stop the attack or infestation but also to protect the wood against future similar attacks or infestations.

Curative treatment use the same products as preventive treatments but the concentration may vary. The procedure depends on how serious the attack or infestation is and the size of the surface area needing treatment. In the case of small surface areas, the product can simply be brushed on. When dealing with large surfaces, a different method must be used. First, holes are drilled in a chequerboard pattern in the surface of the parts to be treated. The depth and width of the holes must obviously not endanger the strength of the wood. The wood preservative is injected into

the holes. It is very important that the product should penetrate as deeply as possible in the wood.

This is particularly important in countries where there are termites. If a building is affected by termites, the whole edifice has to be protected against them by a termite barrier. Built round the whole building, it involves the walls as well as the soil. Unlike woodworm, which lives in the wood and are killed by injecting wood preservative inside the holes, termites live in termite nests away from buildings and they operate in the soil.

To build a termite barrier, holes are drilled in all the supporting walls at intervals of 25 to 35 cm (10 to 14 in) in which poison is injected. Poison is also injected into the open soil to a depth of 60 cm (24 in) because below that level the pressure of the soil is such that termites cannot survive there.

Wood diseases and parasites

Abnormal growth

As living things, trees are exposed to many different diseases and health problems during their lifetime. Some of them are able to surmount these problems easily, whereas others suffer serious damage, which sometimes diminishes the wood's usefulness as a raw material for woodworking, carving or building.

Wood is considered healthy and usable if a transverse cut through the trunk shows regular, well formed, uniformly distributed annular rings. This indicates that a tree has not suffered significant ups and downs in its life from serious diseases or pests, which certainly would have left their mark.

If the sapwood is very soft, it needs to be removed quickly once the tree has been felled in order to protect the wood from the immediate effects of destructive agent such as fungus and insects.

After a trunk has been cut down, the timber is subjected to intensive checks designed to detecting any possible defects or anomalies, which might otherwise cause significant problems during the processing of the wood.

Some of the commonest wood diseases and parasites are described in this section.

Eccentric heartwood or growth rings

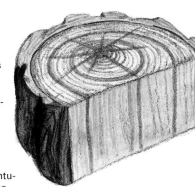

In tropical regions, 75% of trees suffer from this defect. In temperate climate zones, it is found in 50% of the population. It is often caused by constant exposure to strong winds or intensive sunshine coming from one direction. In response to these factors, the heart wood may grow out of the centre, thus shifting the distribution of the growth rings, and eventually leading to non-homogeneous wood with abnormal physical and mechanical properties. The occasional development of two separate heartwood cores enhances this kind of defect. If the deviation from the centre of the tree is not too pronounced, and the bole is not strongly distorted, this defect may not give rise to any serious problems.

Twin sapwood

If a tree is exposed to low temperatures over a longer period of time it will suffer progressive decay as the flow of lignin breaks down. This amorphous polymer provides rigidity and together with cellulose forms the woody cell walls and the bonding material between them. Decaying portions of a tree can be identified by a pale colour, which turns reddish in time as well as by the characteristic odour generated by the decay of the fibres. Such portions of a tree must be rejected, as they affect the strength properties of the wood and are a potential source for further decomposition. If the decayed portions cover a large extent of a tree it is best to reject it altogether in order to avoid processing problems.

Ring check

This is a defect in lumber similar to *twin sapwood*, as it is characterised by alternated live and dead growth rings or knots. This defect is often the consequence of an interruption in a tree's vital functions during extended exposure to low temperatures. As vitality breaks down, the sap clogs up, affecting the growth rings by diminishing their strength with a distorted structure. Trees showing this defect should be rejected, as their wood is not up to the required standard for processing.

Faults in the pattern of growth rings

This defect may arise from different factors: sudden changes of climate, drought, excess or lack of sunlight, repeated transplantation, disease caused by parasites as well as fire and other traumatic injury. These changes affect the regular width of the growth rings without influencing their concentric distribution. If this defect is not too strongly pronounced, it should not cause any serious problems. But if the distribution is clearly irregular this may affect the wood's structure by generating zones of reduced density and strength.

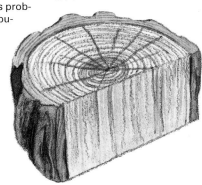

Hollow heartwood

This defect is found when the centre of the tree dries off and the neighbouring growth rings crumble. This phenomenon is know as brown rot, and results from a fungus damaging the heartwood until it crumbles and eventually disappears. Trees suffering brown rot show differences in consistency, which lead to a loss of resistance and strength as the bonding between the radial and tangential fibres is affected. In such cases the outer wood-layers may be usable, as long as the splits which tend to occur along the rays do not cover the entire cross-section.

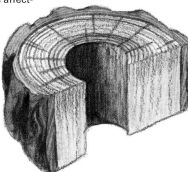

Shakes

Internal stresses in a growing tree or wood being seasoned can cause large splits known as shakes. This defect arises from extended exposure to low temperatures or drought. Shakes often originate in the bark and expand towards the centre of the tree. High wood density may prevent shakes from expanding further, which otherwise eventually causes the death of the tree. Even though they may not have reached the heartwood, trees should be rejected if more than 50 % of the cross-section is covered by shakes, as the wood is not suitable for working.

Cock's claw

This defect can be found both in living trees and in timber. Cracks originating at the centre of the tree develop perpendicular to the growth rings in the direction of the bark. This defect is usually an indicator of decay.

Cup check

This defect arises from the sudden melting of sap frozen between two layers of concentric growth rings, thus generating an equally concentric crack. Insects and larvae are often attracted into such cracks. As the crack expands towards the bark, the heartwood suffers separation, thus affecting the density and mechanical properties of the tree. This defect is normally observed in trees with a high level of tannin, such as chestnut and oak.

The effects of xylophagous insects

Many different species of insects lay eggs in wood, since it represents an excellent source of nutrients for the larvae. The larvae are most commonly found in fallen or seasonally shed timber, which offers little resistance to penetration, thus facilitating the formation of narrow passages into the sapwood high in nutrients. Wood infested by these species therefore has many small holes and narrow galleries, made by adult insects and their larvae.

Different species infesting wood can be distinguished by their specific behaviour patterns, determining the shape of the holes and galleries, the formation of sawdust and the properties of the faeces of the insects.

The pests most threatening to construction material belong to the species of coleopterous xylophages, mainly wood-eating beetles. Termites are the common wood insects in tropical and subtropical countries. Since larvae have a much higher consumption of nutrients, they are the most voracious wood predators, penetrating the sapwood to devour the starch contained in it. Prevention of xylophagous pests is achieved through fumigation.

The commonest and most devastating xylophages are described in this section.

Old house borer
(*Hylotrupes bajulus*)

This is a coleopteran, which attacks the sapwood of coniferous woods. In particular those with a thin bark are infested and often completely riddled, as opposed to the more robust pines and cedars. Life cycles between 3 and 11 years are observed among these insects, which grow to a size of 8 to 20 mm (⅓ to ¾ in). The old house borer beetle is black and has two large feelers. Typical size of larvae varies from 13 to 30 mm (½ to 1¼ in), with a diameter of about 6 mm (¼ in). Holes in wood in which they are commonly found have a diameter of 5 to 7 mm (about ¼ in) and are oval shaped. Galleries made in wood by this insect are filled with sawdust when abandoned.

The female old house borer beetle is capable of laying up to 200 eggs in outer cracks of the wood at the same time. Larvae hatch from the egg of this insect within one to three weeks and remain in the wood, altering in size while going through several moults. They are finally transformed into chrysalis from which the adults emerge.

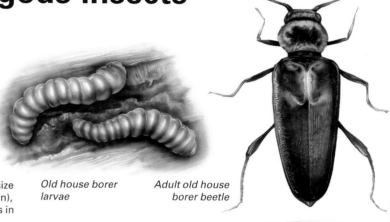

Old house borer larvae

Adult old house borer beetle

Image of wood infested by the Great Woodworm

Powderpost beetle (*Lyctus brunneus*)

This species commonly infests and severely damages deciduous trees, in particular those with particular properties (vessels with a diameter of 0.07 mm or greater and a moisture content between 6 and 32%).

Female insects of these species lay 20 to 40 eggs in porous wood.

Pale coloured larvae 4 to 6 mm (⅙ to ¼ in) long hatch from the egg after a 8 to14 days. Adult insects are 3 to 6 mm (⅛ to ¼ in)long.

The larvae are voracious wood predators, carving narrow galleries along the grain and deep into the wood thereby amassing a fine floury sawdust similar to the talc they excrete.

This insect leaves external signs of attack on the wood's surface by carving ovally shaped holes with a diameter typically of 1 to 1.5 mm (about ¹⁄₁₆ in).

Moths have a life cycle of 1 year, although it may not survive more than 3 to 4 months if they are regularly exposed to inappropriate temperatures.

The presence of moths is only revealed by the external signs of attack. Dry wood being seasoned as well as porous wood is often infested by powderpost beetle, in particular when the size of pores matches the size of the female insect thus enabling it to lay eggs among fibres high in starch.

Adult powderpost beetle

Wood attacked by powderpost beetle

61

Woodworm
(*Anobium punctatum*)

The common woodworm is a coleopteran which mainly attacks the sapwood of pines and deciduous trees and occasionally their bark, in particular when it shows signs of rot. Woodworms are among the smaller wood insects, as adults reach only 3 to 8 mm (⅛–⅓ in). Larvae are 4 to 6 mm (⅛ to ¼ in) long. Female woodworms lay 40 to 50 eggs at a time. Upon hatching from the egg, larvae carve narrow galleries into the wood, which they later abandon filled with sawdust and faeces.

The life cycle of the woodworm lasts 1 to 3 years. Adults emerge from the wood through holes with a diameter of 1.5 to 3 mm (about ¹⁄₁₆ in). Sawdust is pressed through the galleries to reach the surface, where it visibly accumulates.

Cold and dry environments are recommended to prevent this pest, since larvae cannot survive without moisture.

Woodworm larva

Adult woodworm

Termites (*Reticulitermes lucifugus*)

Like bees and ants, termites also populate large colonies under the control of an egg-laying female which lays about 4,000 eggs a day. Larvae hatching from the egg pass through several moults of winged sexual forms, wingless sterile workers and soldiers, finally being transformed into a chrysalis from which the adults emerge.

Adult termites have a sharp very strong mouth pincer, which is their main working tool. Ideal conditions for the existence and reproduction of termites are provided by humid soils at moderate constant temperatures. Termites dig multiple galleries into the soil, through which they finally reach wood in order to extract both bark and sapwood for nutrition. No distinction is normally made with regard to the kind of wood, although a certain preference for resinous wood has been observed.

Termites can reach a length of 4 to 6 mm (⅛ to ¼ in). Signs of termite attack are small cavities carved in the direction of the grain covered by a layer containing saliva, faeces and wood particles. Unfortunately, the wood often has to be broken to reveal termite attack.

Worker termite

The carpenter bee

Insects belonging to these species have different colours: the genus *Sirex juvencus* is typically metallic blue, while those belonging to the *Sirex gijas* genus are yellow-black.

The carpenter bee has a notably prolonged body and a pair of clearly visible feelers. It excavates galleries with dimensions continually adapted to the size of the growing larvae. Adults are from 15 to 39 mm (⁵⁄₈ to 1½ in) long. Larvae are usually about 30 mm (1¼ in) long.

Carpenter bee larva

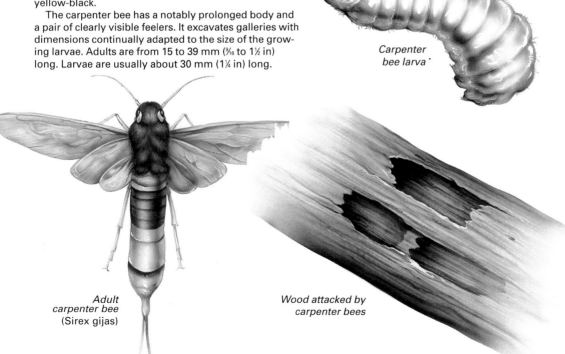

Adult carpenter bee (Sirex gijas)

Wood attacked by carpenter bees

Fungal attack

Fungi grow and reproduce in environments with particular characteristics. Attacks occur where there is a sufficient degree of moisture, enough oxygen and the right temperature, and a strong infection or source of infection. Trees or timber being seasoned are often attacked by fungi in such conditions. Two of the most common species are described in this section.

Xylophagous fungi

These species produce enzymes capable of degrading wood into its components of lignin and cellulose, which form the cell walls of wood. Given favourable levels of moisture and acidity, the components are metabolised, thus generating the nutrients for the fungi. As a result, the wood's outward aspect changes. It loses colour and weight as it becomes more and more porous. The texture as well as the conductivity (both thermal and electrical) and the mechanical properties are affected following fungal attack. This not only reduces its suitability for use, but it may lead to the complete destruction of trees and timber, both while it is being seasoned, and once it has been used to make furniture, buildings, bridges and so on. Propagation is promoted by decay.

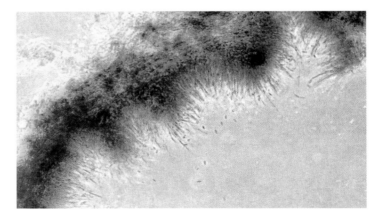

Microscope-view of a xylophagous fungus, showing its ability to penetrate and destroy wood.

Chromogenic fungi

These species contain various pigments in their cellular structure, which result in different colours depending on the kind of wood. The worst are the so-called blue stains, for their action provokes an increase in permeability. This causes the wood to be more hygroscopic, thus affecting its mechanical properties.

Unfortunately these species are found in many different environments, thus making prevention quite a complicated problem.

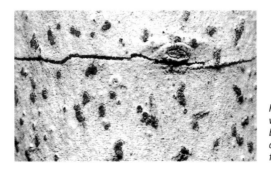

Fragment of wood attacked by blue-coloured chromogenic fungi.

Manufactured products

The man-made wooden boards described in the following pages are the result of the successful search to solve the problem of a world-wide shortage of wood while constantly improving on existing materials. Developing these new materials, wood experts have tried to achieve the following:
• A homogeneous behaviour of the wood with reduced 'movement' (such as warping) under different conditions.
• To solve or at least to reduce the problem of the shortage of wood in the world.
• Maximum use of wood as far as quantity is concerned by further processing the various elements of wood and its fibres.
• Maximum use of the wood as far as quality is concerned through the development of veneer.
• The development of smooth surfaces in the form of large panels which would be difficult or impossible to produce from the natural tree trunk .
• The use of smaller trunks including those of recently planted trees (such as when clearing forests and woods, and thinning plantations).
• Recycling existing materials.

Blockboard

These are boards made from wooden strips of similar or different length which have been glued together. The strips are visible at the sides of the board while the top and bottom are covered with veneer. They were mainly developed for indoor use and are used in the manufacture of furniture, doors, work-tops and so on.

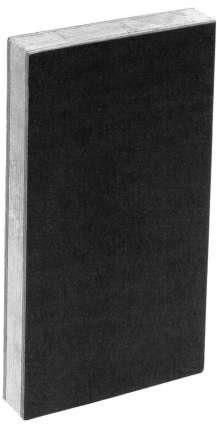

Blockboard

Sheet of ordinary plywood

Plywood boards

Plywood boards (veneer) consist of several layers of wood glued together whose fibres always run at right angles to each other. Because the fibres run against each other in this way, plywood cannot shrink or become deformed. In addition, the board has a greater stability as far as warping and strength is concerned. The thickness of the individual layers of wood on each side of the core must be the same to ensure that the board does not warp. The numbers of layers glued together is always uneven (3, 5, 7, 9...) so that the fibres of both top and bottom surfaces run in the same direction.

Plywood boards have several advantages over natural wood. While wood which grows freely in nature has branches, cracks and resin deposits which cause deficiencies and imperfections on the surface of the wood, plywood is manufactured as a stable, lasting material which does not suffer from climatic fluctuations of temperature and humidity. In addition, the wood industry is constantly looking to improve and develop materials to suit an increasingly large range of applications. That is why plywood is so reliable, safe and versatile in its application.

Normal plywood boards

These are boards consisting of several layers of wood glued together, arranged at 90° to each other. This type of board has very good mechanical properties and a constant stability in the main directions. Depending on the glue used, this type of board can be used, indoors, outdoors and even in shipbuilding.

Plywood is divided into different groups,

depending on the treatment of the surface: unpolished, polished and coated. Plywood is used for all kinds of things: general indoor use, lining, furniture, flooring, and many other purposes.

The types of wood used to make plywood range from black poplar to birch and various types of pine as well as well as tropical woods. Normal plywood is made from knife-cut veneer, Sawn veneer is only used in plywood intended to be used in high quality furniture.

Plywood with phenolic resin coating

This type of plywood is coated with phenolic resin on both sides, mainly to protect the wood against water. An important use for this type of plywood is to make shuttering or formwork for pouring concrete. The quality and strength of such boards is so great that they can be used wherever water would affect the durability of ordinary plywood.

Vibration-absorbing plywood

The only difference from the previous types of plywood is the addition of a layer of rubber inside the plywood which absorbs oscillations and vibrations. This type of ply is therefore particularly suited for floor coverings, vans, buses and other uses where vibration and noise are to be avoided, such as in partitions separating noisy rooms.

Extra-thick plywood boards

These differ from the usual plywood boards only in their thickness which exceeds 40 mm (16 in). Because of their thickness they have particularly good mechanical properties. They are used in places subjected to particularly heavy loading, such as especially wide stairs or wherever great strength is a particular requirement.

Because of its striking appearance, this material is increasingly used in furniture. Its only disadvantage is the rather high cost of this type of plywood.

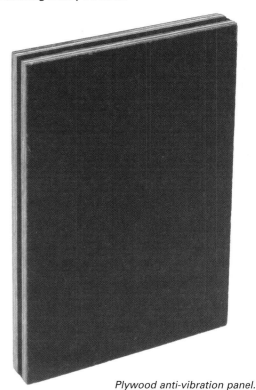

Plywood anti-vibration panel.

Plywood panel with phenolic resin coating.

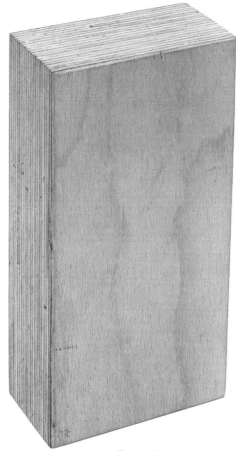

Extra-thick plywood panel.

Plywood with non-slip coating

Plywood boards coated with non-slip phenolic resin are available in various thicknesses and different wood compositions depending on the intended application. It is used mainly for floor coverings in factory, catwalks, supporting structures and scaffoldings, tiered terraces in sports grounds and any place where slipping represents a serious danger. The plywood board can be treated with different kinds of anti-slip coating and is therefore very versatile.

Plywood panel with non-slip coating.

Resin-impregnated high-density plywood boards

Beech plywood boards, pressed and impregnated with phenolic resin is a product with surprising properties. Its density is very high with excellent mechanical properties, being almost completely water-resistant because the resin has filled all the capillary vessels inside the wood, thus preventing water from penetrating the surface and damp from affecting the plywood.

Originally developed as a floor covering for high-load high-traffic areas such as the working areas of merchant ships, its high mechanical resistance and great water-resistance has led to a whole new range of applications. For instance, it is now used as a floor covering in public areas, as cladding for facades and also as floor-covering in buses. However, there are problems with nailing, screwing and joining it.

Resin-impregnated high-density plywood boards for facade cladding

Facade-cladding is one of the applications which had not been originally foreseen because at first it did not provide protection against the sun. In spite of that, it was used to clad the facades of a few buildings. The boards faded and began to decay. Today manufacturers have developed cladding which is completely weather-resistant to wind, rain and sun. In this way the problem has been solved and the results are very satisfactory.

Fire-resistant resin-impregnated high-density plywood boards

In order to meet the requirements of fire regulations, manufacturers were obliged to develop fire-proof plywood boards which could be used practically anywhere. The product is classed as technically safe and non-flammable.

The sheet of plywood illustrated below is also sound-absorbent because of the holes in it.

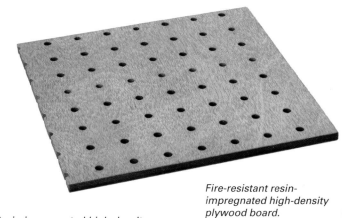

Fire-resistant resin-impregnated high-density plywood board.

Resin-impregnated high-density plywood board for cladding facades.

65

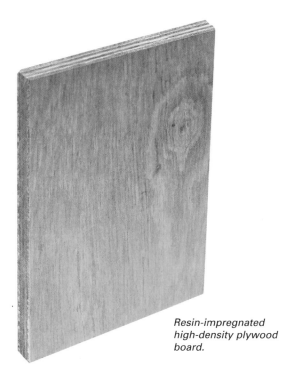

Resin-impregnated high-density plywood board.

Bullet-proof resin-impregnated high-density plywood boards

This bullet-proof plywood board serves a completely different purpose. Like other plywood boards, it consists of several layers of wood, arranged at 90° to each other. However, in this instance, they are thinner than in normal plywood and therefore also more numerous. This type of plywood has a very high density and has successfully passed official tests with a shotgun, 9-mm pistol and .44 Magnum. Their use in banks has been recognised technically.

Resin-impregnated high-density plywood boards made for floor-covering

This is the same type of plywood as that described above. A diamond-shaped pattern is added during the pressing stage with the aim of improving the anti-slip quality. In many cases, the coating which creates the pattern is made from rubber which not only improves the non-skid properties but also increases its sound-absorption. This type of plywood board is used in many countries as floor covering in buses. Because of its pleasant appearance, it is also used decoratively in public buildings and in furniture manufacturing.

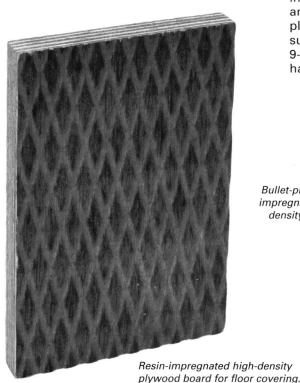

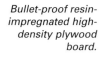

Bullet-proof resin-impregnated high-density plywood board.

Resin-impregnated high-density plywood board for floor covering.

Particle boards

These boards consist of sawdust, wood shavings or wood fibres which have been glued together under high pressure. This produces a material which is a useful replacement for wood in many cases with a wide range of applications and which is also very inexpensive to produce. These particle boards were first produced industrially in 1950 since when they have become increasingly popular because of their great advantages and versatility. They are very widely used in the manufacturing of furniture and in the building trade. Particle board is a homogeneous material which consists of up to 90% wood. In many cases the quality and properties reflect those of natural wood and they are sometimes even better. Many problems which arise when working with natural wood can be avoided with particle board.

To meet the new demands of the market, the industry is constantly producing new types of particle boards to satisfy the requirements of particularly situations or purposes. Among the many qualities of particle board, a few should be mentioned such as:

• Its greater stability of form compared to plywood because of the numerous different directions of the fibres.

• There is no jointing in the manufacturing process.

• They are moisture-resistant because of the impregnation of the fibres during the manufacturing process.

• They can be weather-resistant and immune to fluctuations of the temperature.

• Very large boards can be made, up to a size of 5.40 x 2 m (18 x 6 ft 6 in).

• The average homogeneous density is high.

• They are resistant to mildew, pests and fungi because the components of the board are amorphous and bound in resin.

• They are easy to store in a warehouse.

Medium-density fibreboard (MDF)

These panels consist of compressed wood fibres bonded together with a synthetic resin. The fibres are produced by putting wood chips in a refiner. Like other boards made from wood shavings, medium density fibreboards are extremely versatile in their application. Besides the ordinary MDF boards there are also some which are produced to meet particular requirements, including fire-resistant boards which can be identified by their red colour, and pest-resistant boards treated with a special product. Several types of synthetic glues are used to bond MDF boards: carbamide-formol, carbamide-melamine-formol and phenol. One of the main features of MDF is that it is easy to work and very versatile. The greatest disadvantage of MDF is that it is not water-resistant; if it gets wet, it swells up and frays.

Hardboard (HDF)

This consists of compressed wood fibres with a very high density. During the drying process, the wood fibres are impregnated with binding resins and consolidated under heat and pressure. If this process takes place wet, the wood's own natural resins bond the fibres together. Hardboard panels are usually not thicker than 10 mm (⅜ in).

Hardboard is used mainly in furniture construction, for instance for the bottoms of drawers and the backs of cupboards.

Chipboard

Chipboard consists of fine wood-shavings glued and pressed together under heat and pressure. This type of board makes full use of wood as a raw material since it is made from wood waste, chippings, twigs, thin trunks and even recycled wood. Besides ordinary chipboard, there are also varieties with properties to meet particular requirements such as water-resistance (usually green-coloured); fire-resistance (red-coloured); and impregnated with a product against fungi and pests. There are also coated chipboards, covered with natural wood veneer or melamine, used for work tops and cabinet construction.

Hardboard panel.

Water-resistant chipboard.

Fire-resistant chipboard.

Medium density fibreboard panel.

66

Tubular chipboard

Usually the press works vertically onto the surface of the board. This causes the numerous wood elements to lie parallel in the ready-made board, that is parallel to the surface of the board. In the type of board illustrated below, parallel metal tubes are used in the casting-mould before pressing. After the pressing stage, the tubes are removed, leaving behind round channels which lie lengthways along the board. These boards have a maximum thickness of 5 cm (2 in) and are mainly used to make light partitions or doors.

Cement-bonded chipboard

These boards are made in the same way as the previous boards but the bonding agent is cement. The appearance of such boards hardly looks like wood any longer, their surface now being smooth, grey cement. Mineral bonded chipboard is a hard, heavy material with a very high density. It is resistant to pest infestation, weather-resistant and absorbs very little water. It is interesting that even when it does absorb water, this does not make it expand. It is officially declared fire-resistant because it does not ignite. These boards are used when other simpler boards are not sufficiently sound-insulating. However, there are problems with nailing, screwing and joining parts together.

Pressed boards made from wood shavings

The development of chipboard anticipated the needs of the market by producing a reasonably priced board with smooth surfaces, achieved by using low-cost materials. In order to produce a veneer for plywood, whole trunks of a particular diameter are needed. The pressed chipboard, on the other hand, can be made from thin trunks, twigs and wood waste. Its properties are not quite as good as those of plywood but this is compensated to a certain degree by the smooth surfaces and reasonable prices.

There are two types:
• O.S.B. board (oriented strand board) with shavings 80 mm ($^{5}/_{16}$ in) long and 1 mm ($^{1}/_{32}$ in) thick. Almost 70% of these wood shavings are arranged lengthways which gives O.S.B. its excellent properties such as flexibility which is almost as good as those of plywood and considerably better than chipboard and MDF boards.

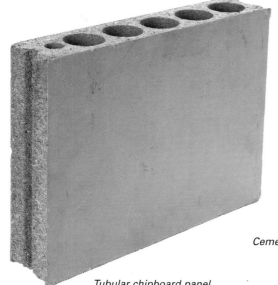

Tubular chipboard panel.

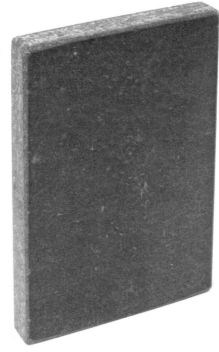

Cement-bonded chipboard.

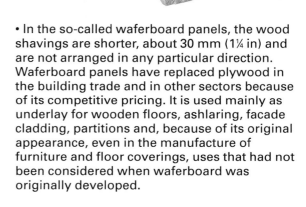

Oriented strand board (O.S.B).

67

Tubular chipboard with sound insulation properties

Like the boards described above, these are also used for sound insulation. They are usually covered with a natural wood veneer. The internal channels are open at one side. These open channels further improve the sound insulation. This is why they are often used as sound-proofing in restaurants, sports centres and leisure centres. This type of board is also very resistant to warping, shrinking and other deformations. If not all the channels are open, the degree of sound insulation changes. They are therefore available in different versions.

Tubular sound-insulating chipboard.

Waferboard.

• In the so-called waferboard panels, the wood shavings are shorter, about 30 mm (1¼ in) and are not arranged in any particular direction. Waferboard panels have replaced plywood in the building trade and in other sectors because of its competitive pricing. It is used mainly as underlay for wooden floors, ashlaring, facade cladding, partitions and, because of its original appearance, even in the manufacture of furniture and floor coverings, uses that had not been considered when waferboard was originally developed.

Other types of wood panels

These are structural wood composites which are not new in themselves but rather the result of further development of the composite panels already described, either through the combination and mixing of existing properties or as a result of taking a new approach to the treatment of wood.

Parallel Strand Lumber (PSL) or Parallam (which was its first trade-name

This a new kind of product. Strips 2 cm (¾ in) long strips are cut from normal wood layers 2 mm (¹⁄₁₆ in) thick. An optical device sorts out the faulty strips. The remaining strips are sprayed with water-proof adhesive and fed into a continuous press. The result is lumber whose length is only restricted by the limitations of transport. Usually, it can be up to 20 m (66 ft) long.

PSL is used for beams of up to 178 x 457 mm (7 x 18 in) and for pillars with a cross-section of 178 x 178 mm (7 x 7 in). Its properties are very similar to those of solid wood: it can be sawn, screwed and nailed. The mechanical features resemble those of natural wood except that being processed wood it does not have the defects which usually occur in natural wood such as branches, cracks etc. This guarantees the standardised quality of PSL.

Larger pieces can also be supplied to order. Thus beams, planks and other structures can be produced – as they would be from solid wood – but with lengths which would be hard to find on the market if solid wood was used.

Malleable boards

The basic materials of this product are boards with a fibre mass 6 to 9.5 mm (¼ to ⅜ in) thick (HDF or MDF). On one side these boards have parallel cuts a few millimetres apart which run across the entire width. These cuts make it possible to bend the board as necessary.

When the board had been bent to the required shape, the process is as follows:
• The side with the cuts is secured with glue.
• Two such panels, coated with glue, are pressed together with their glued sides together so that they are both given the required shape at the same time.
• Pressure is maintained until the glue is dry.
• As soon as the glue is dry the panel is ready.

In order to obtain a good and, if necessary, reproducible result, the procedure is to work with a master which can be used to press subsequent boards in the desired shape. This ensures that the curve of the boards is always the same.

Finished piece of curved wood covered with a veneer of natural wood. The perfection of the curved surface achieved is evident.

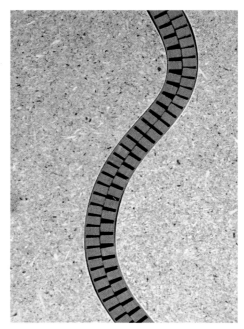

Detail of curved panels being glued, held in position by the formers which give the desired curve like a mould.

Parallam® Parallel Strand Lumber (PSL).

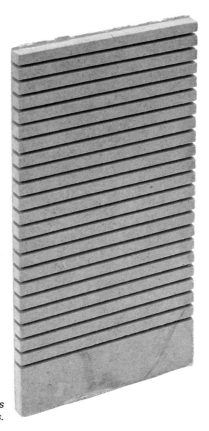

Curvable panel with parallel cuts on one of its sides.

Multi-layered boards

The wood industry is forever looking for new applications and ways to meet new requirements and find new solutions while keeping prices reasonable.
• This type of board consists of a middle layer of glued wood shavings and two outer plywood layers. This multi-layered board lags slightly behind real plywood as far as quality is concerned but the price compensates for this. It can easily be substituted for normal plywood in many areas of applications because the two outer plywood layers are quite thick and very resistant.
• There is also a board with thinner layers of wood enclosed by two layers of bonded fibres (HDF or MDF). The layer of plywood gives the product stability and the MDF can be waxed, varnished or painted without difficulty.

Panel consisting of particle board covered with two sheets of plywood.

Panel covered with two sheets of fibreboard (hardboard or MDF).

Facade cladding

Facade cladding includes a wide range of cladding specially developed for cladding facades. These panels look like varnished or painted solid wood. These product have the advantage that they reduce maintenance and subsequent painting or varnishing, in other words they are easier to maintain and much cheaper than solid wood products. They include hardboard, MDF and stranded boards which have been treated to look like natural wood or other material, finally coated with a layer of weather-resistant plastic which ensures a durability of about ten years.

Building panels for indoor use

These boards are similar to those described above. They imitate solid wood panels and are used as decorative panelling. They include various products made from hardboard, MDF or stranded board, coated with layer of high-quality wood, and also plywood with a first-class quality top layer while the remaining layers consist of ordinary wood. Most of them are tongue and groove boards which are very easy to handle.

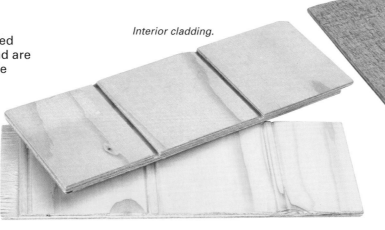

Interior cladding.

Cladding for facades.

69

Floor coverings

In this section a few types of floor covering are described, from simple parquet squares or rectangles to high-quality wooden floor covering consisting of several layers of wood. This is not a complete range of the products available but just a representative selection of the main products used. Several of the products illustrated here show how manufacturers have tried to reduce the need to 'work' the wood by adding incisions in the bottom layer or arranging the layers so that the fibres lie at 90° to each other. It also illustrates the search to reduce the use of expensive, high-quality wood by only using a thin layer on the top surface, the rest of the layers being made of cheap wood or mixed products such as chipboard panels, MDF or plywood of various kinds.

Mosaic parquet floor

This floor covering consists of solid wood pieces, placed one next to other. These can be arranged to form different geometric shapes which are then glued to the floor. The illustration below shows the thickness of the pieces of wood which in this case are oak. The underside of the wood has been treated to reduce the absorption of moisture and thus reduce the risk of the wood warping or shrinking.

upper side

underside

edge

Solid wood

upper side

underside

This flooring is made up of pieces of solid wood 20 mm (¾ in) thick, with tongue-and-groove on four sides. The underside has been machined to minimise the risk of deformation.

upper side

underside

Similar to the previous example, but using hardwood. The underside shows the grooves which have been machined in it to reduce the risk of warping.

edge

upper side

underside

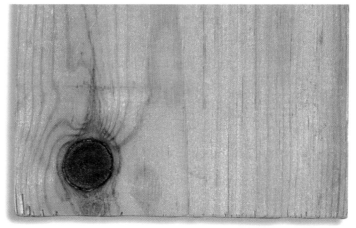

'Copper treated' pine. This is a deep impregnation treatment which increases the durability of the wood when used outdoors. The green tone is characteristic.

edge

Plywood

This page illustrates several products designed to be used as floating floors. They consist of sections made up of strips of wood joined to each other by tongue-and-groove edge joints.

upper side

Beech wood floor 22 mm (3/4 in) thick, finished with several layers of polyurethane varnish.

upper side

underside

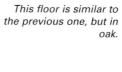

This floor is similar to the previous one, but in oak.

underside

edge

edge

upper side

Floor treated with a layer of special non-slip varnish.

upper side

underside

This flooring has a rubberised black strip attached to one edge to give the appearance of the deck of a ship with dark joints between the planks.

underside

edge

edge

Parquet for floating floors

upper side

underside

edge

Piece of flooring consisting of three layers with an overall thickness of 12 mm (½ in). The underside is a layer of softwood 1.5 mm (1/16 in) thick. It is glued to the next layer which is made up of strips 25 x 7.5 mm (1 x ¼ in) thick, arranged at an angle to the upper and lower surfaces so as reduce any tendency to warp. The upper side is finished with iroko wood 3 mm (⅛ in) thick, varnished in the factory.

upper side

underside

edge

upper side

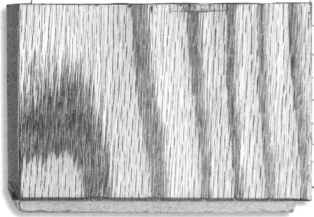

Laminated floor of three parts. The underside is covered with granular neoprene, with a layer of fibre glued to an intermediate layer 10 mm (⅜ in) thick made of MDF or other material. The top surface is beech, 3 mm (⅛ in) thick, covered with polyurethane varnish.

underside

edge

(Above and below) Flooring similar to that shown top left, but 15 mm (⁹/16 in) thick. The wood of the upper side is oak, 3.5 mm (⅛ in) thick, and the centre part is 10 mm (⅜ in) thick. Both are commonly used for floating floors.

upper side

underside

edge

TOO

Whatever the woodworker's level of skill, an indispensable part of bringing a project to a satisfactory conclusion is experience and knowledge of how to carry out the various operations involved in making a piece. But evidently even these are not all that is required, because the woodworker's hands alone, however skillful they may be, are not in themselves capable of achieving the end result. Woodworking involves many operations, such as measuring, marking out, cutting, smoothing and so on, whose achievement would not be possible, or at the very least would be extremely difficult, if they could not be executed with the assistance of an appropriate tool capable of carrying out each stage of the operation, as an extension of the worker's hand.

Since time immemorial mankind has been stimulated by necessity to create special tools designed and constructed to carry out the particular functions expected of them. Many hand tools used today are basically the same as those which existed centuries ago, although not surprisingly they have been improved and perfected since then. Modern research and advances in technology have given rise to the birth of new tools which carry out the work more quickly and accurately, saving the user a considerable amount of effort.

In view of the main purpose of this book and limitations of space, it is not possible here to describe in detail every tool related to woodworking which exists. But all the fundamental ones are described in this section, and the basic tool kit of any woodworker should include almost all of them.

Hand tools

The proper hand tools are essential to high quality woodworking. Other basic conditions for successful woodworking are knowledge and experience, enough space in which to work and the correct types of wood as raw material for the kinds of projects undertaken. But none of these is any use without good tools. Special tools are designed to enable easy, accurate woodworking to be carried out in every phase of the work. The transformation process whereby wood from the timber merchant is converted into finished items and pieces of furniture is performed through a considerable number of steps, each one being directly linked to the next.

As woodworking tools have developed through history, the function and design of many have been continuously adapted to the particular requirements of contemporary woodworking. Nonetheless, some needs are unchanging and many tools used today would be recognised by woodworkers from medieval or even Biblical times. Like skills, their tradition feeds imperceptibly into the work of today.

The tools are described in this section roughly in the order in which they are used in making a project.

Measuring tools

Making measurements is always the woodworker's first step, to achieve the size decided on for the project and to ensure that pieces fit together. Some measuring tools are used to measure distances and others angles.

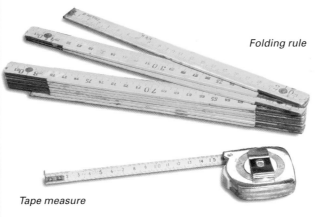

Folding rule

Tape measure

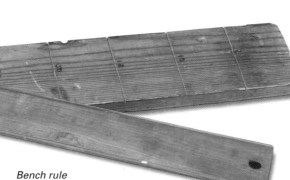

Bench rule

Squares

To check that a line or piece of wood is at right angles or 'square' to another, a try square is used. It is also used to mark such an angle.

The try square consists of a stock and a blade joined at an angle of 90°, and it may be made of wood, metal, or a combination of both. The large wooden square shown at the left has an additional diagonal brace to resist possible deformation. Metal squares are less fragile, and the leg is often divided like a rule. The best cabinetmaker's squares have a rosewood stock faced with brass, and a blued steel blade. The stock is often thicker than the blade, so it can be pushed firmly against one edge.

Different types of try squares.

Occasionally the woodworker may make additional tools as templates to transfer measurements from one piece to another. The following layout tools are commonly used in woodworking.

Rules

As indicated in the introduction, it is evident that rules are the tools most commonly used in measuring, drawing and marking the lines to be cut. Various types and kinds of rules can be used to give an accurate measurement:

• The folding rule is available in various lengths. On wooden folding rules the units of length are normally printed, in other cases the scale is stamped into the metal or plastic.

• Tape measures have a flexible, retractable metal blade upon which the markings are printed. Various lengths are available for workshop use, from 2 metres or 6 feet to 4 meters or 12 feet. The blade is coiled into a case and held there with a spring. Like all measuring tools, they are available with metric or inch measurements, or a combination of the two which is often very useful.

Steel rules

Steel rules are similar to bench rules. The scale is stamped or etched into the metal along one edge. They can be used not only to take measurements, but also as a cutting guide while using a utility knife. Due to their weight, steel rules are also used to keep wooden pieces from sliding while they are cut.
They are available in various lengths.

Bench rules

Bench rules are made from knot-free wood of high compressive strength with a stamped-on scale. They usually have protective brass ends. Bench rules should be wide enough for the edge to be dressed after prolonged use.

They are normally available as metre sticks or yard sticks, 100 cm or 36 in long respectively. even longer measurements exist, for marking lines on boards, but today the retractable measuring tape is often used, in conjunction with the metre or yard stick used repeatedly. Apart from this basic application, bench rules are often used in combination with other tools to check the evenness of surfaces.

Mitre gauge

The mitre gauge designed for woodworking is commonly used for measuring and marking out corner joints. It is similar to a try square but the angle is set to 45°. They are usually made of wood and are available in various different types. The lower example illustrated has two blades forming adjacent angles of 45° and 135°.

Vernier calliper

Sliding bevel

Similar to the square and the mitre gauge, the sliding bevel tool consists of a stock and a blade. The difference is that the sliding bevel is adjustable so it can be set to any angle and held in position by tightening the screw. This tool can be used to measure and transfer both acute and obtuse angles, that is, angles under and angles over 90°.

Two types of Sliding bevel.

Vernier callipers

This is a very accurate measuring instrument with one fixed and one movable jaw. The lower part measures external dimensions and the upper pair internal ones. The movable jaw moves across a scale marked in millimetres or sixteenths of an inch. The small scale attached to the moving jaw enables even finer intervals to be read by counting which of its lines coincides exactly with a line on the main scale.

Vernier callipers are useful for measuring screw sizes and so on, as well as in turning and positioning metal fittings.

Marking tools

Measuring and marking out are basic procedures performed together to achieve the desired shapes and dimensions of a product.

The measurements on a scale drawing should be transferred to the workpiece by accurate measurement and marking out.

Wood pencils

Pencils are widely used to mark the work at various stages in its progress, to mark cutting lines and to indicate areas to be removed (waste) or be used in a certain position (such as the face side of a piece of timber). The advantage of pencil marks is that they can be sanded off easily when no longer needed.

The traditional carpenter's pencil is oval with a chisel-shaped lead to last longer without sharpening, but most people find ordinary pencils just as good and easier to use. They are available in varying degrees of hardness and softness, the softer ones making a thicker, blacker line and lasting less long before they need to be sharpened.

Mechanical pencils such clutch pencils have a fine lead and are normally used for drawing on even surfaces or scale drawings.

Improvising a rule.

How to improvise a rule

It is possible to mark a straight line parallel with the edge of a piece of wood simple by holding a pencil as shown in the illustration and running it smoothly along the length to be marked. The fingers act as a guide.

Using a wood pencil to mark the position of a hinge.

Awls

Scratch awls are among the oldest and simplest woodworking tools, consisting of a pointed steel shaft set in a handle. They are available in several sizes, and are used to scribe a line more permanently than a pencil, and also to mark the centre of holes.

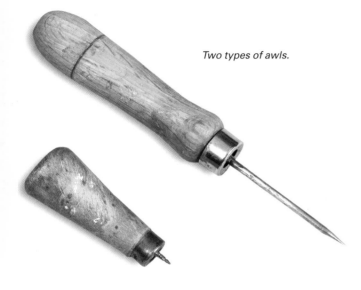

Two types of awls.

Marking gauges

A marking gauge is used to scribe a line parallel to an edge, along the grain or on end grain. It consists of a beam with a pin set in one end, and a stock which slides along the beam, acting as a fence. A thumbscrew or wedge fixes the stock in the chosen position. The stock is sometimes faced with brass to protect it from wear. The steel pin at the end of the beam marks the line.

The marking gauge can be set to a given measurement with a ruler. Even more conveniently and accurately, it can be set to an existing part and used to transfer this measurement to the wood being marked up. This is an excellent way of marking out joints.

A cutting gauge is like a marking gauge but has a cutter instead of a pin. It is used for marking across the grain, and also for cutting strips of veneer.

A curved-edge gauge has a special fence which enables lines to be scribed on a curved surface.

A mortise gauge will mark both sides of a mortise or a tenon at the same time. When used to scribe both parts of the joint without alteration, it ensures that it is marked as accurately as possible. Some kinds of mortise gauge can be used as a marking gauge by holding it in such a way that only a single pin is touching the work.

A frequent operation with a marking gauge is to find the centre of the edge of a piece of wood. This is done by setting it to an estimated position and then making a small mark with the pin from each side of the work. The gauge is

An adjustable mortise gauge and a home-made fixed mortise gauge.

adjusted and the operation repeated until the pin makes a mark in the same place from each side. The line is then marked.

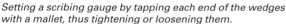

Setting a scribing gauge by tapping each end of the wedges with a mallet, thus tightening or loosening them.

To mark a line using a mortise gauge, use both hands to apply the necessary pressure for the pin to penetrate into the wood and slide it smoothly along the wood being marked.

To draw a longitudinal line using a marking gauge is more difficult, since the tool has to be moved along a longer path.

Compasses and dividers

Workshop operations may be simple or complex. Different types of compasses are therefore used to draw curved lines, small or large circles or semi-circles, depending on the situation. Compasses and dividers are used to draw or scribing circles and arcs, and for transferring measurements. Dividers have two sharp pointed legs while a compass has a pencil or a pencil lead set in one leg. Large circles and arcs are drawn with trammels or a beam compass.

Inside and outside callipers have blunt ends turned inwards or outwards. They are used for measuring the outside or inside diameter of round items and, in particular, turned work, where they can be set to the drawing and used as a gauge to determine when the part being turned is the correct diameter.

Different types of compasses or dividers used for a variety of purposes in woodworking.

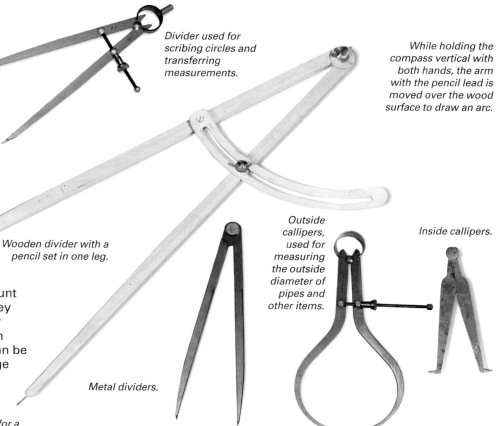

Divider used for scribing circles and transferring measurements.

Wooden divider with a pencil set in one leg.

Outside callipers, used for measuring the outside diameter of pipes and other items.

Inside callipers.

Metal dividers.

While holding the compass vertical with both hands, the arm with the pencil lead is moved over the wood surface to draw an arc.

77

Cutting tools

When constructing a project, one of the first steps is to mark out the sizes of the parts on the selected pieces of wood and cut them roughly to size with a saw. These are then smoothed and joints may be cut in them to assemble them into the finished design. Many different sorts of hand saws and other cutting devices have been developed and improved throughout history to achieve these tasks, according to the technology of the time. Some of the traditional tools are now in becoming obsolete, while others already belong in a museum. But many traditional cutting tools such as saws, planes and chisels continue to be useful and to be used.

Handsaws and backsaws

Saws are used to make straight and curved cuts, and on the whole different types are required for each purpose. Straight cuts are made with ripsaws, crosscut saws and backsaws. Curved cuts are made with keyhole, compass and coping saws. The frame saw is capable of doing both, depending on the blade it is fitted with.

A saw consists of a steel blade with teeth and a handle. The shape and size of the teeth varies with each saw, making each one useful for a different purpose. The number of points per inch (25 mm) of a saw blade also varies. (Saw teeth are still normally measured in points per inch, in spite of metrication.) A fine-cutting saw will have small, fine teeth and many points per inch, whereas a rough-cutting saw will have a smaller number of larger teeth, and will cut much faster. The teeth are sharp, and when moved across the board they cut the wood fibres.

On some saws the number of points per inch is stamped on the heel. There is always one more point per inch than there are teeth per inch; for instance an eight-point saw has seven teeth in one inch.

The teeth on the saw are set, meaning they are alternately bent to the right and to the left all the way along the length of the blade. The result of this is that the kerf, the groove cut by the saw in the wood, will be wider than the blade itself. This prevents the saw from binding in the kerf.

A close-up of a saw blade, showing the set of the teeth.

Far right, side view of saw teeth.

Frame saws

Frame saw

The narrower the blade, the weaker it becomes, which inevitably leads to a compromise in the design of saws. A solution that has been in use for centuries is to hold the blade under tension in some kind of frame. Frame saws with the blade in the centre of the frame were used by the Romans, while the cantilever principle of the modern frame saw was known and in use as far back as the 13th century. The blade in the frame saw is held between two uprights or cheeks that pivot on each side of a central stretcher rail. The blade is tensioned by pulling the tops of the cheeks together by means of a twisted cord and toggle or a twisted wire tensioned by wing nuts. Coarse- and fine-toothed blades can be used and it can be swivelled to allow the saw to cut parallel to the edge of a board. This gives it a versatility making it preferable to a panel saw in some situations.

Sawing is normally done in a vertical fashion, using both hands, one to direct the saw and the other to support the cheek.

The same frame saw can be used to cut around a curve with a narrow blade.

Sawing is a skilled process, especially when two workers use a frame saw together. In this case one worker guides the saw, while the second one provides support.

A skillful worker can use a frame saw putting both hands on the operating handle.

Mitre saw

Ripsaws

A ripsaw is used to cut with the grain of a board. It should never be used to cut across the grain, because the cut will be very rough and ragged.

The teeth of the ripsaw are filed in such a way that they are flat at the bottom. The outer edges cut the wood fibres. The flat bottom removes the wood in chips rather than as fine sawdust. A ripsaw commonly has 5 points per inch.

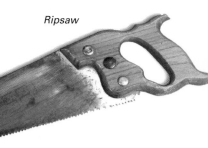

Ripsaw

A widely used sawing tool, the crosscut saw makes a rapid cut across the grain.

Mitre saw

The adjustable mitre saw makes very accurate corner cuts with great ease. It consist of a table and fence set at an angle of 90°. The saw is like a frame saw. It is mounted in a metal frame which can be rotated 45° to the right and the left. The wood being cut is held firmly against the fence. The cut is bound to be at the correct angle and at right angles to the base, so the joint being cut will be accurate.

Crosscut saw

A crosscut saw is used to cut across the grain, with 6 to 8 points per inch.

The panel saw is a finer version for cutting panels including man-made boards, and also for general use. It has 10 to 12 points per inch.

Backsaws

Backsaws are used for fine work work such as joints. They have a stiff blade held rigid and flat by a heavy metal back of brass or steel. Dovetail saws are a smaller variety of backsaw with a very fine blade, usually 15 to 18 points per inch. They produce a very fine cut with a thin kerf. Some very small general purpose saws are also shown below, one of which is offset and can be reversed for cutting flush with the surface.

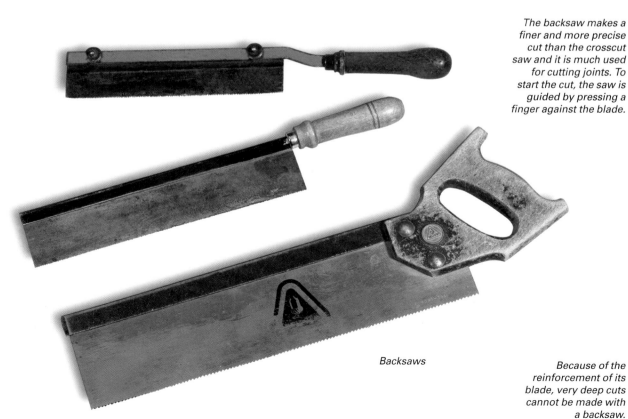

Backsaws

The backsaw makes a finer and more precise cut than the crosscut saw and it is much used for cutting joints. To start the cut, the saw is guided by pressing a finger against the blade.

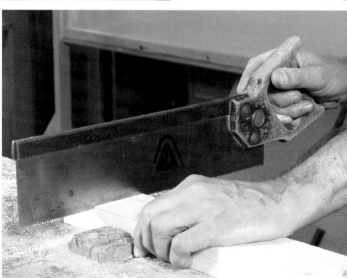

Because of the reinforcement of its blade, very deep cuts cannot be made with a backsaw.

Coping saws

Coping saws have a very narrow blade held under tension in a U-shaped frame and are used specially for cutting curves in wood. A coping saw with its narrow blade can tackle curves of very small radius, but its use is confined to thin woods and the softer metals. Fretsaws are similar but have a longer frame, enabling cuts to be made further from the edge of the work. Both with the coping saw and the fretsaw, rigidity is determined by the quality of the steel with which the frame is made. It has to hold the blade tight and rigid or it will easily break.

Internal curves are cut by drilling a small hole in the area to be cut out, threading the blade through it and fixing it to the saw again.

Compass and keyhole saws

Curves are cut with the compass, keyhole or coping saws. They have narrow or very thin blades, which help them turn as they cut along a curve. Compass and keyhole saws are used to cut curves having a large radius. The compass saw has 8 points per inch and it will cut curves with a radius of 15 cm (6 in) or larger. The keyhole saw is smaller, with 10 points per inch. A selection of blades is available. Thinner blades have finer teeth and are used to cut sharp curves in thin wood; heavier ones are used for thicker wood.

Compass or keyhole saw

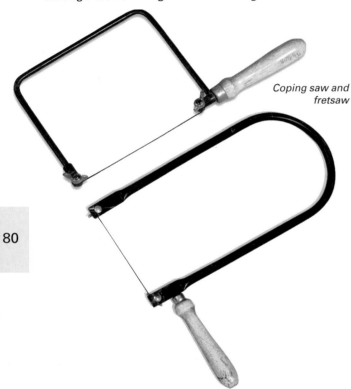

Coping saw and fretsaw

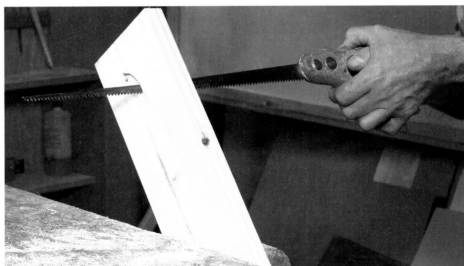

The keyhole saw is used to saw holes in a piece of wood with fairly wide curves. To start the cut, a hole is drilled for the saw first.

Saws with interchangeable blades

For occasional use, saws with interchangeable blades are acceptable. The one shown below combines the functions of a small panel saw, a back saw, a keyhole saw and a hacksaw. The blades all fit the same handle. However, for serious use it is very much more convenient to have purpose-made saws of each type. They will then be ready for use immediately.

Veneer saw

A veneer saw is a specialist tool consisting of a fine-toothed blade with a wooden handle used to trim veneer flush. The operating handle is tilted against the blade in order to produce a precise, fine cut more easily.

Saw with a variety of interchangeable blades for different purposes.

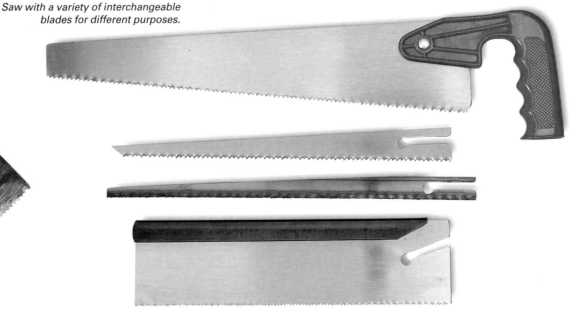

Veneer saw

Tools with a cutting edge

After roughing out, the parts of a project are further processed by planing, jointing, sanding and finishing. Different tools are used for these jobs, many of them tools with a cutting edge. The common principle of these tools is that they have a cutting blade, and these can be classified in two groups: guided cutting tools, such as planes, and freehand cutting tools controlled entirely by the user, such as chisels.

Guided cutting tools: planes

The blades of planes are either tool steel laminated to soft steel or of solid tool steel. They are ground on one side only and the cutting edge may be very slightly curved, depending on the purpose. The blade is mounted in a wooden block and retained by a wedge. Simple or jack planes have only the blade while smoothing planes and jointers have a cap iron or counter blade on top and just behind the cutting edge to break the chip and prevent the wood from tearing out. The blade protrudes from the sole of the plane through the mouth. Its size is critical to the job being performed. Jack planes have a large mouth leaving plenty of room for thick shavings while smoothers have a very narrow mouth to help break up the chip and make as smooth a surface as possible.

Planes

The plane is a guided cutting tool, guided by its sole which restricts its cut, and designed to make wooden surfaces smooth. Planes are made of cast iron or wood. The traditional plane is made of hardwood such as oak, hornbeam or beech. Each plane has a purpose: the jointer is used to plane long boards and joints; the jack plane is for roughing and general work; and the smoothing plane is a finishing plane.

Jointer or try plane

At 60 cm (24 in) long or more, the jointer or try plane is the longest plane generally available. This exceptional jointing tool usually has a blade 6 cm (2⅜ in) wide and a cap iron. It is perfect for squaring up long boards and for making accurate, tight joints for edge gluing or rubbed joints when making wide panels.

Jointer plane

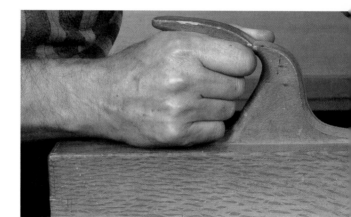

The correct position of the hands when using a jointer plane. One hand pushes it from the rear, while the other hand guides it at the front.

Jack plane

Similar to the jointer plane but smaller, about 350 mm (14 in) long. It is a general-purpose plan for jointing and final smoothing.

Jack plane

Wood smoothing plane

Smaller than a jointer or a jack plane, it is more manoeuvrable than either. It is one of the most commonly used carpentry tools. It may be solid or have a glued-on sole of hornbeam, holm oak, or other hardwood. Models with cap irons are called smoothers and they are used for finishing surfaces. They may be wider and often have a steeper blade angle. There is also a 'Reform' smoother which has an adjusting screw similar to an iron plane.

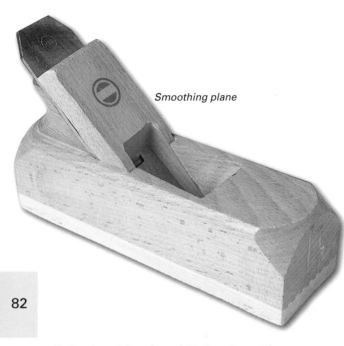

Smoothing plane

82

End grain and the edges of thin boards must be supported to prevent the wooden fibres on the edge from breaking away. The stop on a shooting board will provide the necessary support. Hold the plane centrally using both hands and allow the wood to overhang very slightly. Place one hand on the heel to push, and the other one on the nose to guide the movement of the plane.

When using a plane to smooth concave surfaces, do not move it against the grain. To avoid this, plane down the convex surface, moving it from top to bottom following the curve. Otherwise tears may be caused during planing.

For delicate work, such as putting a chamfer on an edge, use a hand plane held at an angle (45°). Take small chips first to establish the direction of the grain; then, if the grain permits, make longer strokes, lifting the plane off the wood and moving it back at the end of each stroke.

Wide surfaces are normally planed to achieve a uniform, even surface. At first move the plane diagonally to the direction of the grain, alternating directions first across the entire surface one way and then across the other. Once the surface is even, it is finished by planing with the grain.

When planing end grain, be careful not to plane over the edge but only halfway from each side. Planing beyond the edge of the end grain will cause the edge to split off.

Use a toothing plane to roughen the surface before gluing, to increase the area in contact with the glue.

Planes with curved soles

These tools are similar to a regular plane, but with a convex sole. They are designed for planing the inside of curved faces, where the radius is larger than that of the plane. The wooden compass plane has been widely replaced by an adjustable metal one, but neither is much used today.

Large fluting plane, and a convex compass plane.

With the compass plane, planing should normally be towards the lower end of the curvature of the parts with the material to be removed.

Iron planes

Various iron planes are shown below: two block planes and a general-purpose smoothing plane.

Toothing plane

This type of plane is very different from the others in that it has a serrated or toothed blade. It is used to roughen a wooden surface before gluing, thus promoting the strength of the glued joint. It is normally used with veneer.

Detail of the toothed blade of a toothing plane.

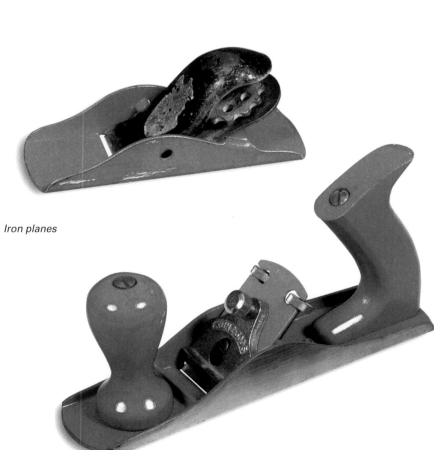

Iron planes

Toothing plane

After planing to size, the project may be worked further with rebate, shoulder, and moulding planes. These planes differ from hand and block planes in that the blade is flush with one or both sides, so that it can plane a clean sharp

Moulding planes

shoulder. They have no box, so the shavings emerge from an opening at the side above the mouth. Both rebate and shoulder planes are

available with straight or skewed mouths. The skewed mouth is better suited for cross-grain planing. Moulding planes have blades ground to the desired shape, and a sole of similar profile.

Shoulder plane

Rebate plane

The blade of the rebate plane is the same width as the body and flush with the body on both sides so that it can plane flush with the shoulder in either direction. It is used to clean and adjust rebates to size. Because it can plane in either direction, it is never necessary to plane against the grain.

Rebate plane

Shoulder plane

The shoulder plane is larger than the normal rebate plane; the sole has a side fence to adjust the width of the shoulder to be planed. Some also have a fence on the side to regulate the depth. Because of its size and the fences, it is relatively easy to use. It is used only to make rebates.

The shoulder plane is used to plane rebates on the workpiece.

Working with the rebate plane flat on a vertical rebate surface.

Working with the rebate plane flat on a vertical rebate surface.

Fluting plane

Fluting plane

The fluting plane has a rounded sole matching its arc-shaped blade. There are many sizes. It is used to plane flutes or rounded grooves in wood. With fluters of various sizes and a shoulder plane, many different mouldings can be generated.

TOOLS

hand tools

Moulding plane

The sole of the moulding plane and its blade have the shape of the moulding to be made. Each type of moulding requires a separate plane.

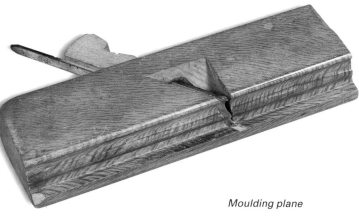

Moulding plane

Like the fluting plane, the sole of the molding plane has the same profile as its blade. Every moulding requires a special plane. For some very common profiles, especially those that are intended to fit together, planes are made in pairs.

Plough plane

The plough plane has interchangeable blades enabling it to make grooves of different widths. It has a side fence to set the distance of the groove from the edge of the workpiece, and a depth fence to set the depth of the groove. Usually the side fence is supported by two large wooden screws and ring nuts to lock it. It is used to make all manner of grooves as long as they are in the direction of the grain.

The plough plane can accept blades of different widths.

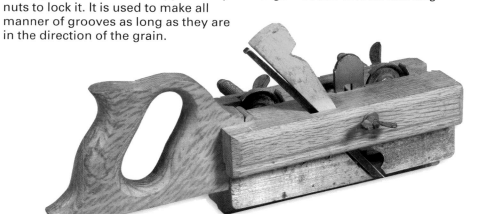

Plough plane with several blades of various widths

Tongue-and-groove plane

This a special plane with two blades facing in each direction; it is actually two planes in one. One side planes the groove, and the other the tongue to fit that groove. It is used to make tongue-and-groove boards to be joined together as panels for cabinet backs, wainscoting, floor boards and so on. It is important to use it from the correct side of the wood so that the boards all end up flush on the face side.

It is not adjustable for width or depth. Because of its shape, the tongue-planing side requires some effort to use, so a proper stance with one foot in front of the other should be adopted.

This type of tongue-and-groove plane combines planes for making each part of the joint in one tool. Using the plane in this direction makes the tongue.

Tongue-and-groove plane

Using the plane the other way round makes the matching groove.

Freehand cutting tools

These cutting tools have tempered steel blades bevelled on one side to create a sharp cutting edge. A wood chisel is an edge tool used to trim wood joints and cut recesses in wood.

At the other end the blade is formed into a tang which fits into a turned handle. Chisels are tools that require some practice to use skillfully, which is why they are referred to as freehand cutting tools.

Firmer chisels and bevel-edge chisels

Firmer chisels are heavier while bevel-edged chisels are lighter, the bevels enabling them to cut more easily into corners and angles. Chisels can be used to cut wood in any direction, chopping across the grain or shaving it off, to make joints, to fit hinges and locks, and so on. They can be used with either or both hands. Working with only one hand, the second should always be kept behind the tool, to avoid injuries.

Blade widths range from 3 mm to 50 mm (⅛ to 2 in), and a well equipped tool box should include firmers and chisels in a range of blade widths. Firmer chisels are designed for heavier work where a mallet is used. Because of its thin, tempered steel blade, a bevel-edged chisel should not be used as a lever.

In making deep cuts, tap the handle with a mallet. Never strike a chisel a hard blow but rather change the angle of the blade slightly between strokes, as the blade may otherwise be damaged.

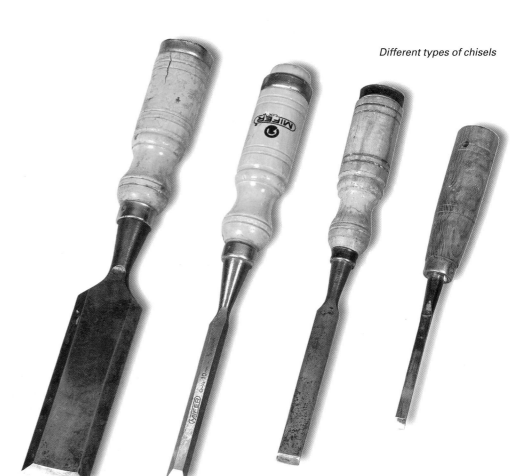

Different types of chisels

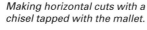

Making horizontal cuts with a chisel tapped with the mallet.

With a firmer chisel it is possible to cut wood in any direction. In the picture, vertical cuts are being made with hard mallet blows.

To finish off a cut, the tool is guided with precision and strength by both hands.

Mortise chisels

Compared with a firmer chisel which is used for similar purposes, a mortise chisel is a long heavy tool with a blade width ranging from 6 to 12 mm (¼ to ½ in) but thicker than it is wide. It is designed for making deep cuts such as mortises and other joints too deep for a firmer chisel. The cut is made with hard mallet blows on the tool which is then levered to tear off the chip. To facilitate this kind of work, the blade is much thicker and the turned handle is reinforced with a metal ring round the top to prevent chipping or cracking.

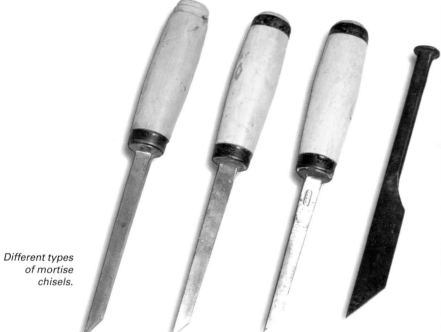

Different types of mortise chisels.

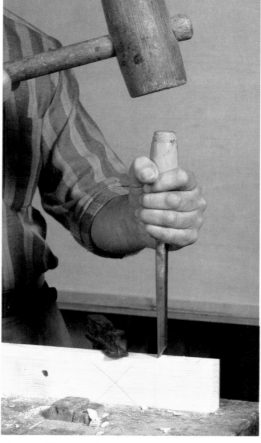

Mortise chisel here being used to make a haunched mortise, with the power delivered by the mallet. Once some vertical cuts are made, a lever action is used to break the chip.

The other end of the mortise socket is cut in a similar manner.

Gouge

A gouge is similar to a chisel but with a blade of curved cross section. Out-cannel gouges are ground with the bevel on the outside while in-cannel gouges have it on the inside.

It is the most important tool for carvers and sculptors who have a large collection of them in varied forms and sizes to meet all their needs. In carving, the tool is worked with a back-and-forth movement, aided by blows to the handle with a mallet. The gouges come in different types, flat, bent, out-cannel, in-cannel, spoon, and so on. Heavier gouges are used for woodturning.

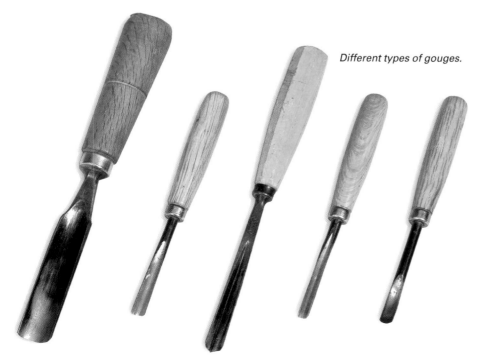

Different types of gouges.

To make the first cut with a gouge, a mallet is sometimes necessary.

To obtain a neat outline, the gouge is held and controlled with both hands.

Tools for drilling and screwing

The easiest way to make a hole in a piece of wood is to drive a sharp punch into it, but this may cause the wood to tear or split, because the wood is not removed but compressed. This problem can be avoided by using a drill bit with a spiral flute which removes the stock from the hole as it is cut away. However, for small screw holes, a punched hole is perfectly satisfactory.

Awl

A tool similar to a punch. With its shape it can make holes in wood while removing some of the stock. It only drills shallow holes with a small diameter, the result being rough coarse holes, unlike those made with twist drills or gimlets.

Awl

Gimlet

This is one of the oldest drilling tools in woodworking. It consists of an auger lead screw which draws the tool into the wood. After the tip, the shaft is fluted to shave the proper diameter of the hole. The shaft has a tang fitted in a wooden handle at the end.

Another version of the gimlet is the auger, which is much larger device used to drill large, and deep holes. It has a hole at the top end through which a circular rod is inserted to make the tool rotate with both hands, applying more torque. They are available in various diameters and lengths.

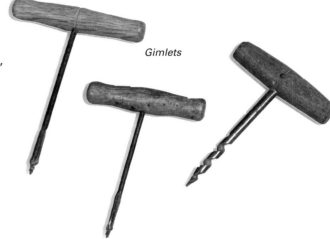

Gimlets

Brace

The brace is designed to work with different types of bits that can easily be changed. It consists of a steel rod formed into a U-shaped crank and is operated by giving it a circular movement with the hand. It has freely-rotating wooden or plastic handles at the top and in the middle of the crank, and a device to accept bits with a fastening screw or a chuck. There are many variations of this tool, some of them having a ratchet which allows drilling in difficult corners with short back-and-forth movements of the crank.

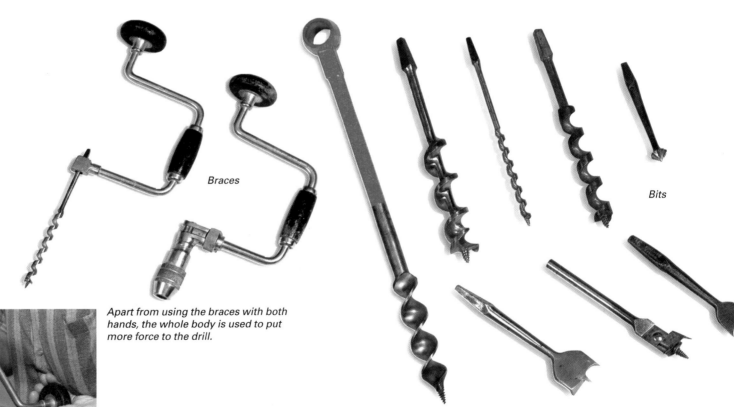

Braces

Bits

Apart from using the braces with both hands, the whole body is used to put more force to the drill.

Drill bits

Bits with flat or square tangs can be used in braces, while those with cylindrical shafts can be operated in hand and electric drills. To drill cleanly, the bit should be as close to a right angle as possible so that the spur cutters can scribe the circumference before the cutters start to lift the chip. There is a large variety of bits for different purposes and the various drills available.

Illustrated are flat bits and auger bits. The auger bits are for deep holes made with a drill brace or a hand drill, as is the adjustable expansive bit shown between the two flat bits. The flat bits can be used in a power drill. Not shown are spade and Forstner bits. With these, it is necessary to empty the hole often so as not to clog or bind the bit.

88

Hand drill

The larger hand drill at the right has a closed gearbox, a breastplate, and a side grip. It can be used for quite large bits and twist drills. Usually it has two speeds. The smaller one shown is the typical open type suitable for small twist drills only.

There is another, older, simpler kind of drill called an Archimedean drill. This has a coarse screw thread between the chuck and the knob at the top. A small collar, threaded inside, slides up and down the threaded rod, rotating it. This makes the drill bit turn clockwise and anti-clockwise. It is only suitable for small-diameter bits.

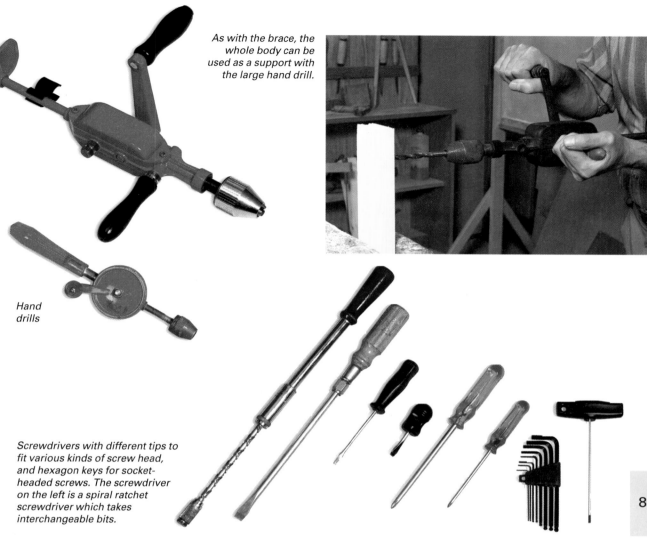

As with the brace, the whole body can be used as a support with the large hand drill.

Hand drills

Screwdrivers

Screwdrivers consist of a metal shank inserted in a grooved wooden or plastic handle, sometimes secured with a metal ferrule and a bolt-pin. At the end, the shank is forged and hardened to make a blade tip matching the slot or other driving form in the head of the screw, which may be slotted, cross-point, Pozidriv or socket head.

There are grips with various interchangeable shanks, for normal or Pozidriv screws. An example is the spiral ratchet screwdriver which rotates the bit by being pushed.

Screwdrivers with different tips to fit various kinds of screw head, and hexagon keys for socket-headed screws. The screwdriver on the left is a spiral ratchet screwdriver which takes interchangeable bits.

89

Hammers and nail extractors

Hammers, mallets and nail extractors generally exist as separate tools, but sometimes they can be combined. A good example is the claw hammer which combines in one tool the ability to hammer nails in and to remove them. In this section, some of these combined tools are described, as well as the single-purpose tools designed to carry out one particular task and no other.

Hammer

The hammer is a universally used tool whose main function is to drive in nails and, in the case of the claw hammer, to extract them as well.

Although simple in appearance, the hammer too has its critical aspects. In particular, the length and flexibility of the handle are very important. A large variety of hammers exist, ranging from the carpenter's or claw hammer, to the joiner's cross-pein hammer (where the cross-pein is used to start a nail held between the fingertips) and the veneer hammer to name but a few. The hammer head is specifically formed for the work to be done.

Generally the hammering of the nail should stop when the nail just stands out from the wood to avoid leaving marks or damaging the wood. The nail should be driven home with a nail set so that its head is just below the surface of the wood.

When nailing wooden parts together, the nails should be driven at an angle to the wood, with each nail an opposing angle.

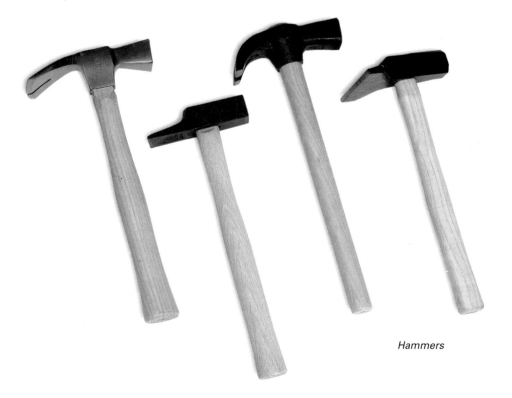

Hammers

Mallets

Mallet

The mallet is a type of hammer but it is used for different purposes. It has a softer head made of wood, leather, or hard plastic, and it is used where it is necessary to hit a piece without damaging it, for instance in assembling frames in projects. Even so, its blows are normally delivered through an intermediate piece of scrap timber so as not to mark the surface of the wood. It also used to apply force to tool handles, notably chisels.

The mallet head may be rectangular, cylindrical or barrel-shaped. Mallets used by carvers are rather different, more like a pestle in shape and shorter, making them more suited for delivering repeated taps to the ends of chisels and gouges.

Pincers

Pincers are used in woodworking to remove nails, particularly one which has become bent as it is being knocked in. It has two sharp-edged bevelled jaws which can grab the nail by the head, even if it barely stands proud. The curved shape of the jaws enables the pincers to be rolled, levering out the nail. A scraper blade or other thin sheet of metal should be placed between the pincers and the wood to prevent marking or damaging it. If the nails are long, a block of wood may be needed to raise the pincers, enabling them to get more purchase on the nail.

Because of their sharp edged jaws, pincers it can also be used to cut wire. A special version (on the right of those illustrated) called an end-cutter is designed specifically for this purpose

Pliers

Pliers are steel tools formed by two arms joined by a pivot, ending with a pair of jaws. The pliers most commonly used in woodworking are engineers' pliers. These have serrated flat jaws with a curved section for holding round work, and wire cutters. They are used for a variety of gripping and holding tasks in woodworking, chiefly those associated with fixings and metal fittings.

Pincers

Pliers and (far left) side cutters

Nail set

A nail set is a simple tool consisting of a steel rod with a tapered, blunt tip. It is used to set nails below the surface without damaging the surrounding wood. It is held in one hand with its tip on the nail, and tapped with the hammer to sink the nail head. The tip should be smaller than the head of the nail it is used on.

Claw or pry-bar

Nail sets

Claw

The claw, also called pry-bar, wrecking bar or case opener, is a steel bar used to open crates and packaging. One of its ends is cranked and tapered for levering planks, while the other has a claw similar to a hammer enabling it to grip and pull nails. Being made of steel and longer than a hammer, it is better for robust work such as lifting floorboards.

Cramping tools

Wood constructions are commonly held together with various kinds of joints. Unless metal connectors are used, these are normally fixed with glue, and until the glue dries cramps are needed to hold the work in position. At the same time they apply the pressure to a glued joint while the glue sets, which is necessary to achieve maximum strength.

There is a wide range of cramps designed for various purposes and in many different sizes. The terms 'cramp' and 'clamp' are synonymous.

G-cramps and corner cramps

G-cramps and corner are used to hold pieces together in position while they are glued, nailed or screwed. The principle on which they operate is that they have one fixed jaw and a second adjustable jaw operated by a screw, which adjusts the opening to the size of the work to be cramped and then applies pressure to the joint with the considerable force of the tightened screw. Cramps are usually made of metal.

A corner cramp is a specially designed modification for gluing mitre joints. Essentially it consists of two cramps mounted on a base at right angles to each other. Each of the two parts to be joined is fixed firmly in the correct position for gluing.

Cramps can sometimes be improvised, for instance by using pieces cut from mattress springs which will apply pressure to a small mitre joint, or with a tourniquet, a length of string or rope twisted with a stick to pull the pieces it surrounds towards each other.

Band or strap cramp, used to cramp irregular parts

Pieces of mattress springs. These can be used to hold mitred corners together.

G-cramp

Corner or mitre cramps, used to hold corner joints while they are glued. These are invaluable for picture framing and any other projects involving mitre joints.

Strap, web or band cramp

This type of cramp consists of a textile or metal band or strap which surrounds the workpiece and is tightened with a screw. It has the advantage of applying equal pressure to all four sides of a mitre joint. It can also be used to hold the turned legs of stool or chair together while the stretchers are glued, a difficult task to carry out with a normal bar cramp.

Pieces of mattress springs are very handy for holding smaller joints together.

A corner cramp being used to hold two panels together at right angles.

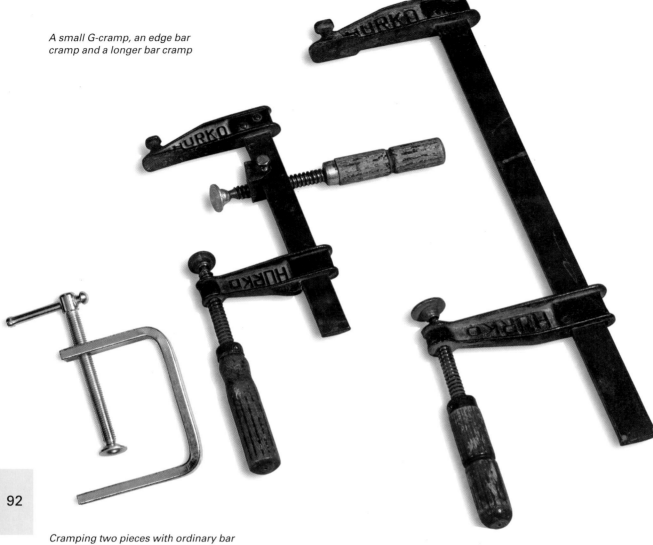

A small G-cramp, an edge bar cramp and a longer bar cramp

Bar cramp

A bar cramp is a quickly adjustable cramp used to hold the workpiece to the workbench while working, or to hold two pieces together for gluing. They are sometimes made of wood but usually they are metal for strength. They are available in many different sizes. The size is quickly adjusted simply by sliding the head along the bar, and then tightening the screw.

Edge cramp

Sometimes attached to an ordinary bar cramp, this has a screw at right angles to the cramp itself. It is used to apply pressure to edges, particularly when gluing lipping to panels.

Sash cramp

This term describes a large bar cramp, used to hold wide pieces such as the parts of a sliding sash window. It has many applications in the workshop, particularly when gluing boards together to make large panels.

I-beam bar cramp

This is identical in principle to an ordinary bar cramp, but the I- or T-section bar is much stiffer and less liable to bend when the cramp is tightened. It consists of a I-beam with a spindle and jaw fixed to one end. The second jaw is fixed in the desired position with a metal peg through one of the holes along the tool. The spindle is then turned to tighten the cramp.

92

Cramping two pieces with ordinary bar cramps

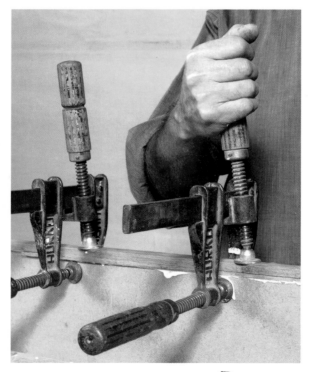

The illustration shows edge cramps being used to glue a piece of solid edge lipping to a panel.

I-beam bar cramp

Smoothing, shaping and finishing tools

To obtain the desired finish on a piece of work, it must be shaped and smoothed before varnishing or painting the wood. These final steps are of the utmost importance to the whole outcome of a piece, because the quality of the whole work will depend upon the quality of workmanship applied to the finish.

This is especially important in staining lacquering or varnishing. If a piece is not properly smoothed, there is no point in giving it a nice finish; it will simply draw attention to its shortcomings.

The tools and some of the materials used in the important finishing stages of any project are described here.

Rasps

A rasp is a kind of tempered steel file with very coarse cutting teeth designed for use on wood. The commonest rasp has one of its faces is flat while the other is half-round. Both faces have a series of large, triangular shaped teeth, widely separated from each other and thicker than file teeth, whose function is to remove material quickly.

Rasps are used to shape curved surfaces which cannot be planed, and to smooth small areas such as joint housings. There are many types with fine, medium or coarse cut. Cross sections also vary, ranging from flat to round, including half round and square.

Files

A file cuts much more finely than a rasp, so it is used to remove any roughness left by tools used previously and to provide a smooth finish. Files can be single-cut or double-cut. Single-cut files have parallel teeth at a small angle to the length, while double-cut ones have teeth crossing each other at different angles. Files are called bastard, second-cut and smooth, names which describe the fineness of the cut from the coarsest to the finest.

Round or rat-tail rasp and file

These have a circular cross-section, tapered to the tip. Both the rasp and the file are useful in the workshop for finishing curves of small radius and to enlarge holes and openings.

Various types of rasps and files.

Rat-tail rasp and file

93

File

Rasps

Scraper

A scraper is one of the simplest woodworking tools. It is a tempered steel blade about 12 cm (5 in) long, 7 cm (2½ in) wide and 1 mm (³⁄₆₄ in) thick. It is the burred sharp edges along the long side which do the cutting.

This tool is used with both hands holding it at each ends, the thumbs bending it into a shallow curve so that the cutting edge itself is slightly curved, and pushing it away from the body. This raises little shavings from the wood.

The tool is excellent for the final finishing of a piece, particularly of wood with difficult grain. It is also much used in furniture restoration.

Scraper

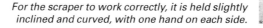

For the scraper to work correctly, it is held slightly inclined and curved, with one hand on each side.

Spokeshave

Hold the tool by its handles with both hands. It is worked by moving it back and forth with a swinging motion, preferably with the grain.

Spokeshave

A spokeshave is a steel blade held in a wooden or iron housing that works in a similar way to the plane. It is used for trimming and smoothing curves, so for this reason it is most widely used by cabinetmaker and chair makers. The spokeshave blade has a cap to break the chip, and both it and the blade can be adjusted for precise working. Spokeshaved surfaces are finished with a scraper

Half-round spokeshave

This type of a spokeshave has a concave cutting blade and it is used for shaping round objects such as spokes. It is the best tool for this kind of job, but a certain amount of practice and skill is required to obtain a good result.

Sandpaper

The general term 'sandpaper' is used to describe various kinds of abrasive paper used to make wood smooth. The sheets of paper are coated with an abrasive powder of glass, sand, garnet, metal oxide, or quartz, in a glue base.

Sandpaper comes in different qualities and sizes, and with different grain sizes ranging from coarse to very fine grit, each suited for a specific work and finishing.

The different grit sizes of abrasive paper are printed on the back, starting at 50 (very coarse), through 100 (coarse), 180 (medium), 280 (fine) and up to 320 and more (very fine). An alternative grading system runs from 1 (very coarse) through 0 (coarse), 3/0 (medium) and so on to 9/0 (very fine).

For flat surfaces, the sandpaper is wrapped around a sanding block, a rectangular block of wood or cork.

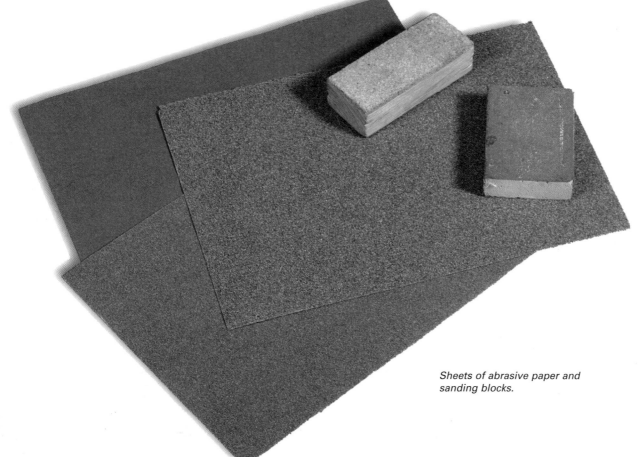

Sheets of abrasive paper and sanding blocks.

Steel wool

After sandpaper, further smoothing can be carried out using fine steel wool. The wool will smooth the wood surface, removing sandpaper marks and leaving the surface with a dull sheen, ready to receive a finish of wax or varnish.

Fine steel wool

Portable power tools

With their small size, great versatility and ability to save labour, the convenience of portable power tools is undeniable. They make light work of many operations formerly carried out manually, or by heavy fixed machinery whose cost and size put it beyond the reach of most users.

Portable power tools meet the requirements of professional and amateur users alike. They have made it possible for many people whose hobby is woodworking to set up an effective workshop in a relatively small space in their own home. For professionals, portable power tools are invaluable for installation and constructional projects carried out on site away from the workshop, such as making and fitting built-in wardrobes or kitchen units. They can be taken to the job itself and used in very varied situations. Battery-powered tools are particularly versatile since they do not need a source of electrical power within reach of the scene of operations.

Portable power tools are divided into two categories. Table-top machinery has to be set up on a carpenter's bench or rigid stand to keep it stable in use. Hand power tools are much lighter and specifically designed to be carried, positioned, guided and controlled by hand. Many are now available with rechargeable batteries.

Compound mitre table saw

This powerful tool makes straight or angled cuts with great accuracy. It has a blade guard which covers the blade completely when it is not in contact with the wood; nonetheless it is potentially dangerous and must be used with care.

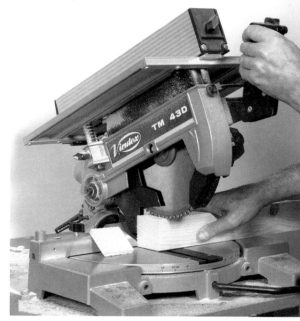

Compound mitre saw cutting wood at right angles. Note that both hands are well clear of the blade.

Compound mitre saw mounted on a strong, simple table specially made for it.

Compound mitre saw cutting a 45° vertical angle.

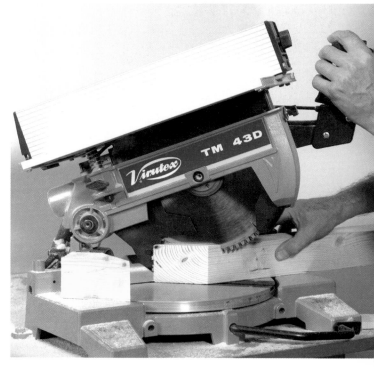

Compound mitre saw cutting wood at a 45° horizontal angle.

Portable power drill

The versatile portable power drill is designed to drill holes in wood, metal and masonry. It has a handle grip at one end, while at the other is an adjustable drill chuck to hold the bit, driven by the motor through an intermediate gearbox. Some drills have an optional hammer action, useful for drilling concrete when fitting built-in furniture. Variable speed models are available (larger drill bits should be used at lower speeds), sometimes with reversible rotation so that they can also be used as power screwdrivers.

Portable power drill with pistol grip.
The chuck is tightened with the chuck key.

Vertical drill stand

This is a metal stand with a drill clamp mounted on a pillar fitted to a base, in which almost any kind of power drill can be fitted. The height is adjustable and the drilling is controlled by a lever. It ensures that the hole is drilled in the work exactly at right angles.

96

Vertical drill stand, converting a portable drill into a drill press.

The vertical drill stand in use. It is fixed to the bench or other solid surface.

Portable jigsaw

With its thin, narrow saw blade reciprocating rapidly up and down, the jigsaw is used to make right-angled and curved cuts on panels and boards. The shoe is adjustable, enabling angled cuts to be made.

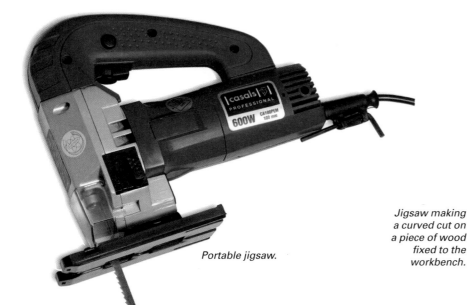

Portable jigsaw.

Jigsaw making a curved cut on a piece of wood fixed to the workbench.

Portable circular saw

The circular saw blade projects through the sole plate, the depth of the cut depending on the amount of projection. The angle of the sole plate is also adjustable. Ripsaw, crosscut and combination blades are available.

Portable circular saw.

Using the circular saw to crosscut a piece of timber fixed to the bench.

Orbital sander

This type of power sander has a base moving with an elliptical motion. Various kinds of abrasive paper are used according to the finish required. The elliptical motion reduces the risk of creating scratches.

Orbital sander.

The orbital sander is moved in the direction of the grain with firm pressure of both hands. It must be moved continually or it will make deep scratches in the wood.

Power edge router

Tool designed specially to mould the edges of boards and panels. The many different shapes of cutter can produce a wide variety of shapes and designs. It is used for both straight and curved edges. It is essential to fix the workpiece firmly to the bench.

Power edge router with rounding over, rebate and cove cutters.

Using an edge router to mould a straight edge. The hand pressure must be consistent so that the moulding is of even depth.

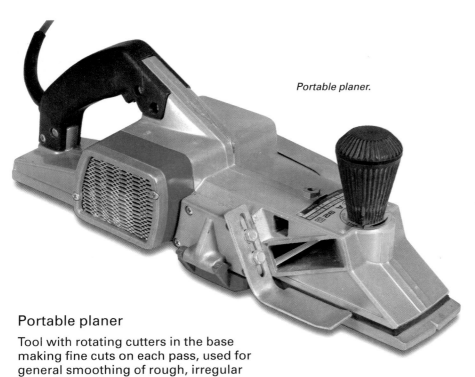

Portable planer.

Portable planer

Tool with rotating cutters in the base making fine cuts on each pass, used for general smoothing of rough, irregular wood. The depth of cut is adjusted by the front handle which moves the front section of the sole, revealing more or less of the cutters. The cutter blades are interchangeable for various finishes.

Power planer mounted on a bench, so that the workpiece can be applied to the tool instead of the other way round.

The depth is set and the plane is then applied evenly to the work, pressing on the front handle and guiding it in straight strokes with the main handle. As the end of the stroke the pressure should be transferred from the front handle to the main handle so as not scoop a deeper cut at the end.

Power router

Tool for making grooves, housings, rebates and moulded edges. The interchangeable cutter projects below the base of the tool, which is adjustable to set the depth of cut. Straight or curved cuts can be made, and it can be used for internal as well as external shapes.

When using the portable power router, it is essential that the area being cut out is not wider than the baseplate of the machine, or it will not be supported. The pressure exerted by the two hands should be equal.

Power router.

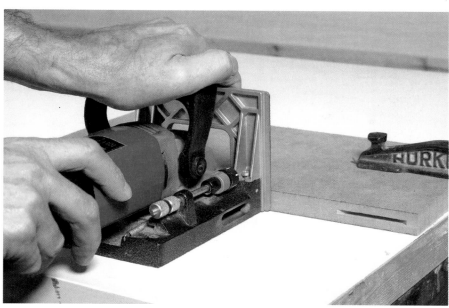

Using a biscuit cutter to cut slots in the edge of a board.

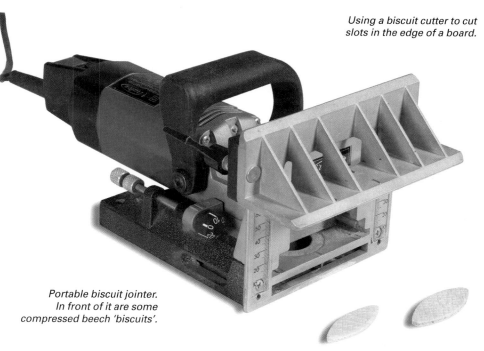

Portable biscuit jointer. In front of it are some compressed beech 'biscuits'.

Portable biscuit jointer

Tool with a small projecting circular saw blade used to make rounded slots in wooden boards or manufactured board panels. Ready-made 'biscuits' of compressed beech are glued and inserted in the slots, making an extremely strong joint.

Biscuit joints ready to be glued and assembled.

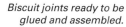

99

Power screwdriver with rechargeable battery

A useful and powerful tool, in spite of its small size. The rotation of the interchangeable screwdriver bits is reversible, so screws can be removed as well as tightened.

Power screwdriver with rechargeable battery.

Portable power drill with rechargeable battery.

Portable power drill with rechargeable battery

Drill with similar characteristics to a mains-powered drill, but with a self-contained power supply which makes it particularly useful for work outdoors. In practice it is convenient everywhere.

Maintaining and sharpening hand tools

Tools should be maintained in good condition at all times, and always kept sharp so that they perform their functions perfectly, with ease and accuracy. This has a great influence on the successful outcome of a project, a fact which the woodworker and cabinetmaker should always bear in mind.

As well as affecting the ease of use, the maintenance, and in particular the sharpness, of tools is also critical to the final finish of an operation, which depends on the quality and accuracy with which it is carried out. Achieving this depends on keeping the tools in good condition, and it is therefore necessary to know the various techniques of sharpening and caring for them.

Looking after tools properly also means using them in the correct manner for the operations for which they were designed. A chisel should never be used to open a can of paint, for instance. The habit of returning them to their proper storage place after use should also be acquired.

The care with which tools are kept and looked after is the mark of a good woodworker or cabinetmaker. This section therefore describes some of the commonest methods of achieving these ends.

Keeping tools clean

With use, it is normal for tools to become covered with wood chips, sawdust, glue and other messy substances. There is a danger that a tool will not work properly or accurately if it is dirty, and with some very tenacious glues there is even the risk that it may be permanently damaged. This is why it is so important to keep tools clean at all times.

Cleaning the striking face of a hammer by rubbing it on a sheet of abrasive paper. This reduces the risk of mis-hitting.

Cleaning compressed sawdust from the teeth of a file with a file card, a kind of brush with steel bristles.

Sharpening

Sharpening a cutting tool consists of wearing away the metal at the cutting edge of the blade so that it makes an acute angle which is almost infinitely thin.

The electric bench grinder. This model has coarse and fine wheels, and it is excellent for sharpening cutting tools before honing them.

Saws are sharpened with a triangular file.

Honing

Once a cutting tool has been ground, the next stage is to hone it to remove the marks and burrs left by the grinding wheel, at the same time producing a perfect edge. This is done by rubbing the blade on an oilstone.

An abrasive stone for honing tools. It is lubricated with oil to float off the metal particles, which would otherwise clog it.

Setting the saw teeth

With use, the teeth of a saw will no longer be bent to each side as much as they were originally, and the saw may jam when cutting. Setting is the process of restoring the cutting teeth to their original positions, alternately pointing to left and right, which provides clearance so that the saw will not jam in the cut it is making. The teeth are adjusted one by one with a tool called a saw set.

Saw sets. The plier-like one sets the teeth to the correct angle automatically. The other design is simpler but harder to use, since the tooth is bent to the correct angle by eye.

Saw sharpening

Sharpening a saw with a triangular file.

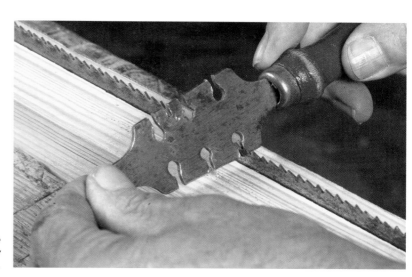

Setting the teeth of a saw with a saw set.

Sharpening the blades of guided cutting tools (e.g. plane blades)

Grinding a plane blade on a bench grinder. Care is needed because this removes metal very quickly. The blade should be dipped periodically in cold water to avoid overheating.

Honing the bevelled edge of a plane blade by rubbing it on a sharpening stone.

Honing the back of a plane blade on the stone. The stone is kept lubricated with oil.

Sharpening the blades of free-cutting tools (e.g. chisels)

Grinding a chisel on a bench grinder. The blade is applied very gently and dipped in cold water from time to time to prevent it overheating with friction.

The honing operation provides a keen edge after grinding. Honing a secondary bevel with a slightly greater angle than the grinding angle gives a stronger result.

Honing the back of the chisel by rubbing it on the stone. For this operation it is important to keep the chisel absolutely flat on the stone.

Sharpening a scraper

The tools needed for sharpening a scraper: a vice with two pieces of wood for clamping the scraper while it is being worked on, files, a sharpening stone and oil.

The scraper is clamped between the pieces of wood in the vice. The edges are then filed to remove any burrs or unevenness.

To finish the edges of the scraper, it is rubbed on the sharpening stone lubricated with oil.

To hone the scraper on the stone, some pressure is needed while making circular movements.

WOODWORKING

This section is devoted to the fundamental techniques a woodworker will call upon in carrying out a project – the preliminary design, planing, sawing, making joints of every kind, sanding and finishing. With these skills of universal application, the execution of a wide variety of projects will become possible, using wood to make pieces designed for storage, for decoration, for comfort, or any other purpose.

Like every skill, that of the woodworker is based on a range of established knowledge and techniques which have been perfected over centuries of use. A long tradition rests on the woodworker's shoulders, a tradition which has passed down a comprehensive range of works full of ingenuity, personality and appeal, as well as accumulating a wealth of experience. This means that woodworking is still a craft in which the nobility of the prime material, wood, is enhanced with the stimulus of creative skill.

The pages of this section are seasoned with a combination of technical skills, advice, suggestions and tips which will help the reader to become a skilled craftsman. The wide range of information will enable the best way of performing an operation to be found, depending on it s function and the part it plays in the finished piece of work. Applying these skills and techniques, the woodworker will take pride in the achievement of a well finished piece of work with the indefinable quality of having been made from the heart.

The woodworker's skills

The workshop

The workshop of a woodworker serves two important functions: it provides a working area with a bench to support the pieces being worked on, and storage facilities for keeping tools and materials good condition, so that they are ready when needed and easily found.

Considered as a trade or skill, woodworking dates back to times when wood was the only material available for building dwellings, for the construction of large mechanical devices such as windmills, smaller ones such as ploughs, and for making equipment such as buckets, and domestic furniture, initially of very rudimentary design. From earliest times, the versatility of wood has meant that the skilled woodworker was much in demand for making every kind of construction or device designed to achieve greater comfort, both indoors and out.

Over the centuries, the techniques related to carpentry have evolved and become combined with those of other trades, such as that of the blacksmith making hinges for instance. This beneficial interaction has enhanced the utility of the pieces made.

Today, the woodworker's workshop will contain tools ranging from traditional hand tools to modern powered versions of them, but the ancient techniques and skills have changed little over the years.

The workbench

The woodworker's bench is the vital support on which the various workshop operations are carried out. It must be solidly built so as to be strong enough to support the weight of the materials and tools, and more importantly it must withstand the forces applied when using tools without wobbling. For strength and resistance to wear, it is usually made of beech, although pine is a possible alternative.

The bench should be situated in an open area of the workshop, free-standing and self-supporting. For ease of working, it is important that the surface should be reachable from any point round it, since it must be possible to operate the tools and handle the pieces of wood being worked on without any obstructions or obstacles.

The height of the bench can vary, but it is best if it is suited to the height of the main person using it. About 90 cm (36 in) is the normal height.

The work surface is usually supported on four solid legs which are attached by double mortise and tenon joints. Sometimes the rear legs are slightly thicker and inclined at an angle to make the bench harder to tip over.

The construction of the bench includes the vice, sometimes attached to one of the legs, which is used to hold a piece of wood firmly while it is being worked on. The other leg may

Saw horses are very useful as a subsidiary bench in a workshop, light and movable yet providing a solid support for large pieces of work.

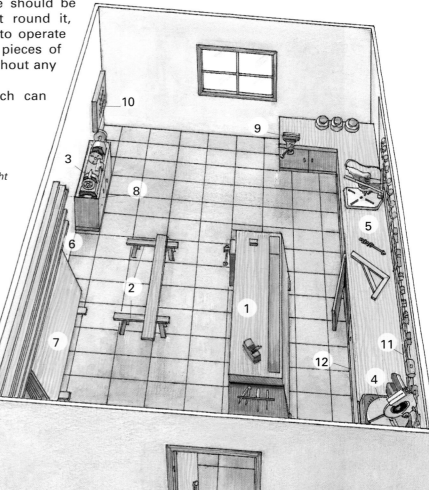

Above and page opposite, two views of a woodworker's workshop with all the basic elements needed, efficiently arranged:

1 Workbench with vice; tool racks on the end

2 Saw horses

3 Woodturning lathe

4 Compound mitre saw

5 Bench drill stand

6 Shelves for storing long pieces of wood

7 Space under the shelves to store large panels

8 Cupboard for storing lathe tools and accessories

9 Vice fixed to the work surface

10 Cupboard for storing tools

11 Racks for storing tools

12 Cupboards for storing tools, abrasive paper, glue, varnish and other materials

have a socket for a holdfast which, with the vice, enables long pieces of wood to be supported.

On the top of the bench is an adjustable bench stop consisting of two wedge-shaped pieces of wood. A collar for a holdfast is useful for clamping work.

The bench also has several places for keeping tools to hand while they are being used on a particular piece of work; there may be a drawer, storage space underneath the bench top, and a tool well on the surface consisting of a narrow channel running all the way along the bench.

Saw horses are portable trestles which are useful for making an auxiliary bench to support very large pieces of wood. Being lower than the bench, they are better suited to some sawing operations.

The bench is the place where most woodworking operations are carried out, such as marking out, planing surfaces, making joints, assembly and gluing.

Storage arrangements

The woodworker's workshop will contain a large quantity of hand, mechanical and electrical tools as well as raw materials such as boards, lengths of timber, mouldings, veneers and so on. To be useful, they must be easy and convenient to find, so orderly storage is essential.

The illustration shows a simple cabinet arranged and fitted out to store many of the tools which are commonly used in the course of particular woodworking operations. The tools of the same kind are stored together and

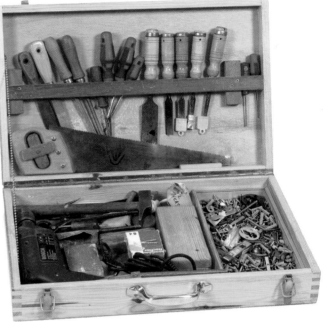

For work outside the workshop there are toolboxes which enable the essential tools and fittings to be carried around easily in an organised way. These toolboxes are very useful in emergencies and for small tasks away from the workshop.

In a workshop neither the size nor the shape of furniture intended for storing tools is critical, but it is important that it should be equipped to store the tools in a logical way, arranged so that when the time comes to use them, they can be found quickly and reached easily. Cutting tools such as chisels should be stored in racks so their blades do not damage each other.

arranged so that the worker does not waste time looking for them. This is particularly important for tools such as chisels, planes, screwdrivers and so on which are numerous and similar in appearance to each other. They should be neatly stored in racks which are always in view and easily accessible.

Lengths of timber require storage arrangements which keeps the pieces out of the way off the floor and horizontal. This can be achieved by strong brackets made of metal or wood, firmly fixed to a wall, spaced at intervals to prevent bending. Large panels can be stored on edge leaning against the wall, raised from the floor by chocks of wood. Other materials such as bands of edging veneer have different storage requirements. It is worth spending time devising convenient storage arrangements for all the tools and materials used.

Fitted to the surface of the workbench is the bench stop, an adjustable arrangement of paired wedges used to hold a piece of wood while it is being worked. Screw-down metal bench stops are also available.

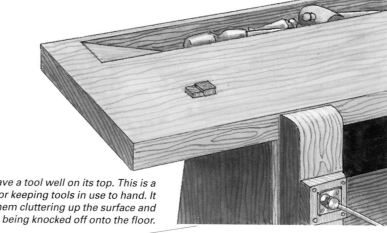

A bench may have a tool well on its top. This is a narrow channel for keeping tools in use to hand. It also prevents them cluttering up the surface and being knocked off onto the floor.

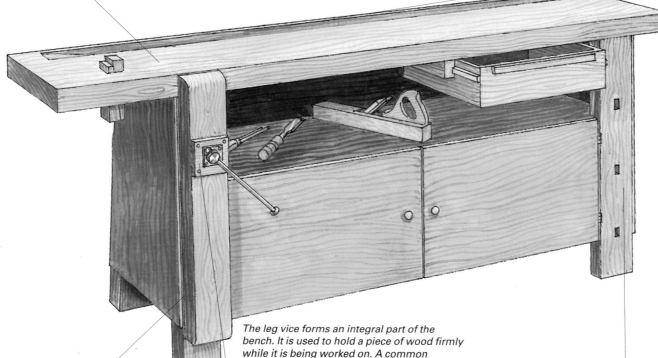

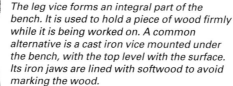

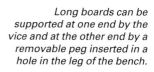

As well as being the essential support for pieces of wood while they are being worked on, the workbench is also useful for conveniently storing the tools being used for particular operations. In this case the bench is equipped with a drawer, a shelf and a large cupboard.

107

To keep its jaws parallel when gripping the work, the leg vice has an adjustable stop at the bottom.

The leg vice forms an integral part of the bench. It is used to hold a piece of wood firmly while it is being worked on. A common alternative is a cast iron vice mounted under the bench, with the top level with the surface. Its iron jaws are lined with softwood to avoid marking the wood.

Long boards can be supported at one end by the vice and at the other end by a removable peg inserted in a hole in the leg of the bench.

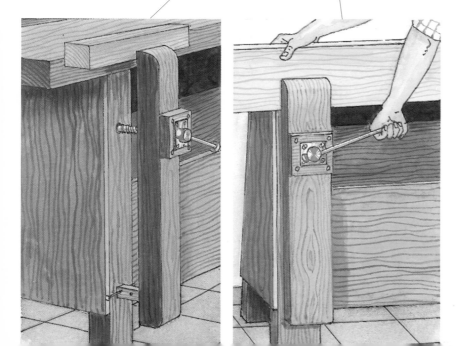

The project

'The project' describes the whole process which culminates in an object or a piece of furniture, the result of a number of steps involving many different tools and pieces of wood in all varieties, shapes and sizes, assembled together using woodworking joints and metal fittings.

If the project is the result of an original idea, it is advisable and indeed essential to make sketches or drawings of all the pieces of which

it will consist, with measurements and, in the case of multiple identical pieces, the quantity needed. If the project is a very complicated one, it is best to draw the pieces in the logical arrangement they will take up.

These drawings should include plan views, elevations and perspectives, depending on the complexity of the work to be carried out. They will be invaluable in deciding what joints to use and the final dimensions of each piece.

When the drawings have been made, the component parts should be listed together with a cutting list of all the materials which will be needed and a list of tools to be used. If full-size templates are required for some of the pieces, these are made in plywood. They are an intermediate step, making it easy to transfer the outline of the drawing to the wood to be worked on by tracing round them. This will simplify cutting out the pieces later.

Preliminary sketches

It is strongly recommended to make preliminary sketches of the project before starting work. These should indicate the proportions and the final appearance as clearly as possible. These sketches will be an invaluable means of acquiring an overall view of how to carry out the work.

Making a template from a drawing of a curved component

First a full-size (1:1 scale) drawing of the component is made on a piece of tracing paper. This outline is then transferred to a plywood panel which is cut out to create the template itself.

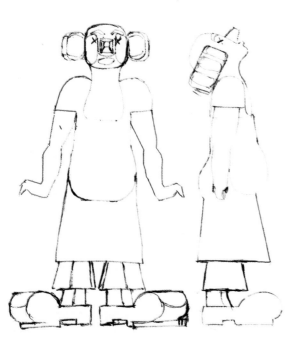

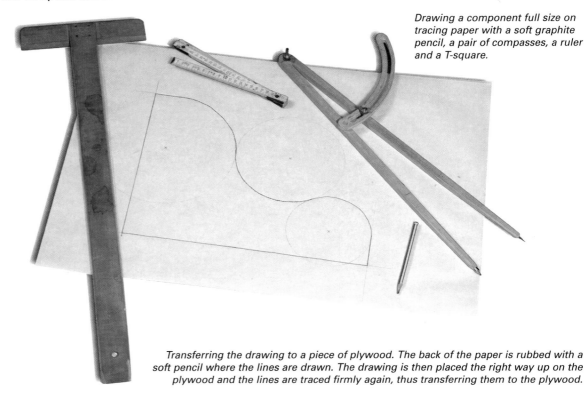

Drawing a component full size on tracing paper with a soft graphite pencil, a pair of compasses, a ruler and a T-square.

Although not exact in every detail, the preliminary drawing give an overall idea of how the piece is going to look. From this starting point the piece itself can be made.

Transferring the drawing to a piece of plywood. The back of the paper is rubbed with a soft pencil where the lines are drawn. The drawing is then placed the right way up on the plywood and the lines are traced firmly again, thus transferring them to the plywood.

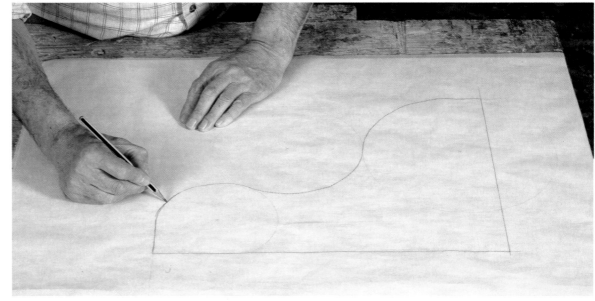

108

The line transferred to the plywood is reinforced and the face side is marked so that there is no doubt which way the template should be applied to the work.

The template is cut out with a jigsaw, keeping the blade to the waste side of the line. This leaves a small margin which is removed in the course of smoothing and finishing the template.

Making templates from a measured drawing

The information for making templates may come from hand-drawn dimensioned drawings and/or plans, details, perspectives and so on, not to scale. All the measurements are taken or calculated from these and redrawn at a scale of 1:1 (full size) on plywood panels which are then cut out to form the templates.

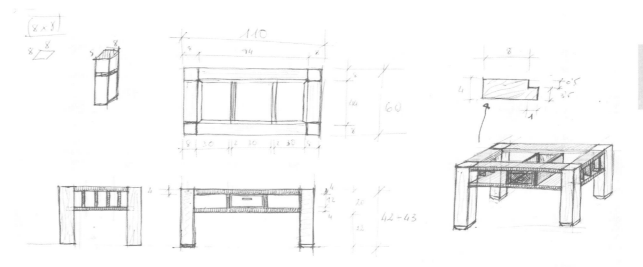

Various measured drawings for a furniture project

Rational arrangement of the pieces for the best use of material, leaving the minimum of waste.

Various templates

Drawing part of a circle on a manufactured board, using an improvised compass made of two nails and a piece of string.

Plywood is also used as a template, particularly to transfer very irregular outlines, since with a jigsaw it is possible to follow a curved line accurately freehand.

The board after the drawn lines have been cut with the jigsaw. The result is a useful, strong template which can be used many times. If several similar templates are needed, it is convenient to make them out of the panel at the same time.

A template need not be used only to draw cutting lines. It is also a very useful method of transferring measurements and angles.

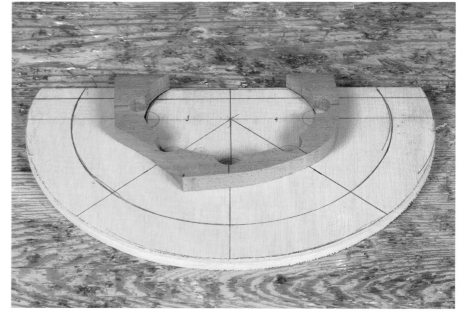

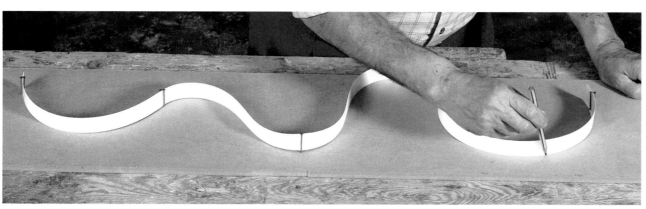

Drawing a complicated curve using a strip of veneer and some nails. These form a sort of pre-template defining the line to be drawn on the plywood template.

Basic woodworking techniques

In woodworking, there are a number of fundamental, basic operations which turn up again and again whenever a different object or piece is made. These include the following:

- All operations directly related to tools which smooth, mark, measure and cut
- The whole range of joints, which multiply the properties and functions of wood
- Operations of Assembly, gluing, installing metal fittings, and applying all kinds of surface finish.

Mastery of these fundamental processes will enable practically any kind of work to be tackled and carried to satisfactory conclusion. They are in a sense the grammar of woodworking, and this section covers these basic operations.

Smoothing the wood

Smoothing is the fundamental technique by which the piece of wood to be worked is given a surface suitable for being measured and marked with sufficient accuracy. If the wood to be used is not properly planed, it will be almost impossible to work with because of its unevenness and the lack of continuity of the faces, edges and ends which will undoubtedly exist. Accurate work is only possible if the surfaces are smooth, flat and at right angles to each other.

For these operations, the hand plane is an indispensable woodworking tool. Even if the wood that has been acquired in a planed condition, it will still need to worked so that the surfaces and edges are exactly square to each other. Machine planed wood bought from the timber merchant is often marked with repetitive ridges and these too must be removed.

The processes by which the pieces of wood are brought to this state vary depending on which part of the piece is being reduced. Planing a face surface is different from planing an edge or an end, for instance.

Whatever the task, the blade should be properly sharpened and adjusted before starting work. To smooth wide surfaces, different types of plane are used in succession. The jointer plane has a fairly long and wide sole and it is the first plane to be used, to even out the most prominent irregularities. The jack plane has a shorter sole and gives a finer finish. The hand plane is even more finely adjustable, and this is used to achieve a perfectly smooth finish.

The rough, uneven surface of a piece of wood, as it might arrive from the supplier.

The long jointer plane to carry out the first stage of smoothing, levelling the wood.

Using the jack plane to bring the wood to the second degree of smoothness,

Smoothing plane being used for the last stage of smoothing the squared-off surface.

Sometimes a cabinet scraper is used to make the wood even smoother. In use, it is held bent into a slight curve.

The piece of wood after it has undergone the whole process of smoothing, from levelling to smoothing.

Marking out

Marking out is the basic operation by which the woodworker measures and marks the prepared pieces of wood to show where it should be cut, transferring the measurements specified in the cutting list of materials, or on the plan drawing, whichever is being used. The tools used to do this are a bradawl, to scratch a deep mark on the wood which will not be removed by mistake, or a pencil if the mark is superficial. In woodworking there is a whole range of techniques used for marking and measuring which, in themselves, constitute little processes which are repeated many times in the same work. Although the pieces on which the measurements are marked may vary, the actions will be the same. The important thing is that the face surfaces and the sides should be properly smooth and true, so that the measurements and markings made are reliable and accurate. This will make subsequent operations easier to execute well.

Marking a horizontal line

This is an operation which is frequently carried out on man-made wood panels. A spirit level is used, first to ensure that the vertical measurement of the horizontal line is correctly marked, and then to mark the horizontal line itself.

Measure the point where the horizontal line is wanted, using a measuring tape. In positioning the tape, it is important for accuracy that it should be vertical, and this can be achieved with a spirit level.

Next, mark the measurement. Keep the measuring tape completely taut while this is done.

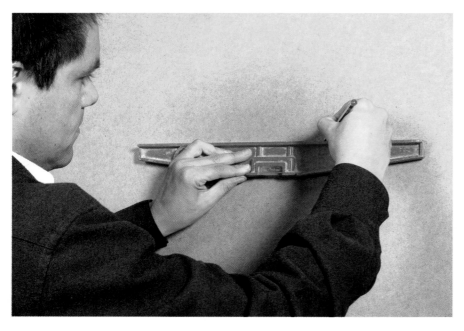

Line up the straight surface of the spirit level with the mark just made. Check that it is perfectly horizontal and then, using it as a ruler, mark the required line.

Truing up a piece of wood

The need to mark right angles arises frequently in woodworking, since it creates a standard angle which enables one part to fit another accurately when cut. A prerequisite is that the wood marked should be true, with edges and faces at right angles to each other.

Fix the workpiece firmly in the vice and smooth the edges with a plane.

The faces of the wood are then smoothed, always following the direction of the grain.

Once the face and sides are levelled, use a try square to mark a line at right angles on each edge and face in turn, starting each new line where the previous one finished.

If the fourth line joins the perimeter round the piece of wood exactly, it means that the piece is square and true, and that the operations making it so have been properly carried out . If the line does not join up, correct the situation by further planing and test again.

Marking an angle

The need to mark an angles arises in many operations relating to the construction of furniture and various other pieces, such as picture frames for example. In marking it out, it is very important to check that the individual pieces are true. If they are not, this will become very obvious when the angle is cut. To perform this operation accurately, a sliding bevel set to the correct angle and a try square are required in each case. 45° is the angle most commonly encountered in woodworking.

The trueness of the wood is essential for using an angle gauge properly, just as it is when drawing a right angle. Here a true edge is being used to mark an angle of 30°.

Many different tools are used for drawing angles. Here a simple angle gauge is being used; its design makes it very easy to draw a number of lines parallel to each other.

To mark an angle cut, the line of the angle must be extended across the edge of the wood. Here a try square is being used to do this. One again, the try square is responsible for checking that the earlier operations have been carried out accurately.

Marking a cutting line

When a right-angled cut is to be marked on a piece of wood or a panel of plywood or chipboard, it is a good plan to cut a physical mark with a knife after drawing a pencil line. This will simplify the cutting operation later, whether a hand saw or power tool is used. Even more importantly, the incision will prevent an irregular or splintered edge.

Mark the cutting line on the panel with a pencil. Then run a sharp cutting knife along it, held at an angle of about 45°. A steel straight edge or rule should be used, to ensure that there is a regular guide for the knife to follow. To avoid accidents, care must be taken that the knife does not slip, and the fingers should be kept as far as possible away from the cutting line.

Using a marking gauge

The marking gauge is designed for marking parallel lines along a straight edge. The more complicated mortise gauge (illustrated) can also mark two lines at once, as in marking out a mortise for a mortise and tenon joint. The tool is also useful for transferring measurements from one piece to another, and it is particularly good for marking the width of an edge on a particular face or on a panel. In many cases, the marking gauge avoids the need to take numerical measurements, accurately transferring a measurement taken from the piece itself.

Before using the marking gauge, the piece of wood on which a measurement is to be marked should be firmly fixed to the workbench.

The distance between the point and the fixed body is adjusted by tapping the end of the stem with a mallet. When set correctly, the wedge (or fixing screw, depending on the type) is tightened to prevent the measurement being changed by mistake.

To mark a line when the gauge has been set, it is held firmly flat and upright against the side of the wood to be marked. It is then turned so that the pin or cutter just touches the wood, and smoothly slid along the wood away from the operator with a steady, continuous arm movement. The mark should not be too deep.

Care must be taken not to let the pin press too hard on the surface to be marked. Otherwise there is a risk of the grain forcing the line out of parallel.

Drawing circles

Constructions in woodworking can involve various circles and curves, requiring the marking out of circles or parts of circles. Consequently, there are various types of compasses to meet the woodworker's needs for pieces which contain circles of different diameters.

Drawing a circle with a rudimentary compass made for the occasion with a nail, a piece of string and a pencil.

Drawing a circle with a wooden pair of compasses

For marking a large diameter circle a beam compass is the most suitable kind to use.

Sawing

A large number of tools have been developed to cut pieces of wood to size. Thee include various types of saw (toothed cutting tools), and various blades (tools for a guided cut), which are essential equipment in every workshop.

Cutting occurs at different stages in the same piece of work, and the basic operations are usually those which take place at the start of the work. In any case a cut of a piece of wood depends as much on the good condition of the tool itself as of its correct support and operation.

Square cuts

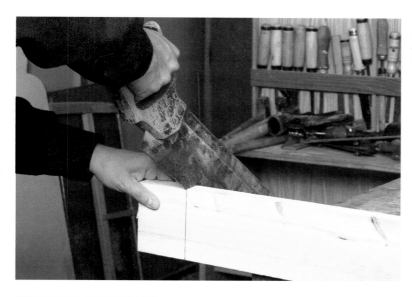

The proper way to make a right-angled cut is to start with the saw at an angle and work from the far to the near side.

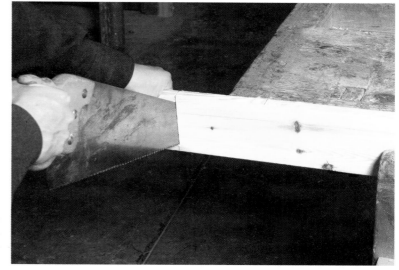

The correct way to finish the cut across the grain, supporting the waste piece with the free hand and sawing slowly to cut the last fibres without tearing the wood.

Cutting along the grain with a handsaw. The workpiece is supported on a pair of saw horses placed close enough together to reduce the vibration created by the saw as much as possible.

Cutting a thin panel across the grain with a handsaw. The panel is clamped to two planks resting on the saw horses, which provide a wider area of support.

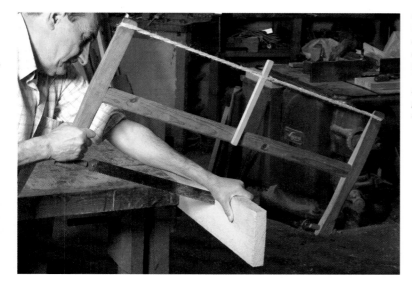

Cutting against the grain with a frame saw. The cutting line is watched carefully all the time, so that the blade follows it. The piece being cut off is supported by the hand passed through the saw above the blade.

Cutting along the grain with a frame saw. The workpiece is fixed to the bench so that part of it overhangs the end.

Making an angle cut

Making an angle cut without a guide. The wood is held in the vice so that the angle cut is horizontal, making it easier to judge the proper angle of the saw. The left hand holding the end of the work is pulling it to keep the sawcut open.

Making an angle cut using a mitre block as a guide. This has a pre-cut slot at the angle required which guides the saw. This simplifies accurate cutting of standard angles such as 45°.

Cutting a rectangular opening

The rectangle to be cut out is marked on the work and a hole is drilled in each corner for a keyhole saw blade to enter.

The rectangle is cut out with the keyhole saw. The holes at the corners enable the direction of the cut to be changed.

Alternatively, a power jigsaw can be used in the same way.

Cutting a curved opening

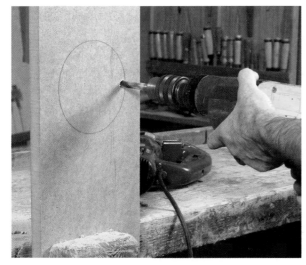

Drilling a hole at the edge of the marked circle which is to be cut out.

A compass saw is used to cut the curve. The cut is started with a few short strokes using the end of the blade, which is narrower.

The curve can be cut with a jigsaw, again starting from the drilled hole. The workpiece must be firmly fixed.

Cutting a curve

The curve is constructed drawing arcs using a pair of compasses, the point of which will make a mark on the workpiece. The method is acceptable if the design of the piece being made means that the mark does not matter, because it is not seen or cut away.

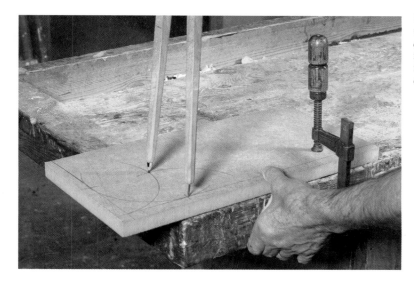

Two curves are drawn with the pair of compasses centred on two marks equidistant from the end and the edge of the workpiece.

The intersection of the two curves marks the centre of the corner curve which is the one to be cut out.

The curve is cut with a compass saw.

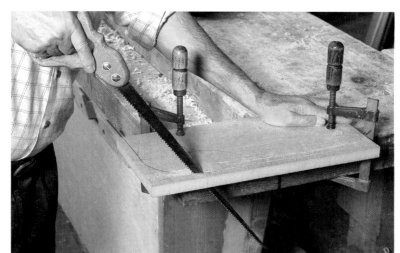

Alternatively, the curve is cut with a jigsaw.

Cutting a curve without marking the surface

This is a way of marking and cutting the same curve without using the pair of compasses; on the workpiece to mark it out. There is therefore no mark made by the compass point.

To mark a curve without using a compass on the workpiece, a plywood template is made. The curve required is drawn on the plywood with a compass and then carefully cut out with a jigsaw. If the wood is thin the free part should be supported with the hand.

The template is positioned tangentially to the edge and end of the workpiece. The curved line is then drawn round it.

The curve marked is cut with the jigsaw. The blade must always remain on the outside of the marked line.

Cutting a concave curve with a frame saw

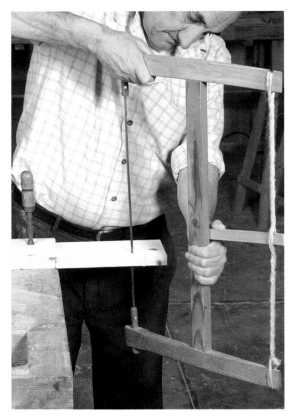

If the curve is being cut out of a piece of wood of a certain size, both hands will be needed to make the cut with the frame saw.

When a curve is being cut out of a thin panel, it should be clamped to the bench with a piece of wood with a V-shaped notch to support it all the time.

Cutting a rebate with a chisel

Rebates are by hand in the workshop are chisels

1. Mark out the rebate using a marking gauge, try square, tape measure and a pencil with a soft lead.

2. With the backsaw, make vertical cuts defining the rebate and a few intermediate cuts, all to the correct depth

3. Next use the chisel bevel side down to start cutting out the waste wood. Work down to the marked line from one side.

4. Turn the workpiece round and continue the same operation from the other side of the rebate. This will leave a triangular base.

6. When the rebate has been cut up to the lines marking the sides and the base, smooth the surfaces with little cuts, tapping the chisel with the palm of the hand.

5. Turn the chisel bevel side up to trim the base flat.

Drilling

Drilling is one of the operations most frequently carried out in the workshop,
used for everything from making a template to assembling the components when they are completed.

Drilling a vertical hole in a piece of wood

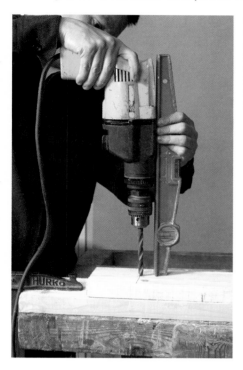

Make sure the drill is perfectly vertical before starting the operation. For really important work this can be checked with a spirit level.

Both hands should be used when drilling, positioned to keep the drill vertical to the wood.

In this drilling operation, the workpiece is cramped firmly to the workbench using bar cramps. These are prevented from marking the work by blocks of scrap wood which distribute the pressure over a wider area. A piece of wood under the workpiece protects the top of the workbench from being damaged by the drill bit.

119

Joints

One of the most significant limitations facing the woodworker is the size and length of the pieces of wood available on the market, as a result of sawing and of the natural size of the trees converted into timber.

For this reason, woodworkers throughout the ages have developed various methods to improve the characteristics of two pieces of wood joined together, such as length, cross section, flexibility, versatility and so on.

The properties which are enhanced by these operations depends on to a great extent on the kind of joint used in each case. Numerous as they are, these joints can be classified into a small number of categories.

In this section devoted to the joints most frequently used for joining two pieces of wood, a simple classification into three groups:
corner and cross joints, and splice joints.

This selection of joints reveals the enormous range of possible solutions there are to endow the joint between two or more pieces of wood with qualities they would not otherwise have. As well as their aesthetic qualities and undeniable utility, joints are a tribute to the ingenuity and skill of the craftsman who has made them.

Edge joints and connectors

The purpose of this kind of joint is to increase the width and/or the length of the piece, so that the resulting dimensions would be almost impossible to supply from existing resources.

Edge joints are basically of two kinds: those made between two pieces planed and glued, and those which are reinforced with tongues, grooves, pins, etc., when what is wanted is a superior resistance in the face of possible contraction than that inherent in the wood itself.

When the joint is made with metal fittings, it is called a connector, which is usually used in the construction of houses.

Splined edge-to-edge joint

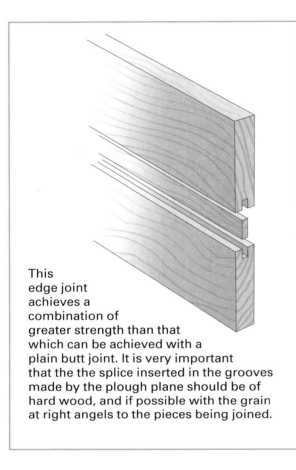

This edge joint achieves a combination of greater strength than that which can be achieved with a plain butt joint. It is very important that the the splice inserted in the grooves made by the plough plane should be of hard wood, and if possible with the grain at right angels to the pieces being joined.

1. Using a tape measure, adjust the marking gauge so that the point traces a width equivalent to one-third of the end of the wood.

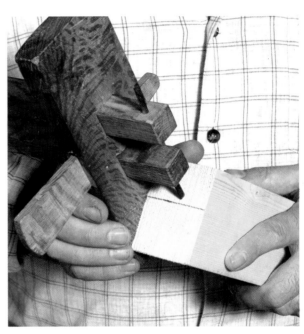

2. Use a pencil to mark the end of one of the pieces of wood with the depth the groove to be made later will reach, about 30 mm (1¼ in) in this case. Then use the marking gauge to mark the end in thirds, and to mark the same divisions along the whole face which is to be grooved.

3. Use a circular table saw to cut a groove in the , set up with a guide which enables the wood to be moved sideways. Make parallel cuts, removing all the material from inside the groove marked on the edge of the wood.

4. Complete the removal of the wood in the groove with a chisel, so that the interior of the groove is free of all wood residue and irregularities which could prevent the splice from seating properly.

5. The splice or false tongue will have the length and width which corresponds to the grooves cut in the two pieces to be joined.

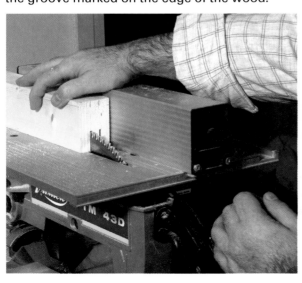

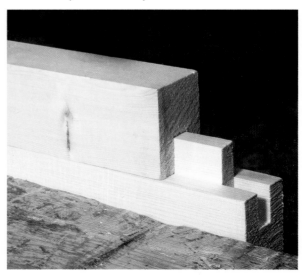

basic woodworking techniques

6. Starting with these measurements, plane a few millimetres off the width and a thin shaving from the thickness of the splice, so that it is loose enough to leave room for the glue to work properly.

7. For the same reasons, chamfer the four corners of the splice. To do this, use a plane held at an angle of 45°, so that the corners are slightly reduced. This means they will not damage or splinter the pieces with which it is in contact.

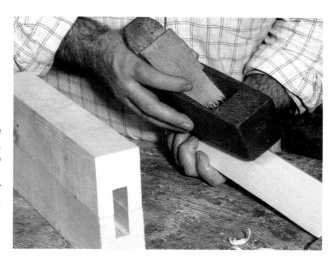

8. Glue the splice and both grooves so that the glue will set firmly round the whole assembly. The overall joint can be adjusted before the glue unites the pieces finally.

121

VARIATIONS ON THE SPLINED EDGE-TO-EDGE JOINT

Double splined edge-to-edge joint

Used on very thick pieces of wood, the double splice provides even greater strength, particularly against warping of the joint.

Splined edge-to-edge joint reinforced with tenons

Used to increase the resistance of the fibres of the wood to splitting, the tenons are set in mortises cut in the length of the groove at distances proportional to the strength to be achieved.

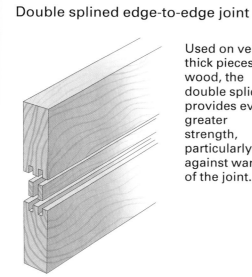

Simple edge-to-edge joint with twin dovetails

An old technique in which recesses are cut in the wood for dovetails made of hardwood.

Edge-to-edge biscuit joint

Butt joint reinforced with prefabricated 'biscuits' of compressed wood, glued into place in sockets cut with a biscuit jointer.

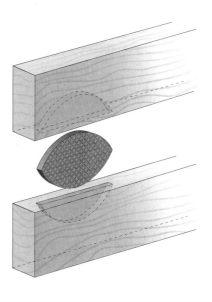

Tongue-and-groove joint

This is a kind of joint used for edge-to-edge jointing of boards. As the name suggests, it consists of an edge with a projection, the tongue, which fits a groove in the edge of the other board. Several boards can be joined together in this way to make a panel of any required width.

1. Fix the board or panel firmly to the bench with the edge uppermost. Use a plough plane to make a groove in the centre of the edge. In this case a combined tongue-and-groove plane is being used. A metal combination plane will include matched cutters to achieve the same result.

2. With a wooden plane, the depth of the cutter can be adjusted by tapping the wedge gently with a hammer.

3. In the same way the tongue is planed on the edge of the other board, using the tongue side of the combined tongue-and-groove plane.

4. When the tongue has been planed, soften the angles by making light cuts with a plane held at 45°. This will ensure that the there is room for enough glue in the joint.

5. This picture clearly illustrates the relationship between the matched moulded profiles of the tongue and the groove, in this case created by the cutters of the combined tongue-and-groove plane.

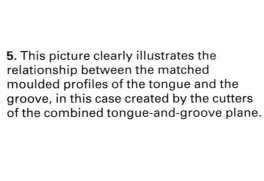

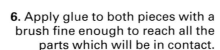

6. Apply glue to both pieces with a brush fine enough to reach all the parts which will be in contact.

7. Use lengthways movements only in assembling the joint. The board acts like a lever so any sideways movements could damage or snap the tongue, which would seriously weaken the joint.

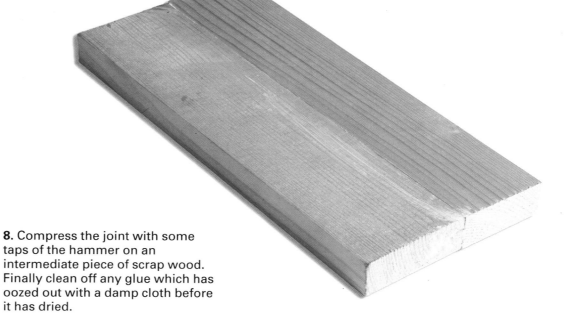

8. Compress the joint with some taps of the hammer on an intermediate piece of scrap wood. Finally clean off any glue which has oozed out with a damp cloth before it has dried.

VARIATIONS ON THE TONGUE-AND-GROOVE JOINT

Twin tongue-and-groove joint

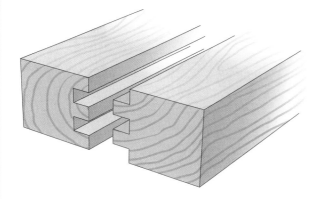

Used to join thicker pieces of wood, the twin tongues make this a stronger joint.

Alternating tongue and groove joint

Each of the pieces to be joined has a tongue and a groove. This provides great resistance to sideways twisting forces.0

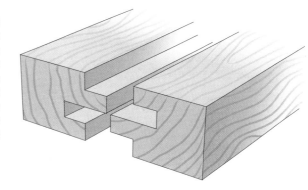

Moulded tongue-and-groove joint

Mouldings help to conceal the effect of any contraction of the wood which would otherwise reveal an open joint. It is often used in cladding, when the boards are secretly nailed to battens instead of being glued together.

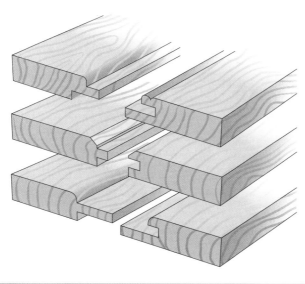

Tongue-and-groove joint with mortise and tenon

Joint used to attach a cross piece to the end of butt-jointed boards to prevent them twisting.

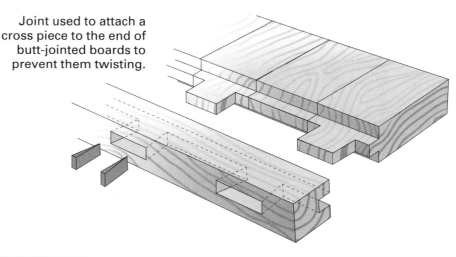

Corner and cross joints

These joints are used to join two pieces of wood at right angles to each other, or sometimes at an oblique angle. Their common characteristic is that the overall thickness of the joint is the same as that of the pieces being joined. They are stronger and better looking than lap joints. The simpler varieties of this kind of joint are stronger in compression than in tension, while the more complex joints are strong in tension as well.

There is a large variety of joints, some being much harder to make than others. Therefore the choice of the one to use often depends on the experience of the woodworker. But usually it is the particular use which is the determining factor, since the correct joint will be the one which best resists the various forces which may simultaneously be applied to it.

T-halving and corner-halving joint

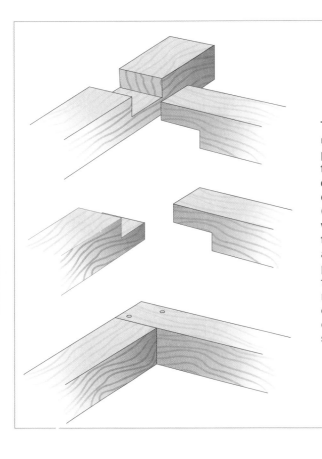

This kind of joint is used when two pieces of wood are to be joined at the corner (upper drawing) or as a T (middle drawing), with the overall thickness the same as that of each piece. The joint is fixed with glue, nails, screws or dowels, depending on the degree of strength required.

1. The first operation is to scribe the depth of the joint on the opposing sides and end of each piece forming the joint. The gauge is set to half the thickness of the pieces, so that it marks the central axis of the wood.

2. With a try square, mark the shoulder of the part to be cut away on each piece. The thickness of the other piece determines the position of this line. On the sides, the line is drawn as far as the depth line already scribed on it.

3. Cut the shoulder of the joint with a backsaw. This will define the amount of wood to be removed, so cut just to the waste side of the marked lines to avoid cutting too far.

4. Complete the cut by using the backsaw to saw the lap, following the marks to complete the removal of the waste wood which is half the thickness of the piece.

5. Finish the sawn edges accurately with a chisel to remove any roughness. Carry out the same operation on the other piece.

124

6. After removing the sawdust with a clean cloth, apply the glue with a brush.

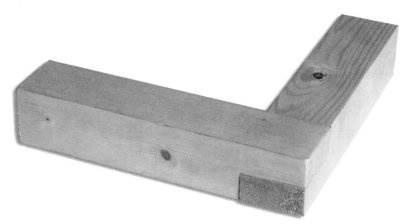

The cross halving joint is made in much the same way as the T-halving joint. The difference is that the waste in the central cavity is removed with a chisel after the shoulder cuts have been made. It is helpful to make one or two extra cuts between them.

OTHER VARIATIONS ON THE HALVING JOINT

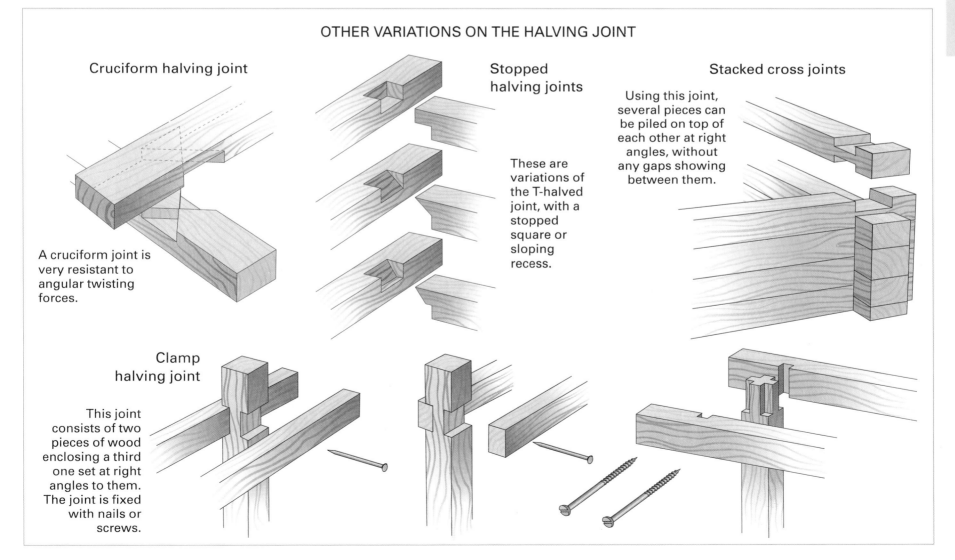

Cruciform halving joint

A cruciform joint is very resistant to angular twisting forces.

Stopped halving joints

These are variations of the T-halved joint, with a stopped square or sloping recess.

Stacked cross joints

Using this joint, several pieces can be piled on top of each other at right angles, without any gaps showing between them.

Clamp halving joint

This joint consists of two pieces of wood enclosing a third one set at right angles to them. The joint is fixed with nails or screws.

Wedged twin through mortise and tenon joint

This is one of the most effective joints in compression and, being reinforced with wedges, it is also performs well in tension. It is used in joinery to make joints between upright and cross members, for instance when a rail meets a leg.

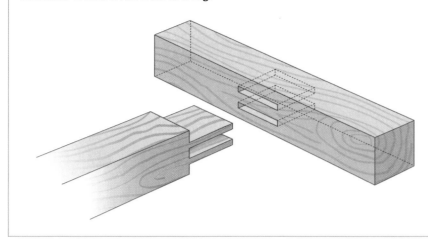

1. Using one piece as a measure, mark the length of the tenons on the other piece. Then stand this piece in position on the other in the form of a T and use it to mark the overall length of the mortises.

2. Reinforce the marks, checking them with a try square.

3. On the marked side, use a marking gauge to mark the positions of the two mortises. This is done by scribing two lines 15 mm (⁹⁄₁₆ in) from each edge, and two lines 10 mm (⅜ in) further in, that is, 25 mm (¹⁵⁄₁₆ in) from each edge.

4. Using a 10-mm (⅜ in) chisel and a mallet, cut out the two mortises which will receive the tenons. Work towards the middle, making cuts alternately from each side. Clean up all the vertical sides.

5. On the side where the wedges will be fitted, make tapering cuts starting 5 mm (³⁄₁₆ in) beyond the marks.

6. Mark out the twin tenons on both sides and end of the piece with lines corresponding to the dimensions and positions of the mortises. Mark the sections to be cut out with a pencil.

7. With a crosscut or tenon saw, make longitudinal cuts for the two tenons, always keeping to the waste side of the marked lines.

8. With the same saw, finish the outer sides of the tenons by making transverse cuts to remove the waste.

9. Use a chisel to cut away the internal part between the two tenons, working first from one side and then from the other.

10. Smooth off and remove any shavings on the tenons. Check for fit and then cover the tenons and shoulders with glue.

11. Assemble the glued mortise and tenon joint. Glue the wedges and hammer them gently with a mallet into the places prepared. When the glue has completely dried, saw the wedges off flush, plane them level and sand the whole area smooth.

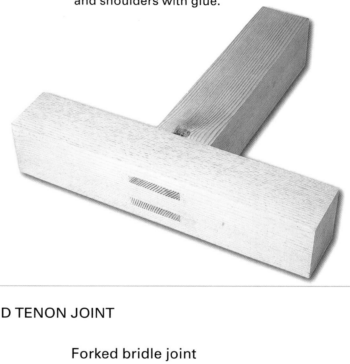

OTHER VARIATIONS ON THE MORTISE AND TENON JOINT

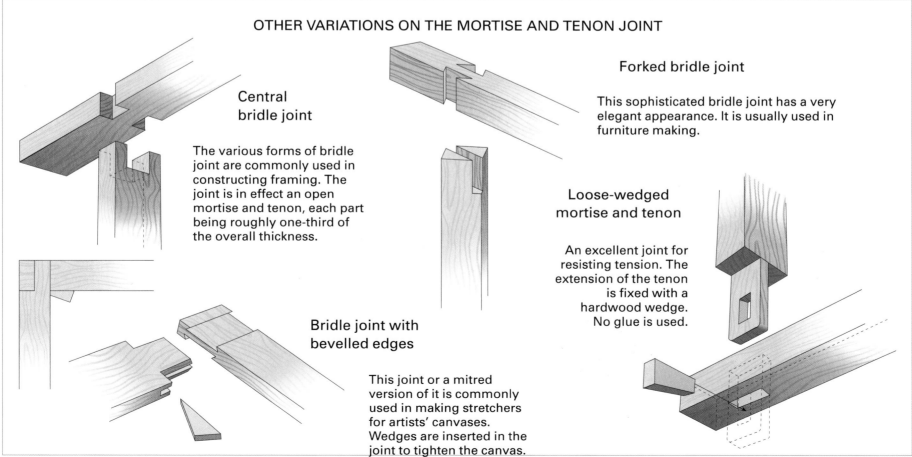

Central bridle joint

The various forms of bridle joint are commonly used in constructing framing. The joint is in effect an open mortise and tenon, each part being roughly one-third of the overall thickness.

Forked bridle joint

This sophisticated bridle joint has a very elegant appearance. It is usually used in furniture making.

Loose-wedged mortise and tenon

An excellent joint for resisting tension. The extension of the tenon is fixed with a hardwood wedge. No glue is used.

Bridle joint with bevelled edges

This joint or a mitred version of it is commonly used in making stretchers for artists' canvases. Wedges are inserted in the joint to tighten the canvas.

Corner bridle joint

This is a joint best used in compression. It is most commonly used for corner joints, in making frames, door and window frames, or in other situations where two pieces are to be joined at right angles. The glued joint is often reinforced with screws.

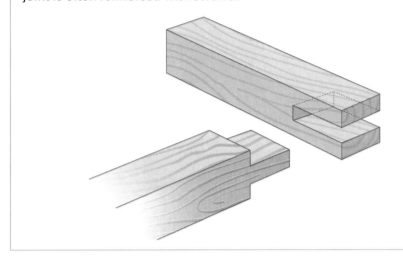

1. Starting with two planed and sanded pieces of wood, mark the good sides with a pencil; these will be the reference sides for all the work. Place one piece on the other and a mark a line, which will be the thickness of the second piece from the end of the first. Repeat for the other piece.

2. Taking this line as a reference, use a try square to mark a line round all four sides. Do the same on the other piece.

3. On the wider side, use a marking gauge to scribe lines dividing the width into three equal bands, extending to the marks already made.

4. With a saw make two vertical cuts along the inner side of the marks, as far as the pencilled line marking the depth. Repeat on the other piece.

5. Clamp the wood firmly to the bench with the face upwards. Use a mallet and chisel to clean out the cuts already made. The width of the chisel should be the same or slightly less than the width of the mortise.

6. For the tenon, clamp the other piece to the bench. Saw up to the outer edges of the marks made earlier.

7. Having cut away the waste wood, smooth the surfaces with a rasp to remove any irregularities.

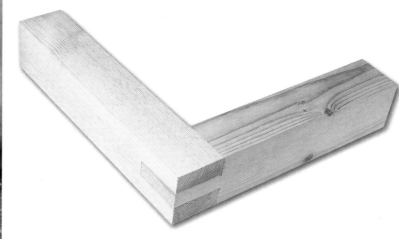

8. Assemble the joint dry, tapping it together with a mallet. Check for fit and adjust if necessary. Apply glue to all the surfaces which will be in contact with each other. Assemble the two pieces, again using the mallet. When the glue is dry, sand all sides smooth.

VARIATIONS ON CORNER BRIDLE JOINTS AND MORTISE AND TENON JOINTS

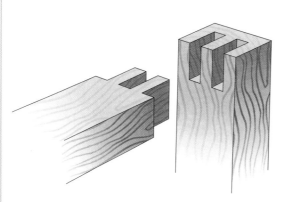

Stopped twin corner bridle joint

Used to join wider pieces of wood, the twin joint provides a greater glued area, making it more rigid. The stopped end gives the joint a neat appearance.

Stopped corner bridle joint with or without sloping faces

There are several kinds of corner bridle joint. Those with sloping faces are stronger when glued, because there is a greater area of contact between the pieces.

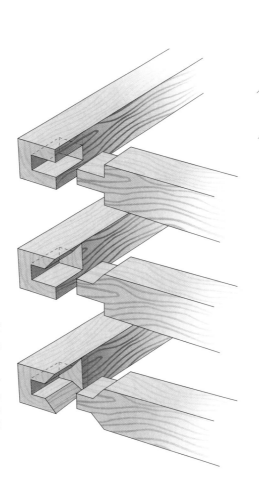

Mitred joint with stub, invisible, or hidden tenon

A joint in which the operational parts are hidden, with a triangular tenon fitting into a corresponding mortise.

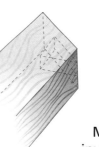

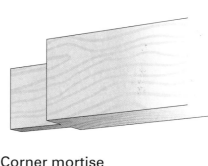

Corner mortise and tenon joint

Used for a strong right-angled joint at the corner of a frame. The tenon is smaller than the width of the rail, so the mortise will not break through the end.

Through dovetail joint with single pin

The through dovetail joint is a modification of the corner bridle joint, compared with which it is superior in resisting tension, while just as satisfactory in compression. In woodworking a single dovetail joint is normally used, while in cabinetmaking multiple dovetails are common.

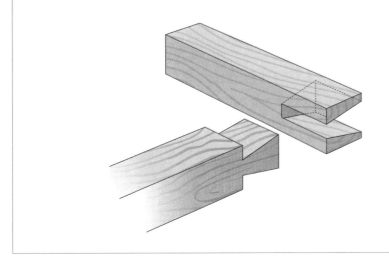

1. The hollow part between the pins (equivalent to a mortise) is marked out first. Using a marking gauge on one of the wider sides, mark two points dividing it into three equal parts. Make two similar marks on the opposite side, half the distance in from each side (that is, one-sixth of the width of the piece). Using a sliding bevel and pencil on the end of the wood, join the two marks on one side with the two corresponding ones on the opposite side.

2. Clamp the piece in the vice and cut down the angled lines with a saw, keeping inside the marks.

3. Use mallet and chisel to cut out the waste and finish it off. Keep the back of the chisel blade flat against the inside faces.

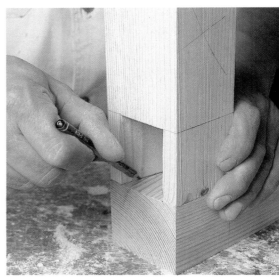

4. Use the completed piece as a template to mark the lines of the pin (equivalent to the tenon) on the faces of the other piece.

5. Once the basic measurements have been transferred, draw the rest of the pin by extending the lines across the end from one side to the other, using a marking gauge.

6. Use the sliding bevel and a pencil to mark out the rest of the pin.

7. Clamp the piece in the vice and make angled cuts from the end to the depth marked earlier. Then clamp to the bench as shown in the picture and make horizontal cuts to remove the waste. Use a flat rasp to smooth the shoulders and faces of the tail.

8. After testing and adjusting for fit, glue all the faces which will be in contact with each other. Assemble the dovetail joint and close the joint by tapping it with a mallet until the faces are firmly in contact.

OTHER VERSIONS OF SINGLE PIN DOVETAIL JOINTS

Dovetail halving joint

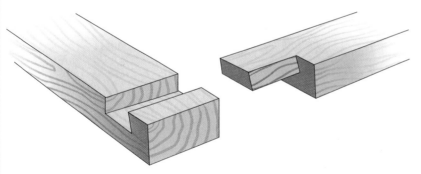

Although easier to make than a full dovetail joint, it is less satisfactory because of its tendency to split the housing.

Slotted dovetail joint

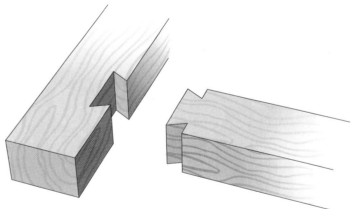

This joint is often used for making braces because it resists tension as well as compression, particularly if the dovetail extends from one side to the other.

Skewed twin dovetail and tenon joint

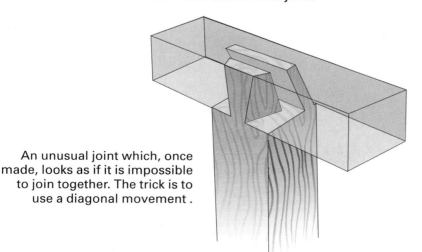

An unusual joint which, once made, looks as if it is impossible to join together. The trick is to use a diagonal movement .

Dovetail pins

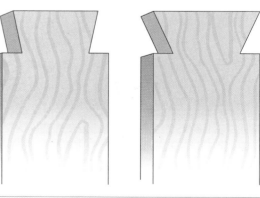

In woodworking, the pins are fairly wide, while narrower pins are customary in furniture making. The slope should be 1:8 for hardwoods (right) and 1:6 for softwoods (far right). A dovetail template is useful for marking out dovetails.

Dowel joints

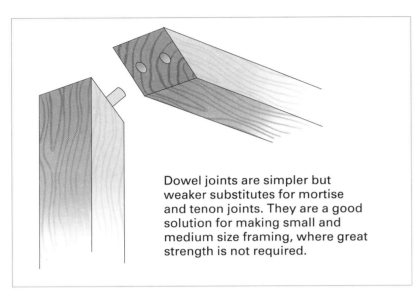

Dowel joints are simpler but weaker substitutes for mortise and tenon joints. They are a good solution for making small and medium size framing, where great strength is not required.

1. On a prepared square-section piece, mark the mitre joint to be made, using a try square and a pencil.

2. The easiest way to cut the mitre joint is to use a compound mitre saw, as here, or a radial arm saw. The blade of the saw should be applied and removed with a fairly rapid movement, so as not to mark the cut faces with burns caused by the saw blade rubbing.

3. Remove any whiskers from the corners of the cut faces with medium abrasive paper.

4. To drill holes in the ends, first fix one of the pieces in the vice with the angled face exactly horizontal. The other piece can be used as a level to align it with.

5. Draw a central line along the face. Divide it into thirds, which will define the centres for the two dowel holes to be drilled.

6. The drill must be held exactly perpendicular. The two holes are drilled 15 mm (⁹⁄₁₆ in) deep with a 6 mm (³⁄₁₆ in) bit. If the dowel size is different the drill size should be chosen accordingly.

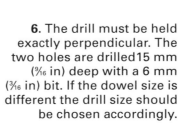

7. To mark the position of the holes in the second piece with perfect accuracy, insert two dowel jigs in the holes already made, so that when the pieces are presented to each other they will mark the second piece in the correct positions.

8. Cover the dowels with glue and insert them in the holes. The dowels must be made of wood harder than the wood they are fixing together.

9. Holding one of the pieces in the vice, glue the faces and the projecting ends of the dowels. Join the other piece to it, using pressure while the glue sets.

OTHER TYPES OF DOWELLED JOINTS

Types of dowels

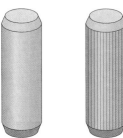

There are different types of dowel depending on the degree of adhesion which is required of the glued joint.

Glued butt joint with wooden pegs

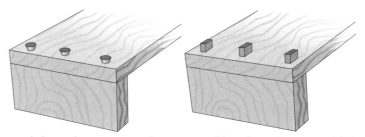

Joint using rectangular or round hardwood pegs, which are driven into holes in the wood. Today these are sometimes replaced with metal fittings.

Corner butt joint with dowels

This joint is a weaker version of the mortise and tenon. It is much easier to make, but less resistant to tension and twisting.

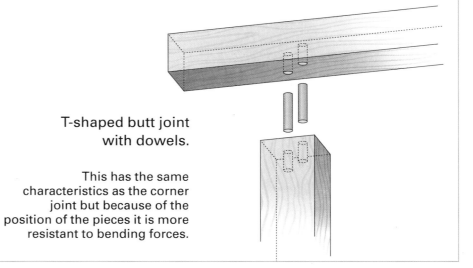

T-shaped butt joint with dowels.

This has the same characteristics as the corner joint but because of the position of the pieces it is more resistant to bending forces.

Splice joints

The basic function of a splice joints to join pieces longitudinally. It is often used in constructions such as porches, arcades and other situations where long straight pieces are required. The type of joint to be used must be chosen according to the forces of tension, compression and torsion (twisting) which the piece will undergo in the position it is used. It is also important that the pieces of wood should have no irregularities or knots where the joint is to be made, since these would reduce the joint's mechanical characteristics.

Splice joint with right-angled tenon

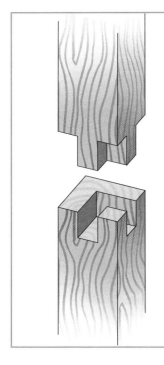

In this type of joint the tenon is a right-angled shape which fits a similar-shaped mortise or socket made in the other piece of wood. This hand-made joint takes time to construct, but it has a very striking appearance.

1. On a square section piece of wood, mark a base line at a distance from the end equivalent to the the width of the piece. This will define the area in which the joint will be made.

2. Use a marking gauge and ruler to mark lines parallel to the adjacent edges. The gauge should be set so that the size of the tenon marked out is 15 x 15 mm (⁹⁄₁₆ x ⁹⁄₁₆ in).

3. Use a backsaw to make horizontal cuts in the parts of the tenon which are to be removed.

4. Fix the workpiece in a vice and saw vertically to release the waste.

5. The same process of horizontal and vertical saw cuts is repeated for the other parts to be removed.

6. To remove the waste from areas which cannot be reached with a saw, use chisels with various widths of blade.

7. Use the chisel to loosen the waste wood with levering movements, alternating with vertical cuts to remove the slivers of wood and finish the shoulder neatly.

8. Clean the inner sides with a very sharp chisel held in the hands, making repeated gentle cuts.

9. Use the finished tenon to mark the other piece for the mortise. Putting the pieces end to end, transfer the measurements from one to the other.

10. Cut out the mortise and remove the waste in the same way as the tenon. Inevitably in this case the operation is a little more complicated.

11. Apply the glue completely, leaving no contact surface uncovered. The brush should be a suitable size for covering all the surfaces which will be in contact with each other.

VARIATIONS OF SPLICE JOINTS

Bridle splice joint	Bridle splice joint with slanted head	Splice joint with alternate tenons	Angled bridle splice joint with tongue
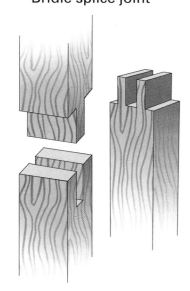		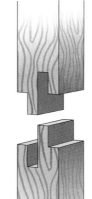	
Much stronger than a halving joint, so long as the width of the tenon member is at least one-third of the thickness of the pieces being joined. If the pieces are large, a joint with twin tenon members is used.	Very similar to the simple bridle splice joint, but with mitred cuts on the head of each piece, giving greater resistance to lateral twisting.	With this joint the contact area of the interlocking pieces is increased.	This needs much patient work with saw and chisel, but the final appearance is very attractive.

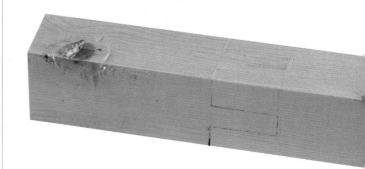

Splice halving joint with simple false tenon

This splice halving joint is a simpler interpretation of the oriental false tenon dovetail joint. It is a joint particularly designed to withstand a tensile force, but it also performs well in compression since there is no danger of splitting through tearing the wood.

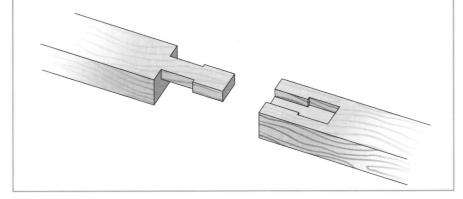

1. Measure the width of the piece of prepared rectangular wood and mark a line across it the same distance away from the end. Then mark two lines with the marking gauge dividing the width into three equal parts.

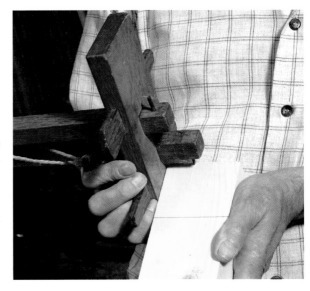

2. Draw another line across the piece two-fifths of the way from the end. Then scribe two lines parallel with the vertical marks and 10 mm (⅜ in) nearer the sides, part of the outline of the false tenon. Mark the depth of wood to be cut away by scribing a line across the centre of the end.

3. With the piece clamped to the bench, mark the outline of the socket of the false tenon which is to be cut away. Then start cutting out the waste using the chisel.

4. Remove the wood by using the chisel blade upside down and chopping it out until the depth line marked earlier has been reached.

5. To complete cleaning the inside faces, use the same chisel but with its blade the normal way up. Make careful cuts, controlling the chisel by hand.

6. Draw the transverse lines of the false tenon which will match the finished socket, using the end of the socket piece as a reference from which to transfer the measurements.

7. Draw the longitudinal lines by positioning the ends of the two pieces of wood together. Transfer the relevant measurements to complete the outline of the false tenon.

8. Before cutting the outline of the false tenon, make a cut halfway through the wood with a backsaw. Make a vertical cut and remove the waste piece. Keep it for the next stage.

9. Use the waste piece just removed as a support while chiselling away all the waste material surrounding the false tenon.

10. Clean the false tenon with careful chisel cuts, turning the workpiece as necessary to facilitate the use of the tool in finishing the wood.

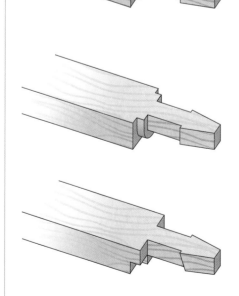

11. The glue is applied with a brush fine enough to cover all the faces which will be in contact with each other.

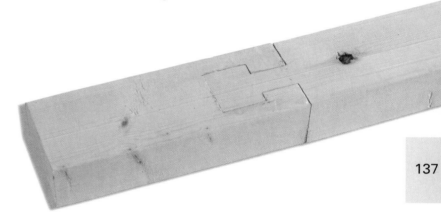

VARIATIONS ON THE SPLICE JOINT WITH FALSE TENON

Splice halving joint with dovetail false tenon

In this joint the tenon terminates with a kind of inverted dovetail. It is a splice halving joint whose length is equal to double the thickness of the pieces.

Splice joint with twin false tenon.

Perfect for woodwork which has to be dismantled easily, at the same time giving an impression of a permanent bond.

Splice halving joint with false tenon, tongue and rebate

A perfected joint based on the simple false tenon joint. The tongue and rebate make the whole joint more rigid, making it very resistant to twisting and bending forces.

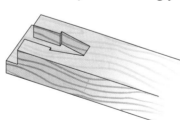

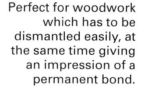

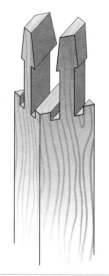

Angled splice halving joint with false tenon

Joint in which the angle of the head of the tenon, makes it easier to assemble. It is good for use where subsequent dismantling may be necessary.

Splice joint with square tenon

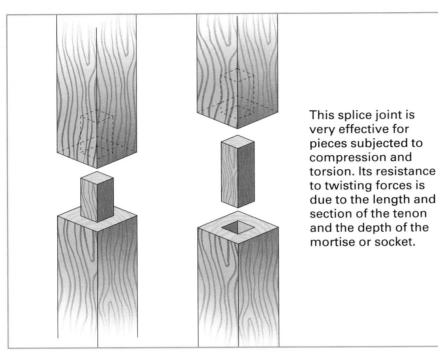

This splice joint is very effective for pieces subjected to compression and torsion. Its resistance to twisting forces is due to the length and section of the tenon and the depth of the mortise or socket.

1. Use a marking gauge to scribe lines on the faces and head. In this case the wood is 40 x 40 mm (1⁹⁄₁₆ in) square and the tenon will have a section of 15 x 15 mm (⁹⁄₁₆ x ⁹⁄₁₆ in).

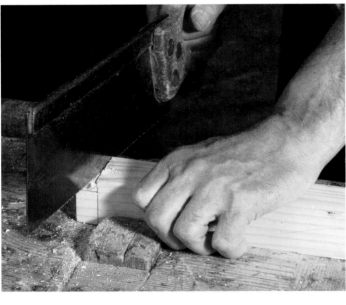

2. After marking out the piece, use a backsaw to cut away the waste wood surrounding the tenon.

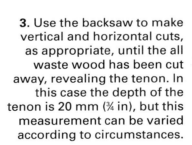

3. Use the backsaw to make vertical and horizontal cuts, as appropriate, until the all waste wood has been cut away, revealing the tenon. In this case the depth of the tenon is 20 mm (¾ in), but this measurement can be varied according to circumstances.

4. Fix the workpiece to the bench and clean up the tenon with a chisel.

5. Scribe the outline of the square socket, transferring the measurements from the tenon.

6. Fix the workpiece vertically in the vice and start cutting out the socket with a chisel.

7. Deepen the socket and remove the waste wood with repeated chisel cuts, until the depth is the same as the length of the tenon.

8. To finish the joint, apply the glue. Be sure to cover every surface which will be in contact with the other piece.

VARIATIONS OF THE SPLICE JOINT WITH FALSE TENON

Quartered splice bridle joint

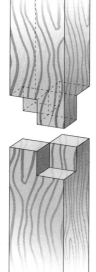

Splice joint with two symmetrical ends, used for pieces with square section. It is excellent for resisting compressive and twisting forces.

Cruciform splice joint

Splice joint with assymetrical ends. The tenon and socket are cross-shaped, ideal for square section pieces subject to compressive and twisting forces.

Double splice bridle joint

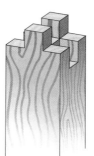

Splice joint which is difficult and time-consuming to make, involving much hand work with back saw and chisels. It has the same properties as the cross-toothed joint.

Splice joint with four tenons

Splice joint notable for its subtle solution to the problem of resisting twisting forces. It is in fact more often used for its appearance than its properties.

Preliminary and final assembly

In every woodworking project, there are normally two or more pieces to be joined together. Before final assembly, a preliminary, temporary assembly is carried out, to check that the various parts fit together correctly and accurately.

To do this, all the pieces are perfectly sanded and checked to see that nothing is missing, since only in this way will the test assembly be a true test, both for the individual components and for the work as a whole. Adjustments may need to be made. Then, when it is certain that the test assembly is correct, the process of final assembly can be carried out, in the course of which all the parts are fixed together permanently with glue, screws (if used), and so on.

In both preliminary and final assembly, various cramps and other tools applying pressure are used to hold the work together. These accurately position the joints and in the final assembly hold them immobile under pressure while the glue is drying.

There are may different methods of cramping, particularly when carrying out the test assembly. These range from the strategic use of pieces of masking tape to more complicated arrangements involving special tools such as web or strap cramps, G-cramps (C-cramps), mitre cramps and bar cramps.

Before starting assembly, all the components must be completely finished and perfectly sanded.

Example of the use of masking tape for a quick test assembly.

Correct use of softening

It is easy to mark or bruise the work with the pressure of cramp jaws during assembly. This is avoided by putting a piece of softening under each pad before the cramp is tightened. The softening must have smooth surfaces and be softer or no harder than the wood under pressure.

Joining two boards edge-to-edge using bar cramps

Before assembly, it is best to alternate the direction of the growth rings of the two pieces to be joined so as to reduce the danger of the wood warping as much as possible.

The correct positioning of a bar cramp for joining two boards, supported on a horizontal surface.

Using scrap pieces of wood as softening will prevent the work being marked, which is otherwise inevitable with the great pressure applied by cramps.

Joining two boards vertically, using the vice of the workbench as one of the pressure elements.

Several bar cramps positioned at approximately regular intervals for gluing together longer pieces.

141

To balance the forces, each of the bar cramps should apply the same pressure to the boards. For the same reason the bar cramps are arranged alternately, at each end of the pieces to be joined, as here, or above and below.

Assembling a frame using bar cramps

Assembling a frame using two bar cramps arranged in parallel and positioned alternately so as equalise the pressure on the work.

Final assembly of the frame using four bar cramps, positioned in such a way that the jaws do not interfere with each other.

Assembling a frame using mitre or corner cramps

Assembling a right-angled mitred corner joint. The first piece of wood is fixed in one of the jaws of the cramp. The other is then fixed in the other jaw of the cramp at right angles to it.

The first mitre joint is fixed in position.

The two pieces forming the opposite corner are fixed in another mitre cramp.

The remaining corners are fixed in the same way. This method of proceeding means only two assemblies are adjusted at a time, which makes the operation much easier.

Holding a right-angled butt joint in position while it is fixed

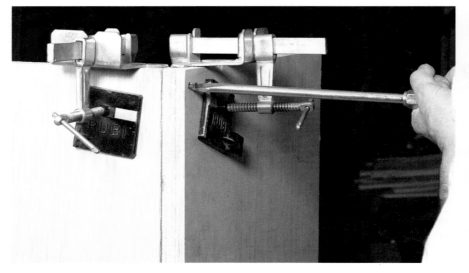

A corner cramp is used to hold the pieces firmly in position. The holes can then be drilled with a power drill, with confidence that they will be perpendicular to the first piece, parallel to the second one, and perfectly aligned.

The fixing is completed by fitting the fixing elements (in this case screws), before removing the cramps.

Cramping using C-shaped springs

C-shaped spring cramps are simply pieces cut from old chair or mattress springs. They act a small cramps applying a gentle pressure. For this reason they are used in the cramping and final assembly of smaller pieces of work.

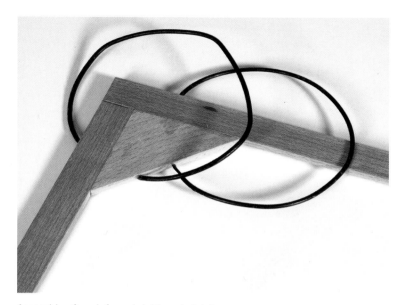

Assembly of a reinforced right angle joint, using the quick and versatile system of applying pressure with C-spring cramps.

Assembly using a circular band cramp

A circular band cramp is used to pull together a four-cornered construction such as a frame. The steel band is adjustable, and when tightened it applies pressure to the corner pieces which are in contact with the work. It is a sophisticated version of a web or strap cramp, or of the tourniquet described below, and although it looks effective, in practice it does not have the versatility of the simpler alternatives.

Use of the strap cramp is recommended in situations where regular circumferential pressure is needed to hold pieces in position together while they are glued.

Cramping a joint using a home-made tourniquet

When the shape of the joint to be cramped is irregular and requires the pressure to be applied evenly at all points of contact, nothing is better than this rudimentary method of applying pressure, known as the tourniquet or Spanish windlass. The only essential requirement is that the position of the tourniquet should allow the tightening stick to be turned.

Preliminary assembly of the joint using a tourniquet.

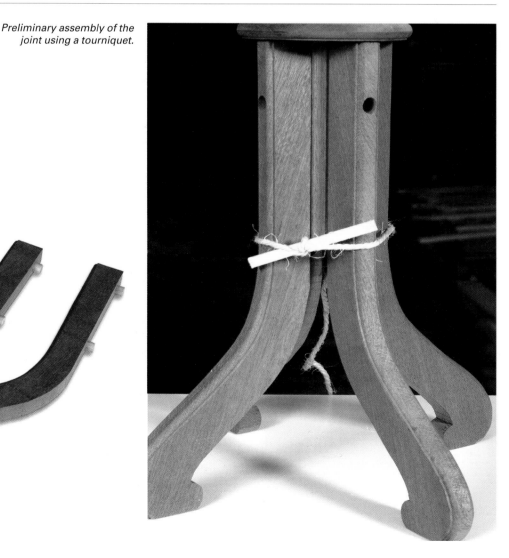

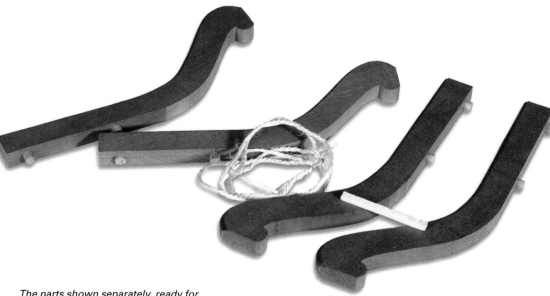

The parts shown separately, ready for assembly in their final position, and the string and stick used to make the tourniquet which holds them together under pressure while the glue dries.

Glued joints and metal fixings

In workshop operations, many of the joints made are glued, but joints using metal fixings are also common. Sometimes both techniques are combined for greater strength. The choice is determined by the practical and aesthetic requirements of each particular case.

Glued joints use the cramping techniques described earlier in the context of assembly. The adhesive normally used for solid wood is PVA (poly-vinyl acetate) glue, commonly known as white glue. This is a non-toxic water-based liquid which is easy to apply, sufficiently slow-drying to allow adjustment, and easily cleaned off with a damp cloth while wet. It dries in 24 hours to make a very strong joint. Water-resistant versions are available for exterior use. To stick laminates and veneers to panels, contact adhesive is used. Both surfaces are coated with adhesive and left to dry. The joint is made immediately the surfaces are joined, so correct positioning is essential.

Diagonal nailing

This is a quick and simple technique for making a joint. Instead of knocking in the nails at right angles to the fibres, which makes a weak fixing since they can easily be pulled out, the nails are hammered in at opposing angles to each other. This makes a fairly strong join.

The pieces to be joined are lined up accurately. The first nail is then hammered in at an angle of about 60°.

To make this kind of fixing stronger, a second nail is inserted pointing in the opposite direction to the first one.

Fixing mouldings with concealed panel pins

This method is employed when it is desirable to use metal fixings but not to see them. It is commonly used for planting mouldings or other visual elements which have no structural function. It is important not to bruise the moulding which would spoil the appearance.

The panel pins must be long enough to secure the moulding to the wood with about 6 mm (¼ in) still projecting. Fix the moulding by hammering in the panel pins only this far.

Use pincers to cut off the projecting part of each panel pin, being very careful not to make any marks on the moulding.

When all the heads of the panel pins have been clipped off, sink each one below the surface using a nail punch, so that the panel pin is completely concealed in the wood. Fill the holes with wood filler.

Screwing components together

The precise location of the screw hole is measured and marked. A number of operations must then be performed before the actual tightening of the screw itself.

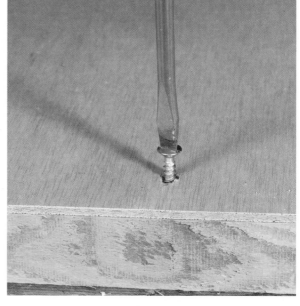

When the pieces to be screwed together are both made of solid wood, the operation is as follows. First make a pilot hole with a drill slightly smaller than the width of the screw thread through the first piece and well into the second. Next drill the top piece again with a drill the same size as the shank (the non-threaded part) of the screw.

Then pass the screw through this hole and position its point in the pilot hole in the lower piece. Finally, tighten the crew with a screwdriver. The drilled clearance and pilot holes make it easy to start the screw perpendicular to the surface of the wood, although it is still important to keep the screwdriver itself vertical.

Sometimes the two pieces to be joined are made of different materials, such as when a plywood panel is screwed to a frame. In this case it is even more important to drill a clearance hole in the upper piece to avoid splintering and breaking the wood.

When countersunk screws are used, the upper part of the clearance hole should be enlarged slightly with a screwdriver, so that the heads of the screws are slightly below the surface of the panel.

Another way of countersinking the pilot hole is by making delicate cuts with a small chisel.

Turn the screw with the screwdriver until the head of the screw is flush with the surface of the plywood.

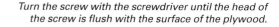

Fixing with coach bolts

Coach bolts are often used to make a strong joint between medium and large sized pieces. They have a flat-domed head and the part of the shank under the head is square in section. This bites into the wood and prevents the bolt turning when the nut is tightened. The simplicity and strength of coach bolts is undeniable, but they are not recommended when appearance is an important consideration. For this reason bolts are usually used for the parts of a piece which cannot be seen, or for objects where appearance is not particularly important, such as a carpenter's bench.

The two pieces to be joined are drilled using a drill bit of the same diameter as the thread of the bolt.

If the piece is to be dismantled in future, it is worth chiselling a short vertical slot in line with the hole with a chisel, so that the head can be extracted from the face with pliers. Normally this operation is unnecessary.

Insert the bolt in the hole and hammer it so that the square part of the shank bites into the wood. This will prevent the bolt rotating when the nut is tightened.

Put a washer on the thread before screwing on the nut. This distributes the pressure evenly and prevents the nut damaging the wood.

Tighten the nut with an ordinary spanner, a socket spanner or an adjustable spanner

Butt-jointing man-made boards with screw connectors

For joining chipboard and MDF panels, a special kind of screw connector has been developed, with a coarse thread and a socket head. It is tightened with a hexagon key. Some versions have a cross-head and are tightened with an ordinary cross-head screwdriver.

The connectors and tools used to join two man-made boards with a butt joint. Fix one board in the vice and set the other precisely in position, then mark the position of the holes.

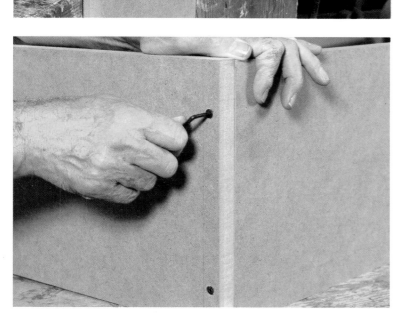

Drill a pilot hole using a bit with a diameter the the same as the screw without the thickness of the thread. Drill through the first board and a little way into the second, so that the screw has something to bite into.

Screw in the connector using a hexagon (Allen) key, until the two pieces are firmly pulled together.

Remove the assembly from the vice and finish tightening the screw connectors on the bench.

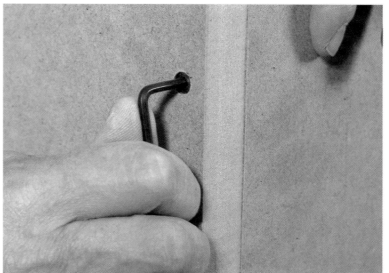

Detail showing the head of the connector pulled firmly into the panel.

Gluing two pieces together

As a general rule, an even but not too thick layer of glue is spread over both the surfaces to be joined. To guarantee a good joint, the surfaces must be smooth; if they have coarse finish they should be smoothed with sandpaper. It is also important that the faces to be glued should be completely grease-free, clean and free of any woody residue such as sawdust.

Having smoothed and cleaned all the surfaces, use a wooden stick or a brush to apply the glue evenly to all the surfaces which will be in contact with each other.

Components joined with joints or mortises should be hammered or cramped together to ensure close contact between the faces. So as not make hammer marks on the pieces, use a piece of scrap wood to receive the blows.

Some of the glue will undoubtedly have oozed out of the joint under pressure. The surfaces should be cleaned up with damp cotton waste or a damp cloth. This must be done before the glue dries.

Gluing two pieces together side by side

Making edge-to-edge butt joints between two boards involves using screw cramps or bar cramps to hold the pieces in position and apply pressure while the glue dries. If the pieces are not too large, the pieces can be joined using the technique of the rubbed joint which needs no cramps.

A rubbed joint can be made when the two faces to be joined are perfectly smooth. The faces are glued and rubbed together to expel the air from the joint. With no air in the joint, the pressure of the atmosphere presses the two pieces together,so cramping is unnecessary.

To make a butt joint between two pieces, one is fixed in the vice. Glue is then applied to both the edges to be joined.

The joint is assembled and cramped with two bar cramps .

Clean off the glue which oozes out under the pressure of cramping before it has dried.

Sometimes the joint is glued and screwed or glued and nailed. In this case the pieces are assembled and glued with the screws or nails already in place. They are then screwed or hammered in at once to apply pressure to the joint.

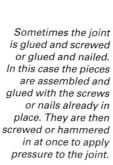

Hammering the nails into an edging strip just glued to the edge of a board.

Cleaning off the glue which has oozed out as a result of the nailing.

Gluing a laminate or veneer to a man-made pane

Contact glue is used to stick the various types of laminate and veneer to man-made boards such as plywood, chipboard or MDF. These laminates and veneers are applied to change the appearance of the board.

1. Some of the items used when veneering a wooden panel: contact adhesive, a scraper to spread it, the veneer and the panel itself.

2. Using a metal scraper or a plastic spreader, spread a thin layer of contact adhesive quickly and evenly over the veneer and the panel to which it is to be attached. Spread the glue from the centre to the edges so as not to create areas with excess adhesive.

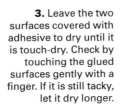

3. Leave the two surfaces covered with adhesive to dry until it is touch-dry. Check by touching the glued surfaces gently with a finger. If it is still tacky, let it dry longer.

4. Position the veneer so that it overhangs the panel by at least 10 mm (⅜ in). A sheet of paper between the surfaces allows the position to be adjusted; it is then removed carefully without moving the veneer.

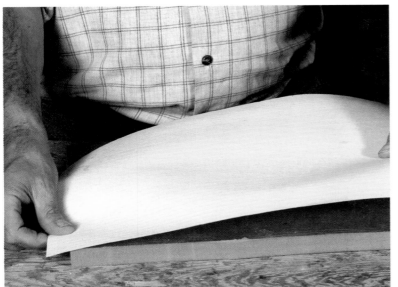

5. Using a piece of scrap wood to protect the veneer and spread the pressure, give the veneered panel a few taps of the hammer to remove any bubbles.

6. Press the veneer firmly to the board, removing any remaining air bubbles. This is best done with zig-zag motions of a veneer hammer, working from the centre too the edges.

7. Trim off the excess veneer, running the edge of a file or chisel along the arrises with an inward slicing motion.

8. Finish and smooth the edges of the veneered face with a sanding block. The veneer is very thin, so be careful not to remove too much.

150

Gluing the edges of man-made panels

The edges of chipboard panels are rough and unattractive, so any which will be visible are covered with a strip of wood or plastic veneer, using contact adhesive. Plywood can be treat in the same way.

1. On a smooth, flat surface, use a chisel guided by a wooden straight edge to cut a strip of veneer slightly wider than the edge to be veneered.

2. Fix the panel upright in the vice and cover the edge to be veneered with a thin layer of contact adhesive, using a scraper or spatula.

3. Apply contact adhesive to the strip of veneer in the same way. Placing the veneer on a raised batten of wood makes it easier to spread the glue thinly, as well as protecting the surface of the bench.

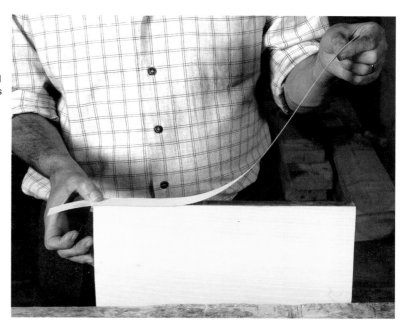

4. When the adhesive on both surfaces is touch-dry, apply the veneer to the edge so that it overhangs each side by the same amount.

5. To eliminate any air which may have be trapped between the glued surfaces, rub the veneer hammer along the edge with short zigzag movements, applying constant pressure.

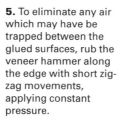

6. Remove the over-hanging parts of the edging veneer, using the edge of a file or chisel like a knife, making short inward movements.

7. After the excess veneer has been removed, smooth the veneered edges with very fine abrasive paper.

8. Gently finish the angles with the sanding block until the join between the panel and the edge veneer is completely hidden.

Sanding

Sanding is an extremely important operation in the process of making any piece, in that the quality of the finish will make a great difference to the final appearance. A bad finish will spoil the effect, no matter how well the earlier stages of the construction process have been carried out. Sanding is the first finishing operation and it must be done well, since the success of all subsequent staining, varnishing and painting depends on it.

The best abrasive paper for most sanding operations is garnet paper, which wears much less quickly than glasspaper. Aluminium oxide paper is harder still and excellent for sanding very dense hardwoods.

Hand sanding

Traditional hand-sanding is the simplest method there is, albeit slower and more laborious than power sanding. It gives the best final finish and is the most effective way of smoothing small areas or parts with irregular high relief. The choice of the correct type and grade of abrasive paper is important, as is the use of a suitable sanding block or other support so that the work is carried out correctly.

Sand a flat surface using a rectangular sanding block, making strokes in the direction of the grain.

Remove sharp arrises with sandpaper and a solid wood sanding block, making even strokes along the angles. The pressure must be even or the chamfer will be irregular.

Smooth the short corner angles in the same way, making short, light strokes across the grain.

Sanding the edges of plywood panels is very important because they are very porous, thus tending to absorb too much of the various liquid finishes. To reduce this tendency they should be made as smooth as possible.

A moulding is sanded with a sanding block shaped to match the curved forms of the piece. The hand movements should follow the shape of the work being sanded.

Sanding another part of the moulding using a smaller sanding block shaped to follow the narrower profile at the edge.

To sand small curved parts and areas with fine details, it is best to use the abrasive paper on its own without a sanding block. Its place is taken by the fingertips, which can achieve great precision.

When a piece of abrasive paper is clogged with an accumulation of sawdust, it can be cleared by banging it smartly on the bench.

For the sandpaper to give a perfectly smooth finish, the grain of the surface should be raised. This is done by moistening the surface of the wood and letting it dry. Sanding is then continued to achieve a very smooth final finish.

To find the direction of the grain, rub the hand across the surface of the wood in both directions. The direction which feels rougher is against the grain (above), while the smoother one is with the grain (above right).

Sanding should always be carried out working in the direction of the grain

Power sanding

One of the main advantages of power sanding is the speed with which medium and large sized surfaces can be smoothed. On the other hand, a very careful professional technique is needed on the part of the operator, since any lack of concentration will cause irregular marks, such as digging in, which will ruin the finish and are hard to remove.

The reciprocating motion of power sanders tends to move the part being worked on. The workpiece should therefore be firmly fixed to a stable support, such as the workbench.

Fix the workpiece firmly to the bench before sanding it with an orbital power sander.

Sanding the surface is carried out by back-and-forth movements always in the direction of the grain.

Fix the workpiece firmly in the vice to sand the edges.

Finish the arrises by holding the sander at an angle of 45° to the faces of the wood. A single very light stroke should be sufficient; it is very easy to sand off too much.

Taking the edge off a corner with the sander requires great control of the machine. It is all too easy to remove too much wood.

A blunt, rounded corner is made by moving the sander in a curve.

Fitting hinges

There is a great variety of metal hinges used in woodworking, many specially designed for particular purposes. The commonest type is the butt hinge, and this alone exists in many variations. The kind of hinge chosen and its positioning is dictated by the design of the piece and the function required.

Conventional hinges may be fitted so that they are proud of the frames they support, or they may be recessed so that they are flush. The second method involves more work but gives a neater, more professional result.

Most hinges are designed to be fixed with screws, so the only tools needed are an awl to make the pilot holes and screwdriver, and a chisel if recessed. It is important to select hinges that are strong enough for the pieces they will support. Fittings which are too light will bend or break if subjected to a load that is too heavy. It is always better to allow for a greater load than is actually required.

Fixing a hinge without a recess

This method is used for furniture, doors, windows and frames where an elegant appearance and a fine finish are not required.

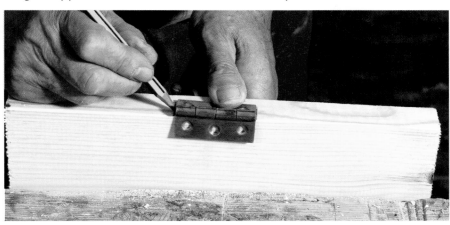

With the workpiece fixed to the bench, use the hinge itself as a template. Mark the outline of one leaf of the hinge, ignoring the diameter of the knuckle.

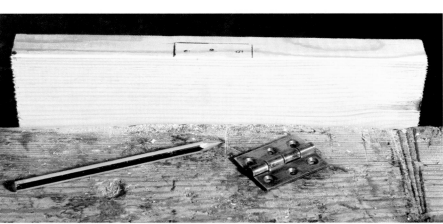

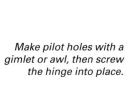

Using the hinge as a guide, mark the screw holes on the edge of the wood.

Make pilot holes with a gimlet or awl, then screw the hinge into place.

156

Once the hinge has been screwed to one of the edges, use it to mark the position on the corresponding piece.

Use a try square to extend the marks made across the edge of the board.

Set the marking gauge to the distance between the edge of the board and the edge of the hinge.

Use the marking gauge to mark the same distance on the other piece of wood.

Place the pieces next to each other and mark the position of the fixing holes, allowing for the thickness of the hinge knuckle.

Make pilot holes in the places marked, using a gimlet or an awl.

The hinge is fixed without being recessed in simple projects where appearance is not of great importance.

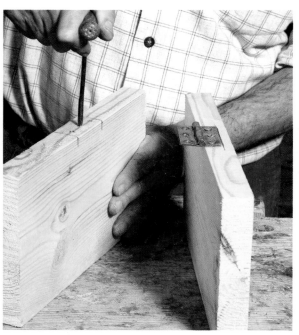

Fixing a recessed hinge

This is a more elegant way of fixing a hinge, used for furniture, doors, casement windows and other frames where appearance is a fundamental requirement. In this case the hinge leaves are recessed so that the surface of each leaf is flush with the wood in which it is set.

Mark the outline of the hinge leaf on the edge in the same way as the previous example. Then set the marking gauge to the thickness of the leaf.

Use the marking gauge to mark the thickness of the hinge leaf on the face which is at right angles to the hinge leaf marked on the edge.

Start making the recess for the hinge leaf, making vertical cuts with the chisel to define the outline.

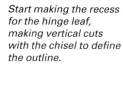

With a very sharp chisel, make some shallow cuts at 60°, about 10 mm (⅜ in) apart within the cut outline.

Detail showing the angled cut of the chisel with the bevel underneath.

Detail showing the levering action of the chisel to remove the remaining wood.

To remove the rest of the wood, work from one side to the other with the chisel, being very careful not to exceed the depth marked with the marking gauge.

After removing all the wood from the recess, check the thickness with the hinge itself. Make further cautious cuts with the chisel until the fit is perfect.

Finish the edges off square by making trimming cuts with the chisel all the way round the outline.

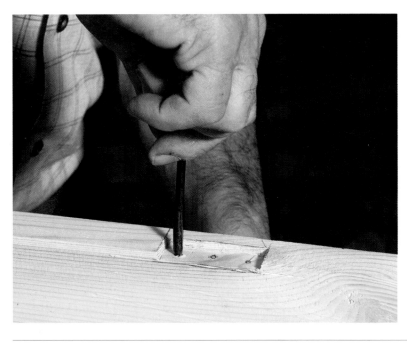

Make pilot holes for the screws with a gimlet or an awl.

Fix the hinge with countersunk screws.

Finishes

Wood can be finished in many ways, the main decision being whether to reveal and enhance the wood itself, or to conceal it with paint. Appearance is usually the main purpose of a finish, but sometimes its prime function is to protect. Many finishes do both.

Applying filler

If the wood is to be painted, any holes, cracks and scratches in the wood must be filled before the work is finally sanded. For this purpose it is best to use a filler with a tone that is similar to the wood on which it is used.

Another aspect to consider is that cumulative finishes alter the final appearance; for example, the number of coats of stain and the use of varnish will give different results. Good preparation is important before any paint, varnish, wax, stain or lacquer is applied.

Traditional gap fillers consist of a mixture of white glue and sawdust from the same wood as the one being treated.

Use a spatula or filling knife to apply gap filler. The paste is pressed hard into the gap or hole to be filled, so that it penetrates properly. Enough filler must be used to stand proud of the surface of the wood, to compensate for the shrinkage which will take place as it dries.

When the filler has dried, rub it with fine sandpaper so that the surface is completely level, smooth and restored.

Another type of traditional filler is made of plaster, glue and yellow ochre pigment. Alternatively cellulose filler and pigment can be used.

To make the paste, the glue, pigment and plaster are mixed together. Sometimes a very small amount of water is needed to make a malleable filler.

The mixture must be sufficiently liquid to fill the irregularities of the wood perfectly, but it must be plastic enough to have texture. Use the filling knife to force it into the crack but leave a small amount proud of the surface to allow for shrinkage. This is sanded smooth later.

Today there are ready-prepared fillers with perfect flexibility for direct application, with a choice of colours to match different tones of wood.

These ready-made fillers are applied in the same way as traditional ones, with the advantage that there is no waste.

Cleaning the surface

After removing the dust made by sanding earlier, some grease marks or fingermarks may be seen. These can easily be removed with a solution of water and turpentine substitute.

Using a cloth moistened with a mixture of water and a few drops of turpentine substitute, rub the surface of the wood to clean off any grease.

Applying a grain filling sealer

Many kinds of wood, such as oak and mahogany, have a fairly open grain with pores which must be filled before applying any kind of finish. If this is not done, an uneven finish will result, first because the pores themselves make the surface irregular, and secondly because the varying porosity will cause a patchy effect. A grain filling sealer will fill the pores and also prevent any absorption of the finish when it is applied.

There are two methods of filling and sealing the wood. The first consists of applying one or more coats of varnish thinned with turpentine substitute or other solvent, using cotton scrim, a brush or a roller. Being transparent, the natural grain of the wood remains clearly visible.

The second consists of directly applying a ready-made grain filling sealer specially prepared for the particular wood involved. This is not transparent, but because it is the same colour as the wood, the effect of the grain is not changed. The filler is applied with a rag.

The materials needed to apply thinned varnish as a grain filling sealer with pieces of cotton scrim.

Applying thinned varnish with pieces of cotton scrim, following the direction of the grain.

Applying thinned varnish with a brush, again following the direction of the grain.

Applying thinned varnish with a high density foam roller, following the direction of the grain.

Applying sealer when the layer of varnish is perfectly dry.

Applying knotting

Knotting is a sealer specially made for knots in the wood which will otherwise ooze resin. This substance is a mixture of shellac dissolved in methylated spirit (shellac solvent). Unless this solution is applied, the resin will bleed through the finish and stain it in a way which is impossible to repair and hard to conceal. There is a simple, ancient method which is also said to be effective: this consists of rubbing the knots with a clove of garlic. But knotting is more reliable.

The items used to apply shellac knotting to prevent knots bleeding.

Applying a fine coat of knotting with a paintbrush, softly dabbing the affected area repeatedly.

Applying wax

Wax should only be applied when the wood has been properly sealed. If this is not done, the wax by itself offers little protection against wear in everyday use. In theory wax accentuates the colour of the wood, and coloured waxes certainly affect its appearance. But it will to a great extent preserve the natural appearance of the wood, enhancing it with a shine which is achieved by burnishing it once it is dry.

Preparing the surface to be waxed by smoothing the sealed surface with a scourer, in this case made of esparto grass.

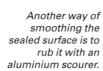

Another way of smoothing the sealed surface is to rub it with an aluminium scourer.

The first coat of wax polish is applied with a piece of aluminium wool using circular movements, followed by further strokes in the direction of the grain.

Once the first coat of wax has dried hard, a second coat is applied with a piece of cotton scrim or a rag.

The wax is left to dry overnight and then burnished to an attractive lustre with a piece of flannel cloth. If a greater shine is required, another thin coat of wax is applied.

Applying wood stains

Wood stain is applied to wood to change its appearance, not to protect it. Both the tone and the colour can be changed with wood stains, and one kind of wood can even be transformed to imitate another. Coloured stains are also available. In all cases, the stain is a transparent finish which allows the grain of the wood to be seen. Stains always darken the wood.

The stains most commonly used are water stains, which are not detrimental to the environment. They spread easily, penetrate well and dry slowly, making it fairly easy to achieve an even colour. Spirit stains dry much more quickly so it is hard to produce an even result unless they are sprayed.

After the colouring process has been completed and when the stain is dry, a transparent varnish should be applied to protect it.

The items needed to prepare and apply walnut stain to a piece of plywood. The stain is made of water-soluble powder stain diluted with water.

The powdered stain is diluted in a quantity of water which varies according to the tone of colour required.

Applying stain with a brush, making rapid brush strokes in the direction of the grain. Flooding should be avoided since this causes variations in tone.

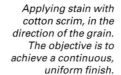

Applying stain with cotton scrim, in the direction of the grain. The objective is to achieve a continuous, uniform finish.

Applying walnut stain to end of the workpiece, using gentle strokes of the brush so that the colour penetrates.

Applying the first and second coats of stain to the surface of a plywood panel in order to achieve the shade of colour which is wanted.

When the colour has been applied but before it has dried, rub a wad of clean cotton over the surface so as to distribute the stain evenly.

163

Applying the water stain may have raised the grain of the wood. This can be smoothed by rubbing with a bundle of esparto grass or a sheet of fine abrasive paper.

When the stain is completely dry, protect it with a coat of clear varnish or lacquer.

Samples of different stain colours being tried out on a panel of veneer-faced chipboard. The range of colours available is very wide.

Applying varnish

There are many varieties of varnish with different characteristics. All of them provide protection against wear and environmental conditions such as moisture which affect wood. Modern polyurethane varnishes are extremely tough, being heat resistant, water-resistant and very hard wearing.

A varnish creates a smooth, colourless surface which may be either glossy or matt, depending on the kind of varnish used. Desirable qualities in a varnish are that it should be quick drying, with a permanent shine, adhering firmly to the surface, not discolouring under any weather conditions, and maintaining its flexibility in extreme conditions.

The items used for varnishing solid wood or wooden panels.

The first coat consists of varnish diluted with 20% white spirit (paint thinner) to ensure greater absorption. Here it is being applied with a wad of cotton.

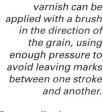

Alternatively, the same diluted varnish can be applied with a brush in the direction of the grain, using enough pressure to avoid leaving marks between one stroke and another.

When a roller is employed, it should be carefully charged with varnish by using a brush, so that the varnish will not drip or harm the surface.

Applying a first coat diluted varnish, using even strokes in the direction of the grain.

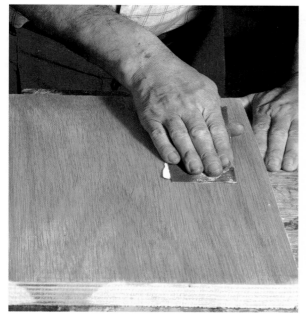

When the first coat of varnish is finished and perfectly dry, it is smoothed by hand with fine abrasive paper, making a perfect surface for the second coat.

Applying a second coat of varnish to the surface. The more coats of protective varnish which are applied, the darker it will become.

Small pieces of wood can be varnished by direct immersion.

Applying paint

Paints for wood provide a coating which is both protective and decorative. They are either oil-based or water-based. Oil paint is fairly slow-drying, but it is best at resisting the expansion and contraction of wood. Water-based acrylic paints are increasingly popular since they are easy to apply, solvent free, and the brushes are very easy to clean since they can be washed in ordinary water. In both cases, the variety of colours available is almost limitless. For the best quality work, primer is recommended both for wood which will be exposed to the weather and for the best wearing qualities in an interior environment. A primer coat seals the wood and provides a smooth base of even absorption for subsequent coats. It is followed by one or two coats of undercoat and a final top coat.

First the surface is given a key by rubbing the panel to be painted with medium grade abrasive paper

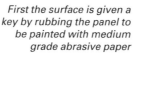

Before applying paint it is essential to clean the surface perfectly of any sawdust and wood residues.

Applying paint to the surface, using brush strokes alternately with and against the grain, and finishing with the grain.

To paint an area with a defined clean edge, use masking tape to protect and isolate the wood which is not to be painted.

When the paint is dry, carefully remove the masking tape.

The sides are painted with repeated gentle dabs of the brush loaded with paint. This ensures that it is properly absorbed by the wood.

Lacquer

With lacquer, wood can be both protected and given a very high gloss. A lacquer is a coating based on coloured varnish which creates a completely smooth surface on the wood, resistant to knocks and atmospheric degradation. Today, lacquers are often two-part cold-cure formulations which set when combined, or in the case of pre-catalysed lacquers, on exposure to the air. They can be applied with brushes or a compressed air spray gun, which produces the best finish by avoiding brush marks altogether. However, a spray gun also has to be skilfully used to produce a good finish.

A mirror finish can be given to lacquer when it has completely set by rubbing it with a burnishing cream.

For a perfect finish without irregularities, the surface must first be carefully prepared by the application of one or two coats of filler or oil-based sealer.

To achieve an even, regular covering, the lacquer should be applied with broad sweeping brush strokes.

High density chipboard panel showing the three stages: in its original state, the intermediate phase with the sealer, and the final lacquered finish.

Distressing or ageing

Sometimes the need arises to give a new piece of wood the appearance of age. This can be done by scorching the surface of the wood with a gas blowtorch. The procedure is much used because of its simplicity, but the heat must be controlled and great care must be taken when applying the flame. Otherwise the surface may be badly burnt, resulting in the loss of too much wood through carbonisation.

Tools used to give the appearance of age to a new piece of wood, in this case pine.

1. Treating a piece of new pine wood to age it. Care must be taken not to burn the surfaces too much.

2. The blowtorch should be held at a constant distance from the surface, to avoid producing unevenly charred areas on the faces and the edges.

3. The charred surface is scrubbed with a brush as a preparation for the desired finish, an operation which removes any loose burnt particles.

4. The process is completed by polishing it with a strong scrubbing motion with a bundle of esparto grass or an aluminium scourer.

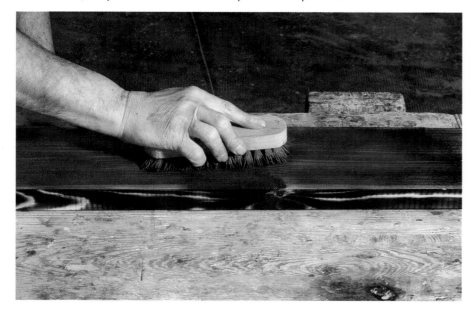

The final finish is created by applying a colourless wax evenly to the faces and edges with a piece of cotton scrim.

Detail showing the appearance before and after the ageing process.

Fixing metal closures (locks, bolts, knobs and handles)

Metal closures for securing doors, drawers and so on are very varied, ranging from the simplest catch, such as a sliding bolt, to the most complicated, secure locks. The simplest types are for convenience, while door locks and window catches often provide security against unauthorised entry as well. The many different designs and shapes cater for various kinds of frames, as well as for the manner in which they are fixed. They can be fitted to the faces of the doors or frames they close, or they may be partially or totally recessed in the edges.

Fitting a sliding bolt

The various types of sliding bolt are among the simplest metal fittings for closing doors and the like, and they are also the simplest to fit.

The items needed to fix a bolt to a panel of high density chipboard.

1. Prepare the screws by rubbing them with a block of wax to make them easier to fit.

2. Line up the two panels next to each other. Draw a line across both panels to mark the position where the bolt will be fixed.

3. Line up the main part of the bolt with the line drawn on the panel and mark the position of the screw holes.

4. Position the bolt housing 2 to 3 mm (³⁄₃₂ to ¹⁄₈ in) away from the edge of the other panel and mark the screw holes.

5. Make pilot holes with a gimlet or an awl and screw the main part of the bolt into position. Complete the operation by screwing the bolt housing into place.

Fitting a cupboard lock in the front face of a panel door

This type of lock is also fairly simple to fit and it has a very neat appearance. It is widely used for pairs of cupboard doors and other kinds of furniture which need a lock but where the security requirement is not particularly high. The lock has a flat bolt which projects behind the other door when the key is turned. The second door is kept closed by interior sliding bolts.

One of the advantages of this kind of lock is that no work is required on the second door with which the bolt engages.

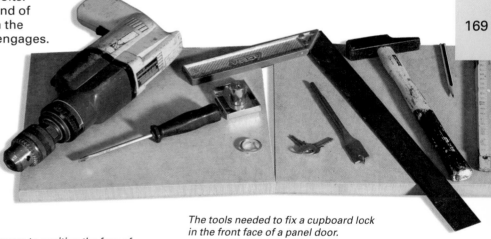

The tools needed to fix a cupboard lock in the front face of a panel door.

1. Use a try square to position the face of the lock about 2 mm (³⁄₃₂ in) inboard from the edge of the panel. This will locate the barrel or cylindrical part of the lock correctly.

2. Holding the lock firmly in position, draw round the perimeter of the lock cylinder which will be set in the wood.

3. Then mark use a try square to mark the centre of the circle which will be drilled to accommodate the cylinder.

4. Use a pair of metal dividers to score round the perimeter of the hole so that the drill bit does not chip it.

5. Drill the cylinder housing using a spade bit of the same width as the diameter of the hole.

6. The drill must be perfectly vertical throughout, and the hole should be drilled in a single operation.

7. So long as the hole is precisely perpendicular, both ends will be exactly the same distance away from the edge of the panel.

8. Fit the lock cylinder into the drilled hole and check that it fits properly.

9. With the lock in position and lined up with the edge of panel, mark the positions of the fixing screws and make pilot holes.

10. Rub the screws with wax to make them easier to turn, particularly in this case where the panel is made of high density chipboard.

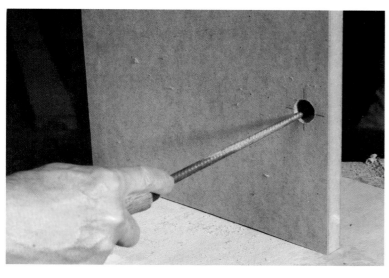

11. Before fitting the lock bezel to the front of the door, ease the edge of the hole with a round rasp.

12. Fit the lock bezel by hammering it into the hole, using an intermediate block of wood so as not to mark it.

13. The finished lock seen from the front.

14. The finished lock seen from the back.

171

Fitting a lock in the edge of a door

This example shows how to fit a conventional lock and the respective door handles to the kind of prefabricated door frequently used for offices and public premises.

1. The components and tools used to fix the lock and door handles.

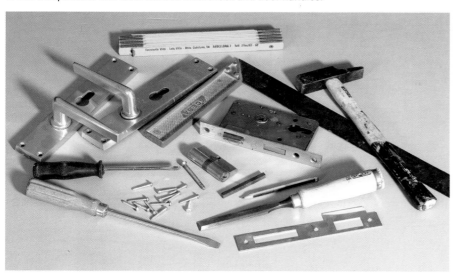

Marking the position of the parts of the lock on the edge of the door

2. Using a rule and try square, mark a line on the front of the door which will locate the central axis of the door handle spindle of the lock, in this case 1.050 m (41 5/8 in)

3. Position the lock so that the centre of the hole for the door handle spindle is aligned with the line just drawn. Using this as a reference point, draw round the lock to mark its outline on the door.

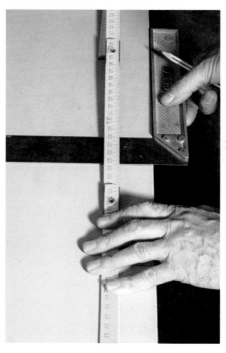

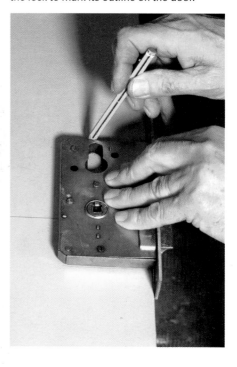

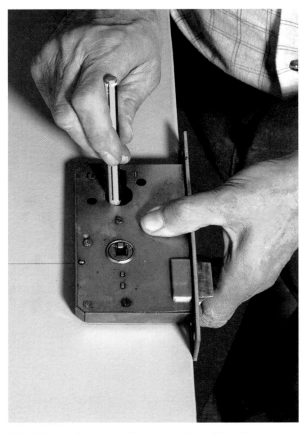

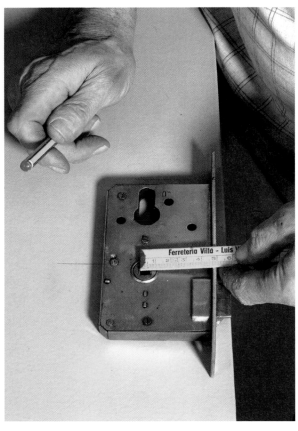

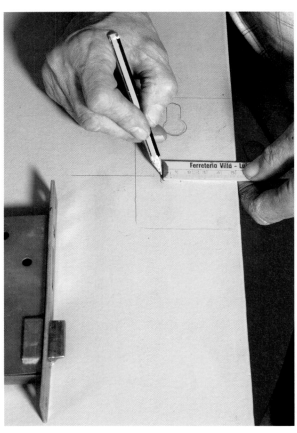

4. Holding the lock in position, mark the outline of the keyhole.

5. Measure the distance on the lock from the centre of the door handle spindle to the front face of the lock, in this case 50 mm (1¹⁵⁄₁₆ in).

6. Transfer this measurement to the line already drawn to mark the height of the door handle axis.

Marking the part of the lock on the edge of the door

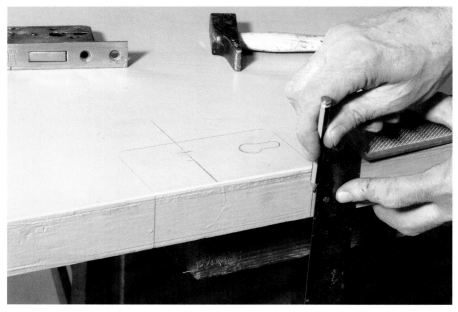

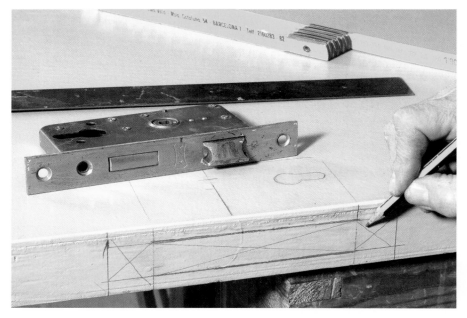

7. The length of the lock is transferred to the adjacent edge of the door with a try square. This will mark the length of the recess to be made in the door for the lock itself.

8. Measure the width of the lock face. Draw two parallel lines the same distance apart, centred in the edge of the door. Measure the length of the lock face and draw lines across the door edge marking the position of the ends of the lock face. The positions of the recess for the lock and the shallower recess for the lock face are now marked.

Cutting the recess in the edge of the door

9. Fix the door firmly to the workbench and chisel out the hole for the lock to a depth of 70 mm (2¾ in), or as required by the lock being used.

10. When the main recess has been cut, carefully chisel out the shallower recess for the faceplate to a depth of 3 mm (⅛ in).

11. Insert the lock, tapping it into place with a hammer if necessary. The front face should be flush with the edge of the door. Insert the fixing screws.

Cutting the hole in the front of the door

12. Cut a hole for the lock with a chisel in the position marked. It should be about 20 x 20 mm (¾ in); the size is not critical so long as it is large enough, since it will be concealed by the backplate. Cut a similar hole for the handle spindle.

13. Insert the lock. Then insert the door handle spindle, leaving enough projecting to engage with the door handle itself when it is fitted.

14. Engage the door handle and its backplate with the handle spindle and lock. When it is correctly positioned, fix it in place with the four screws.

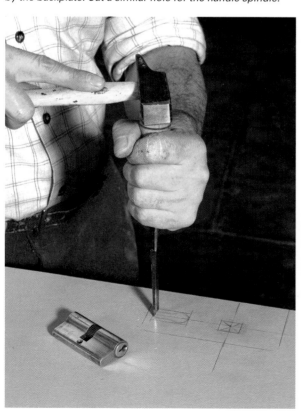

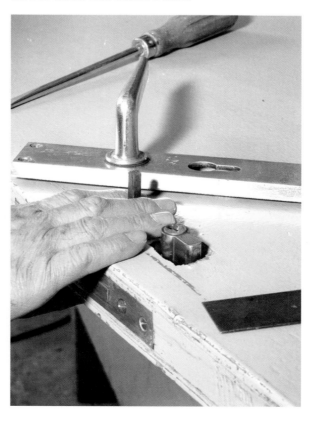

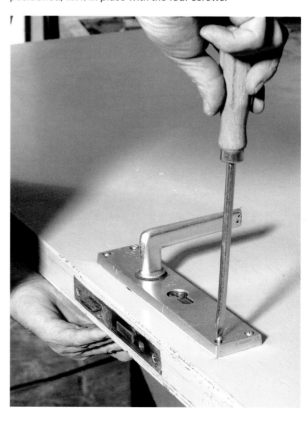

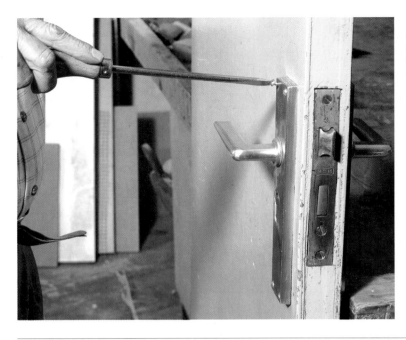

15. Stand the door upright and fit the second door handle to the other side of the door.

16. Check that all the parts are correctly fitted and operate smoothly in all positions.

Fitting a bolt to glazed doors or French windows

This bolt closure for glazed doors is an apparently complicated mechanism, but fitting it does not present any great difficulties. The whole system is operated by vertical rods which raise and lower the top and bottom bolts at the same time.

1. The tools and other parts used to fit a bolt to a pair of glazed doors.

2. Use a tape measure to mark several points an equal distance from the edge of the frame. These will mark the line along which the bolt will be fitted.

3. When at least three marks have been made, join them with a straight edge to make a line along the whole length of the frame.

4. Using this line as the reference, fix the top and bottom guides which will locate the vertical rods.

5. Use the rods themselves to position the intermediate guides correctly.

6. Fit the handle and its connections to the upper and lower rods in the same way.

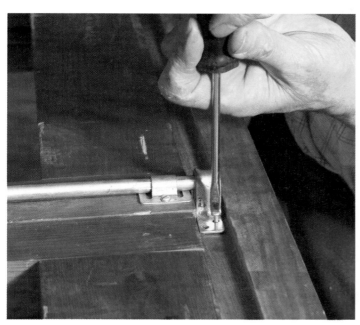

7. Finally, fix the sockets with which the rods engage to the door frame. The exact way of doing this will vary according to their design.

8. The finished bolt fixed in position on the glazed doors.

Fitting escutcheons and pull handles

Escutcheons and faceplates are designed to provide protection to the wood surrounding door knobs, door handles and keyholes from the scratches, knocks and fingermarks which are an inherent part of everyday use. They may be fitted separately or they may be integral with the door handles.

Pull handles are ones which are not part of any closure mechanism; they are used on doors and other parts of a piece of furniture, often in conjunction with simple magnetic catches or sprung hinges.

Escutcheons for door handles and locks

These metal fittings carry out three functions:
• They neatly hide the junction between the hole for the lock and surrounding wood.
• They protect the wood from fingermarks and from scratches made by the key when it is inserted in the lock.
• They have an aesthetic function, improving the appearance of a simple lock or door handle.

A collection of various types of escutcheons and backplates.

Adjusting a protective backplate with an integral door handle.

Knobs and handles

Like escutcheons, knobs and pull handles have an enormous variety of forms, shapes and sizes. The choice is based on their functional and aesthetic relationship with the door, the frame or the piece of furniture on which they are to be installed. They may be made of turned wood, metal, plastic and so on, finished in many different ways.

In general they are not attached to any mechanism; they are used to facilitate opening or closing a door held shut with a simple ball catch or perhaps a magnetic or pressure catch. Handles are often knob-shaped; these are less ergonomic than bar-shaped ones.

Fitting these handles is usually simple, except in those cases where the handle is recessed or contains some kind of a mechanism linked to a bolt or latch.

Fitting a surface-mounted pull handle

A surface-mounted handle is very simple to fit, since apart from drilling the fixing holes, no woodworking operations are needed.

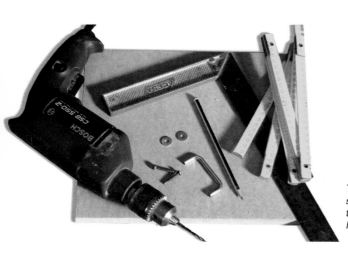

The tool needed to fit a surface-mounted handle, in this case to a door made of high density chipboard.

1. Mark a horizontal line where the central point of the handle is to be. Then make a mark about 30 mm (1⅛ in) from the edge of the door.

2. Using a try square aligned with the measured mark just made, draw the vertical axis of the pull handle.

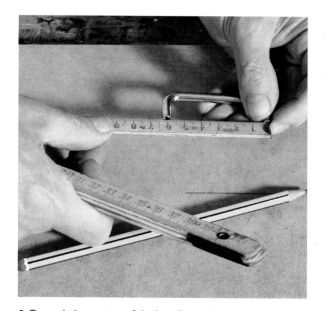

3. To mark the centres of the handle on the panel, measure the distance between the handle's fixing holes.

4. Use the ruler and the measurement just taken to position the holes equally on each side of the horizontal line. Use the handle itself as a template to mark the holes exactly.

5. Drill the fixing holes, using a bit slightly larger than the maximum diameter of the screw shank, to allow a little clearance.

177

6. Put a washer on one screw and push it through the door from the back and screw it a little way into the handle. Repeat with the second screw.

7. Adjust the handle to the correct position and tighten the screws. The washers will prevent the screws sinking into the wood and damaging it.

8. The handle mounted on the door neatly fits the fingers of the hand.

9. The surface-mounted handle fixed to the door.

Fitting a recessed handle

A recessed handle is one which is set in the
surface of the door so both the operating part
and the fixing screws are flush.

1. Place the recessed
handle in the chosen
position on the door,
usually centrally
between top and
bottom, and set in an
aesthetically pleasing
distance from the
edge.

2. Mark lines defining
the top and bottom
of the recessed handle
with a try square.

3. Draw the vertical
axis of the handle. All
the lines must be
square to each other
and parallel to the
sides of the door.

4. Measure the
dimensions of the part
of the handle which
will be recessed into
the surface of the door.

5. Transfer the measurements of the part to be cut
away to the panel. Make a vertical cut with a chisel
all the way round this outline.

6. Cut the recess with the chisel, using it with the bevel
down to split slices of wood away from the recess.
As the work progresses, deepen the vertical cuts
until the correct depth for the recess is reached.

7. Use the same chisel to clean up the recess,
making short cuts by hitting the chisel
handle with the hand to remove any
roughness and irregularities.

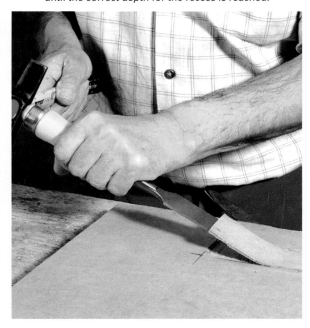

8. Fit the handle temporarily to check that the recess is the right size. Use a protective piece of wood to knock it into position without damaging it with the hammer. Make any necessary adjustments to make the recess deep enough and to achieve a tight fit.

9. To mark the position of the fixing screws, measure the distance between them in the handle and transfer this to the central axis line drawn on the work.

10. Drill pilot holes for the fixing screws, keeping the drill vertical while doing so.

11. With the handle in place, turn the door over and insert the fixing screws through the holes. Tighten them securely.

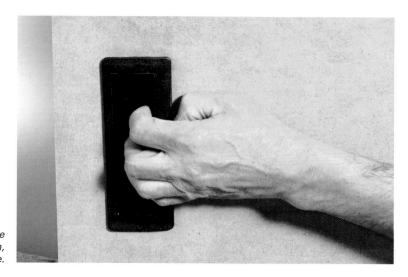

12. The handle fixed in position, showing it in use.

Fitting a door knob with integral surface-mounted backplate

In this example the door knob is integral with the protective backplate which also conceals the holes made for the spindle. This surface-mounted arrangement results in an assembly which is extremely strong and resistant to heavy use.

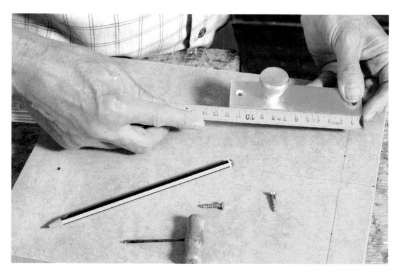

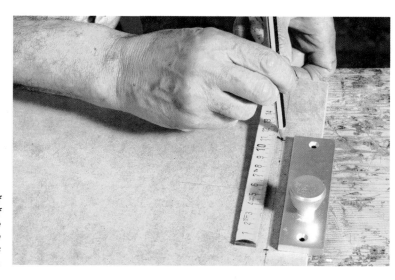

1. Take the overall measurements of the backplate. Draw a vertical line marking the central axis of the fitting. Position this so that there will be at least 10mm (⅜ in) between the edge of the backplate and the edge of the door.

2. Mark the position of the top and bottom of backplate on the vertical line, using the measurements just taken.

3. Double check that the position of the backplate is at least 10 mm (⅜ in) from the edge of the door.

4. With the backplate in the correct place, mark the position of the screws and make pilot holes.

5. With the work supported by a firm, steady surface, screw in the fixing screws until they are flush with the backplate.

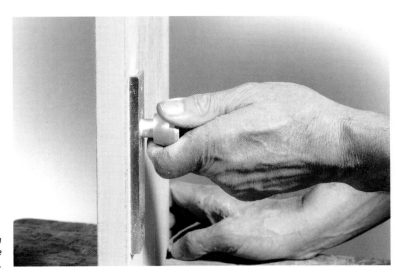

6. The door knob with its integral backplate fixed in place.

Lipping

It is true that panels of wood used for cupboard doors, shelves and similar purposes can carry out their prime function without any additions. But there is not doubt that the application of some extra material can improve both the appearance and the wearing qualities of the item in question. Such is the case with the addition of lipping, a strip of material which is attached round all or part of the perimeter of the piece.

The materials used for lipping include wood or plastic veneer, solid wood and metals.

Metal lipping

In this case, the protective lipping for the high density chipboard panel consists of a lacquered L-shaped metal channel, with dimensions large enough to cover the edge of the panel completely. It is attached to the edge with contact adhesive.

Items needed to fit a protective edge to a chipboard panel.

1. Fix the panel to the bench and remove any irregularities from the edge to be protected using medium grade abrasive paper.

2. To define the areas to be covered with contact adhesive, position the lipping itself on the edge and use it to draw a line on the panel.

3. Fix the panel on its side and apply the adhesive to the edge with a spatula.

4. Put the panel on a horizontal surface and apply adhesive to the area marked, being careful not to go over the line.

5. Next apply glue to the internal sides of the L-shaped lipping. When the adhesive on all the surfaces is dry, position the lipping carefully and press it firmly into position.

6. This shows the final appearance of the panel with metal lipping, which will protect it from abrasion, knocks and damp.

7. Detail of the edge of the panel with its metal lipping perfectly fitted to the size of the piece.

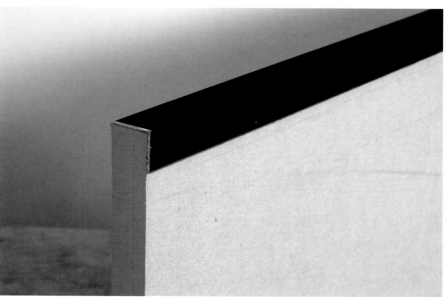

Fitting solid wood lipping to a chipboard panel

In this case, the edge of the panel is protected by an L-shaped wood moulding which will protect the raw edge of the chipboard from knocks, abrasion and humidity.

This kind of lipping can be fixed in various ways, either with contact adhesive, as in the previous example, or glued with white glue and pinned into place, as shown below.

The tools and materials needed to cover the edge of a chipboard panel with wooden lipping using the contact adhesive method described in the previous example.

The tools and materials needed to cover the edge of a chipboard panel with wooden lipping using white glue and pins.

1. Use the L-shaped wooden moulding in position to mark the extent of the area to be glued.

2. With the panel horizontal so that the glue will not drip, apply the white glue with a brush, keeping within the line just marked.

3. Position the edge moulding and fix it firmly with pins at intervals of about 200 mm (8 in). To avoid bruising the wood with the hammer, do not knock them in completely.

4. Complete the process of pinning the edging by using a nail punch to sink the heads just below the surface of the wood.

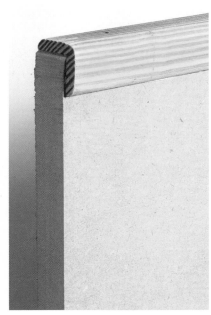

5. Detail of the panel with its wooden lipping covering and protecting the edge.

Solid wood lipping with mitred corners

Sometimes lipping used to protect the edge is simply a rectangular strip of wood the same width as the thickness of the edge of the panel. This kind of lipping has the advantage that it is easier to make mitred corner joints with rectangular shape than with an L-shape.

1. To determine the lengths of wooden strip to be used, measure the dimensions of the piece to be protected. Allow enough extra to cater for the mitred corners.

2. Use a mitre saw to cut the 45° mitres for the corners, or use a backsaw and mitre box to achieve the same result.

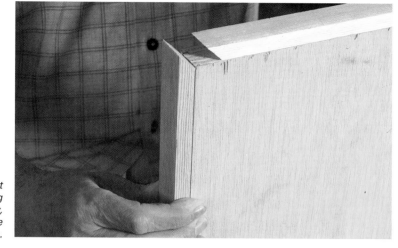

3. Check that the cut pieces of the lipping fit the panel neatly, particularly at the corners.

4. Quickly spread white glue over the edges of the panel. A fine brush should be used so as not to apply the glue too thickly.

5. Position the lipping carefully and fix it in place with pins.

6. The pins apply pressure to the glue so no cramping is needed. As before, hammer the pins only part of the way in.

7. Finish inserting the pins by using a nail punch to sink the heads below the surface of the wood.

8. When the glue is completely dry, finish the work by sanding with medium and then fine abrasive paper.

9. Detail of the protective wood edging showing the mitred corner joint.

Making projects

To complete the section on woodworking, the following pages consist of step-by-step instructions for making a number of practical projects. These examples cover a wide range of woodworking skills and they therefore provide invaluable practice as well as being useful in themselves.

The projects included cover three main areas. Some are projects produced from raw materials in the workshop, while the other two categories include projects which consist of assembling and putting together individual pre-fabricated elements, such as cabinets andinstalling ready-made floor coverings. These illustrate some important changes which have taken place in the last few years in the field of handling wood and making furniture such as kitchen cabinets, in particular with the increased use of man-made boards.

Originally workshop projects included anything and everything that was produced in a workshop, while assembly projects referred to objects that were made outdoors or on-site because of their large size. Assembly projects now describe the numerous pieces of flat-pack furniture where the task involves assembling various pre-fabricated components, available on the market kits. These assembly projects only require a basic technical knowledge.

Other assembly projects include laying parquet wooden floor coverings, where large areas can be covered in a very short time, since the laying process is relatively simple.

Workshop projects

This section contains step-by-step constructional details for wooden objects for various purposes: a garden fence with a gate for the garden, a trellis for covered outdoor areas such as a terrace or balcony, saw horses for the workshop and a wine rack for indoors.

Laying parquet flooring

The techniques used to lay floors are illustrated and described, together with all the necessary equipment. Pre-fabricated parquet and laminates vary enormously in composition and thickness. They are easy to lay and can be used in rooms of all sizes.

Assembling flat-packs

This section explains how to assemble a cupboard, bought as a flat-pack of separate pre-fabricated components. This project is a typical example of the new trend of supplying furniture as non-assembled kits of finished component parts, with all the metal fittings necessary to assemble them

Garden fence

This relatively simple practical exercise with its repetitive stages introduces a section in which a range of objects are produced which will provide an insight into the versatile world of woodworking. This project describes the making of a section of a garden fence, while the next project shows how to make a gate to go with it.

Each stage of the project introduces different tools, such as the bench mitre saw used make the pointed ends of the slats and the try-square used to check that all the slats are the same length. The quantities in the list of materials are for a single section of the fence with five uprights.

MATERIALS NEEDED

For each section of five uprights:

- Softwood planed and squared:
  - For the horizontal cross bars: 2 pieces 2.0 x 6.0 x 100.0 cm (25/32 x 2⅜ x 40 in)
  - For the vertical uprights: 5 pieces 2.0 x 7.0 x 100.0 cm (25/32 x 2¾ x 40 in)
  - For the posts: 1 piece 4.5 x 7.0 x 170.0 cm (1¾ x 2¾ x 67 in)
- Woodworking white glue
- Nails 4.0 cm (1½ in)
- Medium grade sandpaper
- Varnish
- Paint brush

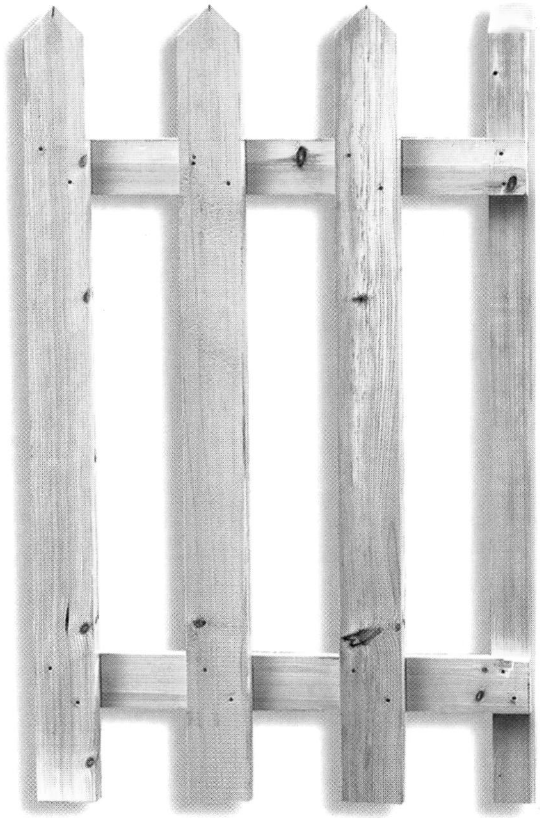

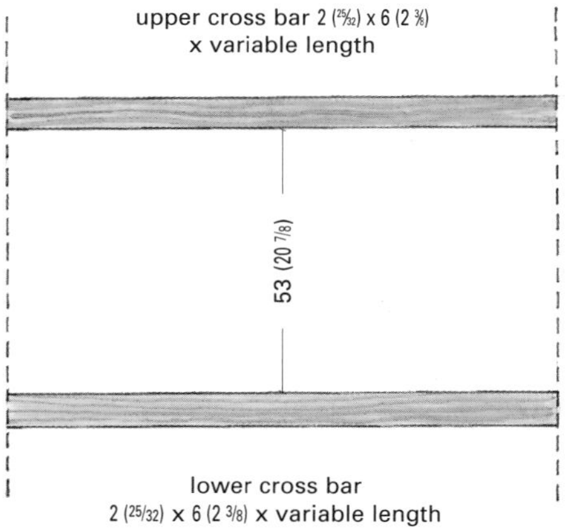
upper cross bar 2 (25/32) x 6 (2 3/8)
x variable length
53 (20 7/8)
lower cross bar
2 (25/32) x 6 (2 3/8) x variable length

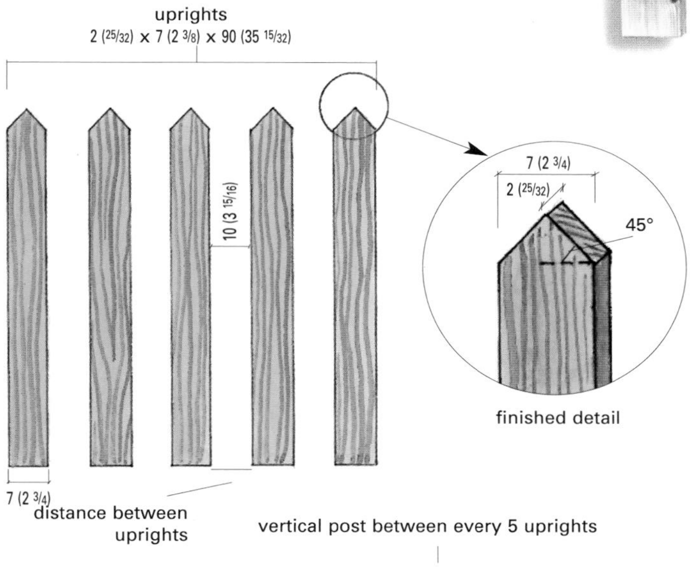
uprights
2 (25/32) x 7 (2 3/8) x 90 (35 15/32)
10 (3 15/16)
7 (2 3/4)
distance between
uprights
7 (2 3/4)
2 (25/32)
45°
finished detail

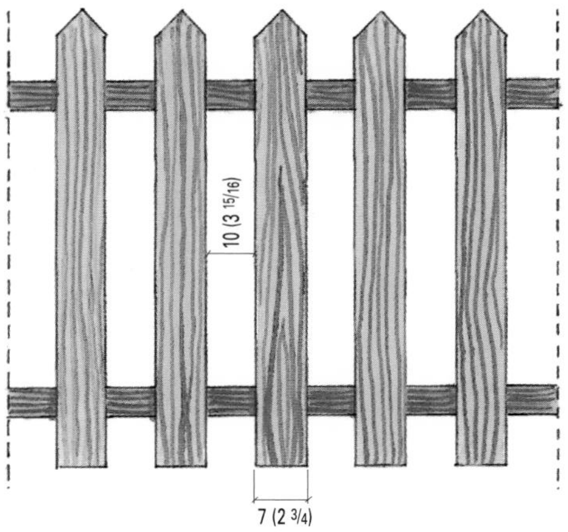
10 (3 15/16)
7 (2 3/4)

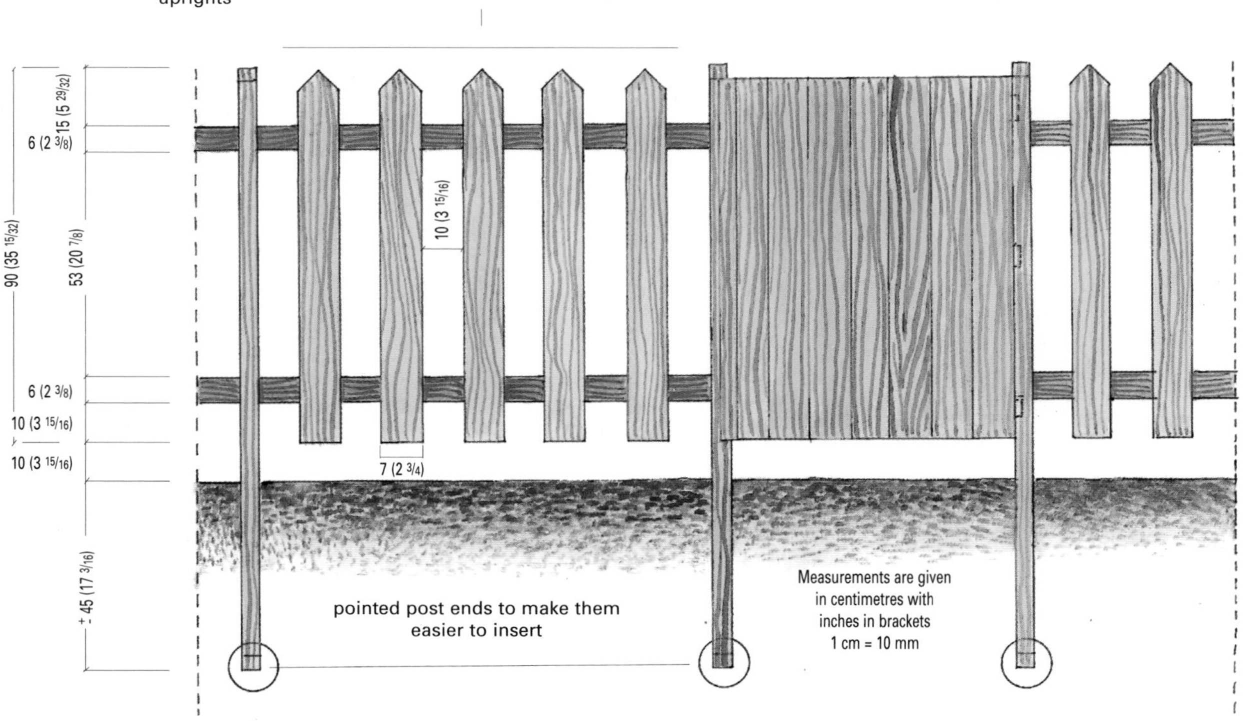
vertical post between every 5 uprights
15 (5 29/32)
6 (2 3/8)
90 (35 15/32)
53 (20 7/8)
6 (2 3/8)
10 (3 15/16)
10 (3 15/16)
± 45 (17 3/16)
10 (3 15/16)
7 (2 3/4)
pointed post ends to make them
easier to insert
Measurements are given
in centimetres with
inches in brackets
1 cm = 10 mm

Step-by-step instructions

Preparing the uprights

1. The tools and materials needed to make a section of the garden fence.

2. With a try square mark a line across one end of the uprights, two or three at a time. The final length will be measured from this line.

3. Make the square cuts accurately, using a bench mitre saw.

4. From the end just cut, mark a line 90 cm (35^{15}/$_{32}$ in) on each of the uprights of the fence.

5. Mark the centre point of the width on each upright.

6. Draw a line at 45° from this mark to each side, making a symmetrical point.

7. Cut along the marked lines to make the pointed ends, using the bench mitre saw for accuracy.

Marking out the joints between the uprights and the cross bars

8. Before making any marks, it is essential to line up the pieces accurately. This is done by aligning the square ends with a try square.

9. Measure a distance 15 cm (5^{29}⁄$_{32}$ in) from the pointed end of the uprights to define the position of the upper cross bar.

10. At this point draw a line across all the uprights with a try square.

11. Taking this line as a reference point, use the cross bar to mark its width, defining the are to be glued.

12. In the same way as for the upper cross bar, measure a distance of 10 cm (3^{15}⁄$_{16}$ in) from the lower end of the uprights to establish the position of the lower cross bar.

13. Mark a line at this point across all the uprights using a try square.

14. Using the cross bar itself, mark its width from the reference line just drawn.

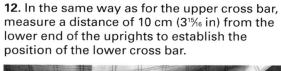

Using the spacer

15. The spacer consists of a piece of wood of the same width as the distance between the uprights, in this case 10 cm (3¹⁵⁄₁₆ in).

16. Begin the process of joining the uprights and cross bars by lining up the spacer and the uprights, with the areas marked for gluing facing upwards.

17. Position the cross bar, leaving an extra amount projecting at the end side to be fixed to the post in the ground later.

Gluing and nailing the joints

18. Apply the glue to the marked areas with the spacer in position.

19. Reinforce the glue by nailing the lower cross bar to the uprights using two diagonal nails.

20. Attach the upper cross bar in the same way, again using two diagonal nails in each joint.

Finishing

21. When both cross bars have been glued and screwed the correct distance apart, smooth all the surfaces with medium grade sandpaper.

22. Since the garden fence will spend its life outdoors, it must be properly protected with two or three coats of weather-resistant exterior varnish.

23. If there is any doubt about the uprights being vertical, it is worth checking with the spacer piece to confirm that the space between the uprights is 10 cm (3$\frac{15}{16}$ in).

24. A completed representative section of the garden fence, ready to be extended with another module or joined to a garden gate.

Here a section of garden fence is terminated and joined to a garden gate. It is attached to the post on which the gate hangs, which is firmly fixed in the ground so that the whole structure is solid and secure.

Garden gate

This practical exercise has been designed as an extension of the previous project for fence sections. Hung between two posts, this garden gate is made by joining individual slats with Z-shaped bracing.

To make this gate you will need a template in order to transfer or check the dimensions and angles of the larger components, and a sliding bevel to mark out and check the angles. The various stages include the preparation of corner bridle koints with mortise and tenon for the frame, and shaping of the pointed ends with mitre cuts.

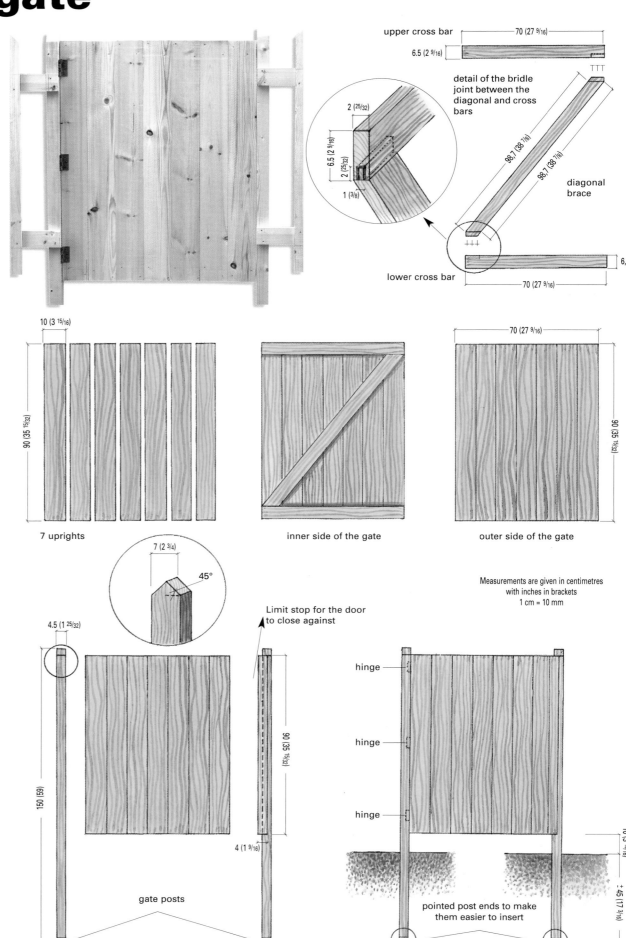

upper cross bar — 70 (27 9/16)

6.5 (2 9/16)

detail of the bridle joint between the diagonal and cross bars

2 (25/32)

6.5 (2 9/16)

2 (25/32)

1 (3/8)

98.7 (38 7/8)

98.7 (38 7/8)

diagonal brace

lower cross bar

70 (27 9/16)

6,5 (2 9

10 (3 15/16)

90 (35 15/32)

7 uprights

inner side of the gate

70 (27 9/16)

90 (35 15/32)

outer side of the gate

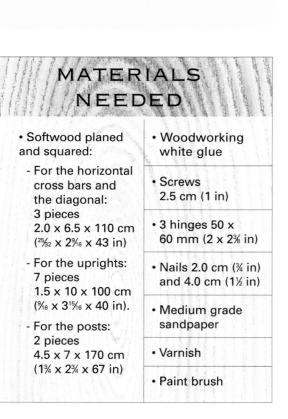

MATERIALS NEEDED

• Softwood planed and squared:	• Woodworking white glue
- For the horizontal cross bars and the diagonal: 3 pieces 2.0 x 6.5 x 110 cm (25/32 x 2 9/16 x 43 in)	• Screws 2.5 cm (1 in)
	• 3 hinges 50 x 60 mm (2 x 2 3/8 in)
- For the uprights: 7 pieces 1.5 x 10 x 100 cm (9/16 x 3 15/16 x 40 in).	• Nails 2.0 cm (3/4 in) and 4.0 cm (1 1/2 in)
- For the posts: 2 pieces 4.5 x 7 x 170 cm (1 3/4 x 2 3/4 x 67 in)	• Medium grade sandpaper
	• Varnish
	• Paint brush

7 (2 3/4)

45°

4.5 (1 25/32)

Limit stop for the door to close against

150 (59)

90 (35 15/32)

4 (1 9/16)

gate posts

Measurements are given in centimetres with inches in brackets
1 cm = 10 mm

hinge

hinge

hinge

10 (3 15/16)

45 (17 3/

pointed post ends to make them easier to insert

Step-by-step instructions

Drawing the template

1. The tools and materials needed to make the garden gate.

2. Place one of the cross bars along the edge of a rectangular panel of plywood and draw its width. The set square will help to ensure that the line is square with the sides of the panel.

3. Having drawn the width and the length – 70 cm (27³⁄₁₆ in) – of one of the cross bars, draw a right-angled line to mark the size of the finished gate.

4. On the opposite side, and at right angles, draw the width of the other crossbar, 90 cm (35¹⁵⁄₃₂ in) overall from the one drawn first.

5. With the upper and lower cross bars marked, draw the diagonal, using the wood itself as a template.

6. Mark the depth of the bridle joint, 2 cm (²⁵⁄₃₂ in), where the pieces meet.

7. The drawing of the template is finished. It shows the correct arrangement of the three cross members used in this kind of gate.

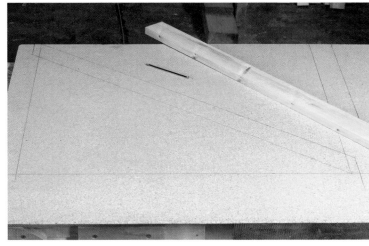

Transferring the measurements

8. To mark out the tenon of the bridle joint, first transfer the lengths to the sides from the lines drawn on the template.

9. Extend this mark round all sides using a try square. This will mark where the cuts are to be made later.

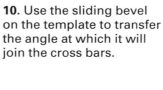

10. Use the sliding bevel on the template to transfer the angle at which it will join the cross bars.

11. On each side of the diagonal piece, draw a parallel line 2 cm (²⁵⁄₃₂ in) from the line already marked, using the sliding bevel. This will define the depth of the tenon.

Cutting the tenon of the bridle joint

12. Using a backsaw, cut the waste away to the upper mark. The workpiece is supported on the bench.

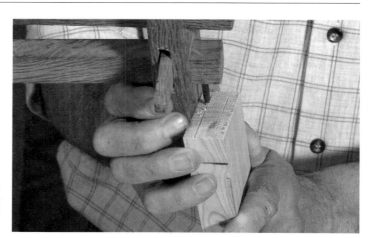

13. With a marking gauge, mark the tenon on the end just cut, centred and 1 cm (⅜ in) wide.

14. Use the marking gauge at the same setting to extend the marks to the corresponding sides, defining the depth of the tenon.

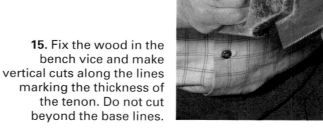

15. Fix the wood in the bench vice and make vertical cuts along the lines marking the thickness of the tenon. Do not cut beyond the base lines.

16. With the piece horizontal, cut away the waste on each side of the tenon.

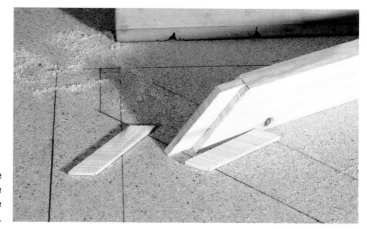

17. The finished tenon of the bridle joint which will join the diagonal member to the upper and lower cross bars.

Cutting the mortise of the bridle joint

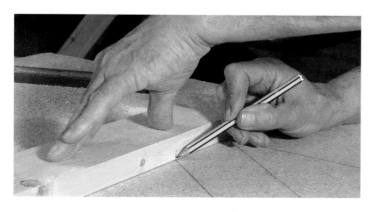

18. With each of the two cross bars cut to 70 cm (27⅝ in) long, use the template to mark the side at the point where it meets the diagonal brace.

19. To ensure that the measurements on the two cross bars are the same, mark both pieces at the same time using a try square.

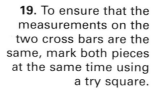

20. At one of the ends, mark the 2 cm (²⁵⁄₃₂ in) depth of the mortise part of the bridle joint which will engage with the tenon of the diagonal.

21. Mark the width of the mortise with the marking gauge set 5 mm (³⁄₁₆ in) from the edges of the narrower edge. The mortise itself will be 1 cm (⅜ in) wide.

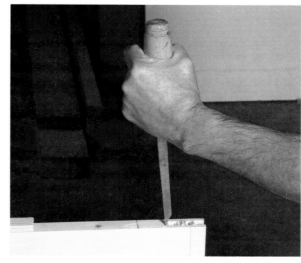

22. Cut out the mortise with a chisel with a blade of the same width. First make vertical cuts with the chisel along the whole length.

23. Then use the chisel as a wedge with the bevel down to remove the waste.

24. When the mortise and tenon parts of the bridle joint are completed, carry out a test assembly before gluing. If necessary, remove any roughness with a rasp.

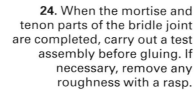

Gluing the cross bars

25. With all parts of the joint sanded smooth, apply glue to the faces which will be in contact with each other.

26. Assemble the joint and press it firmly together, cleaning off the excess glue with a damp cloth to avoid leaving marks.

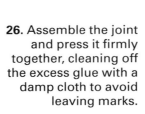

27. Before the glue has set, place the assembly on the template to check that the angles are correct. Adjust slightly if necessary so that it dries in the correct shape.

28. When the assembly has completely dried, cut off the waste part of each joint, which projects beyond the end.

194

Marking and gluing the uprights

29. Arrange the 7 uprights 1 x 10 x 100 cm (⅜ x 3¹⁵⁄₁₆ x 40 in) on the newly completed frame and mark the finished length of 90 cm (35¹⁵⁄₃₂ in), using the frame as a template.

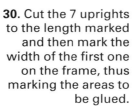

30. Cut the 7 uprights to the length marked and then mark the width of the first one on the frame, thus marking the areas to be glued.

31. Apply glue to the relevant part of the frame.

32. To strengthen the joint, reinforce it with two nails at each end, knocked in diagonally.

33. Repeat the operations of marking out, gluing and nailing until the supporting frame is completely covered, making a continuous, smooth surface. This is the outer side of the gate.

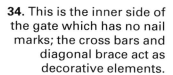

34. This is the inner side of the gate which has no nail marks; the cross bars and diagonal brace act as decorative elements.

Making the posts

35. Cut the two 4.5 x 7 cm (1¾ x 2¾ in) pieces of wood to a final length of 150 cm (59 in). Mark the centre of the wider face and draw two lines at an angle of 45° with a gauge, thus marking a point of 5 cm (1¹⁵⁄₁₆ in) at the end.

36. Cut along the marked angled lines to make a point which will finish off the top of the posts.

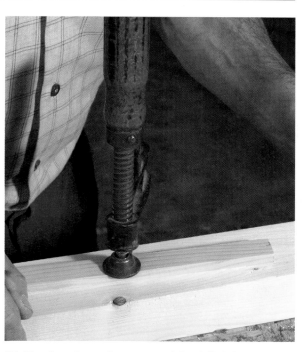

37. To give the points a good final finish, use medium grade sandpaper to smooth the rough edges. Make similar points at the other ends of the posts so that they will be easier to knock into the ground.

195

Fitting the hinges

38. Begin the process of fitting the hinges by offering up the gate to the gate post which will carry it.

39. The gate is lined up with the base of the triangle forming the point of the post and with its centre line, so that it is closer to the outer side, as shown in the photograph.

40. With the position of the gate determined, mark a line 7 cm (2¾ in) from the top. This will locate the top of the upper hinge. Position the second hinge the same distance from the bottom, and the third halfway between them.

41. With the hinges in place, mark the fixing holes using the hinges themselves as a template.

42. Make pilot holes and screw the hinges to the gate post.

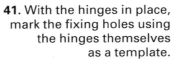

43. Screw the three hinges to the surface of the door

Fitting the stop

44. Now the gate is fixed to the post, mark the other post with the position of the stop which prevents the gate opening outwards. This will be the same length as the gate itself so as to be as effective as possible.

45. The stop is 2 x 4 x 90 cm (²⁵⁄₃₂ x ¹⁹⁄₁₆ x 35¹⁵⁄₃₂ in) and it is aligned with the centre line of the second post. Mark the post accordingly.

46. Glue the edges which will be in contact, position the length of wood and nail it at intervals of about 20 cm (8 in) with 4 cm (1½ in) nails.

47. Sand all surfaces with medium grade sandpaper. Then cover all parts of the gate and the posts with two or three coats of exterior grade varnish.

The finished gate in the fence

The garden gate installed with the garden fence described in the previous project.

The finished garden gate and fence installed in typical surroundings.

48. The finished door seen from the outside.

49. The finished door seen from the inside.

Trellis

This exercise describes the step-by-step construction of a trellis partition. It is true that this is a fairly small trellis but a larger one would be made in the same way. The trellis is perfect in the garden as a support structure for climbing plants, but it can also be used indoors as an elegant room divider to separate parts of the living areas, perhaps with indoor plants climbing up it.

This practical exercise involves arranging and fixing small wood laths, using a square to make and check 90° angles, using laths as spacers, making grooves in the frame with a table circular saw, making and securing corner joints, and handling screw cramps.

MATERIALS NEEDED

- Softwood planed and squared
- for the frame:
  2 pieces 160 x 35 x 35 cm (63 x 13¾ x 13¾ in)
  2 pieces 90 x 35 x 35 cm (63 x 13¾ x 13¾ in)
- for the latticework:
  50 laths of various lengths, 15 x 5 mm (⁹⁄₁₆ x ³⁄₁₆ in)

- Auxiliary pieces (temporary spacers and supports):
  2 or 3 laths of various lengths, 20 x 5 mm (²⁵⁄₃₂ x ³⁄₁₆ in)

- Woodworking white glue

- Panel pins 8 mm long

- Panel pins 25 mm long

- Sandpaper

- Linseed oil

- Varnish

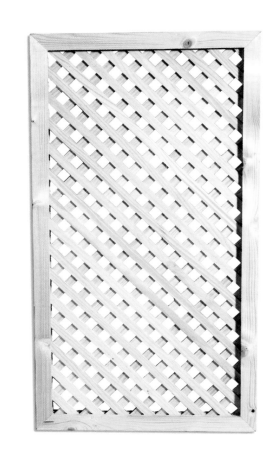

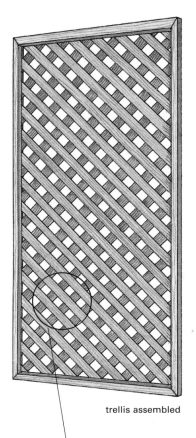

trellis assembled

trellis dismantled

60 (23 ⁵⁄₈)

53 (20 ⁷⁄₈)

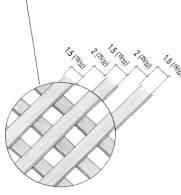

1.5 (¹⁹⁄₃₂) 2 (²⁵⁄₃₂) 1.5 (¹⁹⁄₃₂) 2 (²⁵⁄₃₂) 1.5 (¹⁹⁄₃₂)

detail of the structure

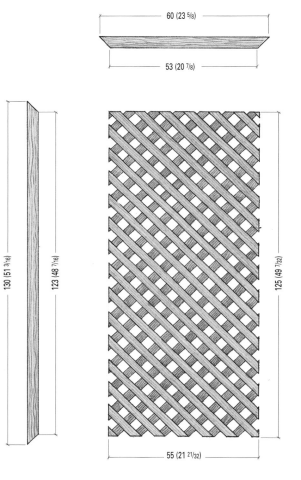

130 (51 ³⁄₁₆)

123 (48 ⁷⁄₁₆)

125 (49 ⁷⁄₃₂)

55 (21 ²¹⁄₃₂)

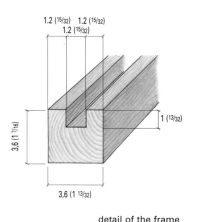

1.2 (¹⁵⁄₃₂) 1.2 (¹⁵⁄₃₂)
1.2 (¹⁵⁄₃₂)

3,6 (1 ⁷⁄₁₆)

1 (¹³⁄₃₂)

3,6 (1 ¹³⁄₃₂)

detail of the frame

Measurements are given in centimetres
with inches in brackets
1 cm = 10 mm

Step-by-step instructions

Making the latticework

1. These laths are used to make the latticework part of the trellis and as spacers. It will be completed with some thicker lengths of timber for the frame which will contain the lattice. The project is a simple one but it demands patience and diligence to make it.

2. Assemble the structure of the trellis on a perfectly flat surface. Start the process by drawing a line on the surface at right angles to the edge. This will be the reference line from which the whole assembly will be taken.

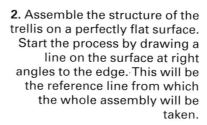

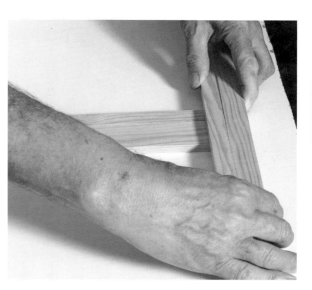

3. Begin the structure by taking two laths for the trellis, and place one of the auxiliary laths as a spacer piece between them. This will keep them 2 cm ($^{25}\!/_{32}$ in) apart and parallel. Align one end of these three pieces and temporarily fix them together with a cramp. This will be the base to which a number of laths will be fixed at right angles.

4. Start fixing the pieces to the base. Use one spacer piece to position the first lath 2 cm ($^{25}\!/_{32}$ in) away from the end of the base piece.

5. The position of the pieces must be checked and corrected with the try square before they are finally fixed. Use the same pieces to mark the area which will be glued, first using the spacer piece on its own to draw the upper line.

6. Finish marking out the rest of the area to be glued by adding the lath itself to the spacer piece and drawing a line. Check that it is at right angles with the try square.

7. Once the area to be glued is marked, apply glue with a fine brush to the two base pieces which will be part of the trellis. Be careful not to get any glue on the spacer piece between them.

8. After glue has been applied to the marked area of the two laths, position the upper lath at right angles. Fix it with two panel pins 8 mm (⁵⁄₁₆ in) long, nailing one to the centre of each joint.

9. Next position the spacer piece and check again that the angle of 90° is maintained, since any inaccuracy will be increased as the number of laths used to complete the task gets larger.

10. The gluing and nailing of the first lath of the upper layer begins to make the structure more rigid. This means that that it will not need to be checked for right angles so frequently, although is should continue to be checked from time to time. Use the separator to mark the upper line for positioning the next lath.

11. Mark the areas to be glued in the same way as before, using the lath itself as a template to draw the line defining the lower limit of the glue.

12. The procedure of gluing is repeated. Apply just enough glue to fix the lath, to minimise the risk of the spacer of the base becoming glued.

13. Use spare spacer pieces to support the horizontal laths so that the pieces being fixed are stable while and after they are fixed.

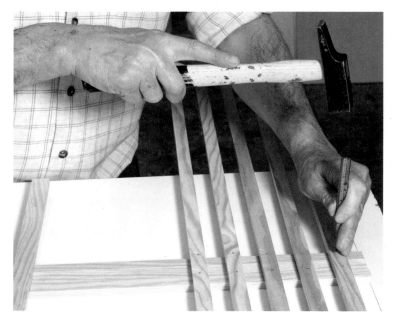

14. When five or six laths have been fixed, use a nail punch and hammer to knock the heads of the panel pins below the surface of the wood. This is done every few laths so as not to miss any.

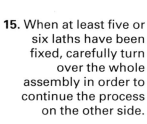

15. When at least five or six laths have been fixed, carefully turn over the whole assembly in order to continue the process on the other side.

16. For the other side of the trellis, carry on in exactly the same way as previously described. Use more auxiliary laths where necessary to support the assembly and keep it stable.

17. The process of marking out will no longer need to be checked with the try square at this stage, because the assembly will now be rigid enough not to be shifted by the positioning of the spacer piece.

18. The gluing must still be applied sparingly to the areas marked, so as to avoid any glue oozing out which would require more work to remove during the finishing stage.

19. As each section of the lattice work is completed, go back and sink the heads of the panel pins with the nail punch.

20. Since the process involves working alternately from one side and then the other, the panel pins will also appear on both sides of the trellis. But as they will hardly be visible after being punched under the surface, this does not matter.

Cutting the trellis and establishing the length of the frame.

21. To mark out and cut the the trellis accurately so that it is at 45°, use the same rectangular base on which the work so far has been marked out and executed. It is important that, to arrive at the correct final size of the trellis, 130 x 60 cm (51³⁄₁₆ x 23⅝ in) the dimensions of the latticework should be 125 x 55 cm (49³⁄₁₆ x 21⅝ in).

22. Fix the latticework firmly to the base so that the laths are at exactly 45° to the frame which will contain it. Mark the required size of 125 x 55 cm (49³⁄₁₆ x 21⅝ in) and cut away the waste with a backsaw.

23. The trimmed lattice is used as a reference from which the lengths of the wood for the frame will be measured, about 10 cm (4 in) longer on each side. A good surplus is required to create the corner joints conveniently and accurately.

Cutting the groove in the frame

24. Use a table saw to cut the groove along the pieces which will become the frame. Set the saw blade to make a cut 1 cm (⅜ in) deep.

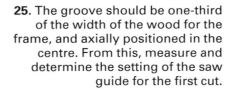

25. The groove should be one-third of the width of the wood for the frame, and axially positioned in the centre. From this, measure and determine the setting of the saw guide for the first cut.

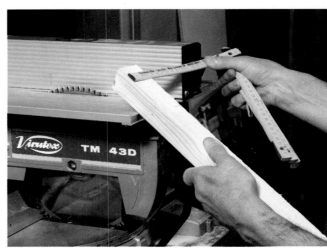

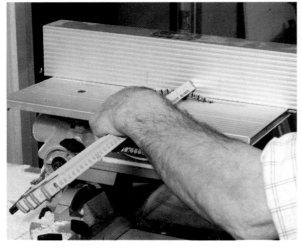

26. Set the saw guide so that the distance between it and the blade is the same as that just measured.

27. For a groove 1 cm (⅜ in) wide by 1 cm (⅜ in) deep, make repeated cuts so as to arrive at the width required. The measurements should be marked accordingly on the end of each piece of wood.

28. Assemble the trellis temporarily to test that the grooves have been correctly and evenly cut, with sufficient depth and width. Move the latticework from side to side in the groove to check that there is no excessive resistance.

Cutting the corner joints and defining the length of the frame

29. To define the point from which the corner mitre is cut, fit the lattice in the groove and mark a right-angled line at the point which leaves an equal amount of waste on both sides of the edge of the lattice.

30. From the line just made, use a mitre gauge or a sliding bevel set to 45° and mark a line on each of the wider sides from the edge containing the groove to the opposite edge.

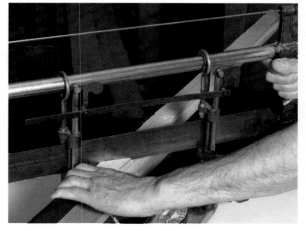

31. Use a bench mitre saw to cut the 45° mitre joint.

32. Use the piece already made as a reference template for marking the other long piece of the frame, transferring the measurements with a try square and pencil. This is a quick and accurate way of marking it out.

33. Line use the long pieces at the cut end and clamp them together. Mark the angles of the corner to be cut at the other end. This is to ensure that they are the same length.

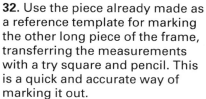

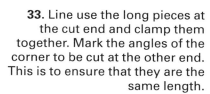

34. Cut the angles at the other end. Then try the latticework in the grooves of the long pieces to check and establish the overall width of the trellis.

35. Measure the exact overall width of the trellis from the outside of one of the long pieces to the other end.

36. Measure, mark out and cut the two shorter pieces together, to ensure that they are the same length.

37. As a check, transfer the measurements of the groove at the corner to the outside of the side pieces, so that the correct position of the lattice structure can be envisaged.

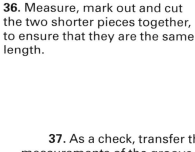

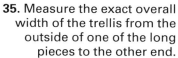

38. Another important check is to confirm that the latticework is at right angles to the frame in which it will be supported.

39. Make a final check by assembling all the pieces on the horizontal surface before gluing the frame.

203

Gluing and nailing the frame

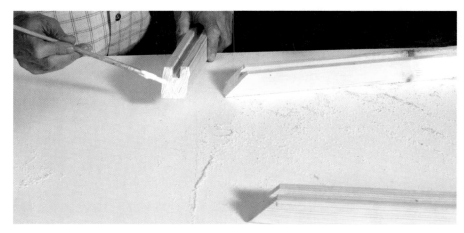

40. Here are all the parts laid out individually, ready to be glued and fixed together.

41. Apply woodworking white glue to the ends using a small brush and being careful not to let any glue get into the groove.

42. Fix the corner joints of one end of the frame in corner cramps and tighten them to apply pressure to the joints.

43. When the glue is dry but before removing the corner cramps, strengthen the corners with nails hammered in diagonally.

44. Slide the latticework into the part of the frame which now consists of one short and two long pieces fixed together.

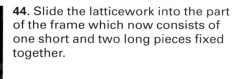

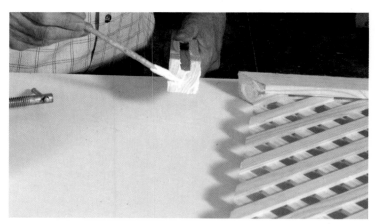

45. Glue the ends of the remaining short side and the corresponding ends of the long sides. The latticework itself is not glued into the grooves.

46. Fix the trellis to the workbench with a cramp so it is stable when the joint is assembled and reinforced as before with diagonal nailing.

Finishing

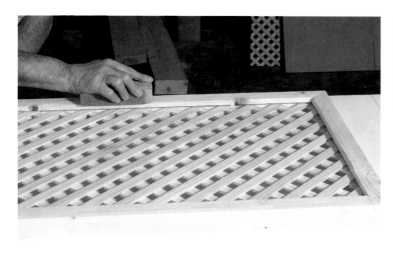

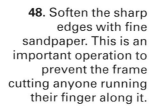

47. Now that the trellis has been assembled, the finishing process begins. First, use a sheet of medium grade sandpaper on a sanding block to smooth the edges.

48. Soften the sharp edges with fine sandpaper. This is an important operation to prevent the frame cutting anyone running their finger along it.

49. Clean off all the sawdust produced by sanding and apply a coat of linseed oil, using a brush to spread it over all the corners of the trellis.

50. To apply linseed oil to the structure, the brush should be nearly vertical and applied with rapid vertical dabbing movements. It is important that it should be worked well into the wood.

View of the completed trellis.

Trestle

This project involves building a sturdy, standard size trestle which is very useful around the house generally and for do-it-yourself jobs. It is a good idea to build two trestles, which with a work top can make a solid trestle table. In the workshop a pair of trestles or saw horses is invaluable for supporting planks, panels and pieces of work which are too large for the bench.

This practical exercise demonstrates how to improve accuracy when dealing with pieces of wood of the same length, and how to deal with different pieces of wood which are at compound angles to each other, joined with modified halving joints. Other procedures include the uses of a sliding bevel, the cutting of housings with a backsaw and sawing sloping surfaces, making sloping housings with a chisel, and smoothing irregular surfaces with a rasp.

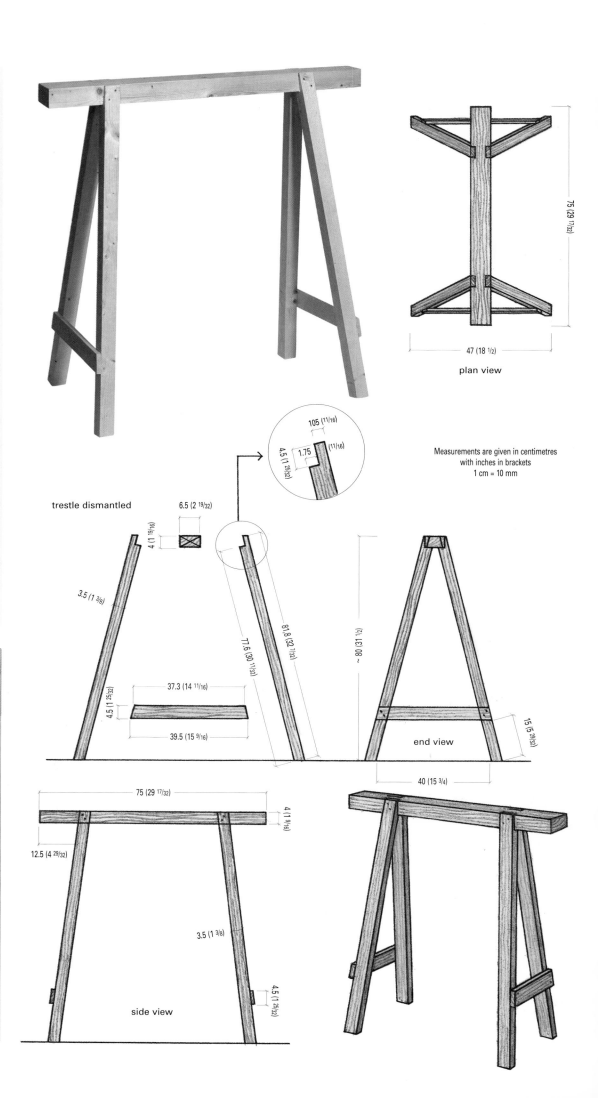

Measurements are given in centimetres with inches in brackets
1 cm = 10 mm

plan view

trestle dismantled

end view

side view

MATERIALS NEEDED

- Softwood planed and squared
- For the horizontal supporting member:
  1 piece 75 x 6.5 x 4.0 cm (29½ x 2⁹⁄₁₆ x 1⁹⁄₁₆ in)
- For the legs:
  4 pieces 85 x 3.5 x 3.5 cm (33⁷⁄₁₆ x 1⅜ x 1⅜ in)
- For the leg braces:
  2 pieces 45 x 4.5 x 1.0 cm (17¹¹⁄₁₆ x 1¾ x ⅜ in)

- Woodworking white glue

- Nails 35 mm long

- Sandpaper

- Varnish

- Paint brush

Step-by-step instructions

Marking out the wood

1. The materials and tools needed to make the trestle, set out on the workbench.

2. Put the four pieces of wood for the legs together side by side and align the ends. This enables them all to be marked for length at once, improving accuracy as well as saving time.

3. Cramp the pieces together with a bar cramp so that they remain correctly aligned. Measure a point 35 cm (13¾ in) from the aligned end.

4. Draw a line across all pieces at the same time. Subsequent operations will all be based on measurements taken from this line.

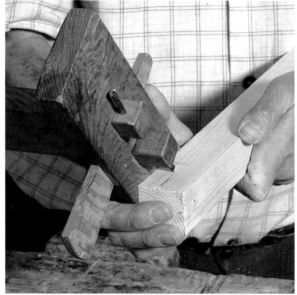

5. Separate the pieces of wood. On each of them, extend the reference line round the other three faces of the wood.

6. Use a marking gauge set to 1.75 cm (¹¹⁄₁₆ in) to mark the depth of the part to be cut out which will engage with the horizontal part of the trestle to be made. Repeat this operation on the other two sides.

7. Reinforce the marks made by the marking gauge with a pencil, so that they are easy to see when cutting the halving joint.

Cutting a halving joint with an inclined face

8. Cut the halving joint at the end of the leg by fixing one of the pieces vertically in the vice and sawing steadily with a backsaw until the horizontal line is reached.

9. Remove the waste piece by holding the leg horizontally in the bench hook and sawing down the marked line until the piece is freed.

10. Clean up the wood with a chisel, making light cuts until the inside surfaces are smooth.

11. With a sliding bevel, draw a line at an angle, starting from one side of the halving joint and displaced 5 mm (³⁄₁₆ in) at the other. The effect of this angle is to splay each of the legs of the trestle outwards, giving it greater stability. It is best to mark these lines in pairs in each 'sense' , so as to end up with the correct orientation of the four legs.

12. Use the bench hook once more to hold the legs while cutting the new angled line. The saw must be carefully controlled while doing this, so that it does not slide off sideways.

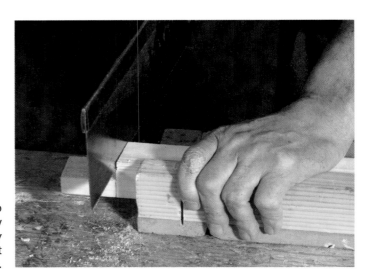

13. Hold the leg in the bench hook while cleaning the new angled face with a chisel. Avoid going over the marked line.

14. At the other end of the legs from the joint just made, mark a line at right angles to the length of the wood. From this line an angled cut will be made, so that the ends of the splayed legs are parallel with the ground.

15. With a sliding bevel mark a line on the foot at the same angle as the cut at the other end, which is therefore parallel to it.

16. Cutting the inclined end of each leg is a delicate task demanding accuracy. Hold the leg firmly in the bench hook while making the cuts.

17. Smooth off any irregularities of the cut end and round the arrises with a rasp.

18. Use medium grade sandpaper on a sanding block to soften the angles along the length of each leg.

Making the halving joint housing in the cross piece of the trestle

19. On the wider side of the wood which will form the cross piece of the trestle, mark a line 12.5 cm (4²⁹⁄₃₂ in) from the end. All the joint's measurements will be made in relation to this reference line. The joint is important because it defines the angles of the legs and the strength of the trestle depends on it.

20. Mark the inclination of the legs on the narrower side of the workpiece extending the line at an angle as with the legs. The slope is given by the difference of 5 mm (³⁄₁₆ in) between the upper and lower face of the wood.

21. Use the sliding bevel to make a parallel line the thickness of the leg, 3.5 cm (1⅜ in), away from the first line.

22. Extend the angled lines marked on the side across the side surface of the wood, using a try square.

23. To define the second angle of the legs, the transverse one, use a marking gauge to mark two different measurements on the cross piece. The first mark is 5 mm (³⁄₁₆ in) from the edge of the upper side.

24. Make the second mark on the lower side of the piece, this time 15 mm (⁹⁄₁₆ in) from the corresponding edge.

25. View of the lower side of the cross piece marked to indicate the pieces to be cut away later.

26. View of the upper side of the cross piece, again showing the parts to be cut away.

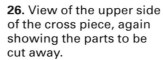

27. Holding the cross piece in the bench hook, use the backsaw to cut down to the bottom of the halving joint. The depth is different at the front and back of the cut, so the saw should be held at an angle to cater for this.

Cutting out the halving joints in the cross piece

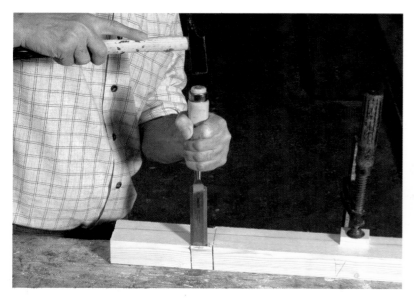

28. To cut each of the four joints in the cross piece, fix it firmly to the bench and use a chisel held at the same angle as the slope indicated by the marks.

29. It is best to fix the cross piece first with the narrower marks upwards. Then make vertical chisel cuts which will not reach as far as the line on the underside. If it is the other way up it is easy to cut too far by mistake.

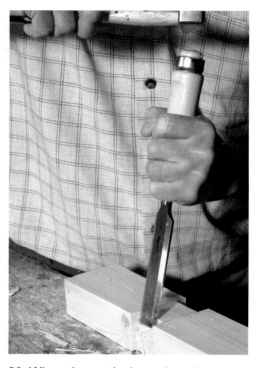

30. When the vertical cuts have been made, turn the piece over. Hold the chisel at an angle and very carefully chisel the slope up to the line.

31. Clean out the joint, using the chisel with short, light cuts as before.

32. The chisel is the best tool for this kind of work, so long as it is razor sharp. If it is not, it is impossible to clean out the joint neatly.

33. Cut and clean up all four joints in the same way. Then soften the arrises of the cross piece with medium grade sandpaper and a sanding block.

Gluing, nailing and fixing the legs

34. Make a test assembly of each joint to check that both transverse and longitudinal angles of the legs in relation to the cross piece are correct. Make adjustments if necessary.

35. Apply woodworking white glue evenly with a brush to the joint of the leg and the corresponding joint of the cross piece.

36. Reinforce each joint after gluing with two nails hammered in diagonally.

37. To position the cross piece firmly while the legs are fixed to it, cramp it to the bench, using a piece of scrap wood to protect the workpiece from being marked.

38. When the legs have been fixed to one side, glue the halving joints of the other side. The legs are pressed firmly toward the underside of the cross piece. It does not matter that part of the leg will project above the surface; this is trimmed off later.

39. While nailing the leg, use the other hand to support it in its final position. This position is defined by the juxtaposition of the inclined surfaces of the joint, so a sensitive touch is needed.

40. After the four legs are firmly fixed, the lower cross braces are made. These will increase the rigidity of the trestle by fixing the distance between each pair of legs. Mark points 15 cm (5²⁹⁄₃₂ in) from the foot of each leg to locate the position of these reinforcing battens.

41. Take a length of wood 45 x 4.5 x 1 cm (17¹¹⁄₁₆ x 1¾ x ⅜ in) and line it up with the marks just made. Mark the angles of the legs on the underside of the batten with a pencil.

42. To mark the areas to be glued, use the same piece of wood and make transverse lines top and bottom.

43. Cut the waste from the transverse pieces using a backsaw and bench hook.

44. Having cut this on one piece of wood, use the wood itself to mark the other piece.

45. Apply glue to the areas just marked.

46. Reinforce the joint with diagonal nailing, protecting the underside from being marked by the bench with a piece of scrap wood.

47. To finish, off, sink the heads of the nails below the surface with a nail punch.

212

Trimming off the waste

48. Use coarse sandpaper on a sanding block to level the ends of the reinforcing pieces to even the ends up with the legs.

49. Remove the waste from the legs which projects above the surface. This is done in three stages. First carefully saw across the waste as level as possible with the surface of the trestle.

50. The second stage is to level and clean the tops with a rasp, smoothing them but leaving the surface itself untouched.

51. The final stage is to smooth the whole with medium grade sandpaper on a sanding block, to achieve a completely even surface.

Finishing

52. To finish off, apply one or two coats of varnish, in this case clear, to protect the wood. It will also prevent the top surface producing splinters when rubbed.

213

Here is the finished trestle. It is very versatile and its many uses include being used as a saw horse in the workshop, a place where it is indispensable.

Wine rack

This practical exercise shows how to build a wine rack of original design in easy step-by-step stages. The wine rack consists of MDF panels and wooden rods which have been imaginatively combined. This examples shows how two different materials can be combined to produce an elegant object.

Each stage of this project makes use of different tools and techniques. For example, the power drill is used to make the holes to insert the rods in one piece, and then to drill through several sheets of MDF at the same time for ease and accuracy. A corner cramp is used to align the panels when fixing the corners, and a screw cramp is often used to hold pieces firmly while they are being drilled or worked on. Countersunk socket-head screws are used to join the sheets of MDF together.

MATERIALS NEEDED

- MDF panels 2 cm (²⁵⁄₃₂ in) thick.
- For the base, top, sides and divider: 5 pieces 30 x 54 cm (11³⁄₁₆ x 21²¹⁄₃₂ in).
- For the supporting feet: 4 pieces 7.0 x 7.0 cm (2¾ in) Wooden dowels 1 cm (⅜ in) diameter
- For the bottle supports: 10 rods 54 cm (21²¹⁄₃₂ in) long.

- Woodworking white glue

- Countersunk socket head screws 4.5 cm (1¾ in) long

- Medium grade sandpaper

- Varnish

- Paint brush

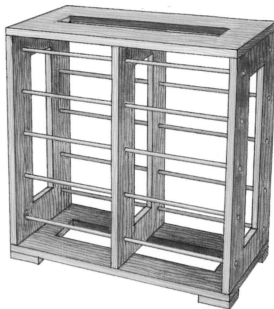

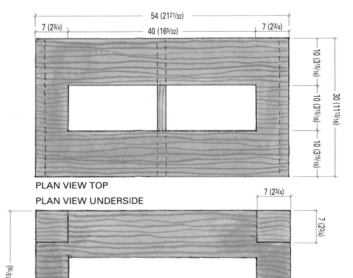

PLAN VIEW TOP

PLAN VIEW UNDERSIDE

FRONT ELEVATION

SIDE ELEVATION

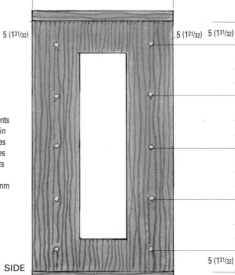

SIDE ELEVATION

Measurements are given in centimetres with inches in brackets

1 cm = 10 mm

Step-by-step instructions

Marking out the openwork on the panels

1. The tools and materials needed to make a wine rack with a capacity of 24 bottles.

2. Start drawing the outline of the openwork in one of the five panels already cut to the finished size of 30 x 54 cm (11³⁄₁₆ x 21²¹⁄₃₂ in). Draw two lines parallel with the short edges and 7 cm (2¾ in) inside them.

3. To complete the outline of the openwork which is 10 x 40 cm (3¹⁵⁄₁₆ x 15¹¹⁄₁₆ in), mark two parallel lines 10 cm (3¹⁵⁄₁₆ in) inside the longer edges.

4. Reinforce the lines by going over them again with a pencil.

5. On each of the five pieces make a cross or other mark on the part which is to be cut out, to avoid confusion later.

Cutting the openwork in the panels

6. This kind of enclosed opening needs a hole to insert the blade of a jigsaw. Drill a hole at each corner using a bit large enough to accommodate the blade.

7. Starting from each of the four holes, use the jigsaw to cut out the inner part within the marked line. This leaves a small excess to be finished later.

8. The waste has now been removed but the openwork needs to be tidied up, since the corners are not square (having been drilled) and the edges are rough.

Finishing the corners and edges of the openwork

9. Use the same jigsaw to cut the corners square, removing any sign of the round drilled holes.

10. To correct the irregularities in the edges, use a rasp or a metal file, being careful not to go over the marked edges.

11. Carry out the final finishing of the openings with medium grade sandpaper and a sanding block, held as shown in the photograph.

12. When the opening of one of the panels has been completed, use it to mark the openwork on the remaining four panels. Repeat the operations on each of them.

216

Marking the holes to be drilled

13. To mark the vertical line of the holes, measure the centre of each side, that is, 5 cm (1$^{15}\!/_{16}$ in) in from the edge. Only the three panels forming the vertical elements are marked in this way.

14. Mark these reference lines with a pencil. The operation is repeated symmetrically on both sides of each vertical panel.

15. Mark the centres of the holes at intervals along the reference axis. From top to bottom, the measurements are: 5, 11, 11, 11, 11 and 5 cm (11$^{5}\!/_{16}$, 4$^{7}\!/_{16}$, 4$^{7}\!/_{16}$, 4$^{7}\!/_{16}$, 4$^{7}\!/_{16}$ and 11$^{5}\!/_{16}$ in).

16. Use a try square to transfer the measurements from one side of the vertical panel to the other.

Drilling the holes

17. When one of the pieces has been properly marked, fix it to the bench to drill the holes. Use a 10 mm (⅜ in) bit and move it up and down two or three times, so that it will be easy to insert the rods later.

18. To ensure that all the holes are in line, put the three vertical panels on top of each other with the one already drilled on top. Mark the sides to record their order and orientation so that they will be assembled in the same way.

19. Fix the three pieces firmly and drill the holes through them all. The top piece acts as a template for positioning the holes in the other too, gaining accuracy and saving time.

Preparing the rods

20. Since the rods are cut from several longer standard lengths, mark them to match the longer dimensions of the top and bottom panels, which is 54 cm (21²¹⁄₃₂ in). It is quickest and most accurate to use the panels to mark these dimensions, rather than a rule.

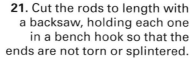

21. Cut the rods to length with a backsaw, holding each one in a bench hook so that the ends are not torn or splintered.

Marking out and assembling the main part of the wine rack

22. Fix one of the vertical pieces in the vice of the workbench and position the top piece on it. Using a pencil and the hand as a marking gauge, draw a line on the top to indicate the thickness of the vertical member. The screw holes will be marked within this area.

23. Check that the line drawn is at right angles and draw another line 1 cm (⅜ in) in from the edge.

24. Mark the points along this line where the three fixing screws will be positioned. The two outer ones are each 4 cm (1⁹⁄₁₆ in) from the edges and the third is midway between them 15 cm (5²⁹⁄₃₂ in) from each edge.

25. Fix the two pieces firmly in position using a corner cramp. It is essential that they do not shift during the drilling operation. Drill the holes carefully, making sure that the drill is perfectly vertical to the work throughout.

26. Before removing the corner cramp, screw in the socket-head screws with a key that fits them perfectly. The screw heads should be sunk slightly below the surface.

27. With one corner assembled, work on the bench to assemble the other side of the wine rack. Repeat the operations of measuring and marking out as before.

28. Use the corner cramp again to hold the joint firmly while the holes are drilled.

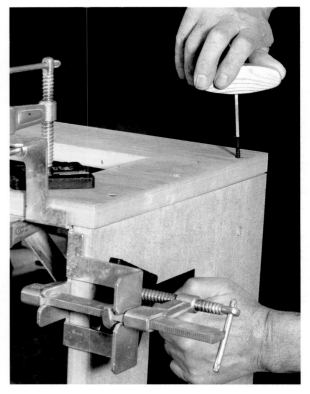

29. The use of the corner cramp, even when working on the workbench, is very important, since the force of tightening the screws could distort the joint if it is not securely cramped.

30. To determine the correct position of the central vertical piece, make a mark at the mid point of the base, which should be 27 cm (10⅝ in) from each end.

31. The mid point is transferred to the edges and upper side of the panel, so as to mark the axis of the two fixing screws clearly. These screws and the equivalent ones on the top surface will fix the vertical panel and make the whole structure rigid.

32. Position the intermediate panel, using the mark made earlier to decide which side is which. Check with a try square to ensure that it is vertical.

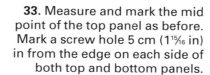

33. Measure and mark the mid point of the top panel as before. Mark a screw hole 5 cm (1¹⁵⁄₁₆ in) in from the edge on each side of both top and bottom panels.

34. It is not necessary to use the corner cramp when drilling these holes, since the joint is now perfectly stable and it would be very difficult to distort it with the frame.

35. The same screws are used as earlier in the project, tightened until the head is just below the surface of the wood.

Inserting the rods

36. When the frame is assembled, soften all the arrises with medium grade sandpaper before inserting the rods.

37. If necessary, rub the ten rods with wax before inserting them, to minimise any rubbing as they are fitted through the holes.

38. Fix the assembled to the workbench and start inserting the rods. Tap them gently in with a hammer, guiding them through the intermediate section and into the holes at the other end.

39. To fix the rods, apply a small quantity of woodworking white glue to the end of each one. Clean off the surplus with a damp cloth so that it leaves no marks.

Making and attaching the feet

40. Take a surplus piece of the same panel used for the top and sides of the wine rack, large enough to make the four square feet, about 30 cm (12 in) by at least 8 cm (3⅛ in). Mark a line 7 cm (2¾ in) from the edge.

41. Using a try square, draw lines 7 cm (2¾ in) apart at right angles to the edge. This will mark out the feet which will raise the wine rack 2 cm (²⁵⁄₃₂ in) off the floor.

42. Cut out the four feet and soften the edges with medium grade sandpaper.

43. Turn the wine rack upside down. Apply glue to the feet with a brush.

44. Strengthen the fixing of the feet with two nails 3 cm (1⅛ in) long for each foot, arranged diagonally.

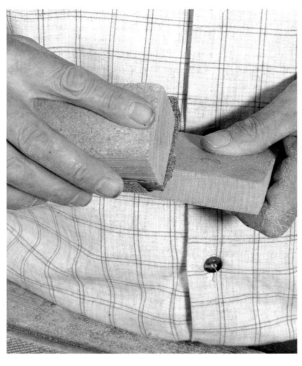

Finishing

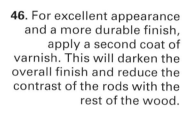

45. Cover all the surfaces of the wine rack, including the rods, with a coat of clear varnish. (Before doing this, clean any wax off the rods with paint thinner.)

46. For excellent appearance and a more durable finish, apply a second coat of varnish. This will darken the overall finish and reduce the contrast of the rods with the rest of the wood.

This shows the completed wine rack.
It is a simple piece of straightforward design which is very practical.

Laying wood flooring

The use of wood as floor covering has a long tradition. Originally, a wooden floor consisted of rough wooden planks and boards laid over an earth or stone floor to protect against the cold and provide a measure of comfort. These elementary wooden floors were followed by floorboards nailed to joists, wood-block paving, and solid wood floors made of a number of smaller individual pieces glued to a solid surface, such as wood block, strip and plank flooring.

The technique for manufacturing and laying wooden floors continued to develop in the course of time, so that today it is possible to lay your own wood floor with a minimum of practical experience. In this chapter we shall concentrate on a few aspects of wood floor such as differences in manufacturing and quality. Ready-made wood is produced either with a solid wood top layer on top of two layers of wood, plywood or MDF. The patterned top layer looking like wood veneer is sometimes produced artificially by photographic methods on sheets of laminated wood.

Composition of wood floor with a solid wood top layer

This type of wood floor has a solid wood surface which varies in strength depending on the quality of the top layer, which usually consists of an elegant hardwood. The supporting layers are also made of solid wood, but of lower quality for reasons of economy. There are usually two supporting layers whose wood fibres running at 90° to each other in order to prevent the boards from warping. Sometimes the supporting layers consist of plywood or fibreboard. They all have a tongue and groove edge by which they are joined together.

Two kinds of floating wood floor whose surfaces are the same apart from the natural variations in the patterns of the wood.

Wood flooring showing its solid wood base. The quality and finish of this side is not as high as the face side since it is invisible.

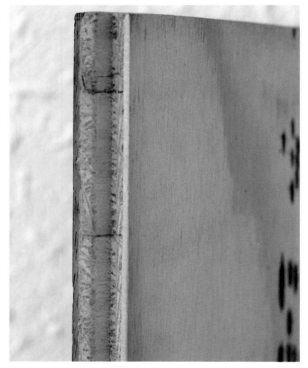

Detail of the edge of a panel of wood flooring, showing the connecting groove cut in the base made of strips of wood glued together with its grain at right angles to the top and bottom veneers.

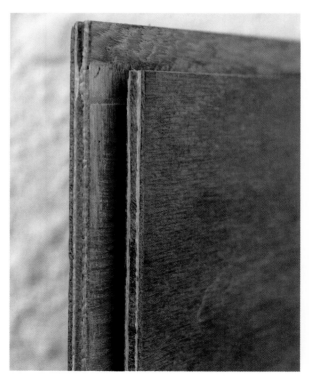

Detail of a wood panel whose base consists of plywood panels, the lower side of one of them treated and sealed to resist the effect of moisture from the surface it rests upon.

Composition of laminated floating wooden flooring with a sub-layer of wood

A floating laminate floor is very versatile as far as application and use are concerned. All that is required is a smooth surface on which to lay it with an underlay of special sound-insulating plastic foam to reduce the noise made by walking on it. Tools and materials needed include special wood flooring glue to secure the tongues in the grooves, a hammer and a wooden device to join them together, a jigsaw to cut the boards, a try square, a folding rule and a pencil. Laminates come in a wide range of wood imitation finishes, colours and patterns. This great variety makes redecorating rooms very exciting because it also makes it possible to combine several kinds of woods and create interesting patterns.

Samples showing some of the different kinds of synthetic wood flooring which are available.

This manufacturer's portable display stand makes it easy to choose the right finish of flooring on site.

Size and packaging of ready-made wood or laminated plank flooring

Although the size of the various kinds of wood plank sometimes varies depending on the manufacturer, there is a generally agreed standard size for pieces of wood plank flooring. This is 20 cm wide and 120 cm long (about 8 x 48 in) long. The thickness varies from 8 to 16 mm ($\frac{5}{16}$ to $\frac{5}{8}$ in). It is packaged in packs of 8 or 10 pieces, ready for laying.

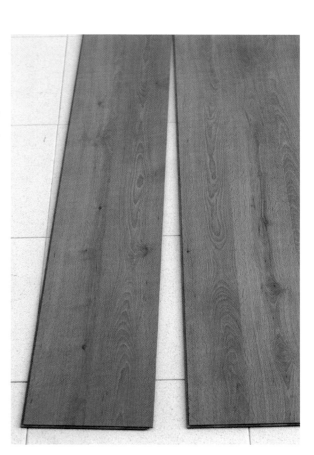

Here there is no doubt that the size of the piece matches the standard, and the effect when laid will be fairly uniform.

A standard pack of pieces of wood block flooring ready for immediate installation. Once laid, it should be noted that this design will give the appearance of being made from smaller pieces of various different sizes. Depending on the circumstances in which it is to be used, this may be seen as a creative opportunity or it may create problems.

In this case the component pieces are smaller and when installed will produce a floor with a non-uniform effect. This will suit some situations better than others.

An extreme example in which the pieces of woods are very varied, giving a fragmented effect imitating the wood strip flooring used in old houses and apartments.

Skirting boards and other uses of wood

The versatility of this kind of wood is enhanced by skirting boards which have the same characteristics as the floor pieces. There is a wide choice of both elements, with a variety of finishes, shapes and sizes.

Since one of the characteristics of this material is its resistance to moisture and to shocks, it is possible to use it as a wall covering, attached directly to a flat surface with synthetic adhesive or dabs of silicone.

A range of skirting boards for this kind of flooring.

A skirting board with the same features as the wood block flooring.

A piece of skirting which gives the appearance of being a continuation of the strip of brown wood enclosing the green part of the floor.

A wall clad in the same material as the the floor, although in terms of colour and tone there is a contrast playing between the vertical and horizontal surfaces.

Laying a wooden floor

Before laying any wooden flooring, there are several things to be taken into account:
• The surface on which it is to be laid must be smooth, flat and dry.
• Like all floating floors, it requires a layer of foam underneath.
• There must be no water leaks of damp patches on the surface to be covered.
• The whole of the perimeter of the area to be covered may be sealed with silicone sealer.

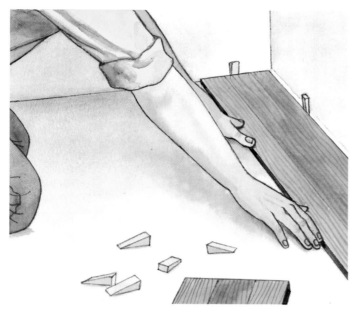

1. Prepare the surface. Begin in a corner and fit the first plank with the groove towards the wall. Use wedges to leave a gap of from 5 to 15 mm (³⁄₁₆ to ⁹⁄₁₆ in), depending on the thickness of the skirting board, between the strips and the walls.

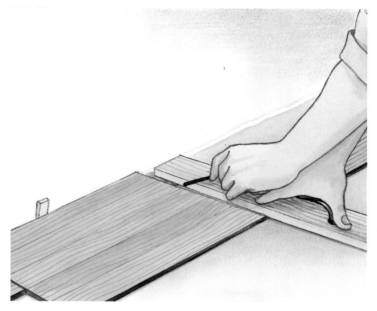

2. To fit the final strip of the first section, take the measurements of the strip to be fitted, mark it square and cut it at the mark. Check the measurement is correct before gluing it.

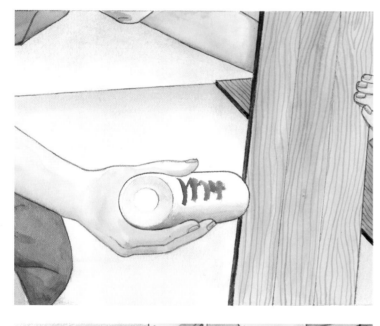

3. Once checked, apply glue evenly to the groove of the tongue-and-groove joint in sufficient quantity for the corresponding edges.

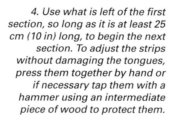

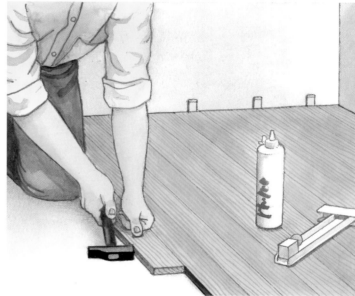

4. Use what is left of the first section, so long as it is at least 25 cm (10 in) long, to begin the next section. To adjust the strips without damaging the tongues, press them together by hand or if necessary tap them with a hammer using an intermediate piece of wood to protect them.

5. On reaching the last section, measure the length to be covered, mark it and cut it, remembering to leave the gap of 5 to 15 mm (³⁄₁₆ to ⁹⁄₁₆ in) between the wood floor and the wall.

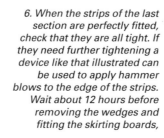

6. When the strips of the last section are perfectly fitted, check that they are all tight. If they need further tightening a device like that illustrated can be used to apply hammer blows to the edge of the strips. Wait about 12 hours before removing the wedges and fitting the skirting boards,

A special jointing system

This kind of wood flooring is very hard-wearing because it consists of a compressed laminate, subjected to high pressure. Even though it is only 6 mm (⁷⁄₃₂ in) thick, it is robust enough to accommodate a thin but strong tongue-and-groove joint all the way round, so two edges of each plank have tongues while the other two have grooves. The glue is applied to the groove with an applicator specially designed for the purpose.

The pieces must be assembled carefully so that they are never used like a lever, which would damage the tongues

The most important thing to remember is that the glues is always applied to the groove, never to the tongue.

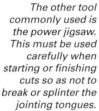

Detail showing how the applicator of the glue is designed to fit the size of the groove to which glue is applied.

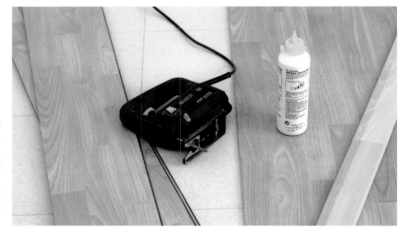

The other tool commonly used is the power jigsaw. This must be used carefully when starting or finishing cuts so as not to break or splinter the jointing tongues.

Some installed floors

For floors with a very large area, over 100 m² (1,100 sq ft), or 12 m (40 ft) long by 8 m (26 ft) wide, expansion joints are recommended. With any floor it is sensible to wait for 24 hours for it to acclimatise and settle before putting very heavy furniture on it. As for the direction in which the floor is laid, the normal practice is for the strips to run in the direction of the predominant natural light which illuminates the appearance of the wood most effectively.

Floor with an imaginative design achieved by combining various types and shades of wood flooring.

Wooden flooring laid in a public place, with a double layer of protective coating to withstand the continuous use which is much greater than domestic traffic.

Wooden floor laid in the sometimes humid environment of a kitchen.

Wooden floor laid towards the natural light, which enhances its light colour.

Wooden floor laid in a gymnasium, with a triple protective layer to survive hard, continuous use, high relative humidity and frequent knocks.

Wooden floor laid in a gymnasium, strong enough to survive the weight of the equipment that is found in this environment.

When there is no natural light to dictate the direction in which the wood is laid, it can be laid diagonally, which produces a sensation of movement.

A synthetic wood floor like this one can be used in a semi-outdoor environment, such as this covered verandah.

Here wooden flooring also used on the ramp connecting the different levels.

Wooden floor beneath a window, which provides the light to pick up the shine which is characteristic of a polished wooden floor.

Assembling kitchen units and bathroom furniture

Both kitchen and bathroom furniture have become very popular items with do-it-yourself enthusiasts. Much of it is now available as pre-fabricated components supplied in flat packs and the instructions are usually clear and easy to follow. The assembly of the individual parts uses relatively quick and easy methods which have replaced the traditional techniques of woodworking. The wood glue of the past has now been replaced with modern formulations, or dispensed with altogether through the use of special clamping connectors which make it much easier to assemble, alter and expand the units.

This development has led to a change in joinery practices. The increasing availability of simple flat-pack units which do not require any particular expertise to assemble has led to a shift in emphasis and specialisation in other areas of joinery.

Some very high quality doors and kitchen units are still made from solid wood, but the cabinets and most doors are now usually made from melamine-faced chipboard. This plastic finish is available in white and in many designs, including some remarkably convincing imitation woods. For the doors in particular, MDF is often used.

This chapter describes the basic methods of assembling flat-pack kitchen units. The methods used for assembling bathroom units are very much the same.

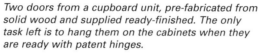

Two doors from a cupboard unit, pre-fabricated from solid wood and supplied ready-finished. The only task left is to hang them on the cabinets when they are ready with patent hinges.

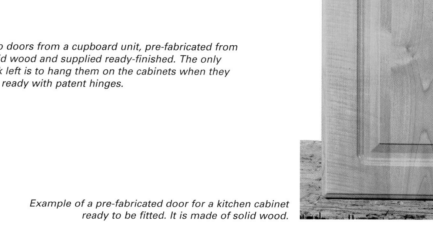

229

Example of a pre-fabricated door for a kitchen cabinet ready to be fitted. It is made of solid wood.

Sample display showing the wide range of finishes available for kitchen cabinets.

Pre-fabricated components and hinges for assembling a kitchen or bathroom cabinet

As was demonstrated in an earlier section, the number and variety of different fittings for joining, fixing, hinging, sliding, closing and locking pieces of furniture is so enormous that it includes a whole section of connectors and other fittings designed specially for use with kitchen and bathroom cabinets. Each of these items is available in a variety of forms, but basically they are all designed to be used with panels of man-made boards. The use of these special fittings is not difficult and they work extremely well.

Concealed hinges for fitting to the moving part of the assembly, usually the door front.

Hinge bases for fitting to the carcass. The hinge itself will be fitted to it.

The two parts of a typical concealed hinge widely used for hanging doors on kitchen and bathroom cabinets. It is adjustable by the screws.

One of the many different handles which can easily be fitted to the door fronts of this kind of cupboard.

The parts of a pair of runners for mounting and fixing sliding elements such as drawers to kitchen and bathroom cabinets.

Adjustable feet (assembled, left, and dismantled) which are fitted to the base of floor-mounted cabinets to level them.

Pre-fabricated plastic adjustable foot with a clip for attacking a skirting to it, as used under kitchen cabinets.

A wide variety of skirting finishes is available, either to match that of the cabinets or to provide a contrast.

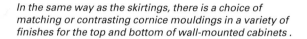
In the same way as the skirtings, there is a choice of matching or contrasting cornice mouldings in a variety of finishes for the top and bottom of wall-mounted cabinets .

A number of shelf supports, which are inserted by hand into some of the prefabricated holes in the insides of cupboards, depending on the height and number of shelves required.

The components used for wall-mounting cabinets in a kitchen.

Typical assembly procedure for a kitchen cabinet

As a typical example, the assembly of a flat-packed pre-fabricated kitchen cupboard has been chosen. This illustrates the method of assembling this kind of construction, from the moment it is unpacked on the bench until it is finished, ready to receive its work top.

Pre-packed pre-fabricated parts for a kitchen cabinet, containing all the parts and hinges needed to assemble it.

Here the parts have been unpacked. The basic structure is made of melamine-faced chipboard.

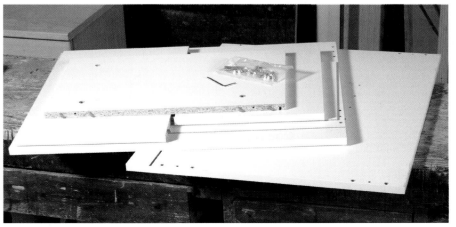

To begin the assembly process, start by fitting one of the narrow pieces to one of the side pieces. They are located with wooden dowels which are inserted into holes pre-drilled in the panels.

The second step consists of fitting the bottom part of the cabinet to the other end of the side piece in the same way. Hand pressure is enough to engage the pegs in the holes.

These three pieces together make a 'U'-shaped structure. A groove runs inside them, in which the thin back panel is now inserted.

The carcass is completed by attaching the other side. The assembly is now ready for the screws to be fitted.

Put a socket-headed screw in each of the holes and tighten them up with the hexagon key supplied.

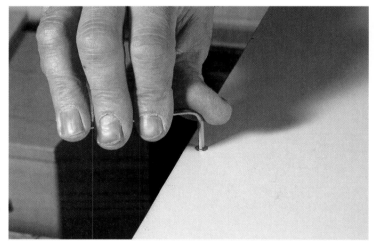

Detail showing a screw being tightened with a hexagon or Allen key.

When the whole cabinet has been assembled and screwed together, fit the mounting base of the plastic feet into the pre-drilled hole in the base

When the base is in place, screw on the foot itself, with its height adjustment system. This works by turning the threaded foot in its housing. Set it half-way; final adjustment will be carried out when the cabinet is in position.

Once the foot is assembled make pilot holes for the fixing screws with a punch.

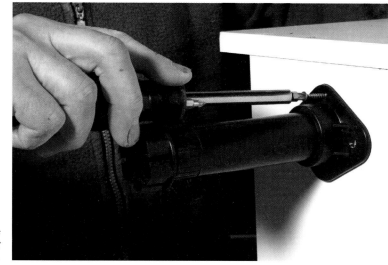

Screw in the four screws which fix each foot mounting in place.

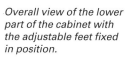

Overall view of the lower part of the cabinet with the adjustable feet fixed in position.

233

Fitting the shelf support by hand in one of the pre-drilled holes at the chosen height inside the cabinet.

Shelf support in position.

Insert four shelf supports by hand and put in place the shelf supplied with the unit.

Parts and tools used for fitting s two-hinged door to the cabinet. Note that the round holes for the hinges had been pre-drilled in the flat-packed piece.

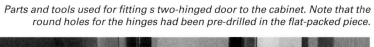

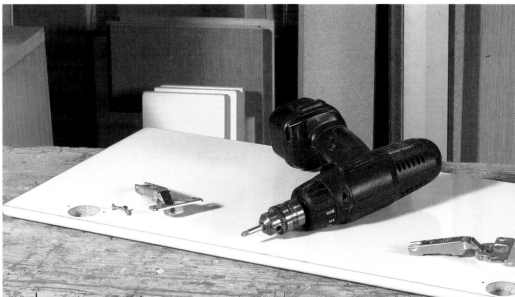

Fit the concealed hinge into the round hole already drilled in the door. Line it up straight and fix it with two screws through the holes in the plate.

Before hanging the door, fit the other part of the hinge to the one just fixed and screw them together. This will be used to locate and mark the fixing holes in the carcass.

Position the door and mark the two fixing holes, using the rear part of the hinge as a template.

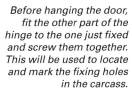

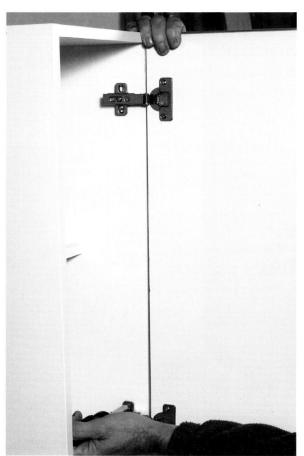

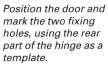

Make punch marks to locate the screws in the holes just marked.

Screw the door to the cupboard, holding it in place with the hand which is not turning the screwdriver.

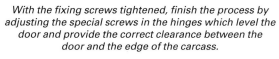

With the fixing screws tightened, finish the process by adjusting the special screws in the hinges which level the door and provide the correct clearance between the door and the edge of the carcass.

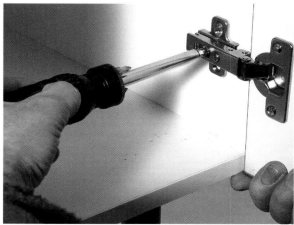

With the door closed, check that the door is centred and any excess width is evenly distributed by passing the hands down both sides.

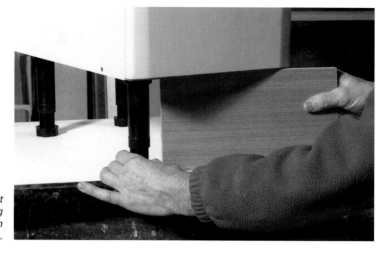

Floor-standing kitchen cabinet 30 cm (12 in) wide with panel door.

Use the adjustable feet to set the height so that the skirting panel just fits underneath without rubbing.

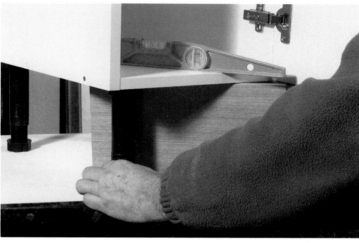

For the final adjustment of the legs, use a spirit level in the bottom of the cupboard to the cupboard is perfectly level. This means that the skirting panel will be vertical.

235

To fit the skirting panel, mark the position of the centre lines of the two front feet on it.

Extend the line across the height of the skirting panel, then measure and mark the mid point.

Fix the clip to the skirting panel with a screw.

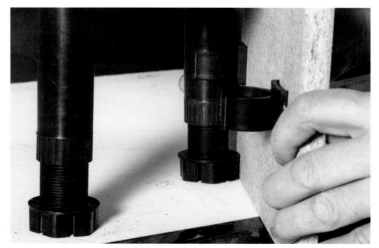

When the two clips are fitted, press the skirting panel onto the feet to fix it in position.

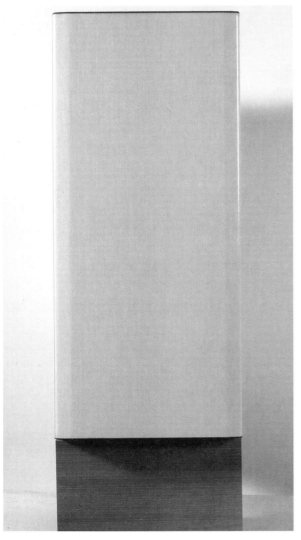

Floor-standing kitchen cabinet with skirting panel.

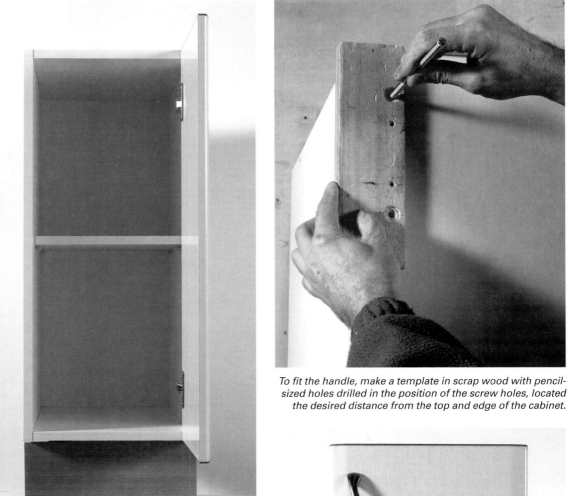

To fit the handle, make a template in scrap wood with pencil-sized holes drilled in the position of the screw holes, located the desired distance from the top and edge of the cabinet.

View of the same cabinet showing the interior.

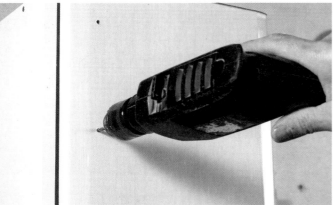

Drill the holes in the positions marked, holding the door partly open to avoid drilling anything inside.

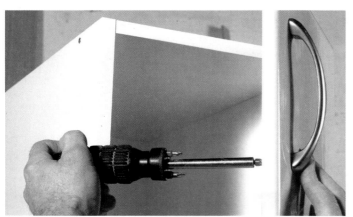

Fixing the handle with two screws.

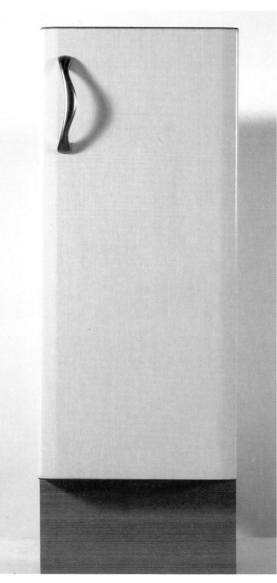

The finished cabinet ready to be fixed in its final position and given a work top. The use of a template to position the handles on all the cabinets ensures that they will all be in the same correct position.

For a wall-mounted kitchen cabinet the procedure is the same as that already described. The only differences are that there may be a cornice, also pre-fabricated, which is attached to the cabinet above the door.

The cornice is fixed with silicone adhesive, applied directly from the cartridge with nozzle to the appropriate area.

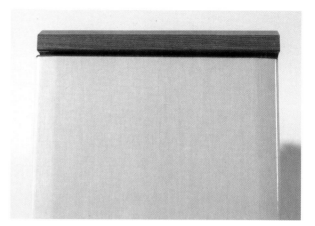

Detail of the finish of the cornice attached to the top of the kitchen cabinet.

Installing the finished cabinets

Everything shown in this section has been included as a general guide which is easily applicable to most kitchen installations. There will inevitably be variations in certain elements (such as the use of plywood instead of chipboard, different hinge fittings, closing mechanisms, feet, skirting panels and so on), since the range of designs is very wide. The choice is increasing by the day, with the creation of new models and the appearance of new features in response to commercial demands and new pressures consumers who aspire to enjoy the most modern lifestyle. All of these things will affect the designs, but the fundamental principles seldom change, and many modifications are easy to understand and implement.

A modern kitchen with a continuous run of floor-mounted units with panel doors and elegant D-handles. The feet are concealed behind skirting panels which are the same colour as the units, making a pleasing effect with the wood floor.

Detail of part of a bathroom in which the warm colour of the floor-mounted units and the doors goes well with that of the wooden floor. The doors have louvres which give them life, avoiding the excessive soberness and monotony of dark plain panels.

View of a rustic kitchen in which the units and other pieces of furniture are designed to relate to the style of the room, including the wooden roof beams.

When chosen well and with an exact idea of how the room will look, wood on its own, without any other element, can create a bright, elegant, minimalist environment like this kitchen.

The atmosphere of this kitchen, fitted out with many pre-fabricated cabinets, illustrates the extent to which commonly available flat-pack units can result in a modern, attractive appearance.

A kitchen in rustic style. The units have fronts framed and enhanced with simple moulding. It is only necessary to acquire similar cabinet doors to achieve a similar effect.

CABINETMAKING

It is difficult to imagine a natural product which is more useful and more important to the life of men than trees. While they are alive, they not only clean the atmosphere and improve the quality of the air we breathe but their beauty, colour, fruit and shade also bring us great joy. When they are felled they provide first class material for building and heating and also the perfect material for items of practical use such as furniture and many other objects of every day life, used for storage, to improve comfort or simply as decoration.

Although this book contains much information on the techniques of woodwork and manufacturing processes, it should be remembered that the information and projects are always presented from the user's point of view. For a woodworker, wood is not a cold, soulless material but a unique, individual material whose qualities only begin to develop as the user becomes aware of the particular characteristics of the wood being worked on. This means that making furniture is not only about the functionality and quality of the finished product but it also concerns its appearance which depends very much on the preparation of the wood.

This chapter deals extensively with the construction of furniture. The practical exercises which are presented here contain many techniques which can be carefully followed. The application of particular techniques and the handling, finish and combination of the various types of wood, as well as the use of the right tools, are always guided by the desire to achieve a single purpose: the construction of successful pieces of furniture which serves its purpose but is also well-made, that is well-designed, attractive and with a presence of its own. In this way, the cabinetmaker will take pleasure in bringing out the best of the wood in the finished product.

Cabinetmaking skills

Cabinetmaking is an ancient craft which takes time and patience, while requiring an observant mind ready to understand the growth and form of trees. It is particularly important for serious, discriminating cabinetmakers that they should know which wood is most suited to the decorative object or piece of furniture to be made.

Besides these skills, the woodworker should be able to produce freehand general arrangement drawings as well as knowing what kind of joint is suitable for each part of a project. The right choice of finish for the surfaces is also very important because they should reflect and correspond to the practical and aesthetic function of the piece of furniture. This is an aspect which must be considered at the very start of a project in order to achieve a result that is not only beautifully in form and appearance but also special and unique.

The following examples include typical aspects of woodworking operations and joints, illustrated step-by-step, which explain how a joiner or cabinetmaker can get the best out of the wood by using the right tools and handling them correctly. The skilled craftsman will succeed in transforming wood into a beautiful object, thus creating the fascination exerted by a well-made piece of furniture.

Cabinetmaking joints

As in other fields of woodworking, the joints used in cabinetmaking can be classified into the same three categories, edge-to-edge joints, corner joints and splice joints.

In the case of cabinetmaking a further consideration enters into play: joints are sometimes chosen for the aesthetic effect they may have on the appearance of the piece, and whether they are intended to be seen or not. It is common in making furniture for a joint to be dramatised for its own sake, or alternatively it may be made in a skillful way which conceals it completely. Discreet elegance is a hallmark of many successful designs.

Here are some typical joints used in making furniture: corner joints for panels, joints to extend the length of components, and dovetail joints.

Corner joints for panels

The use of man-made panels in making furniture has increased with the appearance of MDF (medium density fibreboard), a reconstituted wood product. This can be moulded on its edges, both external and openwork; it can be painted or lacquered, and it can be assembled with self-tapping carcass screws to make a reliable construction. The kind of furniture made with it is not notable for the texture of its surfaces, but the versatility of its properties enables the furniture maker to achieve effects which would not be possible with conventional timber.

Splined wood corner joint for man-made panels

The feature of this method for joining two panels at right angles to each other is that it uses a piece of square-section wood which is joined to the MDF panels by two plywood splines.

1. The tools and materials for making a splined wood corner joint to join two MDF panels at right angles, using a splined wood corner piece.

2. The planed and sanded wood forming the joint is 4.5 x 4.5 cm (1¾ x 1¾ in), and the same length as the panels to be joined. Draw a centre line along the whole length on two adjacent sides.

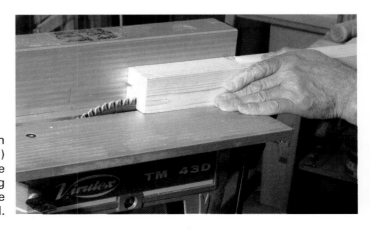

3. Using a table saw with a blade 5 mm (³⁄₁₆ in) thick, make a groove 12 mm (⁷⁄₁₆ in) deep along the whole length of the two sides marked.

4. Mark a centre line along both the edges to be joined of both panels.

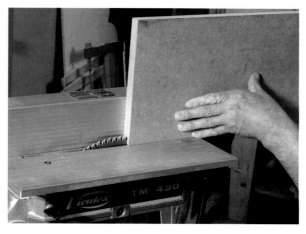

5. Use the same procedure with the table saw to make a groove 19 mm (¹¹⁄₁₆ in) deep in the panels, adjusting the saw guide so that the panel is well supported, enabling the cut to be made safely and smoothly.

6. Cut two lengths of 5 mm (3/16 in) plywood to the width required to fill the grooves. This should be just under the combined depth of the two grooves.

7. Soften the sharp angles of the wooden corner piece with medium grade sandpaper.

8. Apply woodworking white glue to the grooves and the plywood splines. Then assemble the joint and leave it to dry.

The completed splined wood corner joint connecting the two panels.

VARIATIONS ON THE CORNER JOINT FOR PANELS

Corner joint for panels with interior wood reinforcement

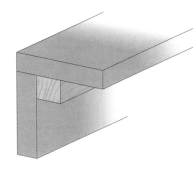

This joint is distinguished by the simplicity of its external appearance, with smooth, uninterrupted surfaces. It is reinforced internally by a piece of softwood fixed with nails or screws long enough to enter the panels but not to penetrate through them.

Lap joint for panels

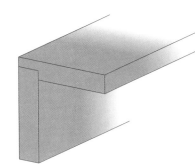

The aesthetic appearance is discreet like the previous joint. The difference is that it does not have an internal reinforcing piece, but gains its strength from a glued lap joint.

Curved splined wood corner joint

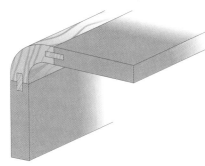

The components of this kind of joint have a smooth continuity, both inside and out. The rounded corner emphasises the articulation of the joint without adding to the thickness of the assembly.

Curved tongue-and-groove wood corner joint

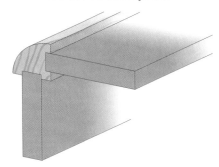

Unlike the previous joint, in this case the articulation is emphasised both by the change of material and by the size and shape of the corner piece, projecting above the panels and giving a framed effect.

Longitudinal joints

Used in all kinds of woodworking and cabinet-making, this joint is used to combine two pieces of wood longitudinally, making them longer. In furniture making, the joint is seldom needed for structural reasons; it is normally used for ornamental or decorative purposes.

Longitudinal joint with a single central dowel

This longitudinal joint is designed to join two long, narrow pieces of wood as invisibly as possible. The secret joint is stylish, but it is not very strong. For this reason its use is normally confined to ornamental applications.

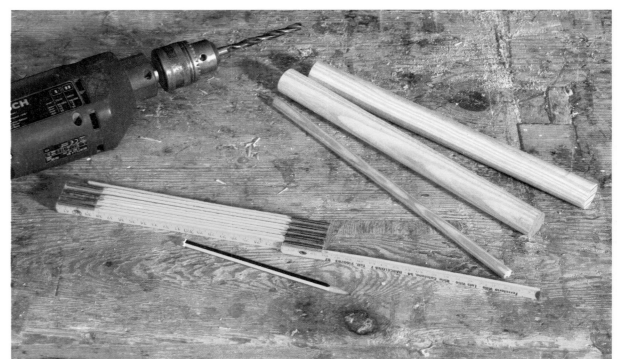

1. The components and tools needed to make a longitudinal joint between two rods 2.5 cm ($^{15}/_{16}$ in) in diameter using a 1 cm ($^3/_8$ in) dowel rod.

2. Prepare the two rods so they are smoothly finished with the ends cut exactly at right angles. Find the centre by scribing arcs with metal dividers, the other leg being held against the side of the rod.

3. Firmly fix the rod vertically in the vice. Drill a hole using a 1 cm ($^3/_8$ in) bit, keeping it exactly parallel with the length of the piece. The depth of the hole should be 3 cm ($1^1/_8$ in) and it is convenient to mark this on the drill bit.

4. Cut a 6 cm (2$^3/_8$ in) length from a dowel rod 1 cm ($^3/_8$ in) in diameter.

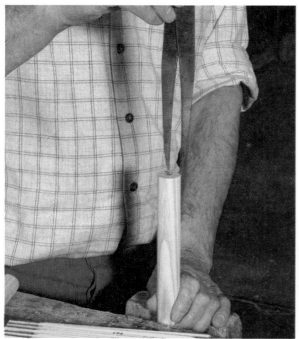

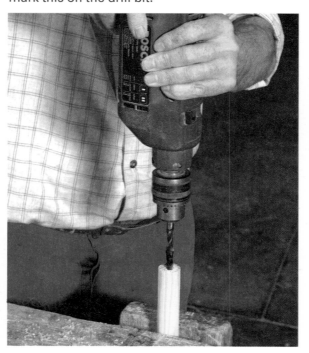

5. Apply woodworking white glue to the dowel and to the hole and end of one piece which is fixed in the vice.

6. Insert the dowel. Using a protective piece of scrap wood, hammer it in to make sure it has reached the bottom of the hole.

7. Complete the assembly by gluing the other piece and knocking it into place.

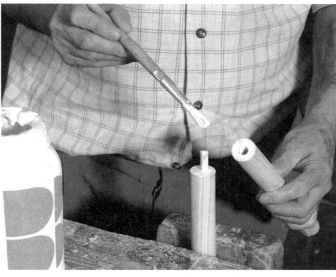

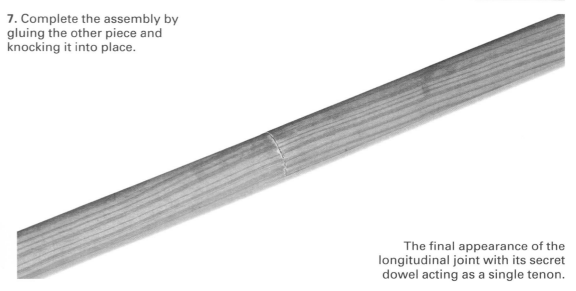

243

The final appearance of the longitudinal joint with its secret dowel acting as a single tenon.

VARIATIONS ON LONGITUDINAL JOINTS

Three-dowel joint

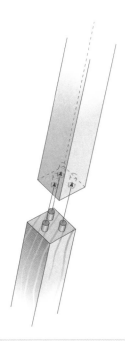

This joint can be used to connect square or curved pieces. Unlike a single dowel, it will resist any twisting forces which would put the pieces out of alignment, but it is not at all strong and should be used for decorative purposes only.

Round peg joint

The peg was made at the end of the cylindrical piece while it was being turned. It fits the corresponding hole in the other piece, the joint being fixed with glue. It is a very good way of finishing off all kinds of furniture.

Screw joint

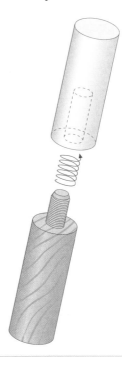

This joint is used where rapid assembly and dismantling is required. It is made without nails, screws of glue, and used for assembling chairs, tables, shelves and so on.

Dovetail joints

This joint is widely used in drawers and chests. Of all the joints used in furniture making, it is one of the strongest when the glue has dried. Its strength is the result of its multiple mortise and tenon joints, reinforced by the dovetail shape in which they are cut. The other feature which makes it popular for furniture is its decorative appearance; or it may be partially or wholly concealed.

Lapped dovetail joint

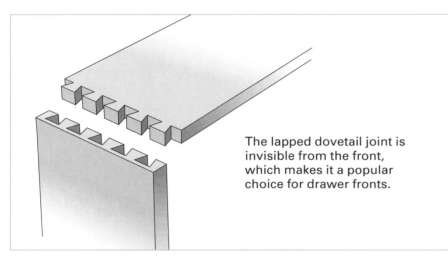

The lapped dovetail joint is invisible from the front, which makes it a popular choice for drawer fronts.

1. Having prepared the pieces of wood for the joint and squared them up, set the marking gauge to the thickness of one of the pieces of wood to be joined.

2. Transfer this measurement to the end of the piece of wood which will form the sockets for the dovetail pins, scribing a line right across the end.

3. At the end of the piece which will receive the dovetail pins, scribe a line 1 cm (⅜ in) from the edge.

4. To mark the sockets, make a mark 1 cm (⅜ in) from each side. Find the centre point and mark sections of 3 cm (1⅛ in) for the sockets and 2 cm ($^{25}/_{32}$ in) for the solid wood between them.

5. To complete the marking out of this part of the joint, use a sliding bevel set so that the inner width of each socket is 5 mm (³⁄₁₆ in) more than the outer width.

6. Begin cutting out the sockets using a backsaw at an angle, as shown in the photograph. Be careful to keep within the lines marked.

7. Complete cutting the sockets by using a chisel, making vertical and horizontal cuts to remove the waste.

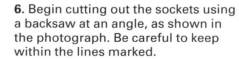

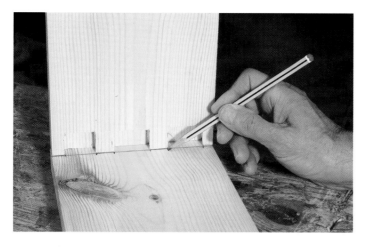

8. To make the dovetail pins, use the piece just finished as a template, transferring the width of the sockets to the end of the piece which will have the pins.

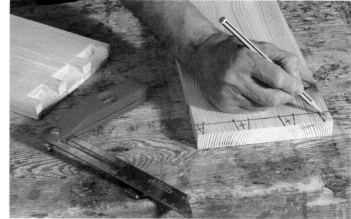

9. Use the sliding bevel at the same angle as previously to mark the sloping sides of the dovetail pins.

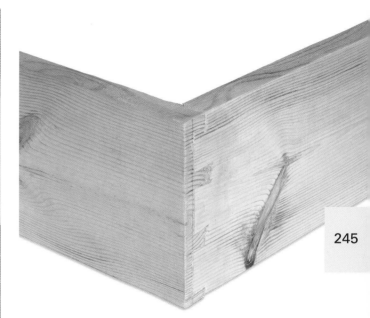

10. Use a smaller chisel to chop out the spaces between the dovetail pins.

11. Test the fit of the joint frequently and make adjustments until it is perfect. Then apply glue to the faces in contact and assemble the joint.

The finished lapped dovetail joint.

245

VARIATIONS ON THE DOVETAIL JOINT

Secret dovetail joint

Secret mitred dovetail joint

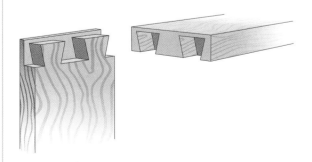

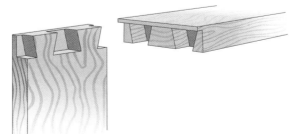

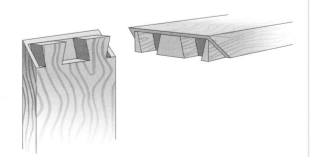

The edge is almost hidden in this version of the dovetail joint; only the thickness of the lap is visible. This is sometimes desirable from an aesthetic point of view, particularly if the two pieces are made of different woods.

The edge of one of the pieces is completely concealed and the thickness of its lap cannot be seen because it is completely covered. It is used to make a front with an uninterrupted appearance, as in the case of a drawer.

Requiring the most work to make, this joint is secret, hiding the corner joint completely. Unlike the previous joint, it is used when both front and sides are required to present an uninterrupted appearance.

Cabinetmaking skills

The great versatility of wood in its uses and applications is explained by its valuable qualities, its flexibility and resistance to wear, together with its friendly, warm appearance. Its versatility has been increased by the development of particular skills which are closely related to cabinetmaking and joinery, introduced to decorate and embellish wooden objects and furniture.

One of these techniques is inlaid wood or intarsia. This technique originated in the East and first appeared in central Europe in the Middle Ages. It involves the use of carefully cut veneer shapes of various woods with different colours which are inlaid in recesses cut in the background wood. Together these form decorative inlaid patterns, or even illustrations.

Marquetry is similar to intarsia. Here too a decorative pattern is produced by using veneer shapes such as panelling with a border. The difference is that the veneer shapes are glued onto a smooth base wood which they cover completely, piece by piece starting from the centre and working outward towards the edges. The 'background' is also formed by pieces of veneer.

Turning is also related to cabinetmaking. It consists of placing a piece of wood in a woodturning lathe and giving it a particular round form by cutting it with chisels and gouges, carried out in several stages. While the piece of wood rotates in the lathe, the shape is created by the use of appropriate tools (firmer gouge, pointed chisel, flat chisel and so on).

Carving is another technique presented in this chapter and illustrated by a practical exercise. The desired shape is obtained by using the appropriate tools to remove and shave off parts of the wood. This technique will enable you to create simple decorative objects or to decorate pieces of furniture.

There are such a large number of such techniques that they cannot all be described in detail in the book but those illustrated will give an insight into the most important related skills, illustrated by short practical exercises.

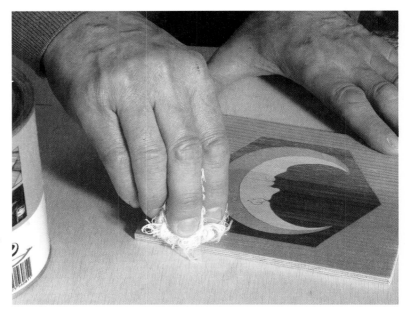

It seems that the crafts of wood inlay and marquetry originated in the East and was brought to Europe by the Romans. At the end of the 15th century, Giovanni da Verona had the idea of treating woods with various ingredients and oils to provide artistic effects.

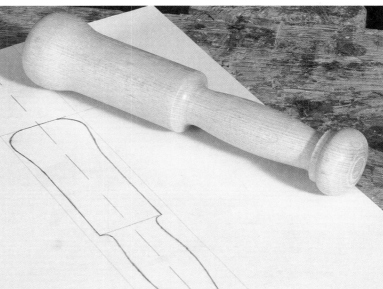

Although woodturning is a very ancient craft, it reached a level of sophistication in the 19th century with the development of industrialisation. This led to the appearance of sophisticated machinery and better tools, opening the way to new possibilities.

Carving was practised by the Egyptians although very few examples of their work have survived. In the west, the craft thrived in the medieval period. It then came to be used for ornamental patterns based on plant themes, such as tendrils, shoots, flowers and leaves.

Marquetry

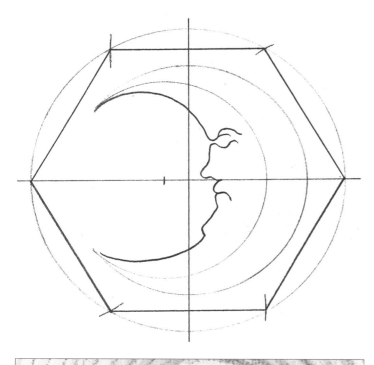

MATERIALS NEEDED

• Sheets of veneer of various woods, each
  16 x 18 cm (6¼ x 7⁷⁄₁₆ in):
- Walnut
- Lemon
- Maple
- Oregon pine
- 2 sheets of complementary veneer of any wood,
  the same size

• 1 backing board 25 x 18 cm (9¹³⁄₁₆ x 7⁷⁄₁₆ in)

• Roll of wide masking tape

• Woodworking white glue

• Medium and fine grade sandpaper

• Varnish

• Pieces of cotton scrim

Drawing the design

1. Draw the design on a piece of paper, identifying the different veneers to be used. The geometrical parts are drawn with instruments while the moon's face is drawn freehand.

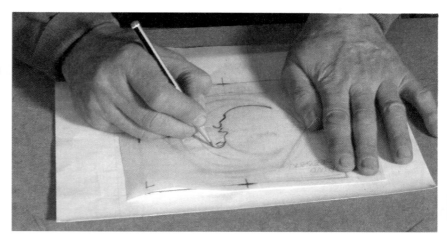

2. From this drawing, trace the part which is drawn freehand onto a piece of tracing paper.

247

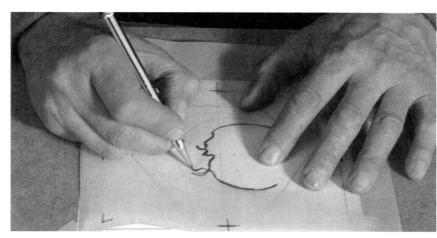

3. Transfer the drawing from the tracing paper to a template with carbon paper.

Preparing and gluing the veneers

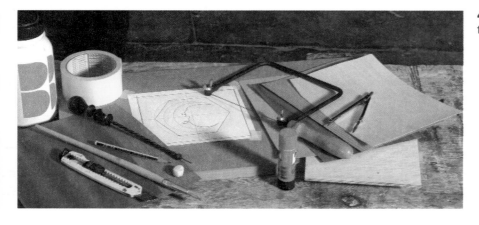

4. These are the materials and tools needed for this exercise.

5. Using a craft knife or scalpel, cut the veneers to a size of 14 x 16 cm (5½ x 6¼ in).

6. Cover each sheet of veneer with overlapping layers of adhesive tape.

7. To ensure that it remains fixed together when cut, cover it with another layer of adhesive tape in the opposite direction.

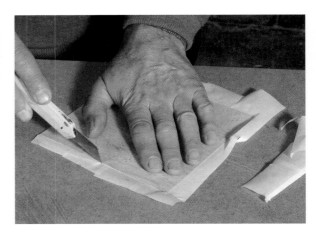

8. Cut off the waste with a scalpel.

9. Use the flat end of a hammer to press the tape down firmly all over the veneer so it is completely in contact.

10. The sheets of veneer, each one covered with tape.

11. Put all the sheets on top of each other and tape them together at the edges.

12. Fold the tape round all four edges of the packet of veneers.

Cutting the veneers

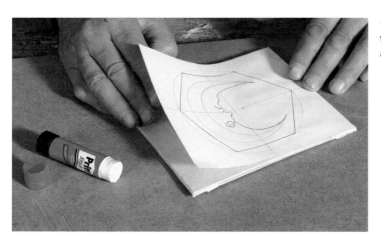

13. Glue the paper template to the packet of veneer with a glue stick.

14. Make small holes with a drill to make starting points for the fretsaw cuts.

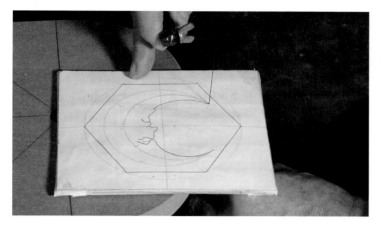

15. Pass the fretsaw blade through one of the drilled holes and re-attach it to the saw frame.

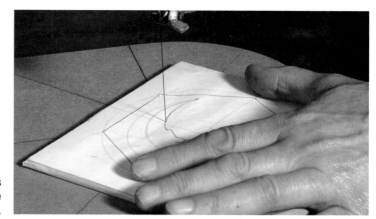

16. Using the template as a guide, saw round the outlines of the drawing.

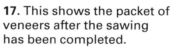

17. This shows the packet of veneers after the sawing has been completed.

18. Carefully dismantle the packet of cut veneers and select the parts of veneer chosen for the work itself.

Gluing and mounting the veneers

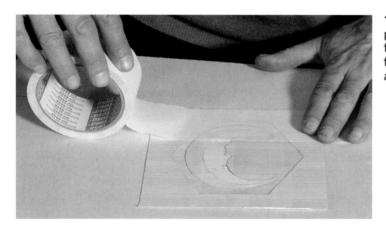

19. Arrange the chosen pieces of veneer in their final position and carefully fix them in place with adhesive tape.

20. Apply a layer of glue to the back of the veneers.

21. While the glue is still wet, stick the veneers to the plywood base.

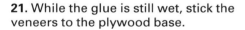

22. Sandwich the backing and veneer between two pieces of MDF.

23. Apply pressure to the work by using two cramps to squeeze the sandwich together.

Finishing

24. When the joint has completely set, dismantle the sandwich and peel off the adhesive tape.

25. Sand the surface of the work with fine grade sandpaper

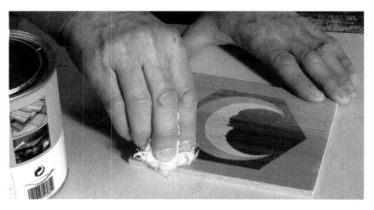

26. Varnish the work using a pad of cotton scrim.

The completed piece of marquetry.

Turning

Making a pestle

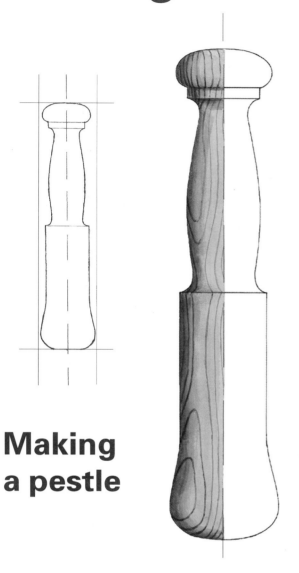

MATERIALS NEEDED

- Solid beech: piece 40 cm (15¹¹⁄₁₆ in) long, diameter 8 cm (3⅛ in)
- Medium and fine grade sandpaper

Tools used for turning

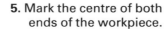

Drawing the design

1. Rule a centre line and then draw half the outline on a piece of card which will be used as a template.

2. Trace the half-outline of the piece on tracing paper.

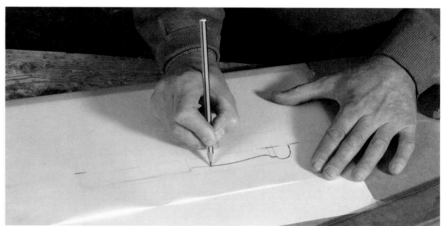

3. Complete the drawing on the card by transferring the half-drawing from the tracing paper.

4. When the template is finished, the work can begin. The tools needed include chisels, gouges and callipers.

5. Mark the centre of both ends of the workpiece.

Turning

6. Fix the wood to the drive centre of the lathe.

7. Slide the tailstock centre up to the other end of the workpiece and clamp it in position. Adjust the pressure with the handwheel.

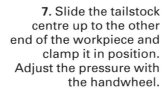

8. When the workpiece has been fixed, position the tool rest and clamp it. The distance between the tool rest and the work should be about 5 mm (3⁄16 in).

9. Switch on the lathe and make the first cut with the gouge to make the work cylindrical. This has to be done before shaping the pestle is begun.

10. Set the callipers to the overall maximum width of the pestle

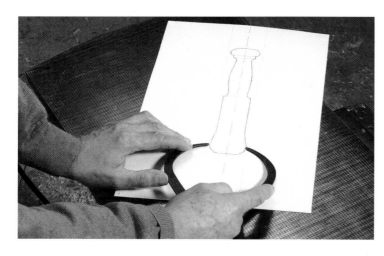

11. Turn the cylinder until it is the same diameter as the opening of the callipers.

12. Take the various longitudinal measurements from the template.

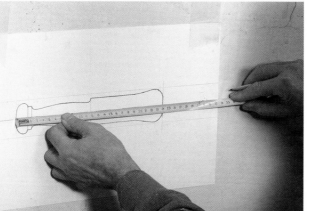

13. Transfer these measurements to the workpiece with a pencil.

14. With the lathe turning, use a fine chisel to make grooves where the pencil marks define the overall length of the pestle. Leave a central core of at least 2 cm (²⁵⁄₃₂ in).

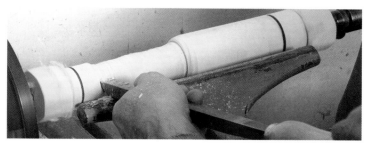

15. Rough out the curves of the pestle, following the measurements and checking the diameter with the callipers.

16. Shape the upper part of the piece, starting at the top and making the moulded shape.

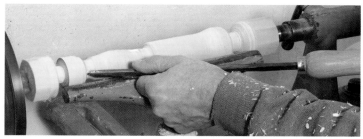

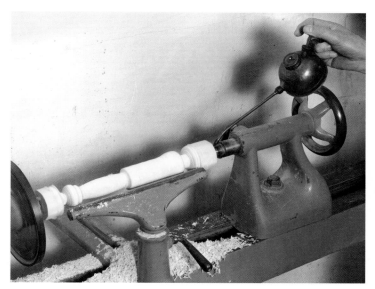

17. Oil the tailstock from time to time.

Sanding

18. When the turning is finished, sand the work with sandpaper. Before doing this move the tool rest well away from the work to avoid accidents.

19. Sand all the mouldings and grooves of the work.

20. Since the pestle will be in contact with food, it should not be varnished. Instead give it a shine by rubbing with the back of a sheet of sandpaper.

21. Cut through the end of the workpiece with a fine chisel.

22. Remove the piece from the lathe and saw through the other end, which has already been partly cut through on the lathe.

23. Clean up the cut ends by rubbing on sandpaper.

The final appearance of the pestle.

Carving

MATERIALS NEEDED

- 1 piece walnut 26 x 13 x 3 cm (10⅜₆ x 5¹⁄₁₆ x 1⅛ in)
- Carbon paper
- Medium and fine grade sandpaper
- Wax and brush
- Pieces of cotton scrim

Preparing the design

1. Materials needed for this carving exercise with the tools to be used: various sizes of chisels and gouges.

2. Use the workpiece to mark its size on a piece of paper.

3. Make the design freehand before transferring it to the workpiece.

4. Transferring the design to the workpiece with a sheet of carbon paper.

5. Go over the transferred design with a pencil to make it clearer.

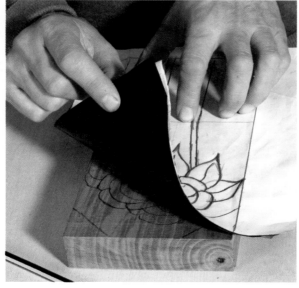

6. Cut the upper corners off the workpiece with a power saw.

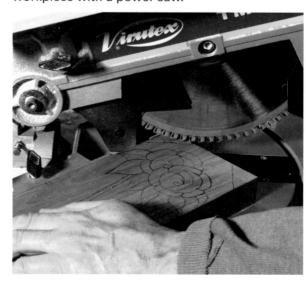

Carving operations

7. With a flat (fishtail) gouge, cut the inner outlines of the two flowers.

8. Use a mallet and small chisel to cut away the inside of the flowers, always working towards the outline just marked.

9. Repeat the previous operation, working the chisel by hand to remove the splinters left by cutting out the wood.

10. Another view of the same operation , cleaning up the carving.

11. Cut the outer outline of the flowers with the flat gouge.

12. On the edge of the work, use a pencil to mark the depth of the background to be cut away round the flowers.

13. With a chisel, cut away the wood surrounding the flowers, keeping to the depth just marked. The final cuts are made by hand.

14. Use the same chisel to complete the removal of the wood, using both hands to control it.

15. Cut out the rest of the area of the petals with a slightly curved gouge.

16. Use a medium gouge to cut out the petals, following the design of the drawing.

17. Cut out the wood from the areas between the petals with a small chisel.

18. To give the flowers realism, round off the edges of the petals.

19. Mark the outlines of the leaves with a gouge and cut away the inner parts.

20. Redraw the lines of the pattern where they have been removed by cutting away the wood.

21. Cut away the wood round the leaves. As a guide, mark the extent to be removed with a pencil.

22. With a small veining tool mark the inner lines of the leaves (representing the ribs).

23. Use a larger chisel to create the outline of the stems.

24. Continue carving the stem, rounding off the edges made.

Sanding

25. Sand the whole surface with sandpaper, including the nooks and crannies created in the course of carving.

26. Use a slightly curved gouge to finish off the central button of the flowers and the spiral lines.

Finishing

27. Apply wax to the whole surface with pieces of cotton scrim.

28. Polish with a brush to remove any traces of solid wax which may have become caught in the details of the carving.

The final carving with floral motifs.

Furniture making

This page introduces an extensive section dealing with building furniture and other decorative and everyday items from wood. Cabinetmaking is a major craft and covers a wide range of objects, ranging from small wooden items to larger pieces of furniture.

Because practical considerations have priority in this book, step-by-step instructions are given for making a number of pieces of furniture which could be useful or decorative in the home.

However, this is not the only aim of this book. The techniques can be applied to the production of a wide range of objects which are introduced in the appropriate chapters.

In this way, the theoretical information is supported by illustrated examples which can easily be translated into practice.

The various projects included in this section are divided into categories according to the rooms in which they are normally found. Naturally this is not intended to be a rigid classification and the table below should therefore only be used a guide or example.

Although these exercises are quite different in some parts, the respective introductions are presented in a standard way. They begin with an introduction to the relevant technique, a list of the materials needed and a workshop drawing showing the individual parts with the corresponding measurements. This is followed by detailed instructions in which the various stages of the project are described and illustrated step-by-step.

The materials and measurements may of course be altered if desired. The type of wood may vary according to what is available, and the dimensions may be changed depending on individual requirements.

These exercises require care and time. It is not a matter of working fast but of doing a good job. Wood is a living, warm material and should be handled accordingly. It is not important that the object should be completed in as short a time as possible but that it should beautiful, very personal and above all radiate warmth. This can only be achieved if the wood is treated lovingly and respectfully – an approach which will be reflected in the end result.

Hall

- Chest
- Longcase clock
- Coat stand

Bedroom

- Bed
- Bedside table

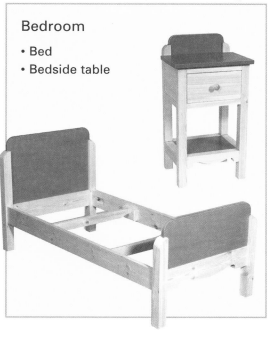

Living room

- Coffee table
- Decorative frame
- Table lamp

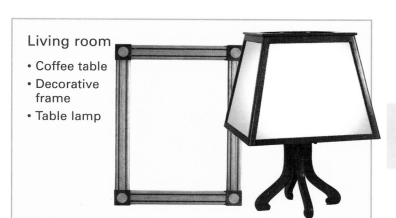

Decorative items

- Pipe stand
- Book rest
- Decorative figure: clown

Useful items and toys

- Shelving
- Toy box
- Chessboard
- CD rack
- Toy aircraft

Chest

This decorative wooden chest is attractive and traditional in appearance. Several simple techniques are used in making as well as a number of more elaborate ones. A wooden chest has been chosen because it is very versatile and will look good anywhere in the home.

This wooden chest is made of a number of softwood boards of various thicknesses. It consists of the 'box' itself, the hinged lid and a decorative plinth with appropriate legs. The boards making up the bottom, sides and lid are joined with tongue-and-groove joints, while the chest itself is assembled with dovetail joints.

To achieve the attractive rustic look, the surfaces are 'distressed' with a hand plane, a power plane and a file after the chest has been completed. This gives the chest an artificial 'used' look which emphasises its rustic appearance. The surfaces are just polished with wax and not varnished, further adding to the effect of age. The hinges too are artificially distressed.

MATERIALS NEEDED

Softwood:
- Sides:
  - 6 pieces 83 x 15 x 1.7 cm (32 5/8 x 5 29/32 x 5/8 in)
  - 6 pieces 43 x 15 x 1.7 cm (16 7/8 x 5 29/32 x 5/8 in)
- Lid:
  - 3 pieces 92 x 16 x 2.5 cm (36 3/16 x 6 1/4 x 15/16 in)
  - 2 pieces 43 x 10 x 2.5 cm (16 7/8 x 3 15/16 x 15/16 in)
- Base:
  - 3 pieces 83 x 15 x 1.7 cm (32 5/8 x 5 29/32 x 5/8 in)
- Plinth front:
  - 1 piece 86 x 12 x 2 cm (33 13/16 x4 11/16 x 25/32 in)
- Plinth sides:
  - 2 pieces 45 x 12 x 2 cm (17 11/16 x 4 11/16 x 25/32 in)
- Plinth back:
  - 1 piece 83 x 12 x 2 cm (32 5/8 x 4 11/16 x 25/32 in)
- Feet:
  - 1 piece 35 x 5 x 5 cm (13 3/4 x 1 15/16 x 1 15/16)
  - 8.6 m 28 1/4 ft battens 2 x 0.7 cm (25/32 x 1/4 in

- 2 pairs hinges with screws
- 1 decorative iron lock and screws
- Steel panel pins 2.5 cm (1 in) long
- Woodworking white glue
- Medium and fine grade sandpaper
- Black shoe polish, paint thinner
- Wax for wood
- Cotton scrim

Step-by-step instructions

1. The pieces of wood for the chest and the jack plane used to smooth them.

2.5 (1)

89.5 (35 1/4)

43.5 (17 1/8)

2.5 (1)   9 (3 17/32)

1 (1/32)

12 (4 3/4)   13 (5 1/8)

40 (15 3/4)

3 (1 3/16)

1.5 (19/32)

80 (31 1/2)

40 (15 3/4)

1.5 (19/32)

37 (14 9/16)

37 (14 9/16)

80 (31 1/2)

40 (15 3/4)

Measurements are given in centimetres
with inches in brackets
1 cm = 10 mm

84 (33 1/16)

43.2 (17 3/32)

1 (3/8)

1.5 (19/32)

1.5 (19/32)

4 (19/16)

10 (3 15/16)

10 (4 1/8)   7 (3 17/32)

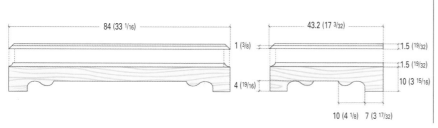

Preparing the pieces

2. Choose the best bits of wood for the front and sides. Where possible pieces with knots should be used in parts of the chest which are not seen, such as the back. Mark the face sides which will be seen so that they can be readily identified.

3. To cut the pieces to length, first adjust the guide to the required distance from the blade.

261

4. Cut the pieces to the lengths set by the gauge.

5. The bench saw cuts off the ends exactly square.

Making the side and front panels

6. Make the grooves for the joints. This is done by making two cuts with the bench saw, so that the groove is centred and of the required width.

7. To make the tongues for the joints, use the groove already made as a reference and adjust the saw guide accordingly.

8. Cut the tongues needed to make the panels of the chest. The depth should be the same as that of the groove, minus about 1.5 mm (1/16 in) to leave room for the glue.

9. When the pieces are all cut, fix one to the bench and apply glue to the groove.

10. Position the tongue in the groove and move it back and forth to distribute the glues.

11. Apply glue to the piece which will engage with the previous one

12. Attach the third piece which will complete one of the panels. A hammer may be needed to make a strong joint.

13. Use the hammer also to position the boards laterally, so that the ends are quite level.

14. Finally, cramp the boards together with bar cramps until the glue is dry. Two bar cramps will be needed.

Matching and sanding the panels

15. With a rule, measure and mark the width of the panels.

16. Use the jack plane to reduce the panel to the mark just made.

17. Smooth the rest of the panel with a plane, removing any differences between the parts making up the panel.

18. Use a power belt sander with diagonal movements to sand the surface.

19. Finally move the sander in the direction of the grain to remove any marks produced by the previous operation.

Making the joints

20. Set the marking gauge to the thickness of the panel, which will be 1.5 cm (⁹⁄₁₆ in).

21. Use the marking gauge at this setting to scribe a line across both ends of each of the four panels.

22. Take a piece of wood the length and thickness of the panels. Mark the centre line.

23. After calculating the distribution of the joints, mark the wood at intervals of 35 mm (1⅜ in).

24. Use the sliding bevel set to a slight angle to mark a line at each point, alternating the direction of the slope for each line as shown in the photograph. The angle should not be too pronounced or the joint may break.

25. Mark the areas to be removed with a cross and extend the lines round the adjacent sides of the piece of wood so they can be transferred to the panels. Use a sharp pencil so that the lines are accurate.

26. Use the try square to transfer the marks from the marked stick to the panel.

27. Once again, mark the parts to cut out with crosses, following the ones made on the marked stick.

28. Use a backsaw to make vertical cuts down to the level of the line marked with the marking gauge.

29. With a jigsaw, cut out the waste. The first cut will be a curved one down to the baseline and along it. The second cut will extend the cut at the baseline to the other vertical cut already made.

30. This is the result after making the first curved cut.

31. When the joints of one panel have been cut, use them as a template to mark out the corresponding pins at the end of the adjacent panel.

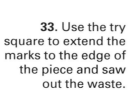

32. Mark the areas to be cut out, using the panel already made as a reference. The pin of one will match the socket of the other.

33. Use the try square to extend the marks to the edge of the piece and saw out the waste.

Making the plinth

34. Take the measurements for the plinth, using as reference the front and side panels to which the plinths will be attached.

35. Mark a line for the corner at the end of the pieces which will form the plinth. Extend this line across the edge at 45° using a mitre gauge or sliding bevel.

36. Working from the face side of the piece, saw the corner halfway through with the backsaw. Turn the wood the other way up and complete the cut.

37. Smooth the saw cut with a plane.

38. Make a template for the shape of the plinth opening. Draw the outline on the wood at each end, then join them with a straight line.

39. Before sawing out the opening, use a moulding plane to shape the top edge of the piece.

40. Cut out the opening with a jigsaw, following the line marked.

Joining the parts of the plinth

41. Saw a length of softwood 5 x 5 cm (1¹⁵⁄₁₆ x 1¹⁵⁄₁₆ in) into four pieces, each 9.5 cm (3¹¹⁄₁₆ in) long. Glue the first one on two adjacent sides.

42. Attach the block to one of the plinth sections, in line with the corner and bottom. Cramp it until the glue is dry.

43. Repeat the operation on the other plinth section.

44. When the glue fixing both blocks has dried, glue the front piece to the side pieces.

45. After gluing the front and two sides of the plinth, attach the back part. Measure the inside length, mark it and cut accordingly.

46. Glue to the back blocks and secure with panel pins.

Assembling the box

47. Apply glue to the joints and assemble the four panels forming the sides of the box.

48. Use a hammer and a scrap piece of wood to knock the joints together without marking them.

49. Cramp the joints with four bar cramps, one at each corner, until the glue has dried.

50. Remove any glue which has oozed out with a chisel before it has set.

51. Fit and attach the base panel with glue and panel pins. The panel pins are spaced at intervals of about 10 cm (4 in) and nailed through the base into the edge of the panels.

Sanding the chest and the plinth

52. Sand the surfaces of the chest with a power sander, particularly the parts where the boards are joined, so that the whole surface is even.

53. Gently chamfer all the edges with a plane.

54. Round the edges with sandpaper.

55. Plane the upper part, so that all the panels are the same level. Then finish off with sandpaper.

56. Assemble the plinth with reinforcing blocks at each corner. Smooth the edges of the plinth with a rasp. followed by sandpaper.

57. Mount the box on the plinth. It is glued and held in position by four panel pins, one at each corner.

Making the lid

58. Using the template, draw the outline on the pieces of wood which will decorate the sides of the lid. Mark one half first and then the other, symmetrically.

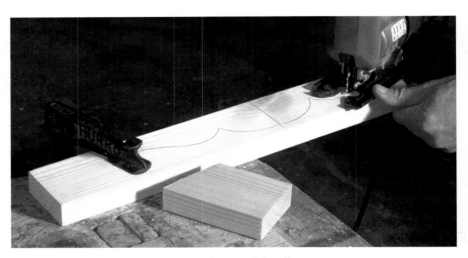

59. Cut out the opening on both pieces with a jigsaw. One piece will be fitted to each side of the lid.

60. Mark the dimensions of the lid. If the chest is 80 cm (31⁷⁄₁₆ in) long, the lid should be about 5 cm (1¹⁵⁄₁₆ in) larger all round, so that it fits comfortably.

61. Attach the two side pieces using glue and panel pins. Leave 2 cm (²⁵⁄₃₂ in) at the back and the remaining 1 cm (³⁄₈ in) at the front.

Sanding the lid

62. Cut off the corners of the lid with a jigsaw, the intention being to give the chest a worn appearance.

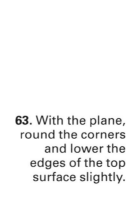

63. With the plane, round the corners and lower the edges of the top surface slightly.

64. Use a rasp to smooth and round the corners.

65. Finish sanding the lid by passing a power sander over the whole surface.

Fitting the hinges

66. The character of age which the chest is being given also takes into account the hinges connecting the lid to the chest. Using the narrow part of a hammer, hit them repeatedly while supporting them on a block of metal.

67. At a distance of 6 cm (2⅜ in) from the edge, mark the position of the hinges on the back panel of the chest.

68. Mark the depth to be cut away, which will be the same as the diameter of the knuckle. In this case it is 12 mm (⅞ in).

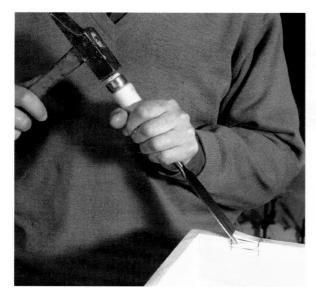

69. Make the vertical cuts with a backsaw and remove the waste with a chisel.

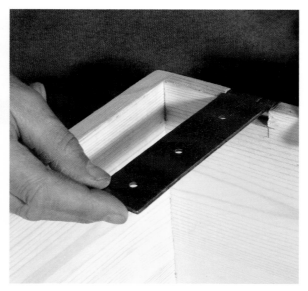

70. Offer up the hinge to check that it fits the housing just made.

71. Make pilot holes for the screws with a gimlet or awl, then screw the hinge into place.

72. Mark the position of the hinge on the lid. To do this, put the lid flat on the bench and place the box with the hinge on it, lined up correctly.

73. Screw the hinge to the lid.

Finishing

74. To give the chest an aged appearance, use black shoe polish mixed with turps (paint thinner). Before applying it to the chest, test it on some a piece of the same wood to decide on the tone required.

75. Next rub on a coat of wax polish with cotton scrim. Leave it to dry for at least 12 hours.

76. Use a scrubbing brush to buff the wax into a shine.

Fitting the decorative lock

77. Mark the centre of the front of the chest where the lock will be fixed.

78. Mark the screw holes and the outline of the keyhole.

272

79. Drill with round part of the keyhole with a power drill.

80. Use the jigsaw to extend the keyhole from the drilled hole.

81. After making pilot holes, screw the escutcheon into place.

Here is the chest completely finished. It is a multi-purpose piece of furniture, good as a decorative storage unit as well as being a decorative object in its own right. It will look well in many parts of the home, fitting in with many different styles.

Clock

As far as construction is concerned, this piece of furniture is one of the most important in this book. It is a piece which will look very handsome in halls and corridors and also in living rooms. The construction of this longcase clock consists of several processes which are more or less complex and will therefore teach the amateur cabinetmaker many techniques in a single project, as an alternative to undertaking a whole series of cabinetmaking projects.

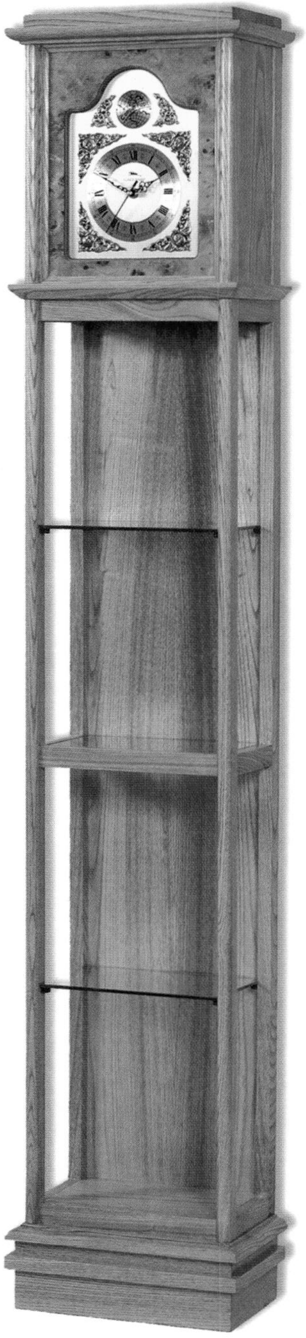

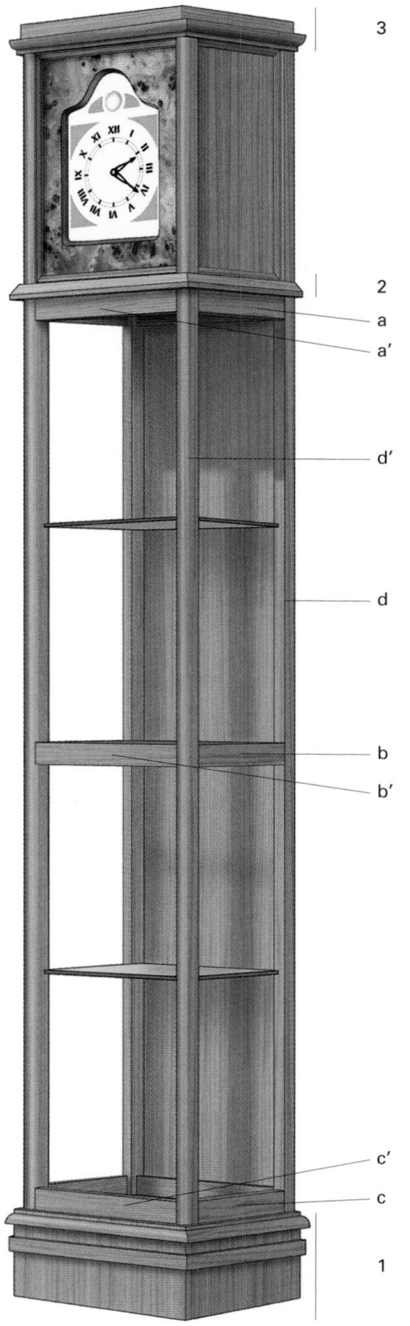

The material used to make this longcase or grandfather clock is almost entirely chestnut because it is a beautiful wood and is also very easy to work. Only a few parts which are not visible are made from lesser woods.

This project includes processes such as the veneering of the decorative frame around the dial, the making of mortise and tenon joints, and making ornamental mouldings in various sizes and shapes as well as rebates. The uprights and cross pieces are connected with mortise and tenon joints. In this project the ornamental mouldings are made with hand tools because they are easier and more comfortable to use.

With its glass shelves and veneered dial surround, this grandfather clock is a handsome object as well as a useful one.

MATERIALS NEEDED

All the pieces of the clock are made of chestnut wood, except the rods, the MDF of the frame of the face, the softwood reinforcing the base and the black poplar root veneer.

• Face:
- MDF 25 x 32 x 1.0 cm (9 13/16 x 12 9/16 x 3/8 in)
- veneer 30 x 35 cm (11 13/16 x 13 3/4 in)
- clock dial with quartz clock movement
- 4–5 m (13–16 ft) softwood battens 1 x 1 cm (3/8 x 3/8 in)

• Clock case:
- 1 piece 29 x 18 x 2 cm (11 3/8 x 7 1/16 x 25/32 in)
- sides: 2 pieces 17 x 32 x 0.5 cm (6 11/16 x 12 9/16 x 3/16 in)
- 1 piece 75 x 4 x 2 cm (29 1/2 x 1 9/16 x 25/32 in
- 1 piece 68 x 2 x 1 cm
- 1 piece 342 x 1 x 1 cm (135 x 3/8 x 3/8 in)

• Back:
- 1 piece 140 x 27.5 x 0.5 cm (55 1/16 x 10 13/16 x 3/16 in)

• Central part:
- Uprights: 4 pieces 165 x 3 x 2 cm (65 x 1 1/8 x 25/32 in)
- Cross pieces: 4 pieces 28 x 3 x 2 cm (11 x 1 1/8 x 25/32 in) and 6 pieces 16 x 3 x 2 cm (6 1/4 x 1 1/8 x 25/32 in)
- 2 glass shelves 27.5 x 14.7 x 0.6 cm (10 13/16 x 5 3/4 x 5/32 in)
- 1 shelf 24.7 x 12.1 x 0.6 cm (9 11/16 x 4 3/4 x 5/32 in)

• Base:
- 1 piece softwood 60 x 10 x 2 cm (23 5/8 x 3 15/16 x 25/32 in)
- 1 piece 77 x 4.5 x 2 cm (30 5/16 x 1 3/4 x 25/32 in)
- 1 piece 32 x 12 x 2 cm (12 9/16 x 4 11/16 x 25/32 in)
- 2 pieces 21 x 12 x 2 cm (8 1/4 x 4 11/16 x 25/32 in)
- 1 piece 75 x 1 x 2 cm (29 1/2 x 1 1/8 x 25/32 in)
- 1 piece 28 x 12 x 20 cm (11 x 4 11/16 x 25/32 in)

• Finishing
- Pieces of cotton scrim
- Woodworking white glue
- Medium and fine grade sandpaper
- Varnish
- Wood wax
- Steel wool
- Screws
- Plastic supports for the glass shelves

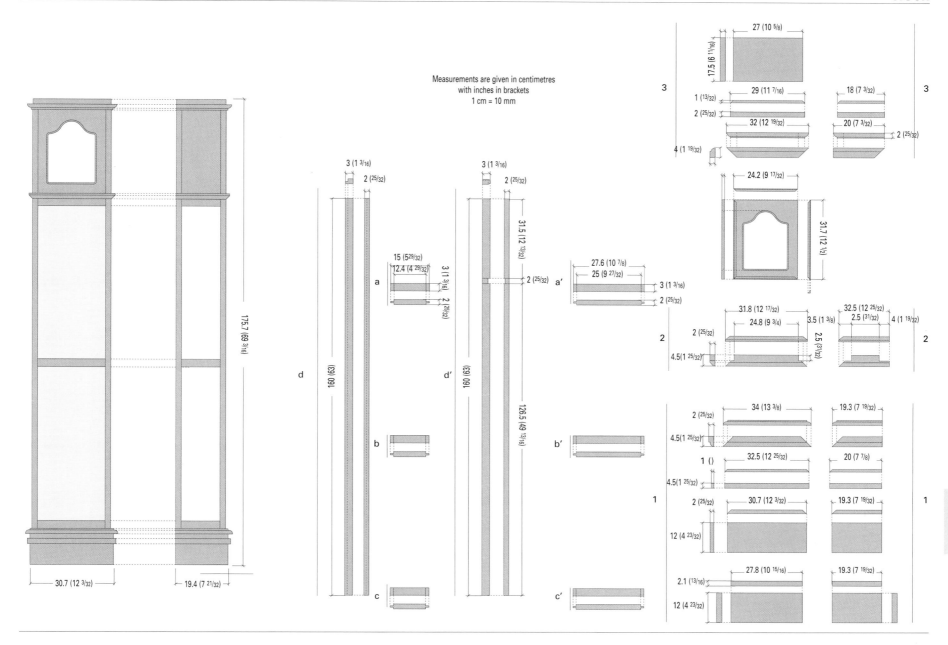

Measurements are given in centimetres
with inches in brackets
1 cm = 10 mm

275

Step-by-step instructions

Making the dial panel

1. This project requires several pieces of chestnut wood planed and squared, a sheet of black poplar veneer and some sheets of MDF.

2. Glue the sheet of veneer on one side with contact adhesive, spreading it with a spatula. Also glue the panel of MDF.

3. Stick the veneer to the panel, smoothing it by hand and pressing it at the same time.

4. Complete attaching the veneer by pressing it firmly with a veneer hammer.

5. For a perfect join between the veneer and the panel, hammer it using an intermediate piece of wood to avoid making any marks.

6. Cut off the excess veneer with a chisel.

7. Mark the central axes on the panel. Then position of the clock face on the back of the panel. There should be a space of 1 cm (⅜ in) all round it.

8. Use a template to draw the curved part of the dial outline.

9. Drill four holes in the corners to enable the inside to be cut out.

10. Fix the piece to the bench and use a jigsaw to cur out the outline marked.

11. Smooth the cut with a suitable rasp and file.

12. Use an edge router to cut the moulding round the inside of the dial frame.

13. Put the frame round the dial to check the fit.

Making the case

14. Select the uprights which will make the case (two front pieces and and two back pieces), making sure that any defects in the wood such as knots are in parts which are hidden.

15. Mark the position of the joints of the case on the faces of the uprights.

16. Mark the positions of the joints on the cross pieces. The 'V' on the side indicates that the piece will be positioned with it facing downwards. The other mark indicates that it is one of the front pieces.

17. Mark the length and the joints of the cross pieces which will make the case.

18. Cut to length and saw off the waste with a backsaw.

19. Mark the sockets of the joints in the uprights with a marking gauge.

277

20. Without moving the position of the marking gauge, mark the tenon of the joint to be made in the cross pieces.

21. Use a bench drill to cut out the waste from the mortises of the joints. Make several adjacent holes and complete the process by moving the piece sideways.

22. Without changing the position of the drill, cut the adjoining socket in the upright.

278

23. Fix the piece vertically and saw to the marks with a backsaw to make the tenons of the cross pieces.

24. Complete the operation of sawing away the waste wood.

25. Use a rasp to smooth off any roughness or splinters created by the saw and round off the tenon.

26. Use the table saw to cut the rebate for the back panel in the two rear uprights.

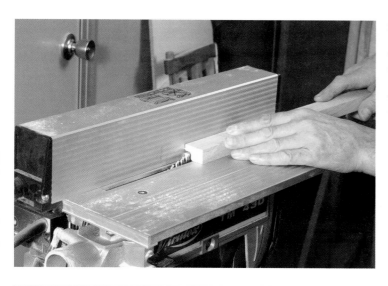

27. Once the first cut is made, turn the piece of wood and make a second cut perpendicular to the previous one. The result will be a rebate 1 x 1 cm (⅜ x ⅜ in).

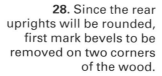

28. Since the rear uprights will be rounded, first mark bevels to be removed on two corners of the wood.

29. Bevel the angles to the marks with a plane.

30. Use the same plane to round the wood between the two bevels.

31. Smooth the whole piece with sandpaper to give a good rounded finish.

279

32. Use a smoothing plane (with cap and back iron) to clean the internal parts of the uprights and cross pieces before assembly. This operation could not be done once the case has been assembled.

33. Final finishing with sandpaper.

Assembling the case

34. Apply white glue to the mortises and tenons of the joints.

35. Assemble the uprights and side pieces of one of the sides of the clock.

36. Before assembling the whole clock, check that both sides are absolutely square.

37. Assemble the rest of the case using a hammer to knock the joints home.

38. Check that everything is square.

Making and assembling the intermediate moulding

41. To fit the piece, first mark the thickness on the uprights. The height of the mark corresponds to the middle of the adjacent cross piece.

39. Mark the area to be removed on the piece by making a bevel.

40. Fix the piece to the bench. Use the plane on the angle to form the bevel.

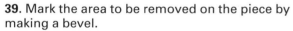

42. Saw to the marks with a backsaw and remove the waste with a chisel.

43. Mark the internal distance between the uprights on the small bevelled pieces.

44. With the mitre gauge, at 45° to the ends of the piece mark a rectangle the same width as that of the cross piece and and the same height as the remaining part of the bevel plus 2 mm (⁵⁄₆₄ in).

45. Mark the length of the internal part of the moulded piece.

46. Saw out the pieces as marked and remove any roughness with sandpaper.

47. Mark the internal distance between the uprights.

48. With the mitre gauge mark the 45° bevels at the ends of the two pieces.

49. Mark the depth 12 mm (¹⁵⁄₃₂ in) from the start of the bevelled angle.

50. Saw to the marks with a backsaw.

51. Offer it up to the frame to check that that the joint fits.

52. Glue the four bevelled pieces.

53. Assemble and cramp while the glue dries.

Fitting the battens

54. Prepare all the battens for holding the side panels. First mark all the lengths where the battens will be fixed.

55. Cut the battens to length with a backsaw.

56. Before gluing, hammer two panel pins part of the way into each batten.

57. Glue and nail the battens into the various parts of the case.

Making the plinth

58. Use the table saw to cut the three pieces of softwood to size.

59. Nail the three pieces together with 5 cm (2 in) nails to make a U-shape. This will reinforce the plinth.

60. Saw the chestnut wood pieces to ize. These will clad the softwood structure.

61. Glue and pin the chestnut pieces to the softwood base. The nails should be 3 cm (1⅛ in) from the top where a moulding will be fixed later.

62. Continue the operation for the side pieces.

Fitting the moulding to the base and upper part

63. Fix the wood to the bench and shape it with a moulding plane.

64. Use the table saw to cut four pieces with 45° angles.

65. With the marking gauge, mark a band 1 cm (⅜ in) wide on the top edge of the plinth. Then glue and pin the moulding to the base.

66. Hold the pieces firmly while they are being nailed so that the mitre joints will be perfect.

67. Mark a line 6 cm (2⅜ in) from the lower part of the base all the way round where the decorative moulding is nailed using headless pins so that they do not show.

Fitting the case to the base

68. Mark the perimeter of the case on the top of the base to position it.

69. Glue the bottom of the case. The joint is fixed with cramps until the glue has completely dried.

Joining the upper part to the case

70. Use the marking gauge to mark the mouldings for the top of the clock 2 cm (²⁵⁄₃₂ in) from the edge. This distance will mark its position in relation to the outline of the case.

71. Glue the moulded pieces to their base.

72. Drill four holes 8 mm (⁵⁄₁₆ in) in diameter and 2.5 cm (¹⁵⁄₁₆ in) deep in the ends of the four uprights.

73. Glue in dowel rods and saw them off 1.5 cm (⁹⁄₁₆ in) from the end.

74. Once the correct location is decided, mark the positions of the four joints.

75. Drill four holes in the top piece.

76. Glue it into place, knocking it firmly into position with blows of the hand.

Side pieces and moulding of the dial frame

77. After cleaning up each piece, glue the rebates which will hold the side pieces enclosing the clock.

78. Use a narrow plane to make the moulding of the decorative battens for the case round the dial.

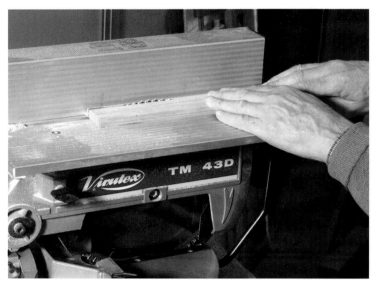

79. Use the table saw to cut the moulded sections.

80. Offer up the mouldings to the frame round the dial. When the fit is satisfactory, glue them into place.

Sanding

81. Smooth all the pieces which allow it with a cabinet scraper. In the photograph is the back piece sawn to the required measurement.

82. Sandpaper pieces which have been planed as well as those which have not, using medium grade paper first, followed by fine.

Finishing

83. Apply varnish to the surfaces with pieces of cotton waste.

84. Sand all the surfaces with very fine sandpaper.

85. Burnish all the surfaces with steel wool, not forgetting the corners.

86. Apply wax to the piece with pieces of cotton. This operation can be repeated several times to achieve the desired final result.

87. Buff up the wax to give the piece a deep, warm shine.

287

Assembling the final pieces

88. Fit the case to the base of the clock.

89. Knock the pieces firmly together with some gentle blows of the hammer.

90. Drill holes 4 mm (5⁄32 in) in diameter in the back panel, positioned at intervals so that it will be firmly fixed in the case.

91. Fix the back panel with steel screws 2 cm (25⁄32 in) long, screwing them in at a slight angle until the heads are flush.

92. Fix vertical battens in the case with panel pins to support the dial.

93. Attach the horizontal batten with white glue.

94. Fix the dial with panel pins.

95. To hold the glass shelves, make a batten with a central mark marked with a nail long enough to reach the upright. Use this to mark the position of the shelf supports.

96. Fix the four plastic shelf supports to the positions marked by the nail. Repeat for the other shelves.

97. Fit the glass shelves. The central shelf is smaller because it is surrounded by the central cross pieces of the clock.

Here is the final appearance of the clock once it is finished. It is evident that, as well as introducing a series of operations used in cabinetmaking, the project has resulted in a multi-purpose piece of furniture. As well as being an object of pride which tells the time, it is also a handsome display piece.

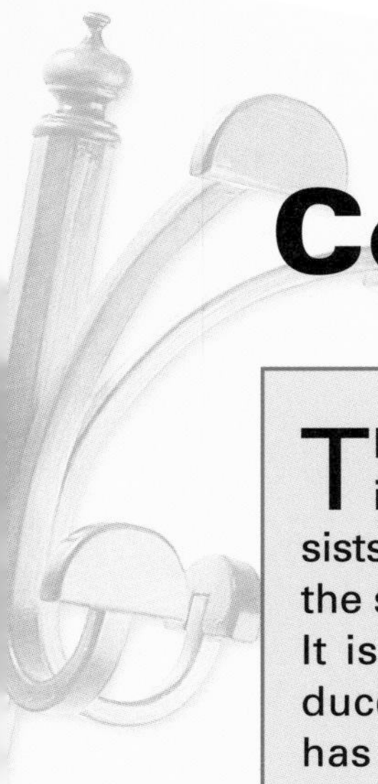

Coat stand

The coat stand for this project, illustrated on the right, consists of a single central column in the shape of a tapered octagon. It is crowned by a finial, produced by turning on a lathe. It has four legs made of laminated wood and four coat hooks, also of laminated wood, each ending with a semi-circular end piece. All the parts of the coat stand are secured by wooden dowels.

This piece of furniture has particular features which may not be apparent at first glance but which will be of interest to the woodworker. There are no metal components at all because all the parts including the fixings are made from wood. This involves two different techniques for securing the various elements to each other, bar cramps and a tourniquet.

The feet and coat hooks are made of laminated wood. The various forming techniques and moulds used to obtain a particular curve in the laminated wood are explained. The shape of these elements, their function and the best way of handling the compression stresses are described. Laminated wood is easier to form than solid wood, and in addition, the gluing of several layers improves the mechanical properties of the wooden elements created in this way, making them much stronger.

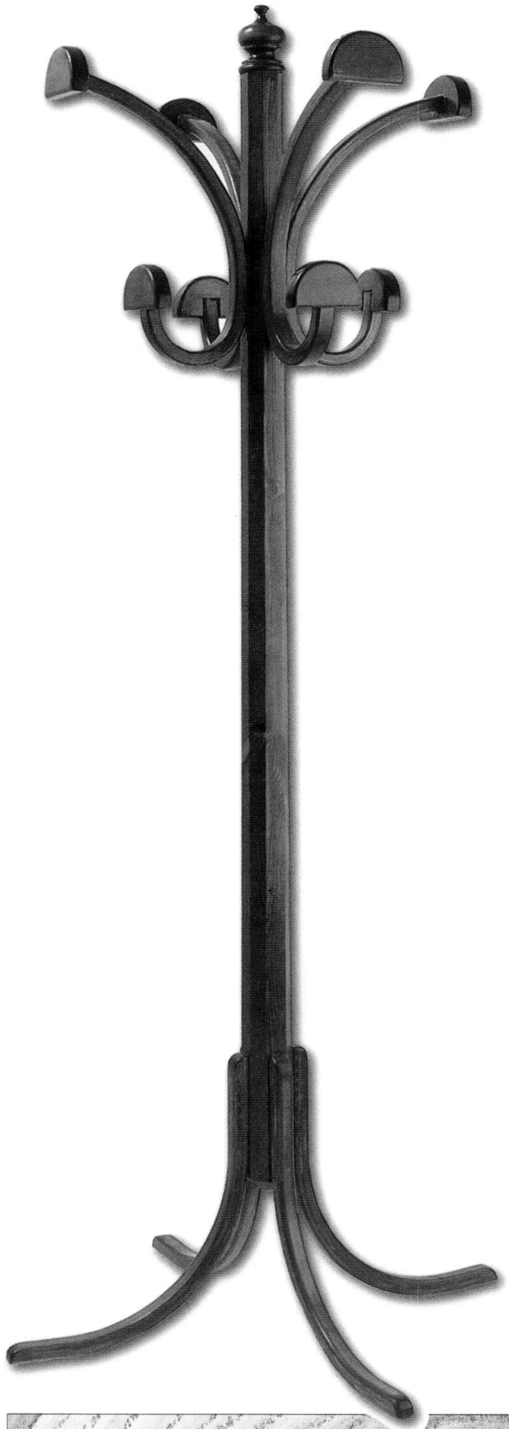

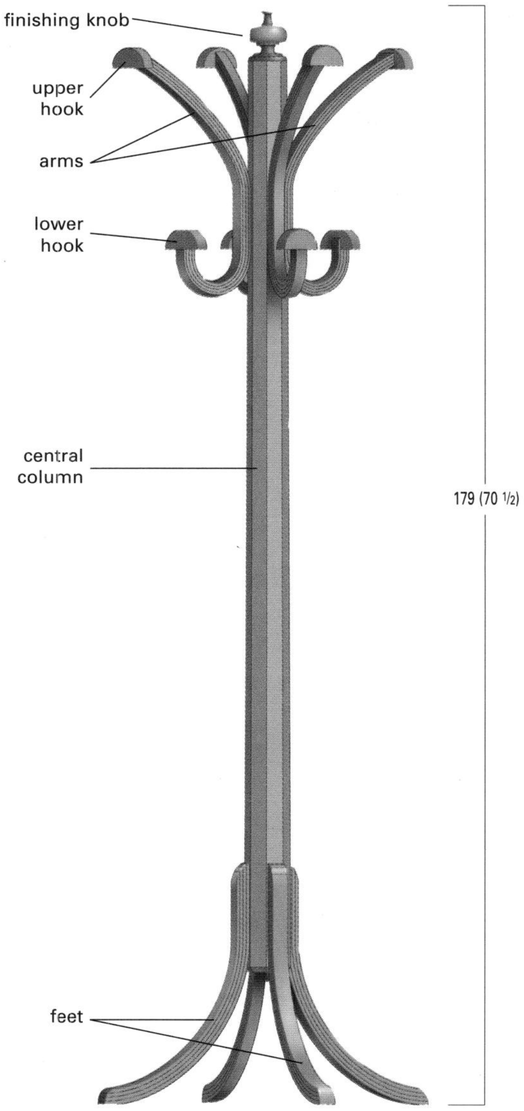
finishing knob
upper hook
arms
lower hook
central column
feet
179 (70 1/2)

MATERIALS NEEDED

• Central column: 1 piece knot-free pine 153 x 7.5 cm x 7.5 cm ($60\frac{3}{16}$ x $2\frac{15}{16}$ x $2\frac{15}{16}$ in)	• 4 feet made of 44 pieces of wood laminate 78 x 3 x 0.2 cm ($30\frac{11}{16}$ x $1\frac{1}{8}$ x $\frac{5}{64}$ in).	• Hook ends: 8 pieces knot-free pine 10 x 7 x 2.5 cm ($3\frac{15}{16}$ x $2\frac{3}{4}$ x $\frac{15}{16}$ in).	• Three supports 62 x 8 x 3.5 cm ($24\frac{3}{8}$ x $3\frac{1}{8}$ x $1\frac{3}{8}$ in) to bevel the central column	• Cord to make a tourniquet • Wood-working white glue
• Knob for the central column: piece of knot-free pine 15 x 7 x 7 cm ($5\frac{7}{8}$ x $2\frac{3}{4}$ x $2\frac{3}{4}$ in).	• 4 arms made of 48 pieces of wood laminate 78 x 3 x 0.2 cm ($30\frac{11}{16}$ x $1\frac{1}{8}$ x $\frac{5}{64}$ in).	• Lengths of 10 mm ($\frac{3}{8}$ in) dowel: enough to make the 20 pegs in the instructions.	• Panel of 3 mm ($\frac{1}{8}$ in) plywood: enough to make the templates indicated in the instructions.	• Spirit stain base colour and walnut water stain • Grain filler/ sealer varnish

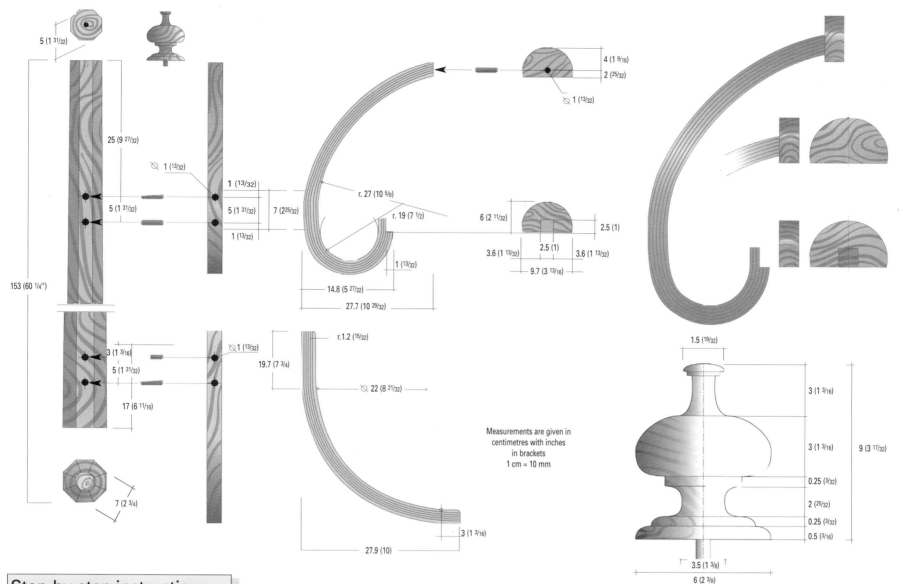

5 (1 31/32)

25 (9 27/32)

⌀ 1 (13/32)

1 (13/32)

5 (1 31/32)

1 (13/32)

153 (60 1/4")

3 (1 3/16)

5 (1 31/32)

17 (6 11/16)

7 (2 3/4)

1 (13/32)

5 (1 31/32)

7 (2 25/32)

r. 27 (10 5/8)

r. 19 (7 1/2)

1 (13/32)

14.8 (5 27/32)

27.7 (10 29/32)

⌀ 1 (13/32)

r.1.2 (15/32)

19.7 (7 3/4)

⌀ 22 (8 21/32)

27.9 (10)

3 (1 3/16)

4 (1 9/16)

2 (25/32)

⌀ 1 (13/32)

6 (2 11/32)

2.5 (1)

3.6 (1 13/32)   2.5 (1)   3.6 (1 13/32)

9.7 (3 13/16)

Measurements are given in
centimetres with inches
in brackets
1 cm = 10 mm

1.5 (19/32)

3 (1 3/16)

3 (1 3/16)

9 (3 17/32)

0.25 (3/32)

2 (25/32)

0.25 (3/32)

0.5 (3/16)

3.5 (1 3/8)

6 (2 3/8)

291

Step-by-step instructions

Central column

1. The project starts by making the central column from a piece of wood 7.5 x 7.5 cm (2¹⁵⁄₁₆ x 2¹⁵⁄₁₆ in), followed by making the laminated legs and arms.

2. With a jack plane, plane two sides at 90° so as to have some regular faces which can be marked and cut with accuracy.

3. Mark each of the sides with a marking gauge so that they will be 7 cm (2¾ in) wide when planed down.

4. The planing should be carried out on opposite sides alternately. To ensure that subsequent operations and the resulting measurements are correct, check that faces are exactly at right angles to each other using a try square.

5. Mark the decreasing width on each of the faces, so that it will end with a width of 5 cm (1¹⁵⁄₁₆ in) when planed. Use a carpenter's rule or other straight piece of wood long enough to draw the whole line in one operation.

6. To plane the column fix it to firmly to the workbench and use a jack plane. The pressure on the plane would vary along the stroke according to the amount to be removed, which is greater at the narrow end.

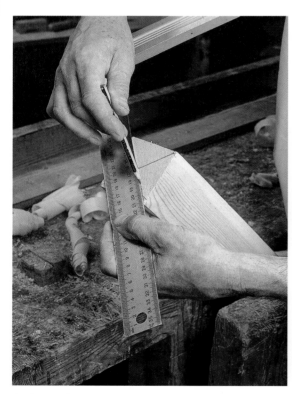

7. To mark the octagonal ends from the squared surfaces of each end, fix the column in the vice. Draw diagonal lines across the end with a rule and soft pencil. Repeat this operation at the other end.

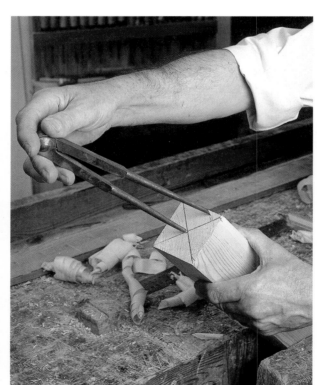

8. Where the diagonals cross is the centre for the compass to scribe a circle on the end with its circumference touching the four edges of the wood.

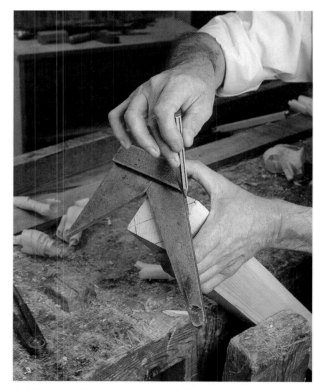

9. With a mitre square or sliding bevel set to 135°, draw four lines tangential to the circle marked. This generates the eight equal sides of the octagon.

10. To mark the irregular prism shape the central column will acquire, draw straight lines joining the corresponding corners marked on the ends. Again, it is best to draw each line in a single operation.

11. Make some supports consisting of 45° wedge-shaped openings which will support the piece by its sides. These supports are made from cleaned pieces of softwood on which the openings are marked with a mitre gauge and sawn out.

12. The supports just made are fixed to the bench. They support the column while the corners are planed with the jack plane. To resist the force of the planing a bench stop is used.

293

Making the arms and feet from laminated wood

13. The planing is completed on all the sides as far as the marks.

14. To make the arms and feet, templates are needed. These are made from a full-size drawing of the shape of each piece. As these have curved outlines, a carpenter's compass is used to draw each piece on a panel. The square and rule are also needed for this operation.

15. When the templates have been drawn, cut them out with a jigsaw, keeping to the outside of the marks so that the sizes of the pieces are not reduced by the cut.

16. To simplify subsequent operations, the templates for the arms and feet are larger than the finished pieces.

17. To make the arms of the coat stand, place the template on an MDF panel 3 cm (1¼ in) thick. When cut out, this panel will act as a mould for the laminates which will make up the finished piece of laminated wood.

18. Cut out the marked area with a jigsaw. The position of the blade must be exactly at right angles to the surface being sawn.

19. When the whole outline has been cut out, there will be two pieces to serve as a mould or former for the shape of the laminated arms. A right-angled piece is cut out of the mould where shown to provide a bearing for a bar cramp which will be used when gluing the laminates.

20. The laminates are moistened, bent to shape and dried with an electric drier. Then they are glued and positioned one after another in the mould which holds them in place.

21. When the stack of laminates reaches a thickness of 3 cm (1⅛ in), fit the other part of the mould and compress them together with bar cramps so that the pressure is as strong and as even as possible. The whole operation is repeated for the remaining arms.

22. Making the feet involves a similar process, except that the mould is fitted with guides to align it when the cramps are applied.

23. The internal surfaces of the mould are covered with was so that the parts of the mould do not stick to the work. This is important in that the mould is used several times.

24. To apply glue to the laminates, arrange them side by side after they have been moistened and dried, and spread the glue evenly over them with a brush.

25. Once the laminates have been arranged in the sliding mould to a thickness of 3 cm (1⅛ in), apply bar cramps to compress them together. The pressure applied should be even so that the glue oozes out everywhere. This should be cleaned off with a damp cloth before it dries.

26. Remove the pieces in their final shape when completely dry. Mark them with a marking gauge to their final thickness of 2.5 cm (¹⁵⁄₁₆ in). Mark one edge first, plane it smooth and then mark the other edge.

27. The laminated pieces must be firmly supported by the bench stop while the edge is being planed.

28. To shape the edges of the pieces of laminated wood, use an edge moulder held in the vice.

29. Round the ends of the feet which will be in contact with the ground, using a rasp and medium grade sandpaper.

Arm end pieces

31. The arm end pieces have a rounded finish. To soften the edges use a hand moulder for the curved arrises.

32. The lower end pieces are joined to the inside ends of the arms with a lap joint cut in the centre of each of the pieces. Made with a chisel, this is 2.5 x 2.5 cm ($^{15}/_{16}$ x $^{15}/_{16}$ in) and half the thickness of the pieces in depth. The operation will be more accurate if the blade of the chisel has the same width as the joint to be cut.

30. For the arm end pieces, make a mould on a piece of finished wood 2.5 cm ($^{15}/_{16}$ in) thick, cutting out the sections with a jigsaw. There are eight end pieces. four for the inner parts and four for the outer parts of the arms.

33. The lap joint is completed by fixing the arm in the vice and using a backsaw to saw away the waste from the lower end.

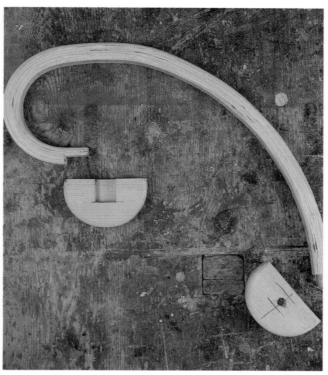

34. The end pieces of the upper arms are attached with dowels. First drill a hole 1 cm (⅜ in) in diameter in the end of each arm to a depth of 2 cm (²⁵⁄₃₂ in).

35. Complete the fitting of the upper end pieces by drilling a corresponding dowel hole in each one. The photograph shows the difference between the lower and upper end pieces, one with a lap joint and the other with a dowel hole.

36. To finish the lower end of the central column, make successive cuts at 45° with the compound mitre saw to leave an eight-sided pyramidal end.

Final operations for joining the arms and feet

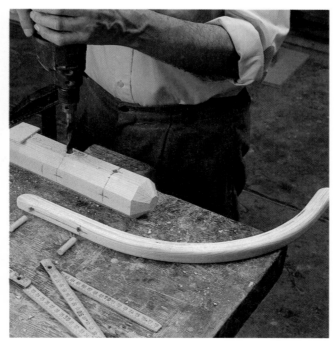

37. The joining of the feet to the central column is by 10 mm (⅜ in) dowels attached to four opposite sides of the octagon. To mark the positions to be drilled, use a sliding bevel and draw a line 17 cm (6¹¹⁄₁₆ in) from the base of the pyramid end. The first hole is 3 cm (1⅛ in) from the line drawn and the second is 3 cm (1⅛ in) from the pyramidal base.

38. To mark the holes in the feet use a similar process, taking care that the upper end of the feet is no longer than the line 17 cm (6¹¹⁄₁₆ in) marked on the central column. The column is fixed to the base with a cramp and the holes are drilled to a depth of 2 cm (²⁵⁄₃₂ in). The depth of the holes in the feet should be no more than 1 cm (⅜ in).

39. Use dowels to assemble the joints of the arms. First flatten the areas which will be in contact with a plane, working on the least curved parts. The flat surface should be about 7 cm (2¾ in) long. Mark two points 1 cm (3/8 in) from each end of the flat surface, with 5 cm (1¹⁵⁄₁₆ in) between them.

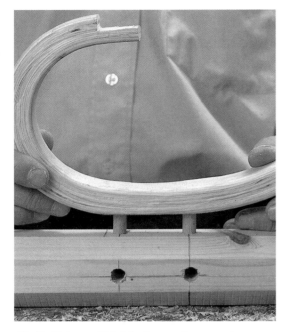

40. Drill 1 cm (⅜ in) holes at these points, 1 cm (⅜ in) deep in the arms and 2 cm (²⁵⁄₃₂ in) deep in the central column.

41. Before assembly, sand the pieces which are going to be joined. On the central column, sanding can be carried out with an electric sander using medium to fine sandpaper.

42. The column must be firmly fixed while being sanded. Use the 45° supports made earlier to achieve this.

43. The finial on the central column can be of any shape desired. The top end of the central column is prepared by marking the centre and drilling a hole 12 mm (15/32 in) in diameter and 2 cm (²⁵⁄₃₂ in) deep for the peg of the finial.

44. A lathe can be used to turn a decorative finial with chisels and gouges.

45. The grooves and rebates are finished with a small gouge specially designed to make fine cuts and irregular mouldings.

46. When the turned piece is finished, sand it and remove any roughness with fine sandpaper held in the hand.

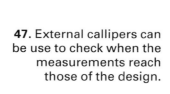

47. External callipers can be use to check when the measurements reach those of the design.

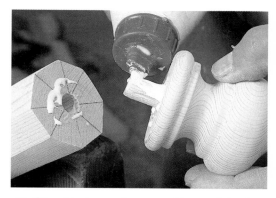

48. Glue the turned peg and insert it in the whole drilled in the end of the column.

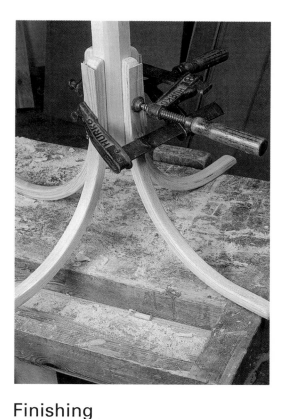

49. The arms are glued to the central column using a simple tourniquet to apply pressure to the joint. The tourniquet consists of a twisted cord and a dowel, applying even pressure to the joints in all directions. After about 30 minutes it can be removed.

Here is the completed coat stand. In carrying out this project, a number of useful cabinetmaking techniques have been covered.

50. Glue the feet to the central column and use bar cramps to apply pressure as evenly as possible to the four feet.

Finishing

51. Apply a coat of stain with a brush. In this case a mixture of spirit die and walnut water stain has been used.

52. When the stain is dry, apply grain-filling varnish with a brush, always following the direction of the grain. After the first coat, sand with very fine sandpaper and then apply a second coat. Finish with a coat of wax polish.

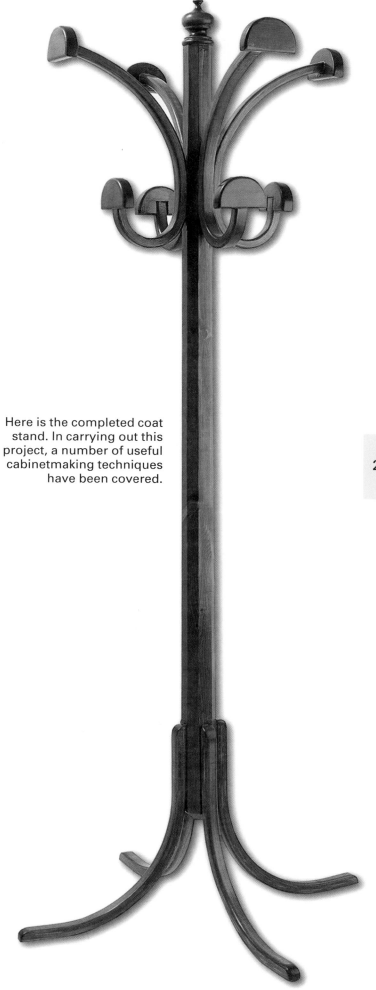

Bed

Building a bed is not as difficult a project as might be imagined. It will be explained in the following exercise, accompanied by step-by-step illustrations. All it needs is a slatted frame and mattress and you will be able to enjoy the comfort of this attractive bed. The suggested measurements of the various elements, listed below, can be altered according the individual requirements and the size of bed which is wanted.

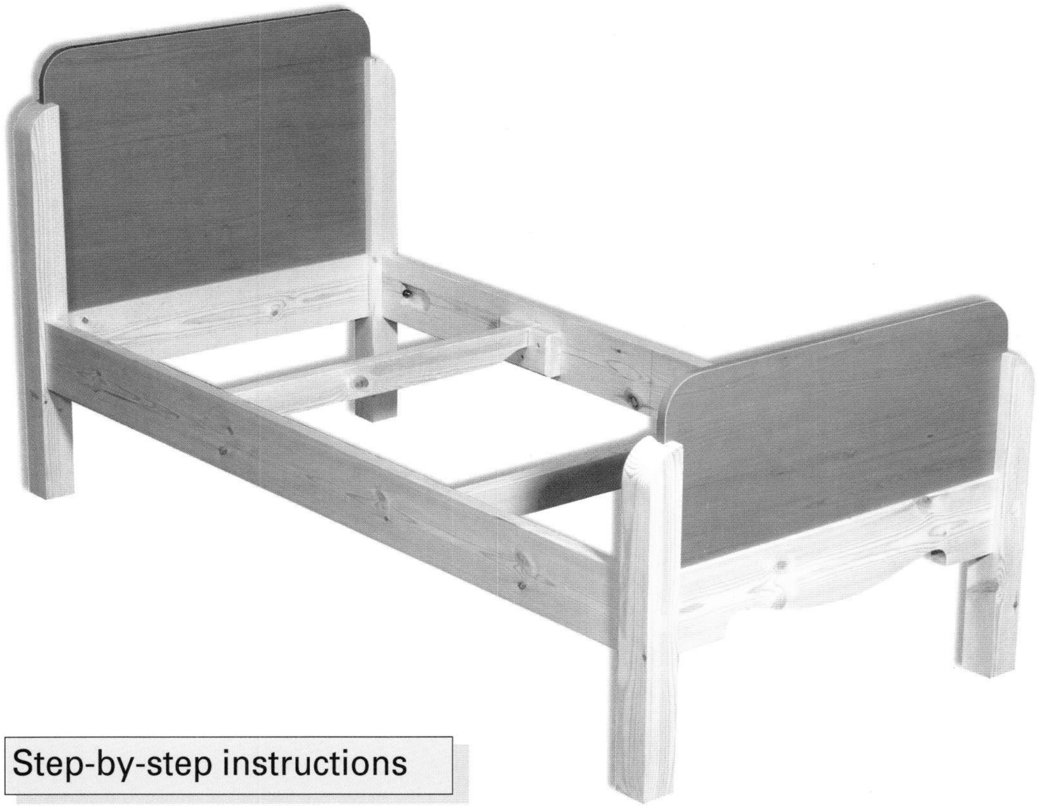

Several tools are needed to make this bed, including a jigsaw to round off the tops of the legs of the headboard and footboard and to cut curved shapes out of plywood. The various techniques used are all clearly explained: the chopping out of mortises of different dimensions with a mortise chisel, the application of edge-lipping to chipboard and the assembly of the frame with special cylinder-screws and fixing plates, which allow it to be dismantled for removal.

MATERIALS NEEDED

• Knot-free softwood 3 cm ($1\frac{1}{8}$ in) thick - For the long members: 2 pieces 15 x 192 cm ($5\frac{7}{8}$ x $75\frac{9}{16}$ in) - For the short members: 4 pieces15 x 80 cm ($5\frac{7}{8}$ x $31\frac{7}{16}$ in)	• Melamine faced chipboard 19 mm ($\frac{11}{16}$ in) thick: - For the headboard and bed-end: 1 piece 34 x 80 cm 1 piece 58 x 80 cm
• Knot-free softwood 3.5 x 7 cm ($1\frac{3}{8}$ x $2\frac{3}{4}$ in) section: - To support the base: 2 pieces 81 cm ($31\frac{7}{8}$ in) long	• 4 cylinder screw and plate fixing devices • Flat-headed screws 6 cm ($2\frac{3}{8}$ in) long
• Knot-free softwood 7 x 7 cm ($2\frac{3}{4}$ x $2\frac{3}{4}$ in) section: - For the feet: 2 pieces 62 cm ($24\frac{3}{8}$ in) long. 2 pieces 85 cm ($33\frac{7}{16}$ in) long.	• Plywood panel 5 mm ($\frac{3}{16}$ in) thick • Melamine edging 2.5 cm (1 in) wide • Woodworking white glue
• Knot-free softwood 3.5 x 10 cm ($1\frac{3}{8}$ x $3\frac{15}{16}$ in) section: - To fix the bed base: 4 pieces 16 cm long.	• Medium grade sandpaper • Varnish • Paint brush • Brush

Step-by-step instructions

Making the templates

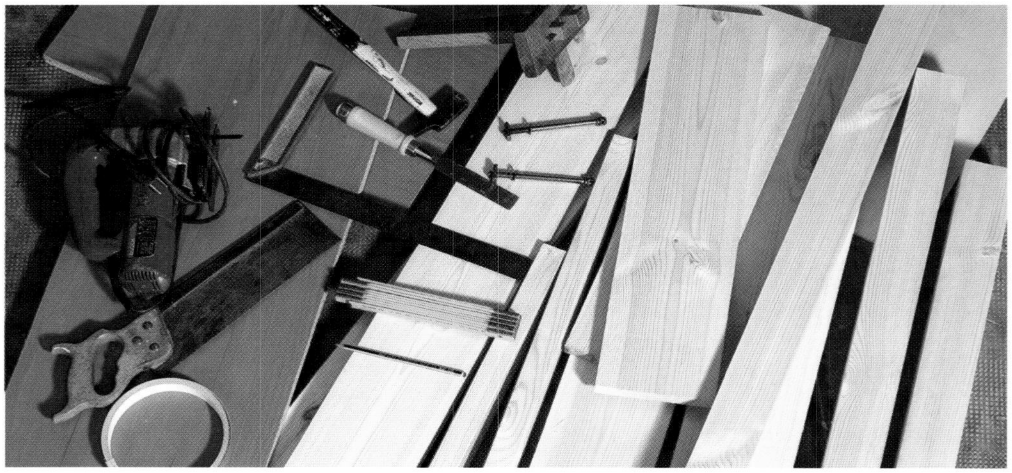

1. The tools and pieces of wood needed to carry out this project.

2. On a squared up piece of plywood 5 mm ($\frac{3}{16}$ in) thick mark a rectangle 4 x 26 cm ($1\frac{9}{16}$ x $9\frac{13}{16}$ in) thick. Make a freehand drawing of the curve for the foot of the bed shown in the photograph.

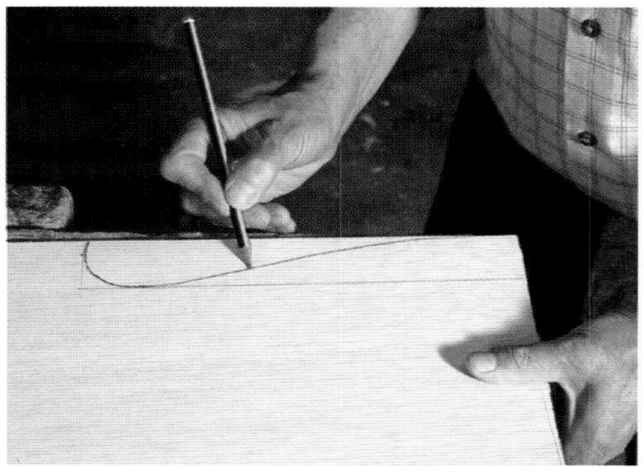

3. With the plywood fixed firmly to the bench, use a jigsaw to cut out the template for the curves.

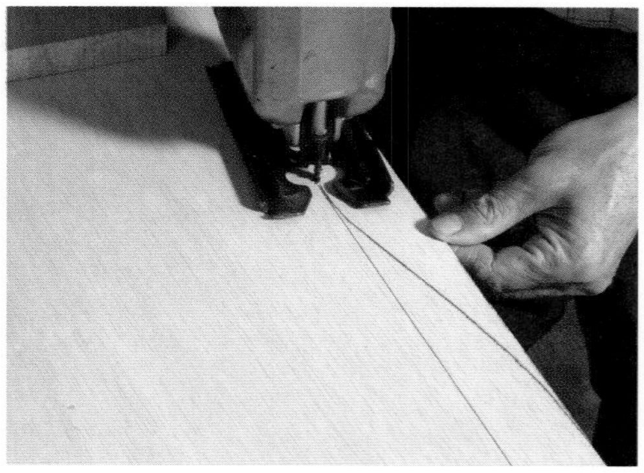

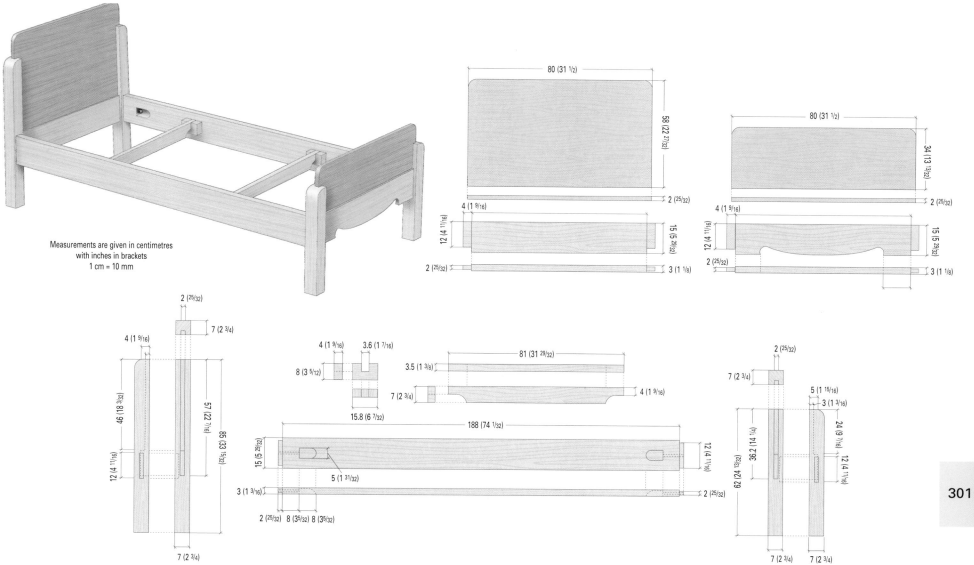

Measurements are given in centimetres
with inches in brackets
1 cm = 10 mm

301

4. When the curves have been cut, smooth the edges with sandpaper.

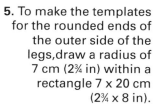

5. To make the templates for the rounded ends of the outer side of the legs, draw a radius of 7 cm (2¾ in) within a rectangle 7 x 20 cm (2¾ x 8 in).

6. As before, cut out the template with a jigsaw, keeping to the outside of the line.

7. Use medium grade sandpaper on a sanding block to smooth the edges of the template.

Making the legs

8. Mark two lengths 62 cm (24¹³⁄₃₂ in) and two lengths of 85 cm (33¹⁵⁄₃₂ in) on pieces of wood 7 x 7 cm (2¾ x 2¾ in) square. Extend the lines round all four sides with a square.

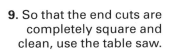

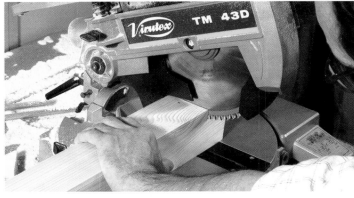

9. So that the end cuts are completely square and clean, use the table saw.

10. With the lengths defined, mark the rounded outlines on the ends of the four legs using the template. Transfer the curve marked from one side to the other.

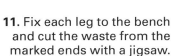
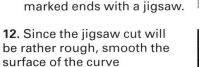

11. Fix each leg to the bench and cut the waste from the marked ends with a jigsaw.

12. Since the jigsaw cut will be rather rough, smooth the surface of the curve vigorously with the rasp.

13. Finish the ends smooth by rubbing with medium grade sandpaper wrapped round a sanding block.

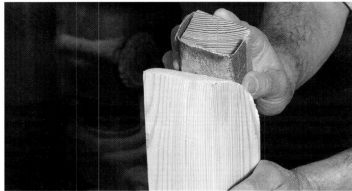

Cutting the grooves for the end panels

14. To hold the panels at the head and foot of the bed, make grooves into which they will slide. These grooves are 26 cm (9¹³⁄₁₆ in) from the lower end of each leg, but the grooves will be of different lengths because the legs at the head are longer than those at the foot.

15. To mark the width of the groove, mark a line 1 cm (⅜ in) each side of the centre line of the relevant side of the leg to make a channel 2 cm (²⁵⁄₃₂ in) wide.

16. Set the table saw to a depth of 2 cm (²⁵⁄₃₂ in) and cut the groove. To achieve the width of 2 cm (²⁵⁄₃₂ in) pass the wood over the saw several times, moving the fence slightly each time.

Making the mortises for the longitudinal pieces

17. To mark out the positions of the mortises, make a line 26 cm (9¹³⁄₁₆ in) from and parallel to the lower end of the legs, and another 12 cm (4¹¹⁄₁₆ in) from it.

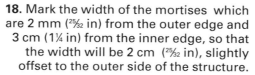

18. Mark the width of the mortises which are 2 mm (²⁵⁄₃₂ in) from the outer edge and 3 cm (1¼ in) from the inner edge, so that the width will be 2 cm (²⁵⁄₃₂ in), slightly offset to the outer side of the structure.

19. Begin chopping out the mortise with a chisel with a blade of the same width. Make a number of parallel vertical cuts.

20. Continue cutting out the mortise and finally use the chisel blade with a mallet to make cuts combined with a levering motion to remove the chips.

Making the mortises for the cross pieces

21. The mortises for the shorter cross pieces of the bed are the same size and position but at right angles to the previous ones. The difference is that the area chiselled out is in the centre of the leg. The depth of the mortise should be 4 cm (1⁹⁄₁₆ in).

22. Finish the surface of the sides in which the mortises have been cut with medium grade sandpaper to remove any irregularities.

Making the cross pieces

23. On pieces with a section of 15 x 3 cm (5²⁹⁄₃₂ x 1⅛ in), mark two lengths of 84 cm (33 in), with the ends exactly square.

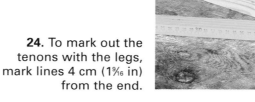

24. To mark out the tenons with the legs, mark lines 4 cm (1⁹⁄₁₆ in) from the end.

25. Mark two parallel lines on the end of the wood so that they are 2 cm (²⁵⁄₃₂ in) apart.

26. Clamp the piece vertically and accurately cut away the waste with a backsaw.

27. Complete the removal of the waste by clamping the piece horizontally and cutting it off as shown in the picture.

28. Now mark the edges to be removed from the tenon. These are 1.5 cm (⁹⁄₁₆ in) from the corresponding side.

29. With the piece vertical, make cuts as far as the depth marked.

30. Complete cutting out the tenon by sawing to the lines marked.

Transferring the template to the lower side of the cross piece

31. An operation which can be carried out before completing the cutting of the tenons is the application of the template which defines the decorative cut out in the cross piece joining the legs at the foot of the bed. Mark a point 12 cm (4¹¹⁄₁₆ in) from the shoulder of the tenon as a point of reference to locate the template.

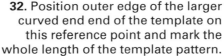
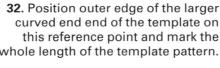

32. Position outer edge of the larger curved end end of the template on this reference point and mark the whole length of the template pattern.

33. Repeat the operation symmetrically at the other end. Then cut out the whole of the curved line with a jigsaw, always keeping to the outer side of the line.

34. When the whole curve has been cut out, sand it with medium grade sandpaper.

Marking out the panels

35. Take the pieces of 19 mm (¾ in) chipboard already cut to size and squared up. Position the template as shown in the illustration and draw the curve. Repeat for the other corners.

36. With a jigsaw, cut round the corners to the lines marked.

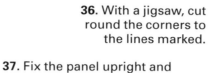

37. Fix the panel upright and smooth off any irregularities with a file.

38. Complete the smoothing process by sanding all the edges with medium grade sandpaper and a sanding block.

Applying the edging

39. To apply the edging, apply a thin layer of contact adhesive to all the visible edges. This should be done smoothly and evenly with a spatula.

40. When the glue is tacky, apply the 2.5 cm (1 in) wide edging strip, positioning it as centrally as possible.

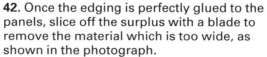

41. To finish off the edging, press them firmly with a veneer hammer to eliminate any air bubbles.

42. Once the edging is perfectly glued to the panels, slice off the surplus with a blade to remove the material which is too wide, as shown in the photograph.

43. The headboard and tailboard are finally finished by rounding the edges very gently with medium grade sandpaper so that they are no longer sharp.

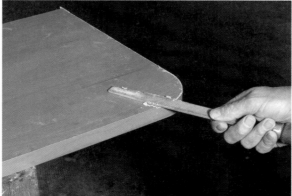

Making the longitudinal members

44. Mark the overall length of the longitudinal pieces at 192 cm (75⅝ in). Ideally these pieces should be even-grained and free of knots, so as to be as strong as possible in use.

45. Cut the ends squarely to length with a table saw, pressing it firmly against the fence.

46. The tenon of the joint is 2 cm (²⁵⁄₃₂ in) deep. Mark both lengths at the same time to minimise the possibility of each piece being a different length.

47. Make two further parallel lines, one 6.5 cm (2⁹⁄₁₆ in) and the other 16.5 cm (6½ in) from the mark of the shoulder. These will be the area containing the special fixing screws.

48. Mark the centre line of the widest face, the reference from which the area to be cut out will be measured.

49. Mark two lines 2.5 cm (¹⁵⁄₁₆ in) from each side of this line, so that the area for the fixing mechanism will be 5 x 10 cm (2 x 4 in).

50. The tenons of the side members are made in the same way as previously described for the cross pieces.

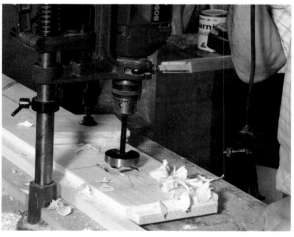

51. When the tenons at both ends have been finished, drill a recess for the fixing mechanism. This is done with a drill press and a cutter 5 cm (2 in) in diameter, to a depth of 2 cm (²⁵⁄₃₂ in).

52. Complete cutting out the recess with a wide-bladed chisel, being careful not to go over the marks made earlier nor to exceed the depth of 2 cm (²⁵⁄₃₂ in) defined by the drill cutter.

53. Mark the centre point, both height and width, on the end of the tenon. This marks the point for the hole containing the tension screw of the fixing device.

54. Drill this hole, keeping the drill completely horizontal and in line with the centre line of the side member.

55. Use a gouge to cut a channel in the lower part of the recess, so that the fixing device can be easily tightened, thus holding the whole bed firmly together.

56. This shows one of the four ends of the longitudinal members with the recess and drilled hole completed.

Making the anchorages for the feet and the side members.

57. Before making the anchorage points for the fixing devices, sand all the face so that all subsequent operations are carried out on smooth, regular surfaces.

58. On the side of the foot which contains the groove and no mortises, drill a hole 1 cm (⅜ in) in diameter through the centre.

59. Centre the fixing plate on the hole just drilled and mark round it. This marks the area to be recessed.

60. Cut out the recess marked, in this case 1 x 1.5 cm (⅜ x ⁹⁄₁₆ in) to a depth of 5 mm (³⁄₁₆ in) using a thin-bladed chisel.

61. Cut some filling pieces of wood thicker than the depth of the fixing device. Insert the fixing plate, glue the filling piece and insert in the hole.

62. When dry, carefully plane off the part of the filling piece projecting above the surface so as to make everything even.

Assembling the headboard and footboard

63. Given that the head and foot of the bed are assembled in the same way, this description covers both. The only differences are the length of the legs and the curved decoration on the bottom of the footboard. Here the tenons are glued after the panel has been fitted.

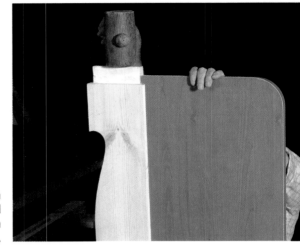

64. To seat the tenons firmly in the mortises, hammer the end with a mallet through an intermediate piece of wood.

Making the pieces supporting the cross bearers and mattress

65. On one of the pieces 3.5 x 7 x 81 cm (1⅜ x 2¾ x 31⅞ in), mark a point 12 cm (4¹¹⁄₁₆ in) from the end. Draw a freehand line from this point curving to the end, leaving not less than 5 cm at the narrowest part.

66. Cut the marked line with a jigsaw to the shape just drawn.

67. Take four pieces 3.5 x 10 cm (1⅜ x 3¹⁵⁄₁₆ in), each 16 cm (6¼ in) long. On them draw the part to be removed, 4.5 cm (1¾ in) deep by 3.5 cm (1⅜ in) wide, centred on the piece as shown in the photograph.

68. To remove the waste from the support for the base, use the backsaw and chisel as before.

69. Soften the angles with a plane, making bevels on all the visible angles.

70. Fix these blocks inside the side members of the by drilling three 5mm (³⁄₁₆ in) holes positioned as shown in the photograph, for the countersunk screws. Countersink the ends with a chisel or countersink bit.

71. Draw a line through the longitudinal axis of the side member and mark the mid point. 35 cm (13¾ in) to each side, make marks which will be the central point of the support pieces.

72. Fix each piece supporting the cross bearers with countersunk screws 6 cm (2⅜ in) long.

73. Before assembling the parts, rub on a coat of grain-filler with some pieces of cotton scrim.

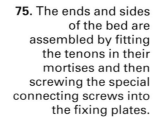

74. Before final assembly, arrange all the pieces in their relative positions so as to avoid getting them mixed up.

75. The ends and sides of the bed are assembled by fitting the tenons in their mortises and then screwing the special connecting screws into the fixing plates.

The bed as it is when finally assembled

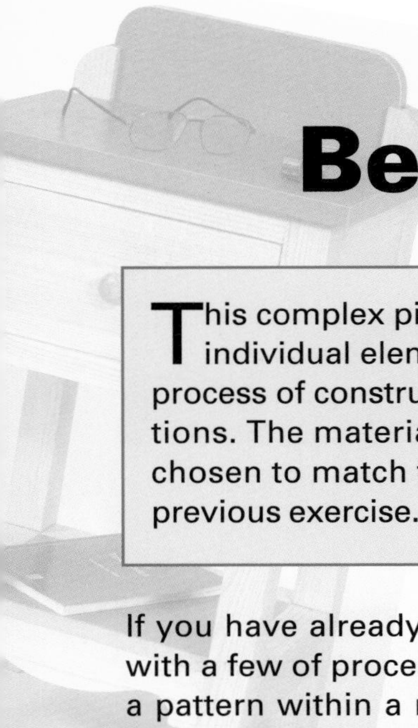

Bedside table

This complex piece of furniture is made up of a large number of individual elements so that it is quite difficult to assemble. The process of construction consists of a range of very different operations. The material, appearance and style of the bedside table is chosen to match the bed whose construction is explained in the previous exercise.

If you have already made the bed, you will now already be familiar with a few of processes used in this project: the freehand drawing of a pattern within a rectangle which is used as reference, the rounding off of the headboard with a jigsaw, the sawing of curved edging out of plywood and solid wood, the hollowing out of mortises of different widths and depth using a chisel and the application of edgeing strip on chipboard. Other techniques include the making of tenons with the front edges bevelled to 45°, the construction of a drawer with runners and the marking of the various similar components to establish the order and position in which they are used.

MATERIALS NEEDED

- Knot-free softwood, 4 x 4 cm (1 9/16 x 1 9/16 in) section:
  - For the front legs: 2 pieces 60 cm (23 5/8 in)
  - For the back legs: 2 pieces 67 cm (26 3/8 in)
  - For the cross pieces:
    Lower front cross piece: 1 piece 32 cm (12 9/16 in) long.
    Lower back cross piece: 1 piece 32 cm (12 9/16 in) long.
    Side cross piece: 2 pieces 25 cm (9 13/16 in) long
- Knot-free softwood, 3 x 4 cm (1 1/8 x 1 9/16 in) section:
  - For the cross pieces:
    Long cross pieces: 3 pieces 32 cm (12 9/16 in) long
    Short cross pieces: 4 pieces 32 cm (12 9/16 in) long
- Knot-free softwood, 2 x 2 cm (25/32 x 25/326 in) section:
  - To support the various horizontal and vertical surfaces
    4 pieces 10 cm (3 15/16 in) long
    10 pieces 20 cm (7 13/16 in) long
    2 pieces 27 cm (10 5/8 in) long.
- Knot-free softwood, 2 cm (25/326 in) thick
  For the side panels:
  2 pieces 20 x 14 cm (7 13/16 x 5 1/2 in)
- Melamine-faced chipboard 20 mm (7 13/16 in) thick:
  - For the top, back panel and lower shelf:
    1 piece 29 x 29.5 cm (11 3/8 x 11 9/16 in)
    1 piece 38 x 26.5 cm (14 15/16 x 10 3/8 in)
    1 piece 27 x 20 cm (10 5/8 x 7 13/16 in)
- Wood drawer pull for gluing in place
- Lost-head nails 4 cm (1 9/16 in) long
- Lost-head nails 3 cm (1 1/8 in) long
- Plywood panel 4 mm (5/32 in) thick
- Melamine edging 2.5 cm (1 in) thick)
- Woodworking white glue
- Contact adhesive
- Medium grade sandpaper
- Varnish
- Paint brush
- Brush

Step-by-step instructions

Making the back legs

1. Tools and wood needed in the construction of this project.

2. Mark a length of 67 cm (26 3/8 in) on squared and planed 4 x 4 cm (1 9/16 x1 9/16 in) for each of the two back legs.

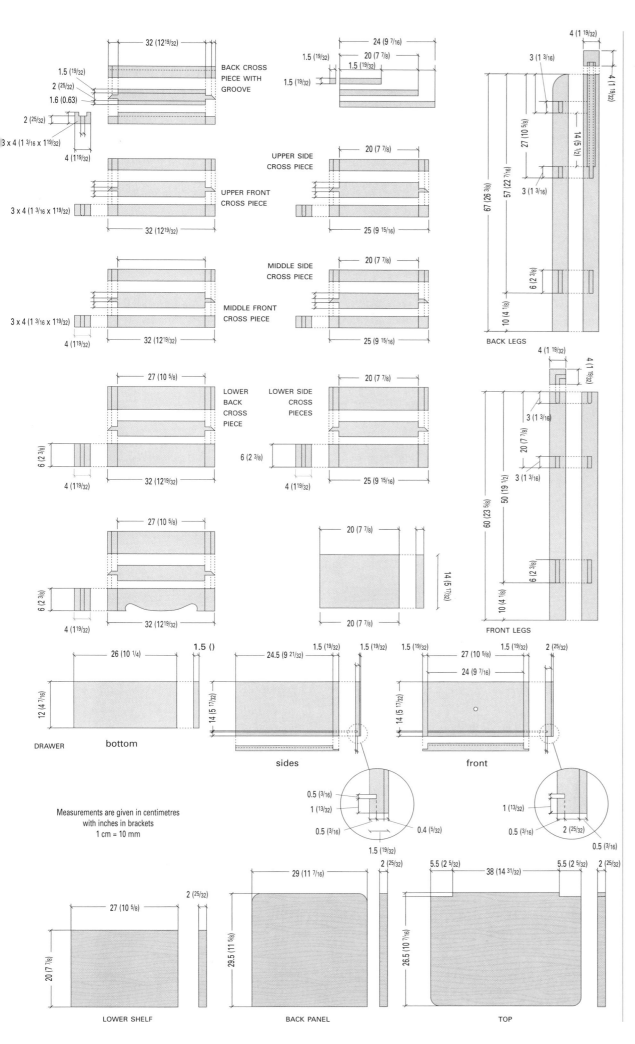

BACK CROSS PIECE WITH GROOVE

3 x 4 (1 3/16 x 1 19/32)

UPPER SIDE CROSS PIECE

UPPER FRONT CROSS PIECE

MIDDLE SIDE CROSS PIECE

MIDDLE FRONT CROSS PIECE

LOWER BACK CROSS PIECE

LOWER SIDE CROSS PIECES

BACK LEGS

FRONT LEGS

DRAWER   bottom

sides

front

Measurements are given in centimetres with inches in brackets
1 cm = 10 mm

LOWER SHELF

BACK PANEL

TOP

3. Make a plywood template for the rounded upper ends of the legs. This consists of a quarter of a circle with a radius of 4 cm (1⁹⁄₁₆ in).

4. Cut the curve with a jigsaw, keeping to the outside of the line.

5. Make the rounded curve smooth with a rasp and then finish it off with medium grade sandpaper.

311

6. On the other side of the two back legs mark a length of 27 cm (10⅝ in). Use the marking gauge to mark two parallel lines 2 cm apart, centred on the face which contains them. This mark will be the groove which holds part of the back panel.

7. At 3 cm (1⅛ in) from the mark made earlier draw another line parallel with it, the same width as the groove. This marks the limit of the area to be cut away by the table saw when cutting the groove.

8. On the same face and at the lower end of the legs mark a line 10 cm (3¹⁵⁄₁₆ in) from the end, and 6 cm (2⅜ in) from this make a similar mark which, together with a central band 1 cm (⅜ in) wide, define the area to be removed to contain the lower back cross piece.

9. Use a chisel to chop out the two areas marked earlier, making mortises 2.5 cm (¹⁵⁄₁₆ in) deep. These marks are transferred to the same surface measurements on the opposite side of the leg. Repeat the operation in the lower part of the leg, making another mortise 2.5 cm (¹⁵⁄₁₆ in) deep.

10. On the adjacent side of the leg, make a third mortise, 14 cm (5½ in) from the end and 3 cm (1⅛ in) long.

11. The three mortises made in the sides of the rounded end of the leg will receive the tenons of the back cross pieces, three in all.

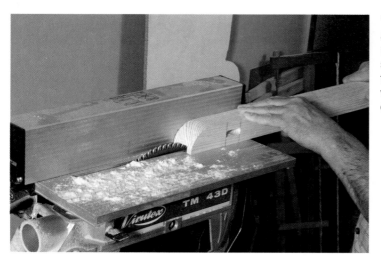

12. To make the groove already marked, make repeated cuts of the table saw, moving the fence, so that a groove 2 cm (²⁵⁄₃₂ in) wide by 1 cm (⅜ in) deep is creates.

13. The lower end of the groove will meet the mortise made by hand earlier with the chisel. This junction must be smoothed and cleaned up, removing any irregularities.

Making the front legs

14. The front legs contain three mortises similar to those made in the corresponding faces of the rear legs, which are used as a measure for defining their positions. The dimensions are transferred from one to the other with a try square.

15. Once marked out, the areas to be removed are identified as before. The top end of the front feet are marked so that they contain L-shaped mortises.

16. As with the rear legs, the marks cut away are transferred to the adjacent faces so that they create joined mortises in which the cross pieces will be in contact with each other.

17. Cut away the end with a chisel so that the L-shaped mortise is 3 cm (1⅛ in) deep.

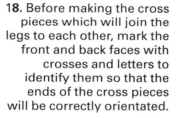

18. Before making the cross pieces which will join the legs to each other, mark the front and back faces with crosses and letters to identify them so that the ends of the cross pieces will be correctly orientated.

Making the upper an lower cross pieces

19. On a piece of wood 6 x 4 cm (2⅜ x 1⁹⁄₁₆ in) mark a length of 32 cm (12⅝ in) and from these lines mark the depths of the tenons, 2.5 cm (¹⁵⁄₁₆ in).

20. When the piece has been cut, mark the width of the tenons, 1 cm (⅜ in) with the marking gauge.

21. Fix the pieces vertically and saw the sides of the tenon to the marks.

313

22. Mark an angle of 45° across the ends of the tenons. Holding each piece in a bench hook or mitre box, cut this angles carefully with a backsaw.

23. In the same way as the fronts of the back legs were marked, mark the face of the cross pieces which will be at the front when the angles of the tenons face the interior.

24. To make the curved front cross piece, make a plywood template 6 x 14 cm (2⅜ x 5½ in). Draw a curve starting 3 cm (1⅛ in) from the end and reaching a maximum of 3 cm (1⅛ in) from the edge, and a minimum of 1 cm (⅜ in). Use this template to trace the line on the work.

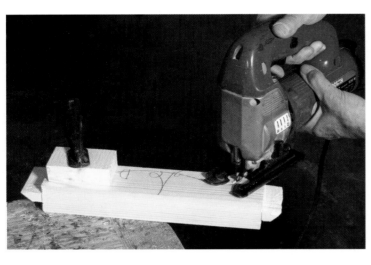

25. With the piece attached firmly to the workbench, cut the waste away from the curved shape with a jigsaw.

26. Clean the curve with a rasp and finish with medium grade sandpaper.

Making the lower cross pieces and the front frame

27. Mark a length of 32 cm (12⅝ in) on a piece of wood 3 x 4 cm (1⅛ x 1⁹⁄₁₆ in). Mark the length of the tenons, 2.5 cm (¹⁵⁄₁₆ in) from these lines.

28. The procedure for marking and making the tenons on these pieces is the same as described earlier, but of course the sizes are to suit those of the new sections. In this case too the front face is marked.

29. With the cross pieces made and the corresponding tenons cut, assemble to check all the joints.

Fixing the supports

30. The front support intended for the lower platform is made of wood 5 x 5 cm (1¹⁵⁄₁₆ x 1¹⁵⁄₁₆ in), the size being the distance between the legs, 32 cm (12⅝ in).

31. The position of this support is marked by drawing a line 2 cm (²⁵⁄₃₂ in) from the upper side of the crosspiece and parallel to it.

32. Glue the support and then nail it so as to reinforce the join.

33. The fixing is strengthened by three nails 4 cm (1½ in) long.

34. To position the supports of the side panels, mark parallel lines 1.5 cm (⁹⁄₁₆ in) from the upper and middle cross pieces. This result in a distance of 10 cm (3¹⁵⁄₁₆ in) equidistant between them.

35. Cut the two support pieces from wood 2 x 2 cm (1¹⁵⁄₁₆ x 1¹⁵⁄₁₆ in) and 10 cm (3¹⁵⁄₁₆ in) long. Glue and nail to fix in place.

315

Making the rear cross pieces.

36. These are similar to the plain front cross pieces except the upper one has a 2 cm (²⁵⁄₃₂ in) groove, here being marked, in its widest side.

37. Cut the groove to a width and depth of 2 cm (²⁵⁄₃₂ in).

38. Make a mark to identify the back face of the cross piece.

39. Fix a support to the lower side, to serve as a support for the lower platform.

40. The supports for the side panels are the same size and position as the similar ones on the front cross pieces.

Marking the front and back frames

41. On the side faces of the front frames, mark letters to indicate which ones correspond with the visible faces of the side cross pieces which will be made later.

Making the lower side cross pieces

42. On a squared and planed piece of wood 4 x 6 cm (1⁹⁄₁₆ x 2⅜ in) mark a length of 25 cm (9⅞ in) and the corresponding marks for the tenons, 25 mm (¹⁵⁄₁₆ in) long.

43. Having made the tenons in the same way as the others, mark the piece for the 2 x 2 cm (⁹⁄₁₆ x ⁹⁄₁₆ in) support which is glued and nailed 2 cm from one of the narrower faces. The length of this piece is 17 cm (6¹¹⁄₁₆ in).

44. Mark the two pieces with letters and numbers to indicate which side of the table they belong to.

Making the intermediate cross pieces

45. On a piece 3 x 4 cm (1⅛ x 1⁹⁄₁₆ in) and 25 cm (9⅞ in) long mark parallel lines 2.5 cm (¹⁵⁄₁₆ in) from the end for the tenons.

46. Once the tenons are completed, glue on supports made from pieces 2 x 2 cm (⁹⁄₁₆ x ⁹⁄₁₆ in) and 20 cm (7⅞ in) long. As shown in the photograph, these are glued and nailed with 3 cm (1¼ in) nails. The result is two symmetrical cross pieces.

Making the upper side cross pieces

47. The upper side cross pieces are identical to the lower ones, except that one of the tenons is not cut an angle across the end; it is a rectangular tenon, as can be seen in the picture.

48. This shows all the side cross pieces: two lower, two middle and two upper, all in equal pairs.

Gluing and assembling the front and back frame

49. On the workbench glue and assemble the frames, in this picture the back one. Hammer the joints together fully using a piece of wood to protect the surface from the hammer blows.

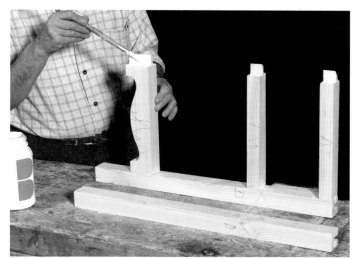

50. Glue the tenons of the front frame and assemble it in the same way as the back one.

Gluing and assembling the side pieces

51. Once the side pieces are firmly glued and fixed, glue and assemble the side pieces, following the letters and numbers marked earlier to ensure that they are correctly positioned.

52. Glue and assemble the pieces without excessively straining the mortises and tenons, or the weakest parts may be broken.

53. Glue and nail the side panels into position. They consist of two pieces of wood 14 x 20 cm (5½ x 7⅞ in), which will hide the drawer.

Finishing the frame

54. Sand all the visible surfaces to remove any marks and irregularities produced in the previous operations.

55. Apply a coat of grain-filler and two coats of clear varnish, sanding with fine sandpaper between the coats.

Making and fitting the platforms

56. On a piece of chipboard 20 mm (²⁵⁄₃₂ in) thick and 29 x 29.5 cm (11⁷⁄₈ x 11⁵⁄₈) in size, draw the outline of two curved corners, using the template made for the rounded top of the legs.

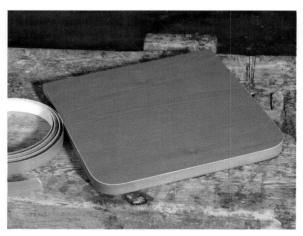

57. After cutting and finishing the rounded corners, cover the visible edges with an edging strip the same colour as the surface.

58. Mark a rectangle 38 x 26.5 cm (15 x 10⅜ in). Mark a section to be cut out 5.5 x 1 cm (2³⁄₁₆ x ⅜ in) at each of the back two corners, for the back legs. Again, once the piece is cut and finished to size, cover the visible edges with edging strip.

59. Glue and fit the lower panel, knocking it into position.

60. Fit the vertical back panel by sliding it into the grooves made in the back legs.

61. Glue the faces of the top of the structure which will be into contact with the panel which covers it.

318

Making the drawer

62. Make the front and back of the drawer from a knot-free piece of softwood 2 cm (²⁵⁄₃₂ in) thick, following the measurements in the drawings.

63. Similarly, make the sides and back of the drawer from a knot-free length of softwood 1.5 cm (⁹⁄₁₆ in) thick.

64. Make the rebates and join the pieces with lost-head nails 3 cm (1⅛ in) long, using two or three in each joint.

65. For the bottom of the drawer, slide in a piece of 4 mm (⁵⁄₃₂ in) plywood 25 x 22.5 cm (8⅝ x 8⅞ in). Then nail on the back of the drawer.

66. Once the drawer is made, mark the position of the handle by drawing diagonal lines across the front. Drill a hole for the peg of the knob where the lines cross and glue it into place.

The finished appearance of the bedside table.

Coffee table

This project describes the construction of an elegant coffee table which is made entirely from sipo wood. At first sight, it may appear to be rather complicated but when looked at in more detail it is soon realised that each stage is quite easy and that many of them are in fact also repeated.

The most striking features of this coffee table are the two horizontal sheets of plate glass which, being 8 mm (5/16 in) thick are extremely stable and strong and therefore sufficiently solid for every day use. The glass gives the table a particular elegance and lightness.

In order to make the coffee table look even more different from traditional ones, the ends of the long sides ends are decorated with vertical strips which at the same time form a link between the top and bottom frames of the table. The various elements are secured with mortise and tenon joints.

The top part of the table is built in such a way that it can easily be removed so as to be able to remove the bottom sheet of glass.

The end result is an elegant, useful and decorative piece of furniture.

MATERIALS NEEDED

All the parts of the table are made of sipo, a hardwood sometimes known as utile.

- Legs:
  4 pieces 6.5 x 6.5 x 43 cm (2 5/16 x 2 5/16 x 16 7/8 in)
- Lower cross pieces:
  2 pieces 7.0 x 3 x 102.5 cm (2 3/4 x 1 1/8 x 40 5/16 in)
  2 pieces 7.0 x 3 x 52.5 cm (2 3/4 x 1 1/8 x 20 5/8 in)
- Uprights:
  28 pieces 26 x 3 x 1.5 cm (9 13/16 x 1 1/8 x 9/16 in)
- Upper cross pieces:
  2 pieces 6 x 3 x 102.5 cm (2 3/8 x 1 1/8 x 40 5/16 in)
  2 pieces 6 x 3 x 52.5 cm (2 3/8 x 1 1/8 x 20 5/8 in)
- Upper frame:
  2 pieces 10 x 4 x 110 cm (3 5/16 x 1 9/16 x 43 1/4 in)
  2 pieces 10 x 4 x 60 cm (3 5/16 x 1 9/16 x 23 9/16 in)
- Glass:
  1 piece 42 x 92 x 0.8 cm
  (16 1/2 x 36 3/16 x 5/16 in)
  1 piece 43.5 x 93.5 x 0.8 cm
  (17 1/8 x 36 3/4 x 5/16 in)
- Finishing:
  - Plywood panel
  - Cotton scrim and cloth
  - Woodworking white glue
  - Fine and medium grade sand paper
  - Solid lacquer varnish
  - Methylated spirits (shellac solvent)
  - Wood wax
  - Steel wool
  - Hexagonal socket head screws

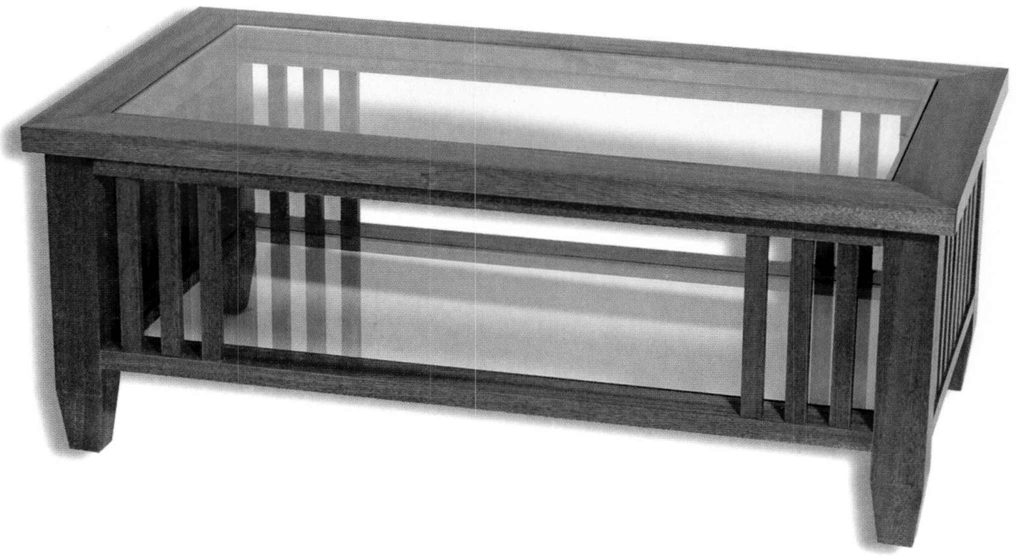

Step-by-step instructions

Making the legs

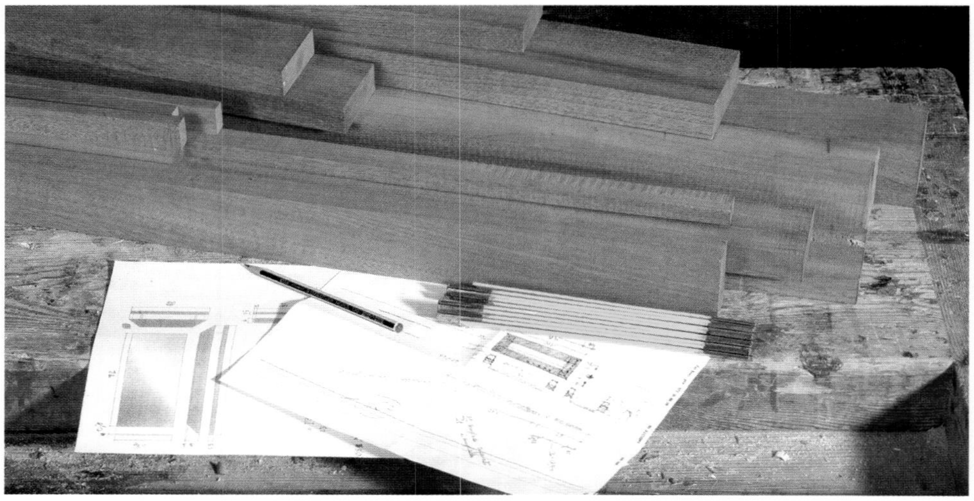

1. To make this coffee table , several pieces of sipo squared and planed smooth are used.

2. Mark the length on one of the four pieces for the legs.

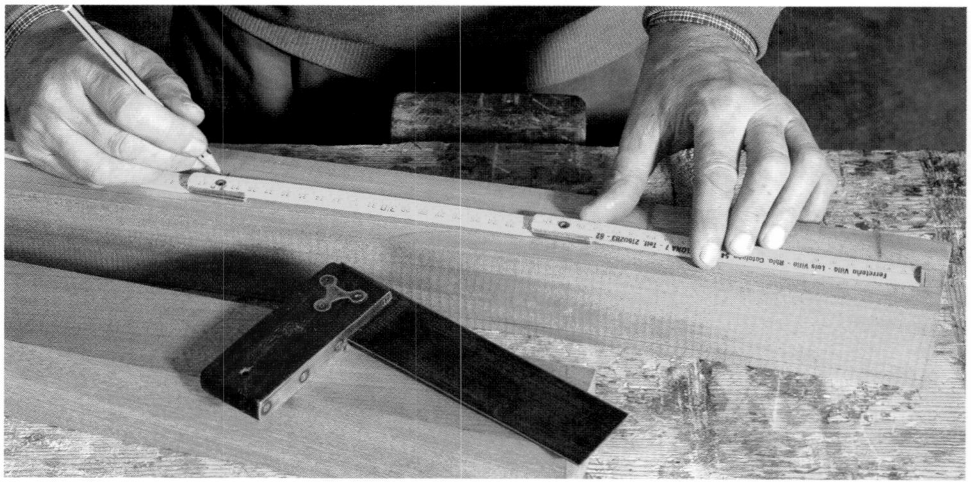

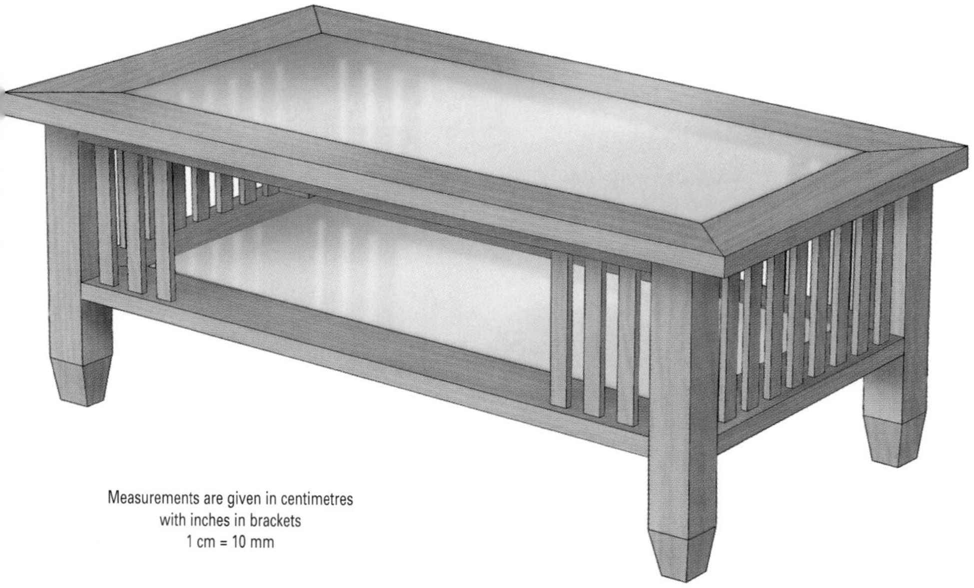

Measurements are given in centimetres
with inches in brackets
1 cm = 10 mm

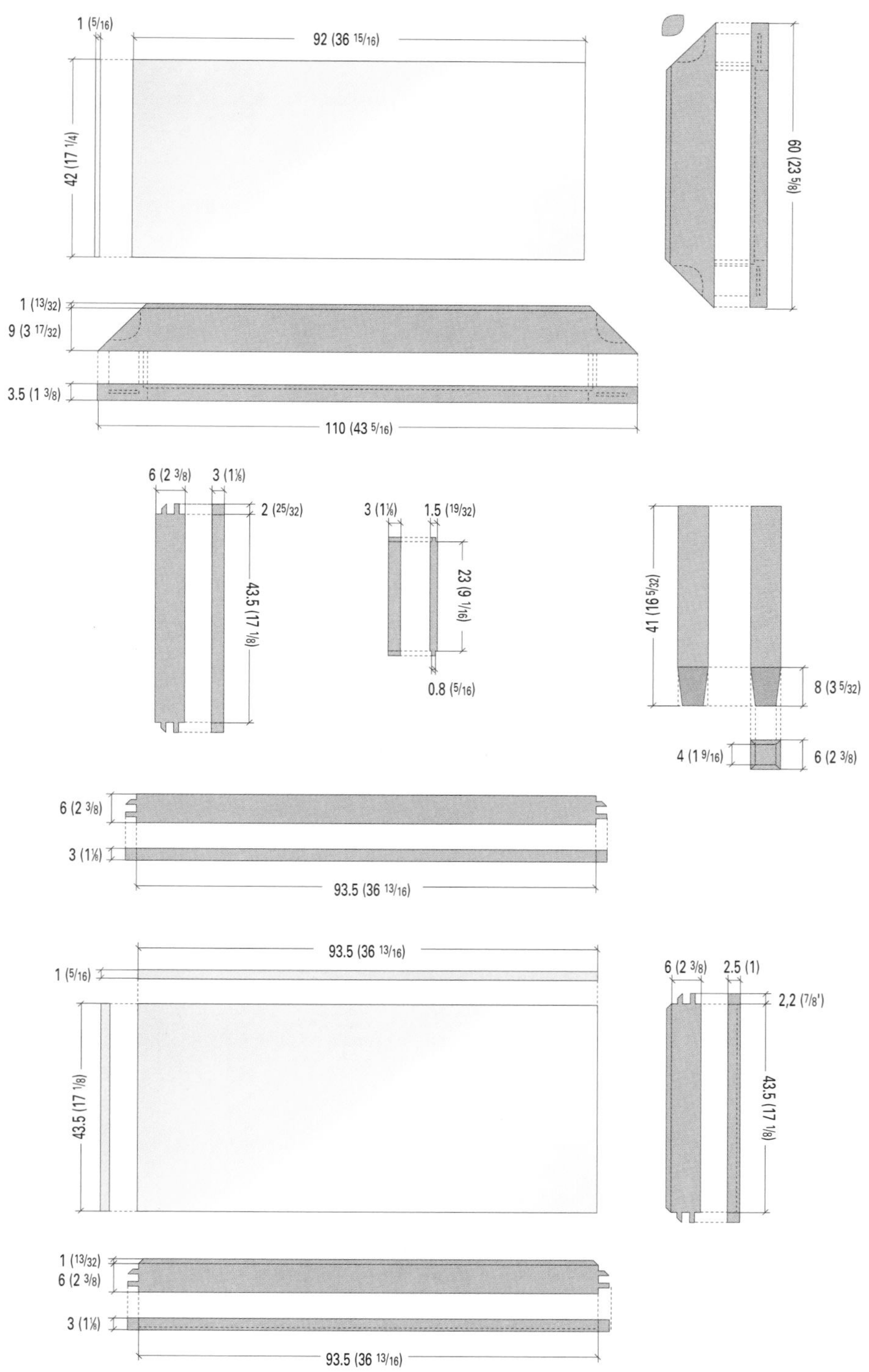
1 (5/16)
92 (36 15/16)
42 (17 1/4)
60 (23 5/8)
1 (13/32)
9 (3 17/32)
3.5 (1 3/8)
110 (43 5/16)
6 (2 3/8)
3 (1⅛)
2 (25/32)
43.5 (17 1/8)
3 (1⅛)
1.5 (19/32)
23 (9 1/16)
0.8 (5/16)
41 (16 5/32)
8 (3 5/32)
4 (1 9/16)
6 (2 3/8)
6 (2 3/8)
3 (1⅛)
93.5 (36 13/16)
93.5 (36 13/16)
1 (5/16)
43.5 (17 1/8)
6 (2 3/8)
2.5 (1)
2,2 (7/8')
43.5 (17 1/8)
1 (13/32)
6 (2 3/8)
3 (1⅛)
93.5 (36 13/16)

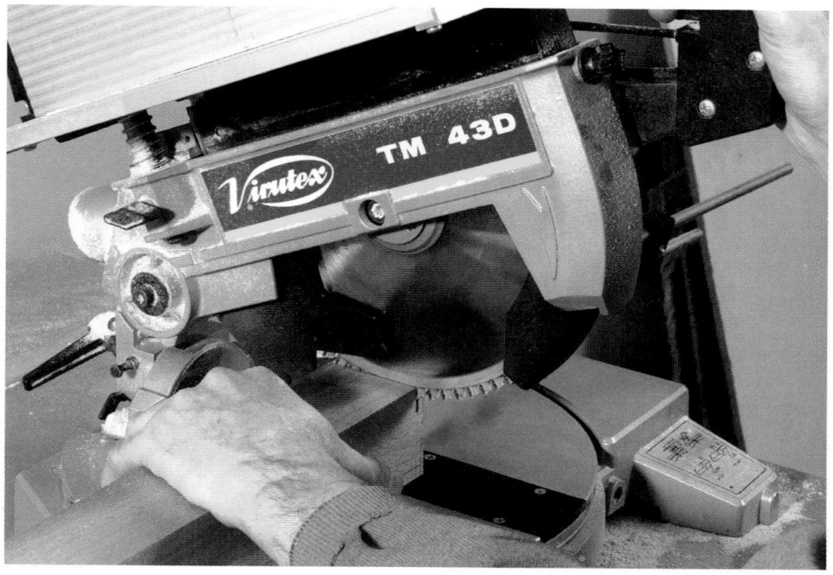
Virutex
TM 43D

3. With a table saw cut the first leg to length following the marks just made.

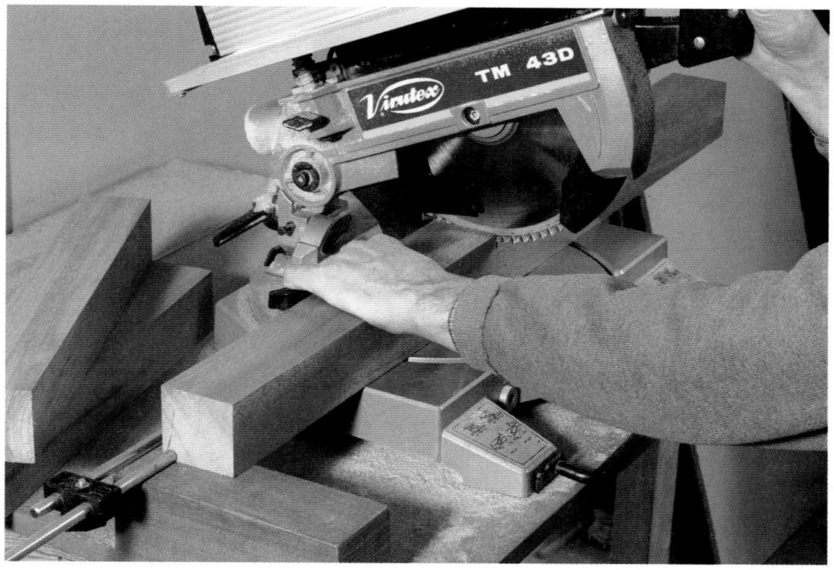
Virutex
TM 43D

4. Use the leg just cut to set the length gauge of the saw. Then saw the other legs to the same length.

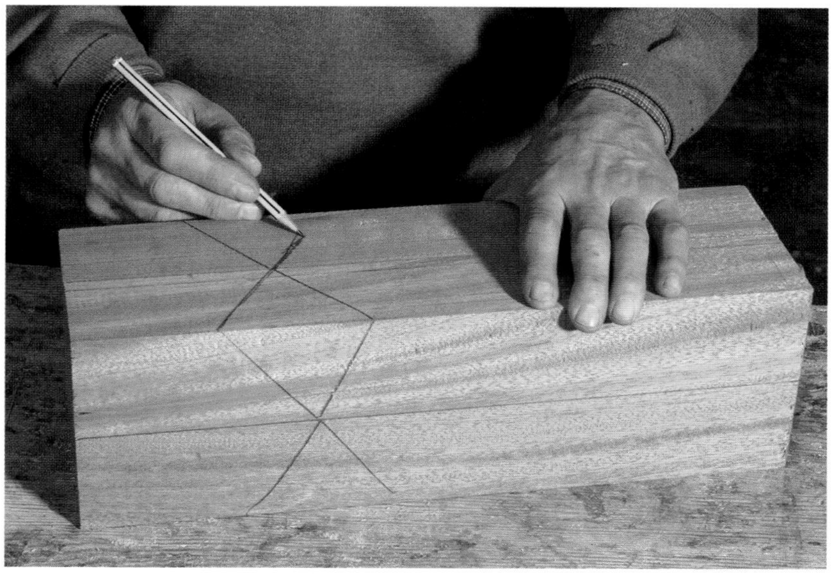

5. Select the best sides of the legs to be the outside ones. Mark them to identify them.

6. On one of the legs mark the thickness of the upper cross piece which will join the legs.

7. Mark the space between the two horizontal elements, which is 23 cm (9 in).

8. Mark the thickness of the lower cross piece.

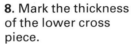

9. Mark the upper end of the bevelling, which is 8 cm (3⅛ in) from the foot.

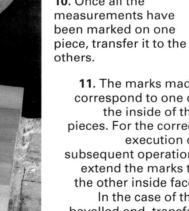

10. Once all the measurements have been marked on one piece, transfer it to the others.

11. The marks made correspond to one of the inside of the pieces. For the correct execution of subsequent operation, extend the marks to the other inside face. In the case of the bevelled end, transfer it to all four sides.

12. Use the marking gauge to mark the mortises of the joints in the pieces which will be the legs.

13. Mark the length of the eight cross pieces, 105.5 cm (41½ in) for the long ones and 52.5 cm (20⅝ in) for the shorter ones.

Making the cross pieces

14. Mark the length of the tenon from the line indicating the length of the piece.

15. Transfer the length of the maximum depth of the mortise to the cross piece and then transfer the mark to the others.

16. Use the table saw to cut the cross pieces to length.

17. Mark the tenons with the marking gauge, using the same measurements as for the mortises.

18. For the lower cross pieces there is a difference. The inner tenon is marked in relation to the foot.

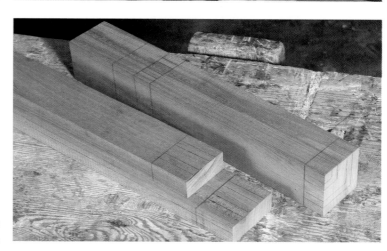

19. These are the pieces marked.

20. With an edge moulder bit in the drill press, set it so that the bottom is the correct depth. Use it to rout out the slots of the tenons.

21. Detail of one of the legs with the cuts made so far.

22. Fix the leg in a vice and saw the tenons with the chain saw.

23. With hammer and chisel chop out the waste to form the tenons.

24. Complete the operation with the backsaw, cutting off the waste at the marks.

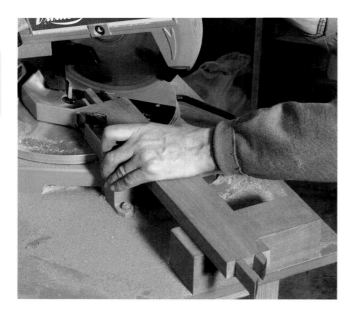

25. Use the compound angle saw to bevel the ends of the tenons at an angle of 45°.

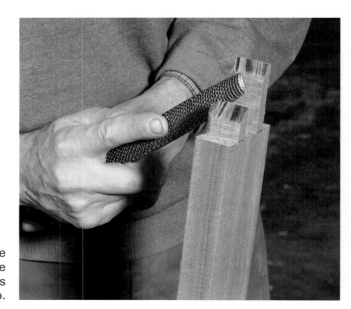

26. Since the mortises were made with a router cutter, they are rounded. Round the tenons accordingly with a rasp.

Preliminary assembly

27. Check that all the joints fit together correctly.

28. At the end of the legs, mark a line 1 cm (⅜ in) in from the edge all round. This marks the end of the taper.

29. Mark the bevelled taper on the four sides by joining the lines.

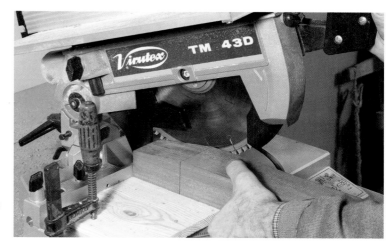

30. Saw the bevels with the compound angle saw.

31. In the four lower cross pieces of the table, use the marking gauge to mark the rebate to be cut for the glass, 1 x 0.8 cm (⅜ x ⁵⁄₁₆ in).

32. With the rebate plane cut the rebate to the lines marked with the marking gauge.

325

Making the decorative uprights

33. Mark the length of the pieces using the legs as reference. Add 1 cm (⅜ in) at each end for the joint.

34. Cut the pieces to length with the table saw.

35. On one of the shorter cross pieces, mark the length occupied by the eight uprights side by side.

36. The length thus marked is divided by nine (8 uprights +1). The result is the distance between the uprights, which is marked on the cross piece, alternating with the width of an upright.

37. Mark the width of an upright. To avoid confusion it is convenient to mark with a cross the parts to be cut out for the sockets for the uprights. In the wide cross pieces there are three uprights at each end.

38. Mark the centre of the width of each cross piece.

39. Since a 8 mm (⁵⁄₁₆ in) bit will be used, make a mark 13 mm (½ in) on each side.

40. Use a marking gauge to mark the part to be cut out 3 mm (⁵⁄₃₂ in) from each side of the line.

41. To form the tenon, mark 1 cm (⅜ in) from each end of the eight uprights.

42. Mark the tenon from the marks made by the marking gauge.

43. Use the marking gauge to complete the marking of the tenon on the uprights.

44. Start cutting off the waste vertically with the backsaw. Then using the same tool cut it off entirely.

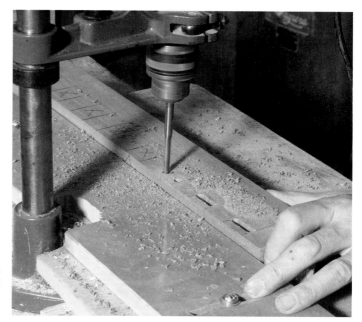

45. Use the drill press and a 5 mm (³⁄₁₆ in) side-cutting bit to cut the mortises. The depth should be 1 cm (⅜ in.)

Sanding and finishing

46. Use a power sander to sand all the surfaces of the pieces.

47. For small surfaces such as the bevelled feet and the uprights, turn the sander upside down and fix it to the bench. Then apply the work to the belt.

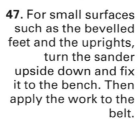

50. Polish the surfaces with steel wool. Do not wax the surfaces at this stage, since it would interfere with the gluing process.

48. Use a sheepswool roller to apply varnish to the surfaces.

49. Sand the varnish when dry with a very fine grade of sandpaper.

Assembly

51. Apply white glue to the uprights.

52. Use a hammer to tap the uprights into place. Afterwards wipe off any surplus glue with a damp cloth.

53. Fit the other cross piece and clamp the assembly with bar cramps, making sure everything is vertical.

54. Glue the feet.

55. Fit the feet. Use the hammer to knock the pieces together, with an intermediate piece of wood to prevent damage. Cramp the joint until the glue has set.

Making the upper frame

56. Mark the good faces.

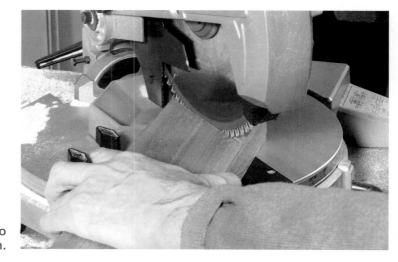

57. Saw the pieces to length.

58. Cut a rebate 1 x 0.8 cm (⅜ x ⁵⁄₁₆ in) for the crystal.

59. Mark the centre of the ends with the square. This will be a guide for making the grooves for the biscuits.

60. Use a biscuit jointer to make the grooves for the biscuits, two at each end.

61. This shows the appearance of the ends after the biscuit grooves have been cut.

62. Before gluing the biscuits. use a power sander on all the surfaces. Use sandpaper by hand in the vicinity of the grooves.

63. Apply white glue to the biscuits.

329

64. Put the biscuits in the grooves, tapping them into place with a hammer.

65. When the biscuits have dried, glue the whole face.

66. Use a frame cramp to apply pressure all round the assembly. Remove it when the glue is dry.

Templates for the glass

67. To make templates for the glass, measure the size of the two frames.

68. Use a sheet of plywood for the template. Saw it to width, then mark the length, taking it from the frame itself as reference. Leave a clearance of 1 mm (1⁄32 in) on each side.

69. If it does not fit exactly, adjust with a plane to correct the width or length.

70. Check that the template fits perfectly.

Final assembly

71. Assemble the sections already glued together.

72. Cramp the joints together until the glue is completely dry.

73. In the centre of the cross pieces, drill four holes to fix the upper frame.

74. Put a length of dowel in each of the holes and saw it off so that 1 cm (⅜ in) projects, to fit into the upper frame.

75. Position the glass in the lower frame.

76. Screw the upper frame into place, as shown in the picture.

77. Install the upper glass once the frame is fixed.

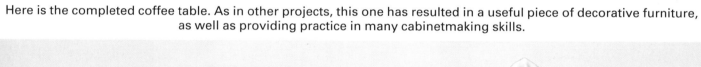

Here is the completed coffee table. As in other projects, this one has resulted in a useful piece of decorative furniture, as well as providing practice in many cabinetmaking skills.

Decorative frame

Several cabinetmaking techniques have been used in this project for making a decorative picture frame, including inlay and ornamental mouldings. Colour has been achieved by combining a number of different kinds of wood.

This picture frame is decorated at each corner with squares of sipo wood with inlaid circles of box wood.

The frame itself consists of four pieces of chestnut wood which are embellished lengthways with two parallel strips of inlaid sipo wood.

The techniques used in this exercise are not particularly common in cabinetmaking. But they are attractive and have been included for that very reason – a woodworker using them will be producing very original work.

The frame as a whole has a harmonious symmetry combined with great elegance.

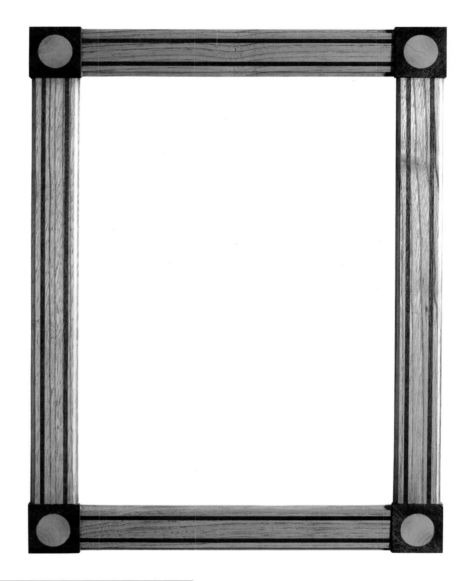

Step-by-step instructions

1. Materials used to make and decorate the frame, including a cylinder of box wood, chestnut boards and sipo wood.

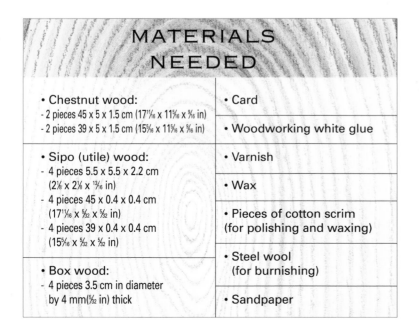

MATERIALS NEEDED

• Chestnut wood: - 2 pieces 45 x 5 x 1.5 cm (17¹¹⁄₁₆ x 11⅝⁄₁₆ x ⅜ in) - 2 pieces 39 x 5 x 1.5 cm (15⅝⁄₁₆ x 11⅝⁄₁₆ x ⅜ in)	• Card
	• Woodworking white glue
• Sipo (utile) wood: - 4 pieces 5.5 x 5.5 x 2.2 cm (2⅛ x 2⅛ x ¹³⁄₁₆ in) - 4 pieces 45 x 0.4 x 0.4 cm (17¹¹⁄₁₆ x ⅝⁄₃₂ x ⅝⁄₃₂ in) - 4 pieces 39 x 0.4 x 0.4 cm (15⅝⁄₁₆ x ⅝⁄₃₂ x ⅝⁄₃₂ in)	• Varnish
	• Wax
	• Pieces of cotton scrim (for polishing and waxing)
• Box wood: - 4 pieces 3.5 cm in diameter by 4 mm(⅝⁄₃₂ in) thick	• Steel wool (for burnishing)
	• Sandpaper

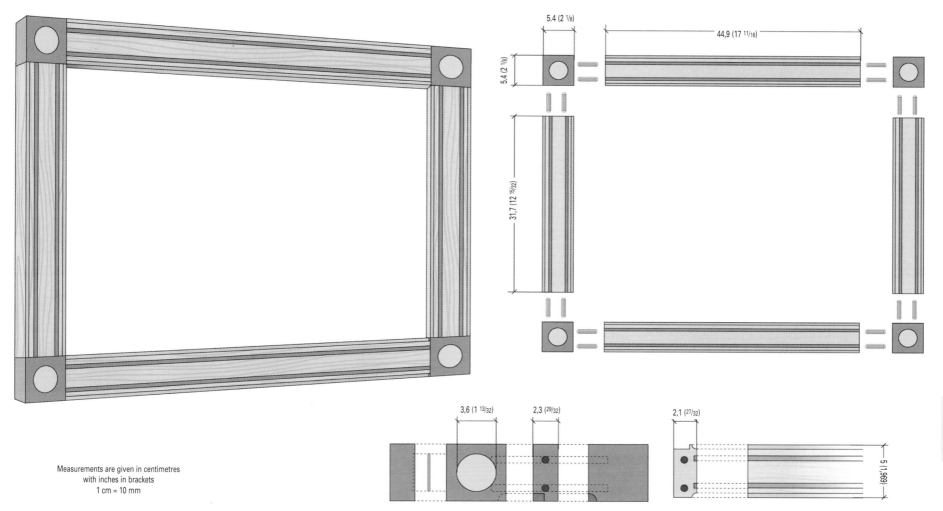

5.4 (2 ⅛)

44,9 (17 ¹¹/₁₆)

5.4 (2 ⅛)

31,7 (12 ¹⁵/₃₂)

Measurements are given in centimetres
with inches in brackets
1 cm = 10 mm

3,6 (1 ¹³/₃₂)   2,3 (²⁹/₃₂)   2,1 (²⁷/₃₂)

5 (1,969)

Making the frame

2. The first task is to prepare the chestnut pieces. The good faces are identified and marked, these being the ones which will be seen when the frame is completed.

3. Mark the lengths of the pieces. It is best to take the measurements from the centre of the length, thus avoiding possible defects at the ends which are very common.

4. Use the saw to cut the pieces to the lengths marked.

5. The same saw is used to cut the decorative grooves in the pieces of the frame. Take the relevant measurement and set the saw fence to it.

6. Start cutting the grooves.

7. Once the grooves are cut in the four pieces of the frame, use the edge moulder \to make the decorative rebate. For ease of working and to achieve a better result, fix the tool in the vice. This enables the work to be moved against the tool with both hands, moving it as convenient.

8. Use the same tool to make the rebate for the glass, the mount and the plywood backing board of the frame.

9. Glue the grooves ready for inserting the strips of sipo wood.

10. For the operation to be carried out successfully, the strip should be fitted immediately.

334

12. Use a cross pein hammer to ensure that the strips are seated properly, continuing until no more glue appears.

13. The operation is completed by using the flat of the hammer on the inlaid strips. It is not necessary to wipe off the glue, since this will be removed when the strips are planes.

14. After waiting at least half-an-hour for the glue to dry, plain the piece so that the surface is smooth.

Making the corner pieces

15. The frame is joined together by square corner pieces with dowels. So that the loss of material produced by cutting the pieces does not reduce the measurements, they are marked out on the diagonal.

16. The pieces are cut to the correct measurements.

17. To make the recess for the box wood, draw diagonals on the corner pieces and punch a pilot hole with a punch and hammer to form a guide for the drill cutter in due course.

18. Fix the workpiece in the vice and drill with a round cutter to a depth of 5 mm (³⁄₁₆ in).

Preparing for assembly

19. Cut the pieces of box. The thickness should not be much over 5 mm (³⁄₁₆ in).

20. Glue the pieces of box. It is only the support which needs to be glued.

21. Mark the lines for the housing in the pieces of the frame, which will be about 2 mm (⁵⁄₆₄ in) larger.

22. Use the backsaw to start cutting the housing.

23. Cut out the housing with a chisel.

24. With the marking gauge mark the centre line of the piece for the dowel sockets.

25. Carry out the same operations on the corner pieces.

26. Fix the piece in the vice and drill the dowel.

27. Glue the dowels and the area on the end of the piece surrounding them.

28. Knock the dowels into the holes with gentle hammer blows.

Smoothing and sanding

29. Before assembling all the pieces, carry out the smoothing and sanding operations. First go over the surfaces with a cabinet scraper. The bench stop keeps the work from moving.

30. Wrap sandpaper round a sanding block and sand the piece. Move from a medium to a fine grade of sandpaper.

31. Smooth the rebates, using folded sandpaper and making sure that it is in contact with all the mouldings, including the most concealed ones.

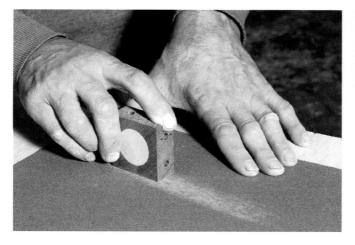

32. To sand the corner pieces, reverse the operation. Put the sandpaper on the bench and rub the corner piece over it, pressing hard enough for the sandpaper to be effective.

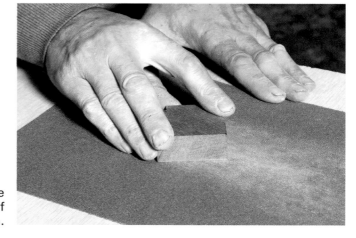

33. To sand the faces, move the piece in the direction of the grain.

Assembly

34. When all the pieces have been finished, assemble the frame by gluing the dowels and the surrounding surface.

35. Fit the frame pieces into the corresponding corner pieces.

36. The last piece, which completes the frame, is the hardest to fit since it requires both hands, leaving none to keep the vertical parts of the frame upright.

37. Check that all the pieces of the frame are perfectly square to each other.

Finishing

38. This stage begins with the application of varnish. All the crevices must be covered.

39. Use very fine silicon carbide paper to rub down the frame once the varnish is completely dry.

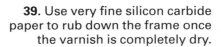

40. Polish with steel wool.

41. Wax the frame with pieces of cotton which will distribute it evenly. Apply another coat of wax and after a few minutes buff it to a fine lustre.

Assembling the back of the frame

42. The first stage is making the system for hanging the frame on the wall. With a tape measure find and mark the centre of the piece. all the steps which follow are carried out from the back of the frame. This means that the front of the frame, the part always seen, is underneath, and to prevent it being damaged it should be laid upon a rug or something similar.

43. Use a saw to mark the sides of the area of wood to be cut out.

44. Use a chisel to remove a channel, large enough to accommodate the hook on the wall.

45. Mark the position of the hanging plate and its mounting screw.

46. Use a panel of 4 mm (5/32 in) plywood for the back. Mark it with the interior measurements of the frame.

47. Before cutting the panel, mark it out with cutting lines using a square.

48. Cut the back panel with a backsaw. Smooth all the roughness off the edges.

49. Mark the glass with a china-marking pencil. The glass should be about 2 mm (5⁄64 in) smaller than the frame so that it an be put in place without difficulty.

50. Cut the glass with a glass cutter and square.

51. Supporting the cut line of the glass on the handle of the tool, press down on the waste side to snap off the surplus. Much care and skill is needed to do this cleanly without cutting the fingers.

52. Mark the card which will serve as the mount. A smooth surface is required for this operation.

53. Use a chisel and square to cut the card. The visible side of the card should be the opposite of that from which the cut is made.

54. Fix masking tape to the back of the mounting card,

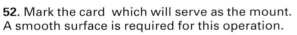

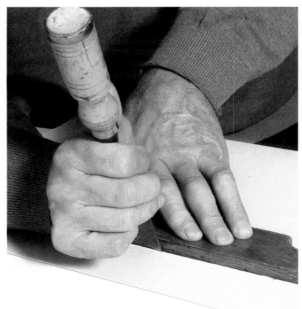

56. Sealing the picture is optional, but it avoids dust entering the glass and the mount.

55. Mount the picture on the card. Fit the glass and the mount, followed by the plywood backing sheet which is fixed by knocking steel pins into the frame. Do this with the hammer on its side.

Final result of the project, with the frame enclosing a print of a building by Gaudi.

Table lamp

The construction of this table lamp includes techniques which require skill and precision, such as for instance the joints for the wooden frame for the shade, and the curved feet of the stand with their attractive moulding. The shade consists of sheets of veneer sandwiched between pieces of glass.

Both the stand and the frame of the lamp shade are made from sipo wood but they are made using very different techniques. The base consists of four pieces of sipo wood and a central part which conceals the electric cable. This creates an excellent arrangement which is not only very stable but also very elegant. The strips of wood used to make the frame of the lamp shade have rounded edges.

The lamp shade is what gives this table lamp its original appearance. Depending on the choice of the veneer, it will let through more or less light, thus creating a warm, homely atmosphere. The result is a simple but very unusual table lamp which will look good almost anywhere in the house.

MATERIALS NEEDED

- All the parts of the lamp are made of sipo wood with the exception of the rods and the plywood for the templates.

- Lamp :
  - Sheet 36 x 26 x 2 cm (14³/₁₆ x 10¼ x ²⁵/₃₂ in)
  - Piece 14 x 4 x 4 cm (5½ x 1⁹/₁₆ x 1⁹/₁₆ in)
  - Piece 12 x 12 x 2 cm (4¹¹/₁₆ x 4¹¹/₁₆ x ¹⁵/₃₂ in)
  - 1 m (40 in) rod 1 cm (³/₈ in) in diameter (sipo cannot be used for this)

- Shade:
  - 8 pieces of glass 40.5 cm (15¹⁵/₁₆ in) wide at the base, 27.8 cm (10¹⁵/₁₆ in) wide at the top and 32.5 cm (12²⁵/₃₂ in) deep (These are exact measurements)
  - 4 pieces of veneer 40.5 cm (15¹⁵/₁₆ in) wide at the base, 27.8 cm (10¹⁵/₁₆ in) wide at the top and 32.5 cm (12²⁵/₃₂ in) deep (These are exact measurements)

- Frame pieces:
  - 4 pieces 43 x 2 x 2 cm (17 x ²⁵/₃₂ x ²⁵/₃₂ in)
  - 4 pieces 31 x 2 x 2 cm (12¼ x ²⁵/₃₂ x ²⁵/₃₂ in)
  - 4 pieces 35 x 2 x 2 cm (13¾ x ²⁵/₃₂ x ²⁵/₃₂ in)

- Upper part:
  - 1 piece 32 x 32 x 1 cm (12⅝ x 12⅝ x ⅜ in)
  - 4 biscuits 7 cm (2¾ in) long
  - 1 piece 25 x 2.8 x 0.4 cm (10 x ¹³/₃₂ x ⁵/₃₂ in)

- Electrical:
  - 1 electric flex 2 m (6 ft 6 in) long
  - 1 plug
  - 1 switch
  - 1 lampholder

- Finishing:
  - Methylated spirit (shellac solvent) and glass cleaner
  - Pieces of cotton scrim
  - Old newspaper
  - Medium and fine grade sandpaper
  - Abrasive sponge
  - Varnish
  - Furniture wax
  - Steel wool

Step-by-step instructions

1. Making this project requires a number of pieces of squared and planed sipo wood, and some black poplar root veneer.

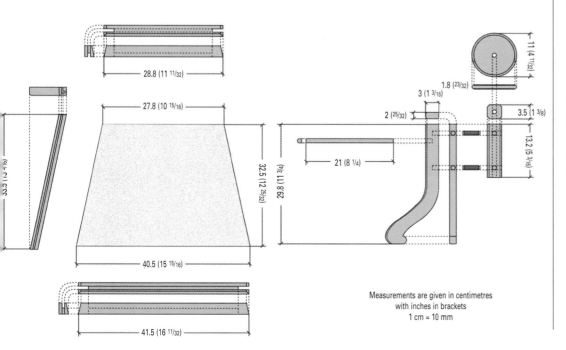

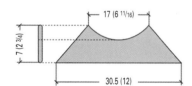

17 (6 ¹¹⁄₁₆)

7 (2 ³⁄₄)

30.5 (12)

28.8 (11 ¹¹⁄₃₂)

27.8 (10 ¹⁵⁄₁₆)

32.5 (12 ²⁵⁄₃₂)

29.8 (11 ¾)

33.5 (13 ³⁄₁₆)

40.5 (15 ¹⁵⁄₁₆)

21 (8 ¼)

1.8 (²³⁄₃₂)

3 (1 ³⁄₁₆)

2 (²⁵⁄₃₂)

3.5 (1 ³⁄₈)

11 (4 ¹¹⁄₃₂)

13.2 (5 ³⁄₁₆)

41.5 (16 ¹¹⁄₃₂)

Measurements are given in centimetres
with inches in brackets
1 cm = 10 mm

MAKING THE LEGS

Templates

2. Using 4 mm (5/32 in) plywood to make templates for the feet of the light. Use a square to draw two lines at right angles.

3. With rule or tape measure, mark the thickness of 3 cm (1⅛ in) which corresponds to the vertical part of the foot.

4. Either freehand or with the assistance of a drawing on paper, sketch out the rest of the outline.

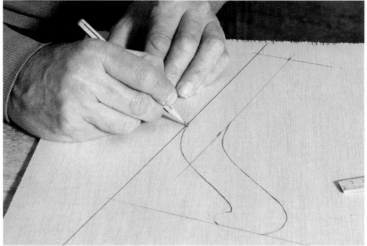

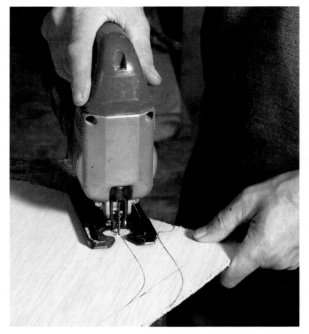

5. Use the jigsaw to cut out the template, starting with the vertical part.

6. Attach the template to the bench and smooth the edges with a rasp to remove the roughness produced by sawing.

7. Smooth the edges further with sandpaper.

Using the templates

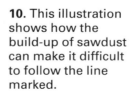

8. Mark the outline of the template four times on the piece of sipo wood, one for each of the lamp's legs. The different legs are arranged on the wood to make the most use of the material.

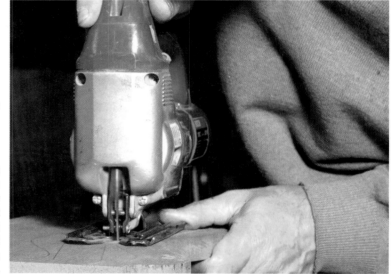

9. Cut out the pieces with a jigsaw. It is a good idea to blow away the sawdust produced which otherwise makes it hard to see the cutting line.

10. This illustration shows how the build-up of sawdust can make it difficult to follow the line marked.

11. Fix the leg to the bench and smooth the edges with a rasp.

12. The most curved part of the foot must be smooth with the rounded side of the rasp to avoid damaging it with its edges.

13. Continue the work with the cabinet scraper. Be careful not to modify the square edge of the foot. After this stage, smooth with sandpaper.

14. Fix the edge moulder to the bench and mould the edges of each of the feet.

Making the central piece

15. Cut the central part, to which the four feet will attached, to a length of 13 cm (5⅛ in) using the compound mitre saw.

16. Fix the edge moulder and mould the four corners of the piece.

17. Mark the centre at both ends and drill a hole 1 cm (⅜ in) in diameter in each end.

18. Mark the centre line of the piece with the marking gauge.

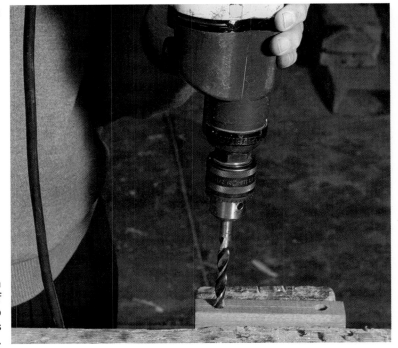

19. Similarly, with the marking gauge mark the points of intersection where the holes will be drilled to attach the feet.

20. Drill holes in the four sides of the workpiece to a depth of half its thickness.

21. Mark the centre lines of the drilled holes on each foot, transferring them from the central piece.

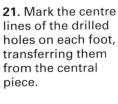

22. Drill the holes in two stages, one from each side of the piece. At the same time drill the holes for supporting the shade.

Sanding

23. Before the feet are assembled, they should be sanded. Hold the piece firmly against the bench stop and sand the wider sides of the pieces with sandpaper and a sanding block.

24. For the curved surfaces, use sandpaper without a block, ensuring that the paper gets to all parts of the piece.

Assembling the feet

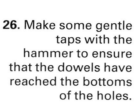

25. Cut the dowels to the correct lengths. They should not be deeper than the thickness of the wood, or they will prevent the passage of the electric cable.Glue the dowels and insert them.

26. Make some gentle taps with the hammer to ensure that the dowels have reached the bottoms of the holes.

27. Next glue the feet to the central piece.

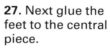

28. To ensure that the whole is assembled properly, fix the various pieces with cramps. Let the glue dry completely before continuing.

MAKING THE SHADE

Templates

29. Using 4 mm (⁵⁄₃₂ in) plywood, draw the trapezoidal outline of the sides of the shade. The measurements are: height 30 cm (11¹³⁄₁₆ in), larger base 38 cm (15 in) and the smaller base 26 cm (10¼ in).

30. Cut out the template and sand the edges smooth.

347

Using the template

31. Having made the template, use the sliding bevel to measure the angle which the pieces of the shade will have.

32. Set the compound angle saw to the angle transferred by the bevel.

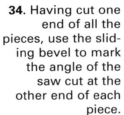

33. Having set up the machine, cut the four vertical pieces of the shade, at the end which corresponds to the lower part of the lamp.

34. Having cut one end of all the pieces, use the sliding bevel to mark the angle of the saw cut at the other end of each piece.

35. Use the back saw to cut the other ends as marked.

36. Use the compound angle saw at the same angle as before to saw the other angle of the head.

37. The result of these operations is a piece with two angled cuts at one end.

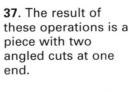

38. Mark the upper and lower cross pieces of the shade, using as reference the size of the template made earlier.

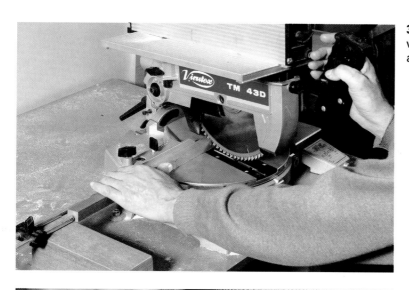

39. Cut the pieces with the same saw angles as before.

40. Modifying the position of the saw, make a groove for the glass and the veneer of 5 mm (³⁄₁₆ in) on the inside edges of the pieces. This operation is carried out on all the pieces, horizontal and vertical. The latter are grooved on two sides.

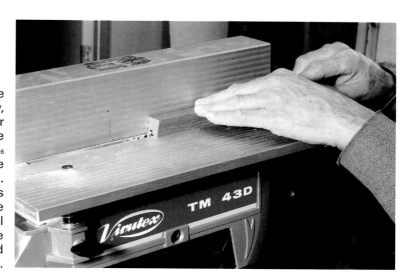

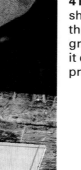

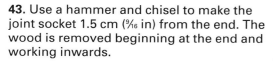

41. Offer up the two sheets of glass and the veneer to the groove, to check that it contains them properly.

42. Make a groove of 1.5 cm (⁵⁄₈ in) deep in the end for the joint socket. This must be done very carefully to avoid injury from the saw.

43. Use a hammer and chisel to make the joint socket 1.5 cm (⁵⁄₈ in) from the end. The wood is removed beginning at the end and working inwards.

44. So as not to damage the lower part of the piece, put a piece of scrap wood in the groove to support it as shown.

45. Make the false tenons with the compound angle saw using the same angle as the other operations.

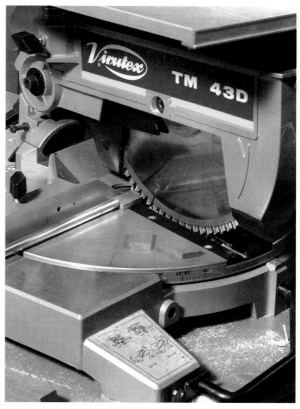

Assembly

46. Glue the false tenons into place with glue, hammering them in firmly with a hammer.

47. When the glue has dried, fix the piece in the bench and use the backsaw to cut the bevel on the tenons.

48. Round the sides of the vertical pieces using the plane.

49. To attach the shade to the feet of the lamp, make a hole in the centre and in each one of the four lower transverse pieces for the rods.

50. Clear out the waste with a hammer and chisel.

51. Before assembling the whole, smooth the inside faces with sandpaper, first medium grade and then fine grade. It is easier to do this before putting the pieces together.

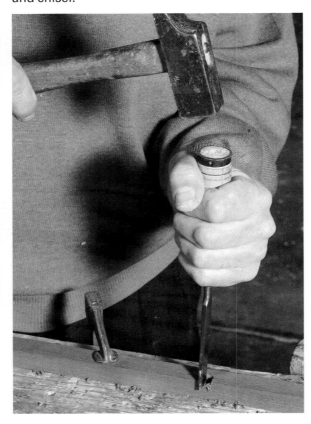

52. Assemble the frame of the shade temporarily. This stage is necessary to check if there is any problem with the cutting or with the false tenons.

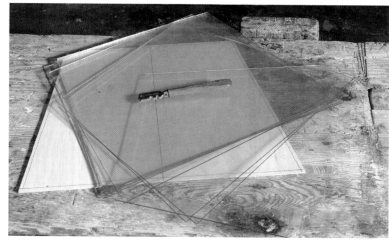

53. Use a glass cutter to cut the glass to the exact size of the template, or have this done by a glazier.

54. Join the cross pieces of the upper part of the shade having glued the tenons. Doing this operation with the lower ones first would make it impossible to fit the glass.

55. Here is the frame of the shade and the fine sheets of veneer for the shade material.

56. Once cut, the edges of the glass should be made less sharp with abrasive paper.

57. Clean the glass very carefully before assembling it.

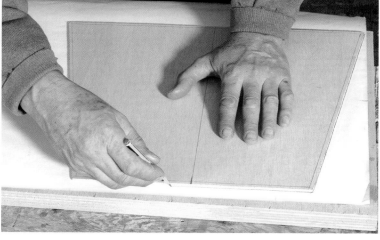

58. Mark the veneer for each side by drawing round the template.

59. Cut out the sheets with scissors.

60. Sandwich the sheet between the two pieces of glass which will form one of the sides of the shade.

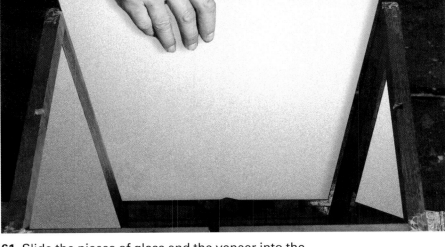

61. Slide the pieces of glass and the veneer into the grooves. Then glue the remaining transverse pieces and fit them into place.

63. Tap the joints into place with gentle taps of the fist so that all the pieces are fitted firmly together.

62. Gluing the last piece.

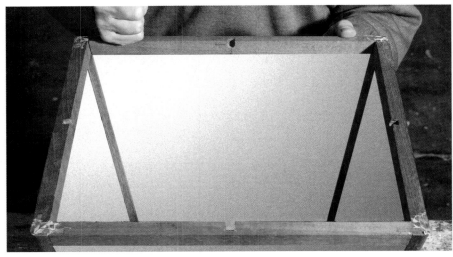

Sanding

64. During the process of sanding and finishing, the glass must be protected with sheets of newspaper. Cut these about 1 cm (⅜ in) smaller all round than the plywood template.

65. Stick these to the glass with masking tape, on both the inside and the outside. Check that the paper fits perfectly so that the wood itself is not covered with the tape.

66. Clean all the surfaces with sandpaper, working from medium grade to dine.

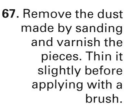

67. Remove the dust made by sanding and varnish the pieces. Thin it slightly before applying with a brush.

Making the upper piece

68. Measure the upper frame with a ruler. Add 5 mm (³⁄₁₆ in) margin all round.

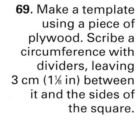

69. Make a template using a piece of plywood. Scribe a circumference with dividers, leaving 3 cm (1⅛ in) between it and the sides of the square.

70. Cut out the template as shown and transfer it to the pieces of wood (four times).

71. Cut out the curved parts of the four pieces with a jigsaw.

72. Set the table saw to 45° and cut the pieces to the sizes marked.

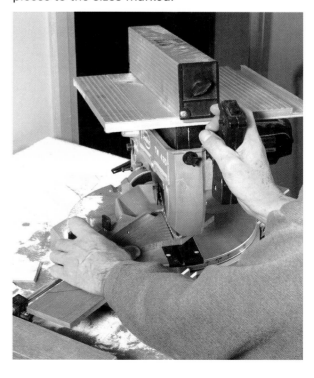

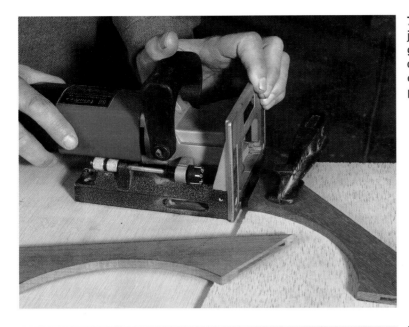

73. With the biscuit jointer make grooves for the biscuits in both ends of each of the four pieces.

74. Round the external edges of the pieces with a plane.

75. Glue the biscuits and fit them in the grooves.

76. Assemble the four pieces. The joints are seated with gentle taps of the hammer, being careful not to damage the wood.

Making the base for the lampholder

77. Mark the circumference of the lamp fitting directly on the wood with dividers.

78. Make a central hole of 10 mm (⅜ in) with a drill. The electric cable will pass through this.

354

79. Cut round the circumference with a jigsaw.

80. Use the edge moulder to mould the disc round the edge.

81. Cut the rods which will support the shade using a backsaw.

82. Sand all the varnished surfaces. An abrasive sponge scourer is used for this operation.

83. The sponge enables the abrasive surface to reach into all the angles.

84. The smoothing operation is completed with fine steel wool.

85. Apply the wax polish with pieces of cotton wool, distributing it evenly. Polish to a lustre when the wax has dried for a few minutes.

86. When these operations are completed, remove the protective paper from the shade.

87. Use a chisel to scrape off the varnish from the area which is going to be glues, about 1 cm (⅜ in) wide.

88. Apply the glue to the area from which the varnish has been removed.

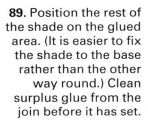

89. Position the rest of the shade on the glued area. (It is easier to fix the shade to the base rather than the other way round.) Clean surplus glue from the join before it has set.

Installing the electrics

90. Join the cable to the bulb holder.

91. Before installing the plug, thread the cable through the inside of the foot assembly.

92. Connect the plug to the end of the cable.

93. Test the installation of the electrics before fitting the shade.

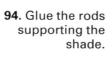

94. Glue the rods supporting the shade.

The finished lamp. As can be seen, with its soft light it is a lamp for creating a warm and friendly atmosphere in part of a room, rather than for providing overall illumination.

Pipe stand

This project involves techniques for sawing opposing curves and for cutting out delicate shapes in a small item. The edges of all the pieces are moulded. Cutting the shapes of this pipe stand demands care and attention, but this is well rewarded by the result.

This piece is made from sipo wood, a high quality hardwood with a beautiful colour. It is ideally suited for the purpose of this project.

The pipe stand consists of an elliptical base which contains the hollows in which the pipe bowls rest. The upper part of the stand holds the stems of the pipes and reflects the flowing, well-balanced design of the lower part. The result is a useful object which is also decorative.

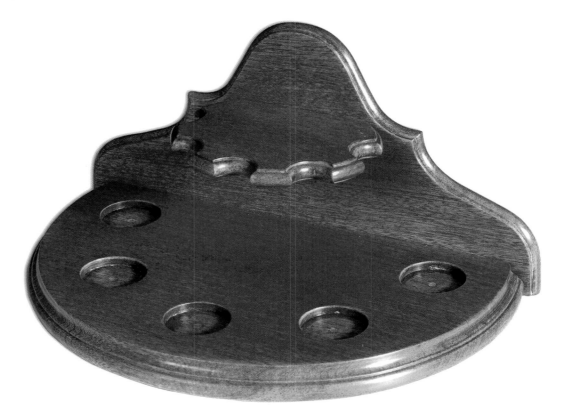

MATERIALS NEEDED

- Pieces of sipo wood:
  - Base: 30 x 18 x 2 cm (12 x 7 x ²⁵⁄₃₂ in)
  - Back: 30 x 15 x 1.2 cm (12 x 6 x ¹⁵⁄₃₂ in)
  - Upper part: 13 x 9 x 1.2 cm (5¹⁄₁₆ x 6 x ¹⁵⁄₃₂ in)
  - Rod 20 cm (8 in) long, 8 mm (⅜ in) in diameter (dowels)

- Templates:
  - 4 mm (⁵⁄₃₂ in) plywood:
    30 x 15 cm (12 x 6 in)
  - 8 mm (⁵⁄₁₆ in) plywood:
    30 x 18 cm (12 x 7 in)

- Woodworking white glue

- Varnish

- Furniture wax.

- Pieces of cotton
  (for varnishing and waxing).

- Steel wool (for polishing)

- Sandpaper

Step-by-step instructions

1. To make this decorative item the following pieces are required: sheets sipo wood 20 and 12 mm (²⁵⁄₃₂ and ¹⁵⁄₃₂ in) thick, and plywood 4 and 8 mm (⁵⁄₃₂ and ⁵⁄₁₆ in) thick for the templates.

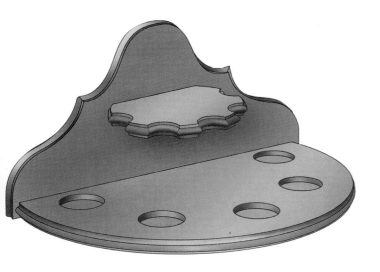

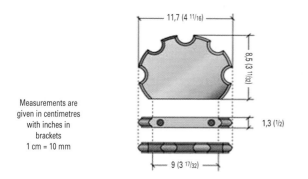

11,7 (4 11/16)

8,5 (3 11/32)

1,3 (1/2)

9 (3 17/32)

Measurements are
given in centimetres
with inches in
brackets
1 cm = 10 mm

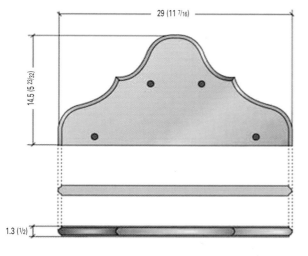

29 (11 7/16)

14.5 (5 23/32)

1.3 (1/2)

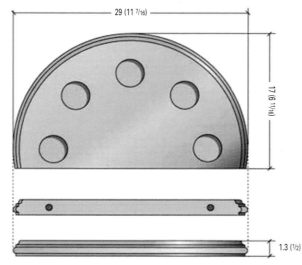

29 (11 7/16)

17 (6 11/16)

1.3 (1/2)

Making the templates

2. The first step in this project is to mark the plywood with the axes and centres of the ellipses which will form the templates for the two elements which support the pipes.

3. Hammer a nail part of the way into one of the centres of the ellipse, to hold one end of the string loop.

4. Repeat the operation for the other centre.

5. Having taken the measurement from one of the points of the ellipse and adjusted the length of the string accordingly, draw the ellipse.

6. Use the jigsaw to cut out the templates for the two ellipses. Fix the panel to the bench with a cramp to prevent it moving while this is done.

7. The finished result with the two templates cut from a single piece of plywood.

8. Smooth the sides of the templates with a rasp to remove the splinters caused by sawing.

9. Finish the templates by smoothing them with medium grain sandpaper.

10. Making the template for the vertical back of the stand. First the centre line is drawn on the piece of plywood. Then the outline of the curved part is drawn freehand. If preferred, the outline can be perfected on a piece of paper first and then transferred to the plywood.

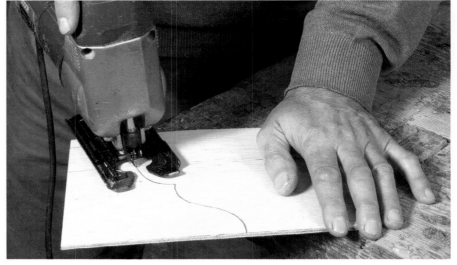

11. Cut out the template with the jigsaw. Remove the rough parts in the same way as before, finishing with sandpaper.

Transferring the templates

12. Mark the outlines of the templates on the sip wood, keeping the template stationary with hand pressure while the outline is drawn with a pencil.

13. Since the shape of the back is symmetrical, first draw a centre line on the wood. Arrange the position of the outline so as to waste as little wood as possible. Draw the outline on one side, then reverse the template and draw the other half.

14. Fix the piece firmly and saw out the shape. Blow away the sawdust produced from time to time so that the line drawn can still be seen.

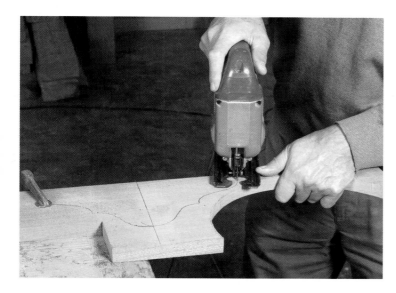

15. Because the shape is made up of several opposing curves, the sawing cannot be carried out in a single operation. A number of cuts are made in separate stages.

16. Making a second cut, where the curve of the pattern changes direction.

17. The second ellipse is drawn in the same way as the first.

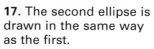

18. The centre line and radiuses shown must also be marked on this piece. This is because the final outline of the upper support contains curves to hold the pipe stems which are too small to be sawn by the jigsaw. The marking is necessary so that they can be marked out and cut by other means.

19. At the points of intersection between the axes and the ellipse, make a fairly deep mark with a hammer and punch to guide the drill bit when holes are drilled.

20. Fix the workpiece to the bench, having put a piece of wood under the workpiece to prevent the drill splintering the exit hole. Drill the points marked. When the shavings drilled change colour, drilling of the hole is complete.

21. Cut the outline of the ellipse with the jigsaw.

22. Smooth the edges first with a rasp, making rocking strokes to accommodate the curve.

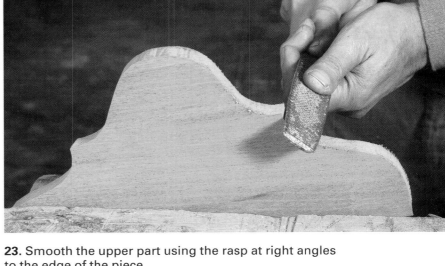

23. Smooth the upper part using the rasp at right angles to the edge of the piece.

24. Complete the operation by sanding the edges smooth with medium grade sandpaper.

Mouldings and joints

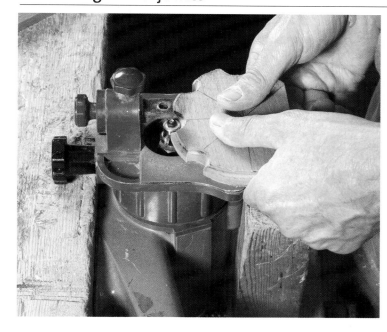

25. Use an edge moulder to shape the edges of the various pieces. For better control of the work, clamp the moulder in the vice and apply the work to it. All three support pieces of the pipe stand are moulded in this way.

26. Use a different cutter for the base moulding which is a different shape from the others.

27. Make the sockets for the joints by first marking a centre line and a centre point within it.

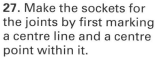

28. Mark the centre of the holes to be drilled at each end, 10 cm (4 in) from the centre mark.

29. With the workpiece fixed in the vice and holding the drill perfectly vertical, drill the holes for the dowels.

30. Saw lengths of dowel rod for the joints with a backsaw.

31. To make the round recesses for the bowls of the pipes, use a special cutter in a drill press. Set the depth stop so they are all the same depth.

32. The separate pieces are now completed and ready for finishing.

Finishing operations

33. Smooth the grooves of the mouldings with fine grade sandpaper.

34. Remove the sanding marks with a cabinet scraper. The dowels are not yet glued in place, but position them where they will be so as not to lose them.

35. The final operation before varnishing is to rub all the surfaces with fine sandpaper.

36. Remove the dust caused by the sanding operations and apply grain-filling varnish with pieces of cotton scrim.

37. When the varnish is completely dry, rub it down with very fins silicon carbide paper.

38. Without removing the dust of the previous operation, polish the surfaces with steel wool.

39. Using the same steel wool, repeat the operation on the edges. In this case work with the fingers to make sure all parts of the moulding are polished.

40. Use pieces of cotton scrim to apply the wax evenly. This will remove any remaining dust.

41. Polish the wax with clean pieces of cotton.

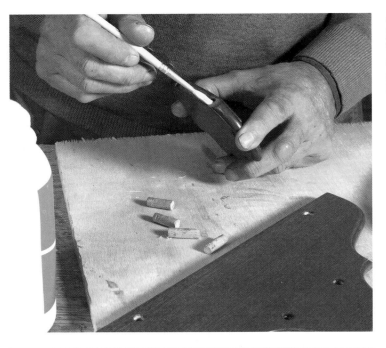

42. Glue the pieces o be joined with a brush and white glue. Put glue in the dowel holes, but not too much, or the dowels will be difficult to fit.

43. Use the hammer to tap the dowels gently into place.

44. If it is found that some of the dowels are too long, correct them now.

45. Shorten the dowels where necessary by cutting them with a backsaw.

46. Glue the back part of the pipe stand.

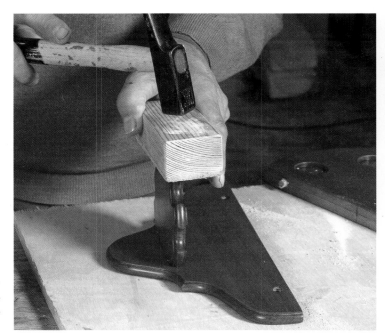

47. Use a hammer and an intermediate piece of wood to assemble the upper piece.

48. Clean the excess glue off with pieces of damp cotton. Do this quickly, before the glue has set on the surface.

49. To make a strong joint, cramp it until the glue has set.

The completed pipe stand, both useful and decorative.

book stand

The little book stand described in this project is an extremely versatile piece. Whether used as a rest for a book or a piece of music, or simply as a decorative object, it will always catch the eye with its harmonious, elegant shape.

This exercise introduces several working techniques, such as the construction of curves with different radiuses and making a piece like a rack with slanting indentations and a movable strut which enable the angle of the stand to be changed. This book stand is made from beech wood which has been previously steamed. Its colour has been strengthened by applying a coat of stain.

It consists of two main parts: a horizontal part which rests on four square feet and is linked to the upright part by hinges. A flat piece of wood is attached at the bottom of the upright which serves as support on which to rest the book.

The fixed central upright contains a movable strut which rests on a toothed track, allowing the user to change the angle of the upright and secure it in the desired position.

MATERIALS NEEDED

• Steamed beech wood:	• Steel pins
• For the base: - 2 pieces 40 x 5 x 1.4 cm (16 x 2 x ⁹⁄₁₆ in) - 2 pieces 25 x 5 x 1.4 cm (10 x 2 x ⁹⁄₁₆ in) - 1 piece 18 x 2.5 x 1.4 cm (7 x 1 x ⁹⁄₁₆ in) - 4 pieces 4 x 4 x 1.4 cm (1⁹⁄₁₆ x 1⁹⁄₁₆ x ⁹⁄₁₆ in)	• Stain
	• Woodworking white glue
	• Varnish
• For the book rest: - 2 pieces 45 x 6 x 1.4 cm (18 x 2⅜ x ⁹⁄₁₆ in) - 2 pieces 35 x 6 x 1.4 cm (14 x 2⅜ x ⁹⁄₁₆ in) - 1 pieces 26 x 6 x 1.4 cm (10¼ x 2⅜ x ⁹⁄₁₆ in) - 1 pieces 25 x 1.4 x 1.4 cm (10 x ⁹⁄₁₆ x ⁹⁄₁₆ in) - 1 piece 40 x 4.5 x 1.4 cm (16 x 1¾ x ⁹⁄₁₆ in)	• Furniture wax
	• Pieces of cotton (for varnishing and waxing)
• Templates: 4 mm (⁵⁄₃₂ in) plywood	• Steel wool (for polishing)
• Two brass hinges 40 x 40 mm (1⁹⁄₁₆ x 1⁹⁄₁₆ in) and screws	• Sandpaper

Squaring the wood and making the frames

1. This project uses small pieces of wood made from a larger one. The work therefore begins with the operations of preparing the wood to the right sizes. Using a power plane, the faces are planed so that all the pieces are 15 mm (⁹⁄₁₆ in) thick.

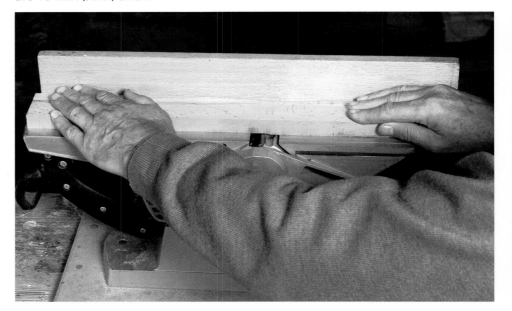

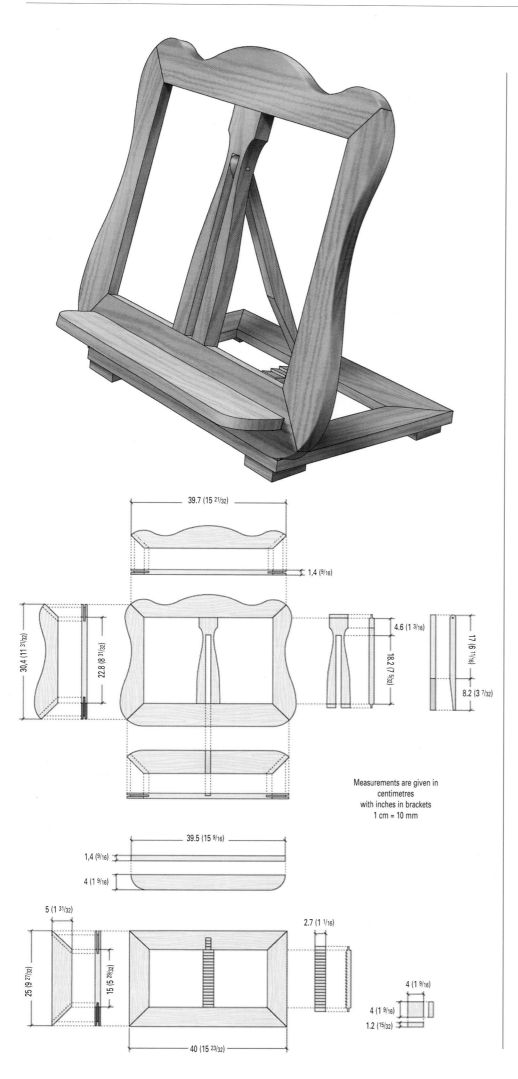

39.7 (15 21/32)

1,4 (9/16)

30,4 (11 31/32)

22,8 (8 31/32)

4.6 (1 3/16)

18.2 (7 5/32)

17 (6 11/16)

8.2 (3 7/32)

Measurements are given in
centimetres
with inches in brackets
1 cm = 10 mm

39.5 (15 9/16)

1,4 (9/16)

4 (1 9/16)

5 (1 31/32)

2.7 (1 1/16)

25 (9 27/32)

15 (5 29/32)

4 (1 9/16)

4 (1 9/16)

1.2 (15/32)

40 (15 23/32)

2. Repeat the same operation for the edges.

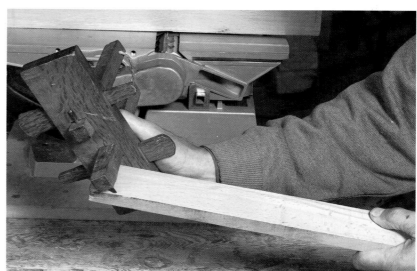

3. Mark the widths of the various pieces required
with the marking gauge.

4. Use the circular table saw to cut
the pieces to the widths marked.

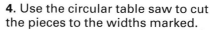

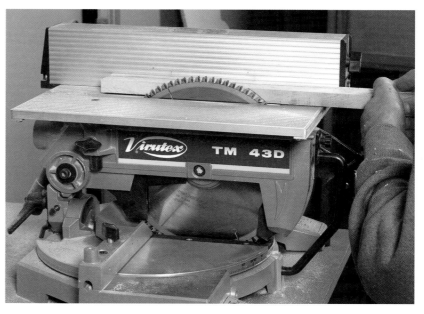

369

5. Here are the pieces prepared in the previous operations, ready to make the book stand.

6. The pieces making up the frame of the book stand

7. To mitre the corner pieces and to ensure that the pieces are the same length as the first one of each type, set the angle of the saw and the end stop.

8. To avoid confusion mark the good faces and their position in the frame.

9. Next saw the grooves for the joints in the ends.

10. Mark the overall length of the tongue of the joint on strips of wood. This should be 2 cm ($^{25}/_{32}$ in) longer than the joint itself.

11. Use the saw to cut the four tongues for the frame.

Templates

12. To make the central part of the frame, make a template on a piece of plywood. The outline of this template is drawn freehand on the plywood, or on paper and then transferred to the plywood.

13. Mark the axis first, since the pattern is symmetrical.

14. Cut out the template with the jigsaw.

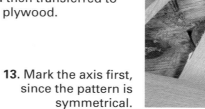

15. Use a rasp on all the edges of the template to remove roughness caused by the sawing.

Using the templates

16. Before using the templates, mark the position of the final joints in the centre of the cross pieces of the frame of the book stand.

17. Mark the outline and measurements of the upper and lower joints.

18. Mark the dimensions on the piece which will be the cross piece of the book stand. Add 1.5 cm (⁹⁄₁₆ in) to each end to accommodate the joints.

19. Mark the lines with a try square, both the length of the piece and of the joint.

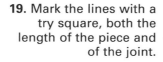

20. Trace the outline of the template on the piece, first one way and then the symmetrical image next to it.

21. Fix the piece to the bench and saw it out with the jigsaw, keeping to the outside of the cut line.

22. To saw the interior part, given the small dimensions, first saw one of the two sides, ending with the curve; then repeat the operation with the other curve.

23. To form the cut to the right shape at the curved end, a rasp of the right size is useful.

24. Fix the piece in the vice and smooth all the surfaces with the vice.

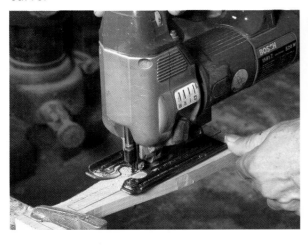

Assembling the frame

25. Use the marking gauge to mark the two horizontal pieces where the cross piece will join them.

26. Mark the area to be cut out of both horizontal pieces, using the try square.

27. To form the mortise, fix the piece in the vice and cut out the marked area with a chisel.

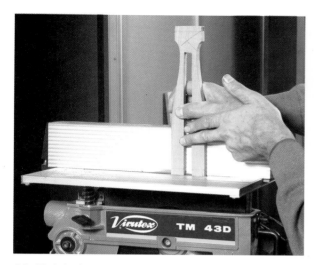

28. Finish the cross piece using the circular saw to make the vertical cuts forming the tenons.

29. Hold it against the bench stop and saw off the waste wood to complete the tenon for the joint.

30. Apply white glue to the tenons and fit them in the lower part of the frame.

31. Complete the assembly by gluing the mitres and the tongues. Press everything firmly together, checking the whole frame is square.

32. Mark the curved outlines on the frame with the template.

373

33. Fix the frame to the bench and saw round the outline with a jigsaw, keeping to the outside of the marked line.

34. To make the joint at the foot of the book stand, cut to the marks made earlier, using a backsaw.

35. Remove the waste with a chisel. This operation should be carried out alternately from each direction.

36. On the piece of wood prepared for the support, mark a curve at one end for the joint in which it will be hinged.

37. Cut the rounded shape with several cuts of the backsaw. Hold the piece on some scrap wood so as not to damage the bench.

38. Finish the curve with a rasp, using rocking back-and-forth movements.

39. Mark the bevel on the end which will fit in the cross piece of the frame.

40. Cut the bevel with a jigsaw to the line marked.

41. Check that the piece fits perfectly.

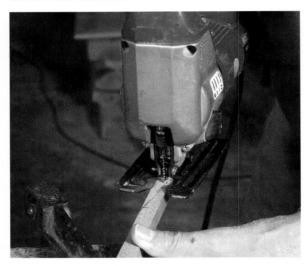

Smoothing and sanding

42. Finish this part of the frame by using a cabinet scraper on all the surfaces, keeping the workpiece stationary against the bench stop.

43. Then rub with sandpaper, first medium grade, then fine.

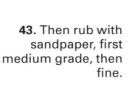

44. Following the same procedure and using the same tools, starting with the cabinet scraper, finish the sides of the frame.

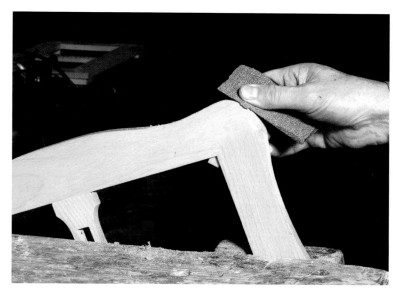

45. Use sandpaper with the fingers to adapt it to the shape of the edges.

Fitting the foot and the book support

46. Holding the frame strut in its final position, make a pilot hole to guide the screw.

47. Using a short screwdriver, fit a screw through the cross piece and the strut.

48. Cut away the exposed parts of the tongues with the backsaw. Smooth the cuts with sandpaper.

49. To make the piece on which the book rests, cut it to length and mark a quadrant at each end with dividers, the radius being the same as the width of the piece.

50. Saw the curves at both ends of the piece with a jigsaw.

51. Smooth the ends, first with a file and then with sandpaper.

52. Use the piece as a template to mark its position on the frame.

53. Draw parallel lines using the fingers as a guide, as here, or using a marking gauge.

54. Cramp the two pieces together.

55. Mark the central line of the book rest on the back of the frame.

56. Mark the positions of the screws, making pilot holes with a gimlet.

57. Screw the piece into place.

Making the base

58. Cut the pieces for the base frame to with their mitred corners on the table saw, and also the central cross piece. As before the face sides and the position of the pieces should be marked.

59. For the rack enabling the stand to be set at different angles, mark parallel lines at intervals of 1 cm (⅜ in).

60. The try square is used to complete the marks.

61. Mark a line along the edge and 4 mm (⁵⁄₃₂ in) from it, either by hand or with a marking gauge. This marks the maximum depth of the rack.

62. Cut the marks to a depth of 4 mm (⁵⁄₃₂ in) using the backsaw and holding the work against the bench stop.

63. To make the rack, cut away the wood with a chisel to make a sawtooth profile.

64. Use the circular saw to cut the feet for the base frame. They are right-angled with the grain at 45°.

65. Hammer two nails into each foot, which will make reinforce the joint.

66. Mark the position of the feet 5 mm (³⁄₁₆ in) in from the edges.

67. Glue and nail the feet into position, making sure the frame does not move during this operation.

68. Each of the nails through the feet should enter a different part of the frame, so that the foot strengthens the joint.

69. When all the pieces are assembled , extend the rack to the frame by chiselling more steps in the frame.

378

70. Clean the whole with fine grade sandpaper. Make sure the paper reaches all the way into the angles of the rack.

71. Fit the hinges which join the base to the frame supporting the book.

72. This is how the piece looks before the finishing operations are started.

Finishing

73. Stain the piece to the colour desired. The satin used is based on walnut stain with water-soluble aniline dyes which produces a brownish colour without an orange tinge.

74. After staining, wax the piece, applying it with pieces of cotton which will distribute it evenly.

The final appearance of the completed book stand.

75. After the wax has dried for a few minutes, give it a shine by brushing it. For a perfect finish, repeat this operation three times.

Decorative figure: clown

When looking at the clown in profile, you will notice the rounded shapes which have been carved from the wood in order to give the figure the required volume. These curves require craftsmanship skills. Manual dexterity plays an important in making this figure as does the skilled use of files which will give the various types of wood their final shape. This project introduces a technique which is more or less unfamiliar to the cabinet-maker who will be using techniques that are usually associated with carving or sculpture techniques.

Different types of wood are used for the different parts of the clown: sipo for the body, mahogany for the hair, the socks and the nose, strawberry wood for the head, mongoy for the trousers and ebony for the shoes. These woods have been chosen for their very different colours. When making the individual parts of the clown, one must be aware of the different degrees of difficulty which should be taken into account when working the various types of wood.

Filing with a rasp to shape pieces is extremely important in this project. The choice of the right kind of rasp and their skillful handling are vitally important to obtain a perfect shape and smooth surfaces. Various techniques are used depending on the shape and size of the individual piece of wood.

Step-by-step instructions

1. This piece is made using several different colours of wood, squared up and brought to the correct sizes to make the different parts of this decorative figure.

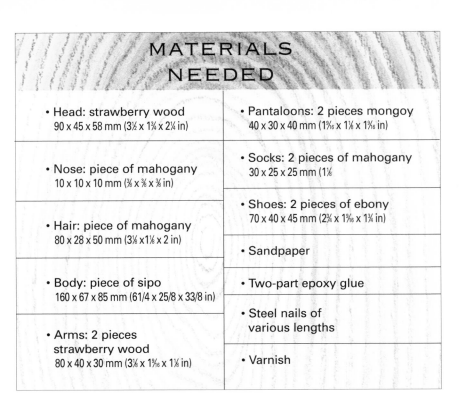

MATERIALS NEEDED

• Head: strawberry wood 90 x 45 x 58 mm (3½ x 1¾ x 2¼ in)	• Pantaloons: 2 pieces mongoy 40 x 30 x 40 mm (1⁹⁄₁₆ x 1⅛ x 1⁹⁄₁₆ in)
• Nose: piece of mahogany 10 x 10 x 10 mm (⅜ x ⅜ x ⅜ in)	• Socks: 2 pieces of mahogany 30 x 25 x 25 mm (1⅛
• Hair: piece of mahogany 80 x 28 x 50 mm (3⅛ x 1⅛ x 2 in)	• Shoes: 2 pieces of ebony 70 x 40 x 45 mm (2¾ x 1⁹⁄₁₆ x 1¾ in)
	• Sandpaper
• Body: piece of sipo 160 x 67 x 85 mm (61/4 x 25/8 x 33/8 in)	• Two-part epoxy glue
	• Steel nails of various lengths
• Arms: 2 pieces strawberry wood 80 x 40 x 30 mm (3⅛ x 1⁹⁄₁₆ x 1⅛ in)	• Varnish

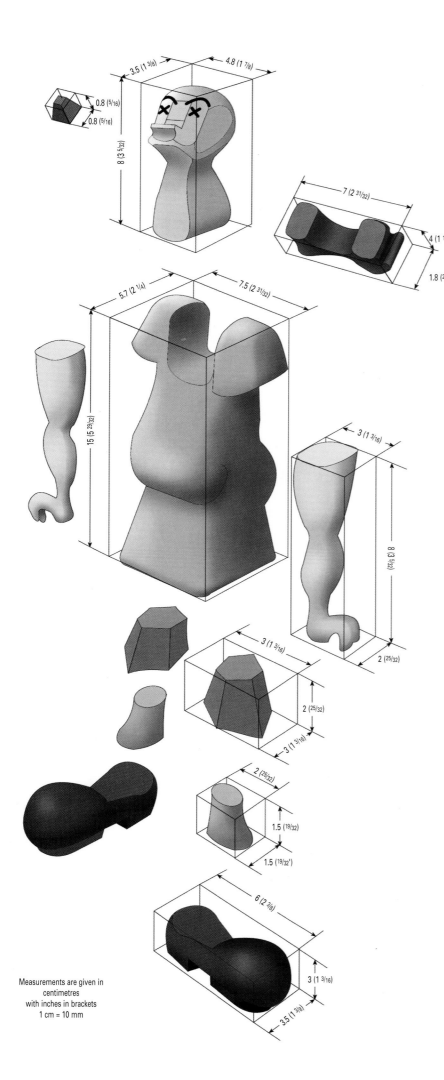

3.5 (1 ³/₈)

4.8 (1 ⁷/₈)

0.8 (⁵/₁₆)

0.8 (⁵/₁₆)

8 (3 ⁵/₃₂)

7 (2 ³¹/₃₂)

4 (1 ¹⁹/₃₂)

1.8 (²³/₃₂)

5.7 (2 ¹/₄)

7.5 (2 ³¹/₃₂)

15 (5 ²⁹/₃₂)

3 (1 ³/₁₆)

8 (3 ⁵/₃₂)

2 (²⁵/₃₂)

3 (1 ³/₁₆)

2 (²⁵/₃₂)

3 (1 ³/₁₆)

2 (²⁵/₃₂)

1.5 (¹⁹/₃₂)

1.5 (¹⁹/₃₂')

6 (2 ³/₈)

3 (1 ³/₁₆)

3.5 (1 ³/₈)

Measurements are given in
centimetres
with inches in brackets
1 cm = 10 mm

381

Templates

2. Draw the figure in front and side view on a piece
of paper or card, which will be used as the basis for
the template.

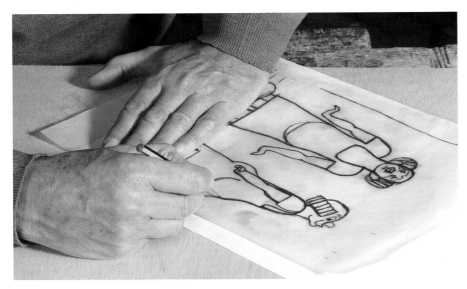

3. Transfer the component parts of the drawing to plywood using carbon paper. A soft pencil is best for this process.

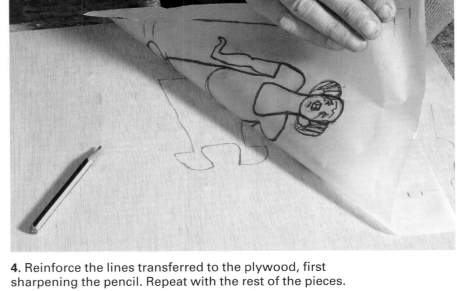

4. Reinforce the lines transferred to the plywood, first sharpening the pencil. Repeat with the rest of the pieces.

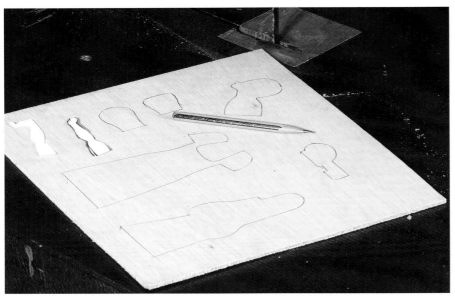

5. The sheet of plywood with the various parts outlined.

6. Before cutting out the individual pieces, saw the plywood into rectangles containing the separate parts, which will make them easier to handle.

8. When the pieces have all been cut out, sand them to remove the roughness caused by sawing. Paper templates can also be used, as shown in the photograph for the arms of the figure.

7. Saw out the pieces one by one, following the drawn outline.

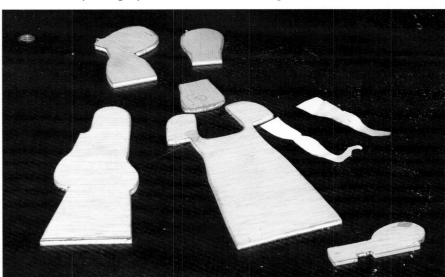

Using the templates

9. Mark the front view of the figure, the largest piece, on the piece of sipo wood.

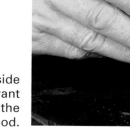

10. Draw the side view on the relevant adjacent face of the same piece of wood.

11. With a bandsaw, saw round the lower part of the piece.

12. Using the same saw, cut round the figure following the outline of the front part.

13. This is how the figure looks when the whole piece has been cut out. The wood has been removed in several cuts.

14. To begin sawing from the adjacent side, tape the pieces together with masking tape.

15. Redraw the lines of the side view which have been hidden by the adhesive tape.

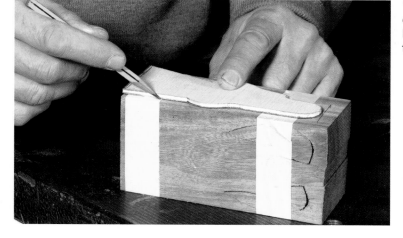

16. Saw the piece from the other direction.

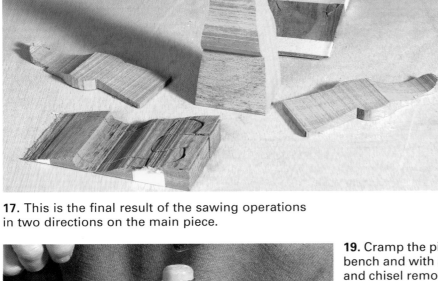

17. This is the final result of the sawing operations in two directions on the main piece.

18. Mark the belly of the clown on the wood with a pencil.

19. Cramp the piece to the bench and with a hammer and chisel remove the material, using the pencil marks as a guide. use scrapwood between the cramp and the piece so as not to damage it.

20. Detail showing the material being removed with a chisel, working with the piece horizontal.

21. Round the shape of the belly with a medium rasp, holding the workpiece firm against the bench stop.

22. Continue rounding the belly of the figure using the same rasp.

23. For the narrowest and/or most curved parts, use a rat tail (round) rasp.

24. Working with different rasps and files, create the final shape. Use fine grade sandpaper to smooth the whole piece.

Making the head

25. With the appropriate template, mark the head of the figure on a piece of wood.

26. Saw the piece following the lines. With small pieces like this, work very carefully to avoid injury. Do not let go of the piece.

27. Saw in the piece in the opposite direction. In this case, because the piece is simple, there is no need to hold it together with tape.

28. Again different rasps are used to shape the head. Here the cheeks are being formed with a medium rasp.

29. It is important to choose the correct rasp for each task, especially for the most curved parts of the figure.

30. The operation is completed by using a very fine rasp.

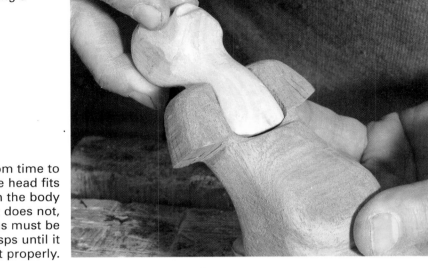

31. Check from time to time that the head fits the space in the body perfectly. If it does not, corrections must be made with rasps until it does fit properly.

Making the hair

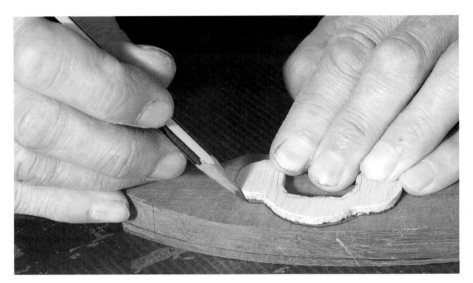

32. Use the template to transfer the outline onto a piece of wood.

33. With a suitable rasp of the correct curvature, shape the piece of hair surrounding the head. Pay special attention to the curvature of the edges.

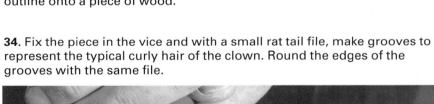

34. Fix the piece in the vice and with a small rat tail file, make grooves to represent the typical curly hair of the clown. Round the edges of the grooves with the same file.

35. Check that the hair piece fits the head correctly. If does not, adjust with rasps until it does.

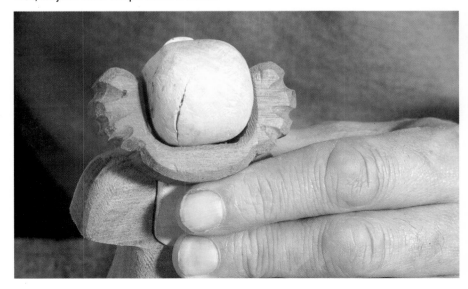

Making the shoes

36. To make the shoes, proceed in the same manner as before. Mark the outline from the template on a piece of ebony and saw it to shape.

37. Again as before, round the edges with various sizes and shapes of rasps.

38. Use the smallest rat tail rasp to make a groove marking the sole of the shoe.

Making the arms

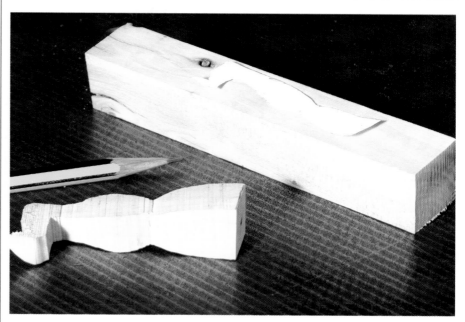

39. Because of its complexity, the choice has been made to use a paper template for the arms. The outline is transferred to the wood as usual. Sawing is carried out very carefully because of the small size of the pieces.

40. Work at the edges with rasps to round them and arrive at the desired shapes.

41. Use the smallest rat tail file to shape the trickiest parts of the arms.

Making the pantaloons

42. Mark the pieces needed to make the pantaloons.

43. Cut out along the vertical lines. Do not cut the pieces off at this stage since they would be too small to work on.

44. Mark the waste parts of the corners to give the pantaloons a rounded appearance.

45. Use the same backsaw to cut to the marks just made.

46. Cut the pantaloons to their final length.

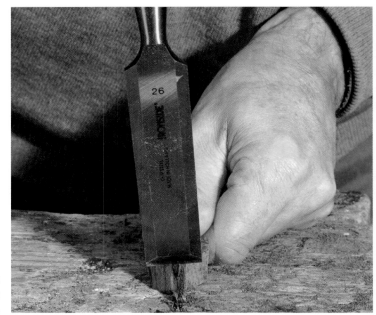

47. Trim the saw marks smooth with strokes of a chisel.

Making the socks

48. Using the shoe as reference, mark the mahogany with the width and length required. Mark the second piece symmetrically to the first.

49. To make the curve, use a half-round rasp .

50. Round the edges using the same rasp.

51. Round the back edges of the socks with a plane.

52. Cut off the two pieces with a backsaw.

Making the nose

53. Given the simplicity of this piece, it does not need to be marked out. First the end of the wood is cut to a pyramidal shape with the chisel.

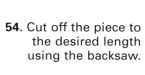

54. Cut off the piece to the desired length using the backsaw.

Sanding

55. When all the pieces have been made, the process of sanding begins. Since the pieces are smaller than usual, it is often easier to put the sandpaper in the bench and rub the pieces on it. Work from medium grade to fine as usual.

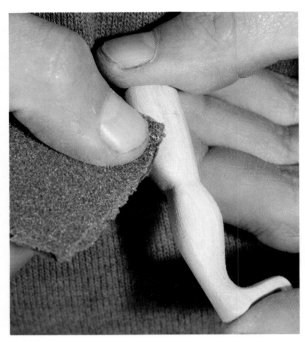

56. For the small, irregularly shaped pieces, use the fingers to rub the paper on every part.

57. Sand the piece forming the body with fine grade sandpaper, having used medium grade on it previously.

Preparing for assembly

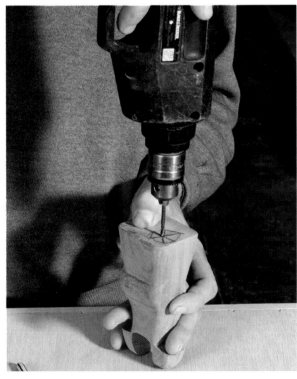

58. Mark the centre and outline of the pantaloons on the base of the body. Use the power drill with a suitable bit to make holes for the metal pins which will connect the pieces together.

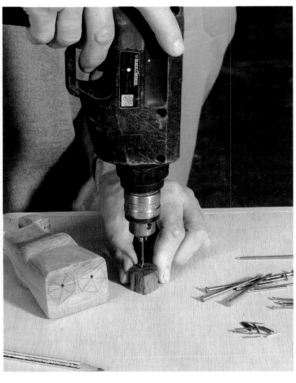

59. Use the same bit to drill holes in the pantaloons, socks and shoes, since they will all be combined together by the same nail. Make holes for the arms an the nose with a smaller bit.

60. Use side cutters to clip the heads off several nails.

61. Before assembling the figure, cut the eyes of the figure, making a single cut with a fluting cutter.

62. Test assemble the piece without glue to check that everything fits in place properly. Make any necessary modifications to rectify the situation.

Finishing

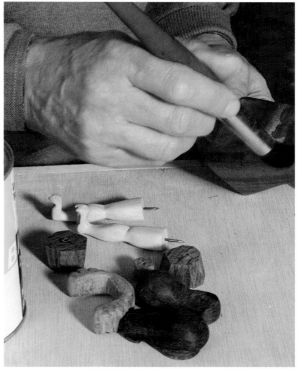

63. Finishing includes the repair of any splits in the wood. For this, special filler is used, mixed with colour to make it the right tone.

64. Apply the filler to the piece with the same spatula as was used to mix it. When dry, sand the repair smooth to hide it.

65. With a brush, apply grain-filling lacquer to all the pieces.

66. Use the nail pins to hold the smaller pieces for varnishing.

67. Before varnishing the head, draw on the eyes and eyebrows.

68. Varnish the head. Prevent the pieces from touching any other surface as much as possible, so as not to alter the finish of the varnish.

Final assembly

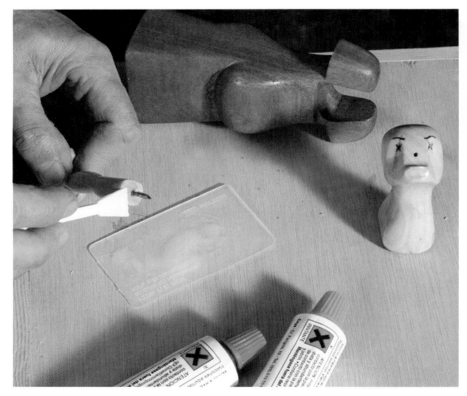

69. Using two-part resin adhesive, glue all the pieces together.

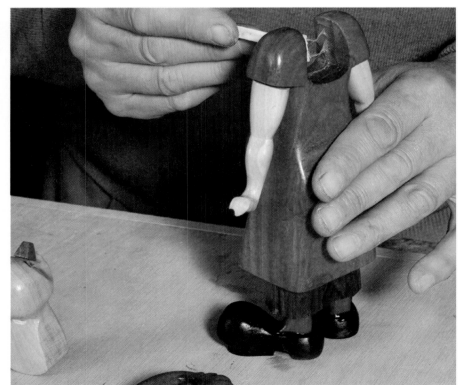

70. Gluing must be carried out as quickly as possible, since this kind of glue can set very quickly.

71. Immediately after applying the glue, clean off the surplus very quickly with pieces of cotton.

72. The last piece to be fitted is the hair. Hold this in position with the fingers while it dries so that it does not slip under the influence of gravity.

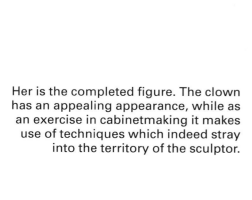

Her is the completed figure. The clown has an appealing appearance, while as an exercise in cabinetmaking it makes use of techniques which indeed stray into the territory of the sculptor.

Shelving

The construction of these shelves with their simple but original design is explained in this project with clear step-by-step instructions.

The shelves are made from one type of wood. In this particular case MDF has been used because of its properties and versatility which are perfect for the purpose.

The end\ product clearly shows that it is possible to make a very versatile and attractive piece of furniture with a small number of very simple materials.

This simple exercise is ideal to learn how to use certain tools such as a jigsaw and chisel. These tools are necessary to cut out the grooves which enable the shelves to slide into each other. Although the various stages are very simple, they must be executed with great care because this will determine not only the correct position of the individual shelves but also the stability of the whole construction.

394

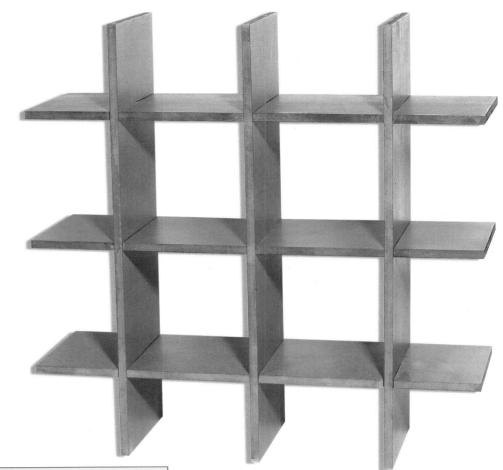

MATERIALS NEEDED

- Sheets of MDF 19 mm (¾ in) thick
- For the structure:
  6 pieces 100 x 30 cm (39⅜ x 11¹³⁄₁₆ in)
- Woodworking white glue
- Medium grade sandpaper
- Grain filler
- Varnish
- Paint roller
- Paint brush

Step-by-step instructions

Making the panels

1. The tools and materials needed to carry out this project.

2. Mark a length of 15 cm (5²⁹⁄₃₂ in) in from the side of one of the six pieces cut to size. (The operations are repeated on the other five panels.)

3. Draw a line through this mark along the length of the shelf, using a carpenter's rule.

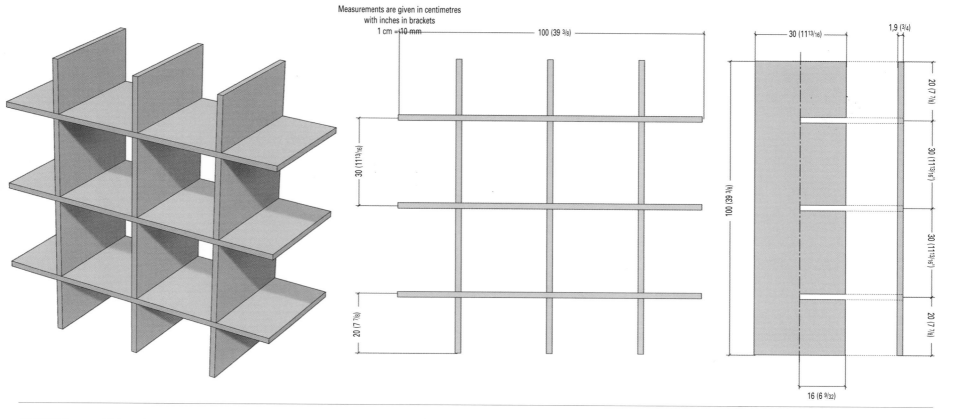

Measurements are given in centimetres
with inches in brackets
1 cm = 10 mm

4. On the axis just drawn, mark a point 20 cm (7⅞ in) from one of the ends.

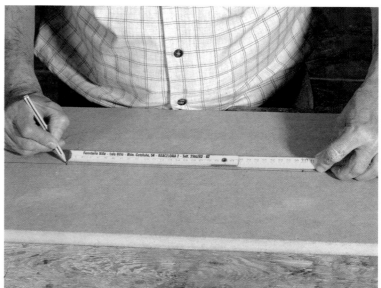

5. Mark another point 30 cm (11¹³⁄₁₆ in) from the point just marked.

6. Complete marking the divisions working from the other end, making a mark at 20 cm (7⅞ in) from the end.

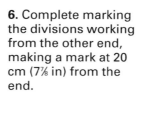

7. Using a try square, draw lines across each of the marks just made. These marks should run from the edge to the centre line.

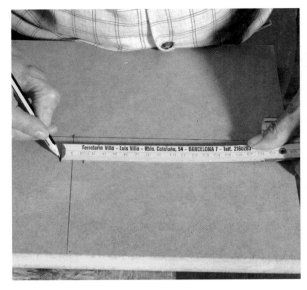

8. Mark parallel lines 1 cm (⅜ in) on each side of the lines just drawn.

9. Use the try square to extend these lines to the edge and centre line. They now define a depth of 2 cm (²⁵⁄₃₂ in) across the board to the centre line, which will accommodate the other pieces when assembled.

10. It is recommended that the areas to be cut out should be clearly marked to avoid confusion.

Cutting the housings for the joints

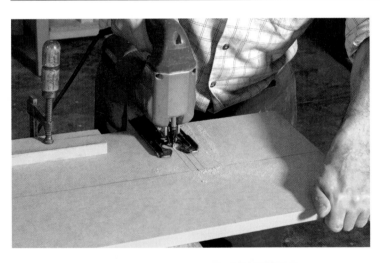

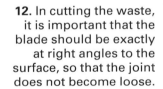

11. With the workpiece fixed to the bench, use the jigsaw to cut out the cross bridle joints.

12. In cutting the waste, it is important that the blade should be exactly at right angles to the surface, so that the joint does not become loose.

13. Complete the removal of the waste with a chisel, applying the blade vertically to define the area being cut out, so that the cut made restricts subsequent ones.

14. Make diagonal cuts with the chisel to complete the removal of the waste.

Cleaning the front faces

15. Use the same chisel to complete the removal of the narrow channels to be cleared.

16. Smooth the interior edges of the housing using the same chisel, making short, gentle, surface cuts.

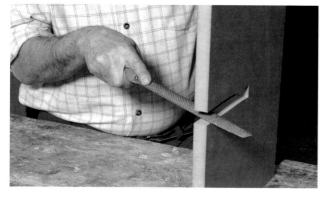

17. To smooth the inner faces of the joint, use a rasp diagonally, as shown in the photograph.

18. Complete the operation by rubbing a sheet of medium grade sandpaper along the channel by hand.

Sanding the surfaces

19. To sand the surfaces of the boards, use a power sander.

20. To clean the edges, use the power sander on the panels firmly fixed in the vice.

21. Soften the edges of the panels with medium grade sandpaper wrapped round a sanding block,

Preparing for assembly

22. Preliminary assembly before varnishing, gluing and final assembly is important because it is essential to check that the

23. If the panels will not interlock, sand the affected parts when dismantled, using a piece of sandpaper supported by a piece of wood.

Applying

24. Apply a coat of grain filler with a roller, followed by one or two coats of colourless varnish to one side of each panel.

25. The roller is also used to apply the grain filler and varnish to the edges of the pieces, which are held vertical while this is done.

26. When the grain-filler and varnish are reasonably dry, the same are applied to the other side. For this operation the panel is propped up with supports of scrap wood.

Gluing the joints and final assembly

27. Glue is applied to the joints with a brush, covering the whole of the inside of the joints. The shelving is then assembled.

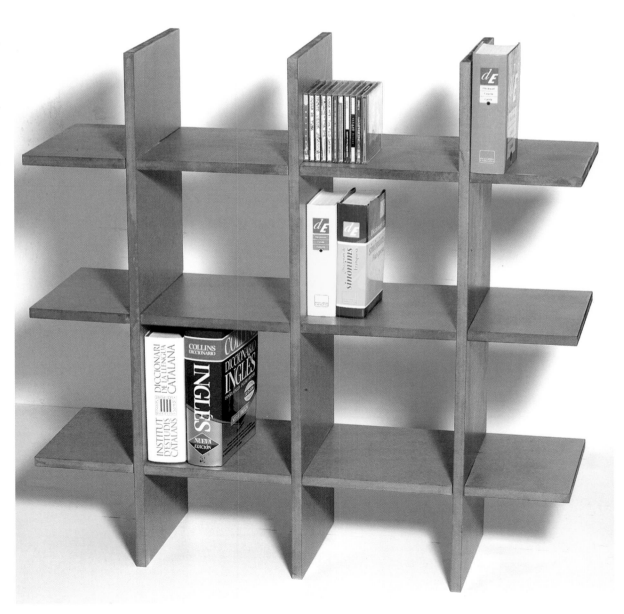

The final result, showing the shelving finished and in use.

Toy box

Anyone who has children knows the problem: what to do with all the toys which are often scattered all over the child's room? In this project the construction of a simple, practical toy box is described with step-by-step instructions. Alternatively the simple container can be used to store other things which seem to accumulate in a child's room, such as clothes for the washing machine.

The construction of this toy box involves several woodworking techniques such as corner joints with uprights and panels of chipboard, bevelling the edges with a plane and the application of edging strip to chipboard.

MATERIALS NEEDED

- Sheets of veneered chipboard
  20 mm ($^{25}/_{32}$ in) thick

- For the sides and base
  4 pieces 60 x 60 cm (23⅝ x 23⅝ in) (side panels)
  1 piece 69 x 69 cm (27³/₁₆ in) (base)

- Pieces of softwood
  6 x 6 cm 2⅜ x 2⅜ in

- For the uprights:
  4 pieces 65 cm (25⅝ in)

- Four rotating castors

- Woodworking white glue

- Grain-filler

- Varnish

- Paint roller

- Paint brush

- Screw connectors 5 cm (2 in) long

- Edging

Step-by-step instructions

Marking out the uprights

1. The tools and materials needed to make the toy box.

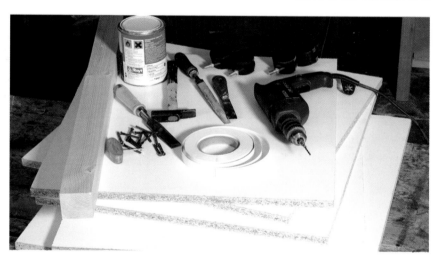

2. On a piece of wood already squared and planed, mark the length corresponding to one of the uprights of the toy box.

3. Use a square to mark the line defining the length at the mark just made.

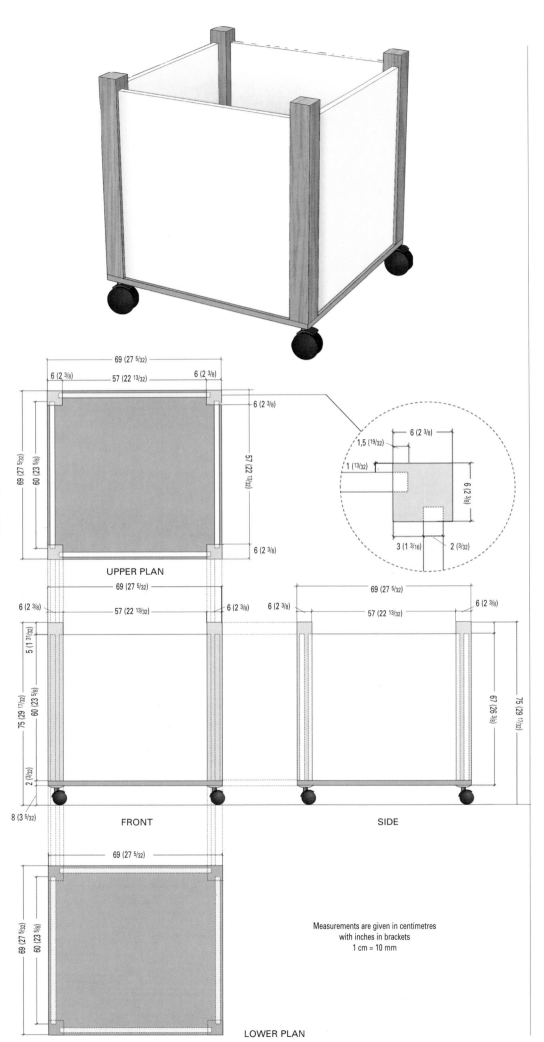

UPPER PLAN

FRONT

SIDE

LOWER PLAN

Measurements are given in centimetres
with inches in brackets
1 cm = 10 mm

4. Cut the pieces to length using the table saw.

5. On one of the uprights mark a point 1 cm (⅜ in) from the edge, the first stage of marking the groove for the panels.

6. Set the marking gauge to this point and run it all along the length of the wood.

7. At a distance of 2 cm (²⁵⁄₃₂ in) from the first mark, mark another mark, the width of the groove for the panel.

8. Set the marking gauge to this mark and scribe a second line along the length of the wood.

9. Repeat these operations on an adjacent side of the upright. Extend both sets of lines to the top end of the wood.

10. Mark the areas to be removed with a cross, as shown.

Cutting the grooves and sanding the uprights

11. Use the table saw to cut the grooves, making several cuts to achieve the width marked.

12. When all the grooves have been made, plane the inner corner of each upright, bevelling it to a width of 1 cm (⅜ in).

13. Use medium grade sandpaper on a sanding block to sand this bevel.

14. Also sand the ends of the pieces, particularly the ones which will on top and visible.

Fitting the edging

15. With the side panels held vertically, cover the top edge (which will be visible) with a layer of contact adhesive.

16. Fit the edging when the adhesive is touch-dry, rubbing it down firmly.

17. When the edging has been attached perfectly, trim off the surplus with the edge of a rasp.

18. Soften the edges of the panels with sandpaper on a sanding block.

19. Remove any traces of contact adhesive with a piece of cotton scrim and some universal solvent.

Gluing and assembly

20. Apply white glue to all the grooves in the uprights with a brush narrow enough to fit in them.

21. Using an intermediate block, hammer two of the uprights to one of the panels.

22. Continue the process until all the side panels are in position. Check that everything is square before the glue sets.

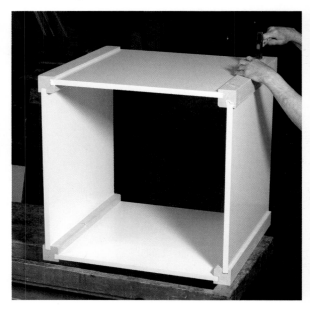

Fitting the bottom and the castors

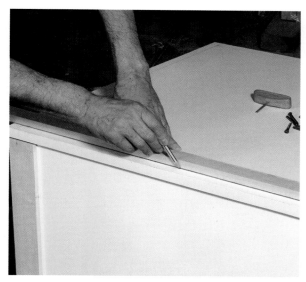

23. At a distance of 2 cm (²⁵⁄₃₂ in) from the edge of the base, rule a line with a carpenter's rule. Repeat on the other three sides.

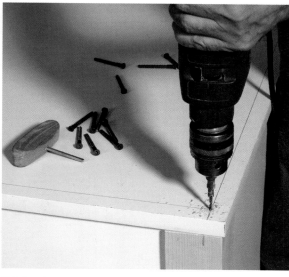

24. In the corners where these lines cross, drill a hole 5 cm (2 in) deep for the connector screws.

25. Insert the connector screws and tighten them up. Then draw the overall dimensions of the uprights on the base, and a diagonal line inwards from the corner. Mark the centre for the castor socket 2 cm (²⁵⁄₃₂ in) from the screw.

26. To make the socket for the sockets holding the castors,use a drill 8 mm (⁵⁄₁₆ in) in diameter. The sockets are inserted with a special key until they are flush with the surface. The castors are then clicked into the sockets.

27. The uprights are protected first with grain sealer and then with varnish.

Here is the toy box completed. To make it more attractive for its users, suitable transfers are stuck to the panels.

Chessboard

In this project the construction of an elegant chessboard is described. The base consists of a piece of MDF, while the surface is covered with veneer. The light and dark veneer squares are used to create the pattern of the chessboard, and it is also framed with other veneers.

To make this chessboard the parquetry-marquetry technique is used. This stage of the work is the most important part of the project and requires the greatest skill on the part of the cabinetmaker.

The choice of the MDF board which will serve as a base for the veneer top is important. Indeed, MDF is ideal for making bevel edges, profiles and so on, and its high density and lack of grain mean that it is very stable. It is also very easy to glue the pieces of veneer onto MDF. For the chessboard pattern you will need two sheets of veneer of different kinds of wood.

The chessboard pattern is a classic design. The board is embellished with a thin border with a semi-circular area at both ends where the players can keep their captured pieces. The edge of the board is finished off with a profiled edge. The last stage is the varnishing of the surface which is then treated with wax to give the chessboard a friendly, pleasant appearance.

MATERIALS NEEDED

- Sheet of MDF
  65 x 45 cm x 19 mm (25⅝ x 17¾ in x ¾ in)

- Sheet of cherry veneer
  45 x 45 cm (17¾ x 17¾ in)

- Sheet of walnut veneer
  40 x 20 cm (15¾ x 7⅞ in)

- Sheet of sycamore veneer
  40 x 20 cm (15¾ x 7⅞ in)

- Sheet of ebony veneer
  4 x 40 cm (1⁹⁄₁₆ x 15¾ in)

- Impact adhesive

- Varnish

- Furniture wax

- Pieces of cotton scrim
  (for varnishing and waxing)

- Steel wool
  (for polishing)

Step-by-step instructions

1. To make this piece, a panel of MDF 19 mm (¾ in) thick is used as a support for four different kinds of veneer. The chessboard itself consists of pieces of sycamore, for the white squares, and walnut, for the dark ones. The line enclosing the board is ebony and the background is cherry.

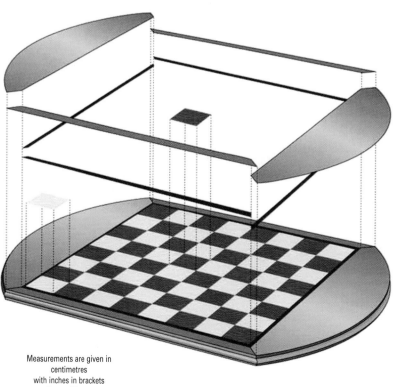

41 (16 5/32)

41 (16 5/32)

58 (22 27/32)

Measurements are given in
centimetres
with inches in brackets
1 cm = 10 mm

Making the chessboard

2. Mark the centre of the panel, so as to establish its overall size.

3. Use a square to check that the centre lines are correct.

4. Using a ruler and square, work outwards from these lines to the edge, marking out the squares of the board. Each square is 45 x 45 mm (1¾ x 1¾ in).

5. Complete the 64 squares of the chessboard.

6. To avoid any confusion between black and white squares, mark the black ones with a cross.

7. To make strips 4.5 cm (1¾ in) wide of the two veneers which will make the squares, prepare a a piece of wood of exactly the same width as a guide. Clamp it on a piece of the veneer to be cut, then cut the veneer on both sides of the guide with a sharp chisel.

8. This is a guillotine for cutting veneer.

9. Set up a stop in the cutter to define the length of the pieces cut. This consists of a piece of wood fixed exactly 4.5 cm (1¾ in) from the edge of the cutter.

10. The first cut is made to square off the end of the veneer.

11. In cutting the squares, make sure everything remains fixed firmly and without moving.

12. Cut the 64 pieces needed for the chessboard, 32 light ones and 32 dark.

Preparing the support and arranging the squares

13. With a large compass mark the two arcs forming the two ends of the board.

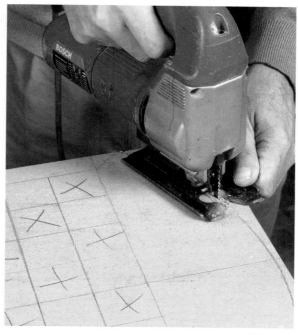

14. Fix the board to the bench with a cramp so ti does not vibrate while being sawn. Cut the curve with a jigsaw, following the line just drawn

15. To arrange and fix the tiles, a smooth surface is need, in this case the same piece of MDF, and adhesive tape.

16. Arrange the square pieces alternately on strips of masking tape. The arrangement is not random; the grain of each piece is aligned in the same direction.

17. Fitting the last piece of the board.

18. The surrounding bands of ebony and the cherry wood edging will now be added.

19. The overall measurement of the squares will determine the length of the pieces of the ebony surround, which have already been cut to the width of 4 mm (⁵⁄₃₂ in).

20. The pieces are cut to the length measured, with the ends at 45° to make a neat mitre at each corner.

21. The border is positioned next to the squares.

22. The strip of cherry is cut to the desired width.

23. Each corner of the cherry veneer is chopped at an angle of 45° at each end.

24. The cut veneer is added to the pieces already assembled, and the same operation is repeated for the other end.

25. To complete the arrangement of the pieces, the remaining border pieces are cut to fit, working from the corner, and placed in position.

26. The ends of the veneer are cut roughly to the diameter of the ends of the panel with a chisel. A clearance of 2–3 mm (about ⅛ in) is left, which will be cleaned off when the veneer has been glued to the panel.

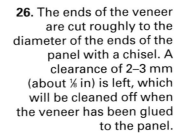

27. This shows the assembly of veneer pieces held together with masking tape. This side is the one which will eventually be varnished and polished.

28. The back of the same, showing the side which will be invisible and glued to the panel.

29. Contact adhesive is used to attach the veneer to the support panel. It is applied with a metal spreader as thinly and evenly as possible. This type of glue is chosen because it contains no water, so the veneer will not expand or shrink under its influence.

30. The glue is distributed by the spreader towards the edges, so as to avoid a build-up in the middle.

31. The panel is also covered with glue, following the same procedure. The two operations should be carried out one after the other, so that the glue of both is at roughly the same state of dryness. To be ready for joining, they should be just tacky, forming a thin thread when touched.

32. To join the surfaces as accurately as possible, put some thin laths between the panel and the veneer, which will keep them separate.

33. Place the assembled veneer sheet on the laths and position it where it is to be.

34. Starting from the end which has been fixed, remove the laths one by one.

35. At the same time as the laths are removed, press the freed areas into contact with each other.

36. When the veneer is all in contact with the support, press it firmly and give it some blows with the flat of the hand to even out any small irregularities produced in joining the two pieces.

37. Complete the joining of the veneer by hammering it through a block of wood.

38. Remove the adhesive tape which has until now held all the pieces in position.

39. Complete the process by smoothing the veneer with a hammer as shown.

Cleaning up

40. Remove the excess veneer round the edge by cutting it with a chisel.

41. Smooth the edges with a file to remove any roughness produced by cutting it with a chisel.

42. Smooth the edges by hand sanding with a sanding block.

43. Use an edge moulder to mould the edge of the panel.

44. Repeat the operation on the other side of the panel.

45. After moulding the edges, clean them with sandpaper, working from medium to fine grade.

46. For the finest parts of the moulding, fold the sandpaper in half and use that.

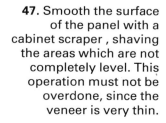

47. Smooth the surface of the panel with a cabinet scraper , shaving the areas which are not completely level. This operation must not be overdone, since the veneer is very thin.

Finishing the piece

48. Before the final finishing operation, clean the surface gently, first with medium and then with fine grade sandpaper. The direction of sanding is not important since any direction will be against the grain of some of the veneer.

49. Remove the dust caused by sanding and then apply grain-filling varnish with a piece of cotton scrim.

50. When the varnish is dry, use very fine silicon carbide paper round a sanding block to sand the board.

51. Carry out the same operation on the sides, but without the wood block and adapting the paper to the shape of the moulding, pressing with the fingers.

52. Without first removing the dust created, polish the surface with steel wool.

53. Use pieces of cotton scrim to apply an even coating of wax. The dust will be removed by applying the wax.

54. The final operation consists of polishing the wax to a good shine by vigorously rubbing it with cotton.

The completed chessboard.

CD rack

This project will satisfy anyone's desire to own a CD rack with an individual character. It will hold a large number of CDs and make a stylish appearance against the wall. MDF has been chosen as the best material for the purpose. It is very easy to handle and to work with, while its texture and colour give the CD-holder a decorative, modern character.

The CD rack consists of horizontal base with the necessary compartments. Its construction involves some quite complicated marking out, cutting the various parts to the right size and assembling them with special screw connectors. In order to improve the functionality and mobility of the CD rack, two castors are screwed on to the base so that it can be rolled from one place to the other. Finally, a coat of varnish, followed by the application of wax will give the CD rack a simple, sleek appearance. This preserves the typical texture and colour of the MDF.

414

Step-by-step instructions

1. The pieces of MDF together with the screws and castors needed.

MATERIALS NEEDED

• Pieces of MDF, 19 mm (3/4 in) - Vertical part: 1 piece 100 x 30 cm (39⅜ x 12 in) - Shelves: 1 piece 120 x 15 cm. - Base: 1 piece 30 x 30 cm (12 x 12 in) - Foot: 1 piece 7 x 30 cm (2¾ x 12 in)	• Woodworking white glue
	• 2-part varnish
	• Wool paint roller
	• Furniture wax
	• Pieces of cotton
• 2 castors 5 cm (2 in) in diameter	• Steel wool
	• Medium and fine grade sandpaper
• 4 screws.	
• 14 screw connectors	• Very fine-grained abrasive sponge.

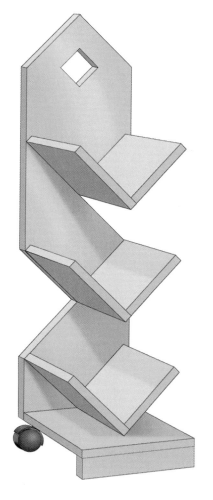

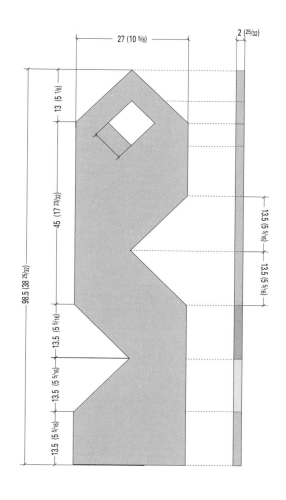

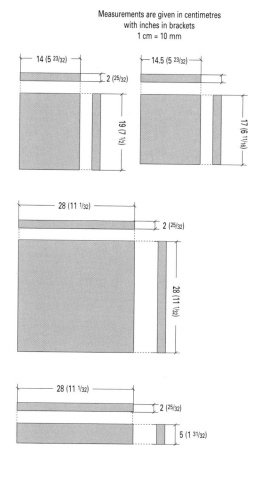

Measurements are given in centimetres
with inches in brackets
1 cm = 10 mm

27 (10 5/8)

2 (25/32)

13 (5 1/8)

45 (17 23/32)

98.5 (38 25/32)

13.5 (5 5/16)

13.5 (5 5/16)

13.5 (5 5/16)

13.5 (5 5/16)

13.5 (5 5/16)

14 (5 23/32)

14.5 (5 23/32)

2 (25/32)

19 (7 1/2)

17.6 (6 11/16)

28 (11 1/32)

2 (25/32)

28 (11 1/32)

28 (11 1/32)

2 (25/32)

5 (1 31/32)

415

Preparing the pieces

2. Mark the width of the piece, 28 cm (11 in) at two points and draw a straight sawing line between them.

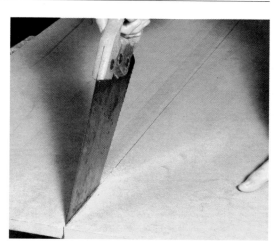

3. The wood is sawn with a panel saw. This is easiest if the wood is supported on two trestles. Given the poor finish produced by the saw, cut at least 2 mm (1/16 in) outside the line marked.

4. Fix the panel to the bench and with a jack plane smooth the sawn edge down to the line.

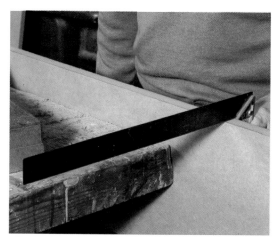

5. Check with the try square that after sawing and planing the edge is still at right angles.

6. Mark the length of the piece, 98.5 cm (38¾ in). The original piece is marked in the centre to compensate in case it is not exactly square. Draw the cutting line.

7. Mark the centre line of the piece.

8. Make two marks 13 cm (5⅛ in) from the upper mark, on the centre line and at the edge. Join the two points.

9. The point of intersection of the between the axis and the new line forms the centre of the square to be cut out. With a sliding bevel draw the two lines between the upper part of the axis and the two ends.

10. Fix the position of the sliding bevel as used in the previous operation and mark a line 8 cm (3⅛ in) from the line which will form one of the sides of the square to be cut out.

11. Complete the square with a line drawn at the same sliding bevel angle.

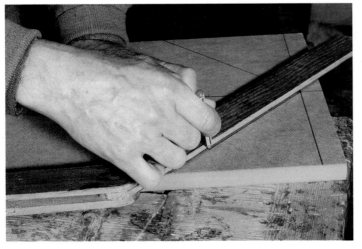

12. Mark the position of the inner shelf with a line at 45°. Do not change the position of the sliding bevel.

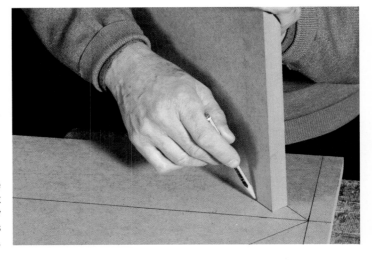

13. A piece of the same material is used to mark the thickness. Finish by drawing the lines positioning the shelf.

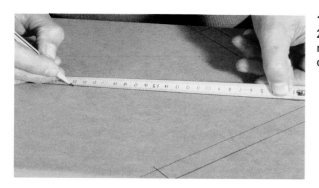

14. On the axis and 23 cm (9 in) from it, mark the upper part of the next shelf.

15. Mark the points to be drilled for the fixing of the vertical piece with shelves 10 cm (3¹⁵⁄₁₆ in) from the base of each one.

16. Mark the points to guide the drill with a punch.

17. Make the holes which must go right through, since the fixing screws are fitted from the back.

Making the shelves

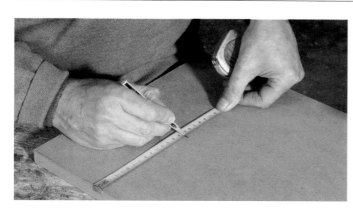

18. Mark the width of the pieces forming the shelves. Repeat the operation for the base piece.

19. With the panel saw cut along the line, but leaving a minimum clearance of 2 mm (¹⁄₁₆ in) to be planed smooth.

20. After marking the line at right angles to the vertical, mark the length of one of the shelf pieces along it.

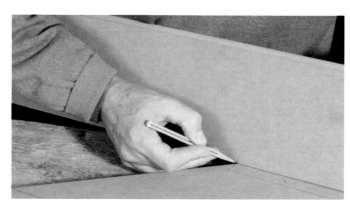

21. In the same way, mark the other shorter line of the shelf.

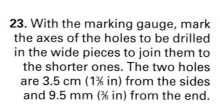

22. Cut all the pieces forming the shelves with the compound angle saw.

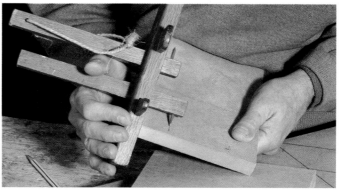

23. With the marking gauge, mark the axes of the holes to be drilled in the wide pieces to join them to the shorter ones. The two holes are 3.5 cm (1⅜ in) from the sides and 9.5 mm (⅜ in) from the end.

417

24. Join the pieces forming the shelves with a corner cramp. Fix the assembly in the vice and mark the holes to be drilled with a punch.

25. Drill the holes with a power drill.

26. This is the end result of the operation. Note the special tool used to drill holes for counter-sunk screws.

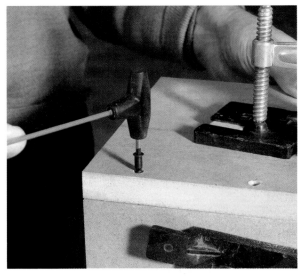

27. Fix the two pieces forming the shelf with the connector screws.

28. Sand the sawn edges smooth, working from medium grade to fine.

29. The shelf where ti will be fixed in position on the vertical piece.

Sawing and cleaning up

30. Use the sliding bevel to mark the pieces to be cut out, as shown on the drawing.

31. Mark the parts to be removed with a cross so as to avoid mistakes in cutting.

32. To cut out the central square, make two holes at opposite corners from which the saw cuts can start.

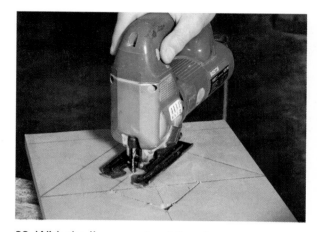

33. With the jigsaw cut out the shape, beginning the cut from one of the drilled holes.

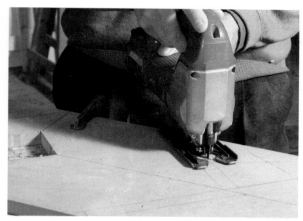

34. Use the jigsaw to cut away the side pieces marked for removal.

35. Plane the edges which can be reached to smooth them.

36. In the areas where the plane cannot be used, use a rasp.

37. Remove any marks with may remain.

Provisional assembly

38. Fix the first shelf in position with a cramp.

39. Turn the piece over and drill the points marked for screws to pass through. This operation is repeated for each shelf and the base.

40. Fit and tighten the screws, in this case with a special key.

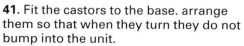

41. Fit the castors to the base. arrange them so that when they turn they do not bump into the unit.

42. Measure the height of the wheels of the castors from the base. Make a piece of MDF with the same height and the width of the piece so that it will stand level.

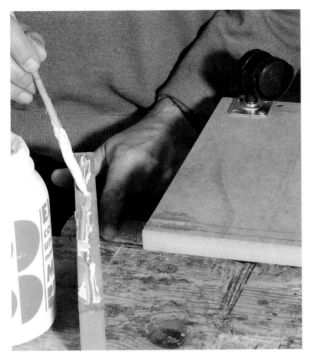

43. Apply glue to the piece and to the base, 1 cm (⅜ in) in from the front edge.

44. Position the piece and fix it with two cramps while the glue dries.

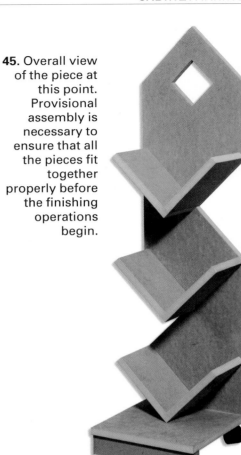

45. Overall view of the piece at this point. Provisional assembly is necessary to ensure that all the pieces fit together properly before the finishing operations begin.

Finishing

46. Prepare the two-part varnish. Follow the maker's instructions regarding the proportions of the base and the catalyst.

47. Apply the varnish with a wool roller. For the angled parts which the brush cannot reach, use a brush.

48. When the varnish is dry, rub it down with very fine grade sandpaper.

49. To continue the operation of smoothing the varnish, use a fine grade abrasive sponge.

50. Polish the surfaces with steel wool.

51. Apply wax with pieces of cotton.

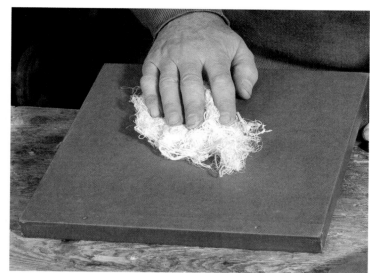

52. Polish the wax with more cotton when it has dried.

Assembly

53. Fit the shelves to the support in the same way as in the provisional assembly. Use a corner cramp to ensure that everything is correctly positioned.

54. Fix the shelves with screw connectors.

The CD rack is now completed. As can be seen, when placed against the wall the wheels are out of sight behind the plinth. They simply make it easier to move the rack when needed.

Toy aircraft

The construction of this object should not present any serious problems because most of the techniques have already been introduced in previous exercises. The small size of the individual pieces makes the work slightly more difficult, but this is useful practice for many kinds of work. The object can be used either as a toy or an ornament.

The different colours of the aeroplane are created by using different kinds of wood (ebony, sipo and beech) to avoid the need for painting or staining.

The greatest difficulty of this exercise is working with very small pieces which requires great dexterity and skill. The preparation of drawings and their correct application are extremely important in this exercise because they determine the shape of the aeroplane. It is also very important to be efficient with a frame saw or backsaw in order to saw the various parts of the aeroplane with great accuracy.

If this aeroplane is to be used as a toy, it should not be treated with paints or varnish which could be poisonous to a child. Because some of the parts are so small, this aeroplane is not suitable for children under 4 years of age.

422

MATERIALS NEEDED

• Fuselage of the aircraft: sipo wood: - 1 piece 27 x 6 x 6 cm (10⅝ x 2⅜ x 2⅜ in)	• Engine, beech: - 1 piece 7.5 cm (3 in) long y 4.2 cm (1⅝ in) in diameter.	• 3 brass-headed nails
		• 2 steel nails
• Wings and tailplane: sipo wood - 3 pieces 31 x 7.5 x 0.5 cm (12¼ x 3 x ³⁄₁₆ in)	• Propellor and wheels: ebony - 1 piece 30 x 5 x 0.5 cm (12 x 2 x ³⁄₁₆ in) and a small piece 2 mm (¹⁄₁₆ in) thick	• Woodworking white glue
		• Medium and fine grade sandpaper
• Wing struts: beech - 2 rods 40 cm (16 in) long and 5 mm (³⁄₁₆ in) in diameter	• Wheel supports: beech - piece 29 x 5 x 0.5 cm (11½ x 2 x ³⁄₁₆ in)	• Varnish
		• Wax
		• Pieces of cotton scrim
		• Steel wool

Step-by-step instructions

Preparing the pieces

1. The various pieces of wood used to make the aircraft.

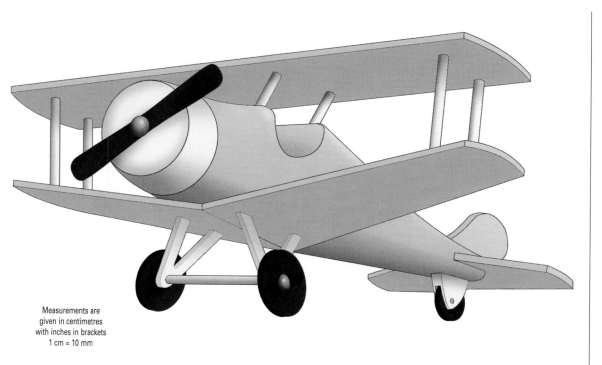

Measurements are
given in centimetres
with inches in brackets
1 cm = 10 mm

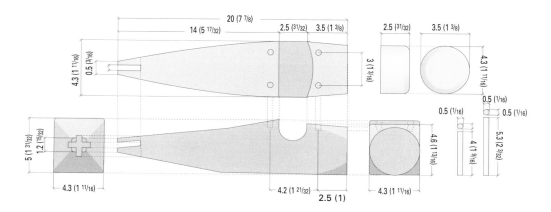

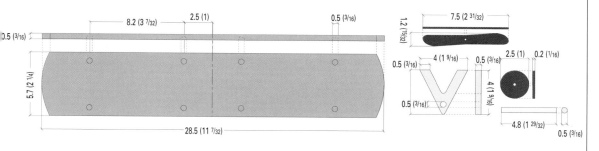

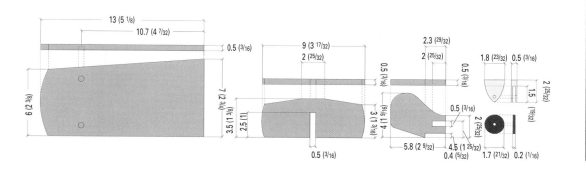

Templates

2. To make this toy, templates are needed. These are drawn on a piece of plywood and cut out with a jigsaw.

3. Sand the edges of the template pieces to remove the roughness caused by the jigsaw.

Fuselage:
Using the templates

4. Position the side template on one face of the piece of sipo wood and draw round it.

5. Position the plan view template, which in this case is drawn on both sides of the piece of wood.

Making the pieces

6. Using the backsaw, cut away the waste from the piece so that it is the correct length.

7. Fix the piece in the vice and use a frame saw to cut to the lines marked.

8. Cut the piece in the other direction with the same saw. This operation could be carried out by a portable jigsaw.

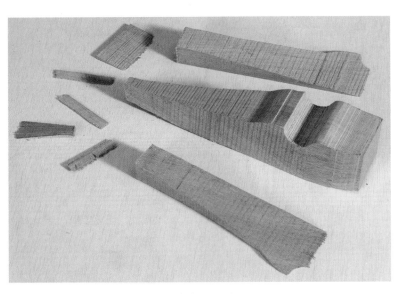

9. This shows the workpiece with the waste pieces sawn off.

10. Use the template to mark the sockets for gluing in the tailplane.

11. With the backsaw, saw to the marks drawn. Because of the small size of the pieces, great care is necessary in doing this.

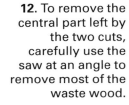

12. To remove the central part left by the two cuts, carefully use the saw at an angle to remove most of the waste wood.

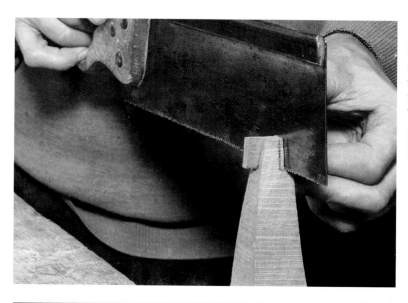

13. Saw the socket at right angles to the first one. To do this, the first cut is temporarily filled with a piece of wood so that the pieces being cut have something to bear against.

14. Mark the centre line of the base of the piece.

15. Plane the underside of the fuselage to a rounded shape as far as the lines marked.

16. Round the upper edges of the piece with a rasp.

Engine

17. After marking the length of the piece with a pencil, use a rasp to round one of the ends.

18. To make the work easier, finish rounding and smoothing the piece before sawing it to length with a backsaw.

Wings

19. Use the templates to mark the shape of the wings.

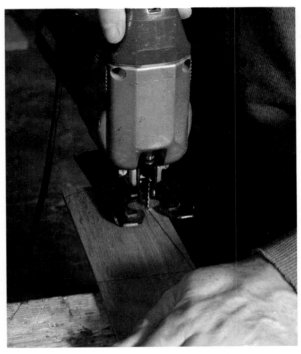

20. Use the jigsaw to cut out all the pieces forming the wings of the aircraft.

21. To make a smoother edge after the sawing, smooth with a plane.

22. Smooth the curves with a rasp.

23. Use the compound angle saw to make the cuts across the wings, since the edges are at a small angle to mate with the shape of the fuselage.

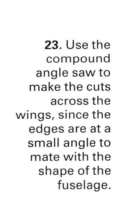

24. The sawing of the surfaces for the tailplane of the aircraft is also carried out with the jigsaw. To avoid the risk of splitting the piece while sawing, cut the trickiest parts first and then the outline of the piece.

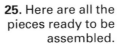

25. Here are all the pieces ready to be assembled.

Preparing for assembly

26. The holes for supporting the wings are made with 18 cm (7 in) between them. The length of dowel is used as a depth gauge to stop the hole being drilled too deep.

27. When the points have been marked, make the holes with a slight inclination.

28. Use a backsaw to cut the dowels which will support the wings. These are also cut at a slight angle.

29. Use the template to mark out the pieces supporting the wheels.

30. Cut out the pieces with the jigsaw. The size of the piece may seem excessive, but this is intentional. If it were smaller it would be too small to saw round.

31. Make all the pieces smooth with a rasp, particularly the insides.

32. Next sand the pieces.

33. Make a hole 5 mm (³⁄₁₆ in) in diameter for fixing the wheels. The workpiece is so small it is clamped between two pieces of wood to hold it while it is drilled.

34. The rods of the landing gear are cut, 4.7 cm (1⅞ in) long.

35. Mark out the wheels on a piece of ebony with a compass.

36. Fix the workpiece to the bench and saw round the wheels with the jigsaw.

37. Drill a centre hole in each wheel 1.5 mm (¹⁄₁₆ in) in diameter.

38. Use the template to mark out the rear wheel support.

39. Saw it out with the jigsaw.

40. Mark the slot for the real wheel in the support. It is 2.4 mm (3⁄32 in) wide.

41. Make the first cut with the backsaw.

42. Make the second cut in the same way. Press the wood with the thumb to prevent it splitting.

45. The procedure for making the propellor is similar. Mark the shape with the template and cut it out with the jigsaw. When these operations are completed, shape both blades with the rasp to give a lifelike appearance to this part of the aircraft.

43. Given the small size of the tail wheel, 1.8 cm (11/16 in) in diameter, draw round a suitable coin to mark it out.

44. Cut out the wheel, clamp it as shown and drill a centre hole through it.

Sanding and assembly

46. Before assembling the pieces, sand them all with medium and then fine grade sandpaper.

47. Knock in a nail to ensure a perfect fixing, then glue the engine and attach it to the front of the fuselage.

48. Glue the lower wings. The joint is cramped with C-shaped springs. follow with the upper wings, reinforced with the struts.

49. Glue and fix the parts of the tailplane.

Final finishing

50. When the glue is dry, remove the C-spring cramps and give the aircraft a coat of varnish.

51. Use a brass-headed upholstery nail to fit the propellor, tapping it in with light taps of the hammer.

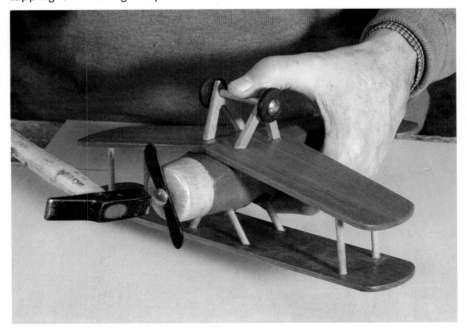

52. Sand overall with fine sandpaper. Follow this by rubbing with steel wool.

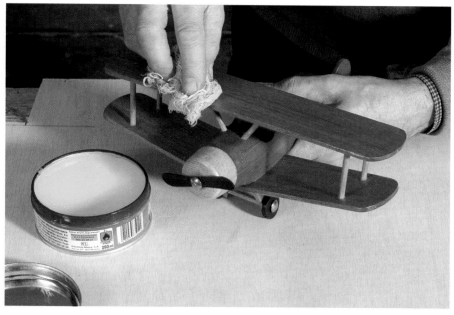

53. Apply a coat of wax to the aircraft, rubbing it well into all the edges of the wood.

Here is the completed aircraft which can be used as a toy
or simply as a decorative piece on a table or shelf.

Restoring a chair

The skill of furniture restoring seems to have arisen from the popularity, over the years, of acquiring more or less ancient pieces of furniture and restoring these to a state of preservation which encourages them to be used again, so that the attraction and interest which they had originally can be enjoyed again. While the range of furniture to be restored is very wide, the commonest are those which are used most often in the home, such as tables, chairs, chests of drawers, and so on.

A characteristic of restorers is the knowledge they must have of the different skills of the cabinetmaker, since a perfect restoration of a piece of furniture implies an understanding of how it was made, step-by-step, how the elements of the piece fit together, and the materials of which it consists.

In this project the example taken is a chair in Victorian style. The passage of time and the results of continuous use over many years has resulted in very evident deterioration which is concentrated in several parts of the chair. There is missing veneer, it has suffered from woodworm, parts of it are broken, there are pieces missing, and so on.

An unusual aspect of this chair is that it has been restored already. At the moment there are some metal pieces in it used to repair broken pieces in the past. This is now actually part of the chair's history and will be retained.

After restoration it will be seen that the chair has acquired the distinction and nobility which is characteristic of all successful restoration, testimony to the attention paid to every detail of this interesting and rewarding work.

Checking the imperfections

The first stage in restoration is the detailed inspection of the piece to determine the materials used, the types of joints, the shapes of the mouldings and so on.

Checking the imperfections through a general overview and a meticulous visual inspection is the second, vitally important stage. This study not only serves to detect all the defects, but it also includes looking at the joints and deciding whether or not the piece should be dismantled, and if so, how. Dismantling is essential in many cases to achieve a good job.

1. This is the general condition of the chair before restoration. The first glance is followed by a detailed examination to decide the degree of deterioration and the steps to be taken to restore it.

2. Checking the kind of wood used originally. For this operation a saw blade is used to scrape off some of the existing varnish. The wood used in this case was mahogany, with pine for the hidden frame.

3. Having seen that some of the joints of the legs with the frame are very weak, one of them is dismantled. This is an essential step to improve the new joint when the pieces are glued together again.

4. Looking at the rest of the legs, the strength of the join with the frame is checked. In this case dismantling is not necessary.

5. The chair back is dismantled, since it was very weak.

6. A detail of a joint in the pine frame. On examination, this is found to be satisfactory.

433

7. Detail of the joint in the chair back, with metal fittings from a previous restoration. It is important to keep any pieces of broken wood, although inevitably many will be missing.

8. It is noticed that the pine frame is covered with mahogany veneer and that at some points some bits are missing which will have to be replaced.

9. Detail showing signs of attack by wood-boring insects (woodworm) in the pine of the frame.

Cleaning and treating

Cleaning a piece of furniture consists basically of cleansing both the exterior and the interior of the wood of which it consists. In this case, external cleansing is carried out with hot water containing a little solvent.

The internal cleansing involves treating the wood against insect attack, by the injection and surface application of an appropriate insecticide.

10. Clean the surface of all the pieces of the chair with hot water containing about 10% solvent. This operation is very effective but because of the toxicity of the solvent, it must be carried out with appropriate precautions.

11. Clean the rest of the chair. Once the material is clean, a difference in colour between the mahogany veneer and the rest of the mahogany is evident. This must be taken account of in the finishing operations.

12. The same procedure is used to remove the rest of the glue from the existing joints.

13. When the surfaces have been cleaned, they are wiped with some pieces of cotton scrim, which will remove the rest of the dirt.

14. Inject insecticide in all the holes made by woodworm to eliminate any possible survivors.

15. Spray a preventative insecticide all over the pieces of wood liable to attack by insects, in this case the pine of the frame.

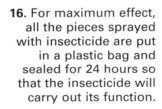

16. For maximum effect, all the pieces sprayed with insecticide are put in a plastic bag and sealed for 24 hours so that the insecticide will carry out its function.

Restoration of the pieces and preliminary assembly

The correct procedure for restoring pieces can be followed if the restorer is familiar with the piece itself, the wood used, the kind of joints which are used, and so on.

17. To restore the pieces of veneer which are missing, the gap is filled with hot glue applied between the veneer and the support.

18. The missing pieces are restored with some new pieces, which are also attached with hot glue. They are hammered to make the joint firm. The pieces of the back are restored before being reassembled.

19. The pieces forming the two uprights of the back are glued with hot glue from a water-jacketed glue pot like a bain marie.

20. The tenons of the centre of the back are glued.

21. The three pieces are joined together. This operation must be carried out quickly, since the glue sets rapidly.

22. The three pieces are cramped together with a tourniquet and left to dry.

435

23. Clean of the surplus glue with cotton. If it has set too hard to be removed, moisten the joints with hot water.

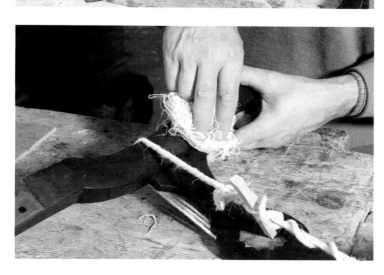

24. Glue the upper piece of the back, taking advantage of the metal pieces existing from a previous restoration.

25. When gluing, glue is applied to both parts of the joint.

26. Cramp the glued pieces together while they set.

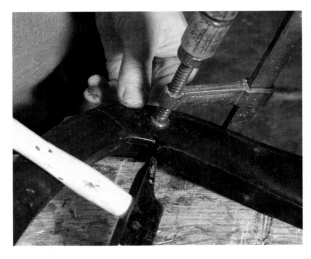

27. Restore and re-glue the pieces of wood. The loose pieces of wood are hammered into place.

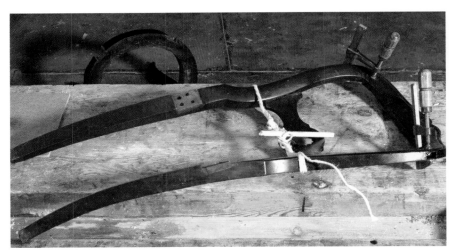

28. A view which shows the back assembled with the broken pieces mended. It will be noticed that some of these were missing and therefore had to be remade.

29. Here is the result of joining the upper piece of the back after it is glued. The missing piece will have to be made.

30. The new piece is made from a piece of the same wood as the original, in this case mahogany. The measurements are taken from the gap to be filled.

31. Use the backsaw to cut a piece of mahogany for making the replacement.

32. Take the measurement of the length of the space to be filled. This must be exact.

33. Use a chisel to clean out the old glue and to tidy up the hole.

34. Check that the replacement piece is large enough to fill the hold.

35. Glue the hole and the replacement piece.

36. Tap the piece into place with a hammer. The clean off any surplus glue.

37. The rest of the missing pieces are restored in the same way.

38. Use C-spring cramps to hold small pieces in place while the glue is drying.

437

39. When the glue is dry, make some holes with a drill and screw in the screws holding the metal plates in position.

Cleaning and final polishing

Restoration should restore the function of the piece of furniture without losing any of its original appearance and distinction. Like all the work of the cabinetmaker, the final result must be agreeable to the eye and give the piece an attractive appearance. Once the damage to the piece has been repaired and possible weaknesses cured, the whole attention must be devoted to cleaning and reassembling the piece as perfectly as possible.

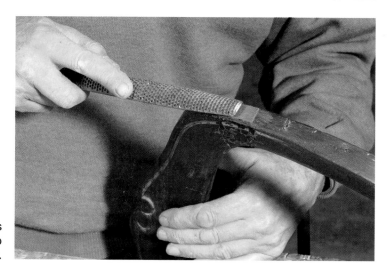

40. After sawing off the surplus wood, it is smoothed with a rasp to the same level as the rest.

41. The piece restored in the curved part of the back is also smoothed with a rasp to match the curvature.

42. The remains of the original tenons of the broken joint are sawn off.

43. The dried glue is removed from the old joint; andy left could weaken the new glue.

44. The two pieces are glued.

438

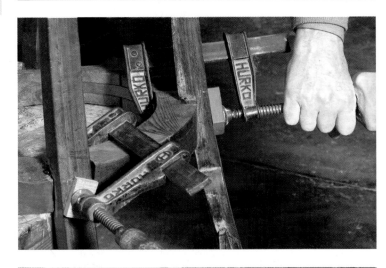

45. The joint is cramped together.

46. The joint between the back and the seat a piece is fitted which acts as a wedge joint.

47. To strengthen the joint between the back and the seat, some bolts will be added, for which holes are drilled.

48. Two hexagon-head bolts are fitted to each joint and tightened with a spanner.

Finishing

The final stage of restoration is the process of finishing the chair. This is the culmination of all that has gone before. The care and attention given at this stage will make all the difference to the impact of the finished result.

49. Here are the materials used for the finishing operations: solid shellac which can be dissolved in methylated spirit (shellac solvent), and pieces of cotton to apply it.

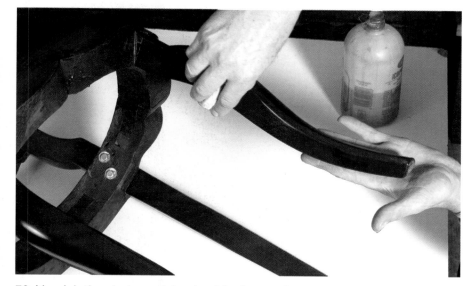

50. Varnish the chair applying it with pieces of cotton and spreading it with a cloth.

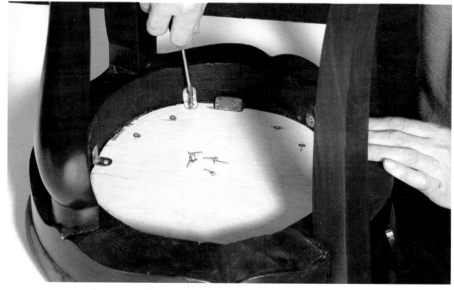

51. The seat of the chair is fitted with metal supports screwed to a plywood panel which is glued to the back.

Here is the finished chair after it has been restored.